# POWER
# PEDAGOGY
# & PRACTICE

# POWER

# PEDAGOGY

# & PRACTICE

*Editors*
Tricia Hedge
Norman Whitney

OXFORD UNIVERSITY PRESS
1996

Oxford University Press,
Walton Street, Oxford OX2 6DP

Oxford New York
Athens Auckland Bangkok Bogota Bombay
Buenos Aires Calcutta Cape Town Dar es Salaam
Delhi Florence Hong Kong Istanbul Karachi
Kuala Lumpur Madras Madrid Melbourne
Mexico City Nairobi Paris Singapore
Taipei Tokyo Toronto

and associated companies in
Berlin and Ibadan

OXFORD and OXFORD ENGLISH
are trade marks of Oxford University Press

ISBN 0 19 437205 7

© Oxford University Press 1996

Typeset in Galliard and Sabon
By Wyvern Typesetting Limited, Bristol

Printed in Hong Kong

FOR
JACK JENNISON
*In Memoriam*
1926–1995

# CONTENTS

## PART TWO: PEDAGOGY
### *Issues in the professional development of teachers*

# PART THREE: PRACTICE
## Issues in curriculum design and development

# ACKNOWLEDGEMENTS

First and foremost, we would like to thank Cristina Whitecross of Oxford University Press and the other members of the Board of Management of ELT Journal, Roger Bowers, Chris Kennedy, Alan Maley, Ron White, and Henry Widdowson, for their guidance and constant support during our time as Editors of the Journal.

We would also like to thank the Reviews Editors, Rod Bolitho and Keith Morrow, and the members of the Editorial Advisory Panel who served between 1988 and 1995: Jill Bourne, Helen Boyle, Martin Bygate, Ron Carter, Janelle Cooper, Tony Deyes, Pamela Frame, Simon Freeman, Stephen Gaies, Kevin Germaine, Jennifer Jarvis, Charles Lowe, Peter Maingay, Patricia Mugglestone, Rob Nolasco, Jenny Pugsley, Esther Ramani, Hilary Rees-Parnell, Euan Reid, Shelagh Rixon, Nina Spada, Kristyan Spelman Miller, Ray Tongue, Brenda Townsend, and Catherine Walter. The hard work of the Panel members and their devotion to the task of reading articles and offering feedback, which often goes unrecognized, are an essential part of the life of the Journal.

We are also grateful to the in-house editors at Oxford University Press during the period 1988 to 1995, Catherine Robinson, David Wilson, and Antoinette Meehan, also the in-house editor of this book, for their work in ensuring that each issue of the Journal appeared on time and in good order.

Thanks are also due to John Clegg, Kristyan Spelman Miller, Barbara Sinclair, and Henry Widdowson for their invaluable comments and suggestions during the planning and preparation of this book.

And finally, we would like to thank the authors whose articles appear in this collection for submitting their work to *ELT Journal* originally and for their permission to reproduce their work here.

Tricia Hedge
Norman Whitney

# INTRODUCTION

The main aims of this selection of articles from Volumes 42–49 of *ELT Journal* are to draw attention to some of the major preoccupations of the English language teaching profession in the period 1988–1995, and to focus on themes and topics which are likely to be of continuing interest and importance in the future. At the same time, we hope to provide a useful resource for teachers, trainee teachers, teacher educators, students, and researchers.

The publication of this book coincides with the 50th anniversary of *ELT Journal*: the first issue of what was then called *English Language Teaching* appeared in October 1946, published by the British Council. There is no attempt here to trace lines of development from that first issue through to today—a historical study of *ELT Journal* would be a research project in its own right. But it is perhaps appropriate to compare the preoccupations of the first editor, A. S. Hornby, and his contributors with those of us, fifty years on, who owe them so much.

As Widdowson (1986: 265) pointed out on the occasion of the 40th anniversary of *ELT Journal*, readers of that first issue might find 'curiosities which catch the eye, dated oddities of another age'. Yet some of the themes and topics discussed then—methodology, audio-visual aids, grammar, pronunciation—would strike a chord today. In that sense, many of the themes and topics in this book cannot be said to be new. So it is not too fanciful to suppose that some of the contributions in the first issue in 1946, for example 'Linguistic Research' (an editorial), 'Linguistic Pedagogy' (an article), and *Language as a Social and*

*Political Factor in Europe* (a book reviewed) might still be relevant and topical today.

Although it would be easy to point an accusing finger at the essentially male, British, middle-class tone of the editor and contributors of fifty years ago, it is important not to forget their explicit commitment to the teaching and learning of foreign languages, cultural exchange, anti-élitism, and internationalism. Readers' attention was drawn to the malevolent power of nationalism, which Otto Jespersen called 'the ghastly malady of our time', and in an editorial in the first issue, Hornby (1946a: 5) wrote

> No nation can afford to live an insulated life to-day. If nations try to live on their own stocks of thought and sentiment, it will not be long before they all suffer from stagnation and decay.

Hornby was speaking from the heart for a generation of Europeans who were, quite literally, tired of war. Given that sort of evidence, ELT theorists and practitioners of the mid 1990s cannot be said to be the first to express interest in what are now called 'global issues'.

Contributions to *ELT Journal* over the years have reflected the interest of ELT theorists and practitioners in a succession of favoured approaches or methods. These have included the structural approach, the direct method, the audio-visual approach, the notional-functional approach, the natural approach, the humanistic approach, and from the 1970s onwards, the biggest and perhaps most influential of all, the communicative approach. In the 1980s, a period called by Rossner and Bolitho (1990: 2) the 'second decade of the communicative era', the communicative approach in its various forms was probably the most easily identifiable issue that substantially concerned the ELT profession. Indeed, by the mid 1980s, the communicative approach, and the methods and techniques with which it is associated, had almost become an orthodoxy in its own right. For even though in reality the communicative approach was by no means established practice everywhere—and is still not to this day—it tended to be the frame of reference within which other activities were compared.

Another feature of the past was that, on the whole, 'experts' led and the rest of the profession followed. Not so in the less deferential, commercial, technological 1990s. This is the era of consumerism, of management and marketing, in which it is common for academic institutions to be called 'providers', textbooks to be known as 'products', and students to be described as 'clients' or 'customers'. Small wonder then that many in the ELT profession today feel it necessary to pay attention not only to the principles and practices of applied linguistics and related disciplines, but also to the principles and practices of commerce.

And for the first time in history, the process of designing courses and materials is facilitated by the apparent freedoms afforded by technology. With the help of word processors, fax machines, computers, data bases, e-mail, and the Internet teachers and trainers can more easily and quickly assemble whatever they feel is appropriate for their own and their learners' needs, always providing they can meet the challenges of taming the technology and navigate their way through the vast amount of information available to them. Today, it would seem, everyone in ELT has the potential to become his or her own expert.

As for the process of writing itself, on-screen composition, rapid deletion, instant editing, and information exchange have released a tremendous amount of energy that, in earlier days, might well have been inhibited by the sheer effort involved in committing pen to paper or using a typewriter.

Not surprisingly, therefore, the late 1980s and early 1990s were particularly exciting and challenging years for *ELT Journal*. The rapid expansion and diversification of ELT throughout the world created an enormous increase in the number of colleagues for whom writing articles became a possible, desirable, and sometimes necessary feature of their professional lives. In the period covered by this book, *ELT Journal* was the beneficiary of a tension between, on the one hand, the reflections of what might be called the third decade of the communicative era, and, on the other, the potential afforded by the commercially and technologically conscious 1990s. It was as if the debate in Volume 39 of *ELT Journal* between Swan (1985a and 1985b) and Widdowson (1985) about the true nature and value of the communicative approach had almost run its course, and that it had been as fully absorbed into the profession as it was ever likely to be. At all events, the profession's centre of gravity gradually shifted from what by the mid 1980s had become relatively familiar discussions about one set of principles and practices towards a growing interest in a greater number of other issues.

Of course, some of the issues of interest to contributors and readers during this time, for example curriculum design, language analysis, language and culture, teacher training, and testing were already familiar, and had been discussed in *ELT Journal* for many years. But others, for example computer-assisted language learning, the use of e-mail, gender, language teaching and imperialism, learner training, management, evaluation, learner autonomy, and self-access were either new, or familiar issues looked at in a fresh light. Naturally, many of them owed a great deal, some their very existence, to the communicative approach.

But for readers of *ELT Journal*, issues are of interest not simply because they are new or newly treated. They need to be written about in the context of the aims of the Journal. These are to 'bridge the gap between the everyday practical concerns of ELT professionals and related disciplines such as education, linguistics, psychology and sociology that may offer significant insights' and to 'provide a medium for informed discussion of the principles and practice which determine the ways in which the English language is taught and learnt around the world'. Between 1988 and 1995 almost 250 articles fulfilled those aims and were published in *ELT Journal*, and it is from them that the twenty-seven articles for this collection were chosen.

The task of selecting the articles was not an easy one. There were many interesting and valuable contributions from authors working in a wide range of teaching contexts and settings. However, our final choice was based on three criteria. We selected articles which we felt were *representative*, in that they illustrate the range of themes and topics which characterized the profession's interests in the period 1988–1995; *significant*, in that they have provoked and continue to provoke debate and discussion among students, teachers, teacher trainers, and researchers, in some cases prompting further study and research; and on the evidence thus far, *influential*, in that the issues they raise are likely to be of continuing interest and relevance.

The book is divided into three parts, called 'Power', 'Pedagogy', and 'Practice'. These are themes which we felt were of particular importance in the period 1988–1995, and which represent long-standing concerns. They testify to the evolutionary nature of change and development in the profession in recent years.

Each of the three major themes is illustrated by articles on different topics, though it is the point of view or overall orientation of each article and not just its particular topic that determines its location in this book. In principle, therefore, a single topic (e.g. learner autonomy) could figure in more than one section, depending on its orientation and treatment by the author.

The articles in Part One, 'Power', deal with issues in the ownership of language and the empowerment of learners and teachers. The theme is illustrated by articles on the debate about native-speaking and non-native speaking teachers, the use of English as a medium in education, language and culture, standard English and other Englishes, empowerment within projects, gender and power, aspects of autonomous learning, and critical reading.

Part Two, on 'Pedagogy', contains articles dealing with issues in the professional development of teachers. Regular readers of *ELT Journal* will know that articles about teacher education and development have always appeared in its pages. Submissions on these topics were particularly numerous during the years 1988–1995, perhaps reflecting the growth in demand and opportunities for training of ELT teachers around the world, and the development of specialized programmes for teachers of young learners, Business English, English for Specific Purposes, and English for Academic Purposes. Topics covered in this section include developing the reflective practitioner, principles for in-service teacher education, issues in teacher education for innovation, the use of diaries on in-service courses, the needs of pre-service trainees, training the trainer, and continuing professional development.

The articles in Part Three, 'Practice', explore issues in curriculum design and practice. The first three articles are concerned with the communicative classroom (particularly with how to create genuine communication in the classroom) the use of role play in literature classes, and the characteristics of communication tasks. The remaining six articles are about teacher and learner roles (with special reference to learner-centred methodology, and moves towards self-access learning), process approaches to writing, the roles of teaching materials (particularly in relation to innovation and authenticity), and evaluation.

Each section is introduced by a Preview which presents the main issues to be discussed and sets the articles in context. The Previews also refer to other relevant articles which have been published in *ELT Journal*, and suggest further reading. The Conclusion pulls together some of the main themes identified in this collection. In addition, we have included a topic index to Volumes 42–49 which lists the articles and survey reviews published in *ELT Journal* between 1988 and 1995.

We hope that readers will find this a valuable guide and a useful resource, that it will serve them in their work and study, and encourage further discussion, debate, and research in the profession.

# PART ONE

# POWER

*Issues in the ownership of
language and the empowerment
of learners and teachers*

# PREVIEW

Empowerment is hardly a new concept in education. There has been a rich tradition of writing on the topic since Freire (1972) argued for an educational methodology which would enable people to look critically at the world in dialogic encounter with others and participate in changing their lives for the better. But it is in more recent years that empowerment has figured as a recurring theme in ELT and *ELT Journal*. Indeed, power is a theme which runs through all three parts of this collection.

It emerges in recent discussions of teacher development in Part Two 'Pedagogy' and in discussions of curriculum practice in Part Three 'Practice'. In this first section, however, the theme of power can be perceived initially in a selection of articles that relate to issues in the internationalization of English. It relates to conflicting views on the ownership of the English language and the issues created by this conflict, for example: how can the ELT profession ensure that appropriate value is placed on the qualities and capacities of non-native teachers and thus secure their empowerment? What constitutes appropriate cultural content in materials? What are the effects of exporting the English of dominant English-speaking countries to other parts of the globe, particularly third world contexts?

The theme of empowerment has also related to local teachers through the development of participatory approaches to project management. There has been much discussion, too, of the empowerment of learners through, for example, autonomous learning schemes or critical approaches to reading. These issues form the substance of this section.

## Ownership of the English language

A recurring theme of the last decade has been power and politics in the ownership of the English language. Kachru (1985) draws attention to the ways in which people around the world have been taking ownership of English and moulding it to suit their own needs and cultures. He conceptualizes an 'outer circle' of countries in which English has been institutionalized as a language and an 'expanding circle' in which English is the primary foreign language. This rapid internationalization of English has posed significant questions for the ELT profession. The articles included here are representative of the questions and the debate which surrounds them.

### The native/non-native issue

One significant question has been whether the traditional distinction between native and non-native speaker is still functional. For RAMPTON (Volume 44/2 1990) the answer is No. Following Kachru (1982a) he advocates displacing the terms 'native speaker' and 'mother tongue'. His concerns are that these terms 'clutter our perception' of the links between speakers and languages and that the dominant notion of the native speaker inappropriately maintains the power of the USA and the UK in ELT. The article clearly mirrors a growing unease with popular professional terminology and the values implicit within it as the internationalization of English proceeds at a rapid pace and the 'non-native teacher' assumes an even greater role in the global ELT profession. PHILLIPSON (Volume 46/1, 1992a) takes up the 'native speaker' concept from a UK perspective and poses two specific questions: is the expertise that British ELT offers really the most appropriate for other countries and cultures? and do native speakers necessarily make the best language teachers? The second of these questions is discussed by MEDGYES (Volume 46/4, 1992) whose paper is sensitive to the limits and potential of both native and non-native teachers. He gives what many teachers may find a constructively balanced view after the years of polemic.

### The use of English as a medium in education

ABBOTT (Volume 46/2, 1992) discusses another issue of our times: does the use of English as a medium in the outer circle of countries contaminate learners with alien ideological values to the extent of devaluing local languages and culture? He suggests that substantial numbers of school children throughout the world in English medium education are victims of a process which one of his sources (Freire 1972) calls 'cultural invasion' whereby 'the invaders penetrate the cultural context of another group and ... ignoring the potential of the latter ... impose their own view of the world upon those they invade'. Although Abbott advises caution in making radical decisions about the role of English, he does suggest the need for studies to illuminate possible links among an imposed language, failing literacy, and underdevelopment.

## Language and culture

ALPTEKIN (Volume 47/2, 1993) considers the complex relationships between language learning, language teaching, and culture. It reflects such questions as: is English language teaching inextricably bound to the culture and values of the inner circle of English-speaking countries (USA, UK, Canada, Australia, New Zealand)? Is it possible to become bilingual without becoming bicultural? Alptekin focuses specifically on the use of the target language culture as a vehicle for teaching the language in textbook materials and considers a series of issues: whether it is possible to teach a language without embedding it in its cultural base; what dangers such embedding might hold for cultural stereotyping; and what the appropriate cultural base would be anyway. Interested readers will find a range of perspectives on culture in language teaching, discussing these and other questions, in recent volumes of *ELT Journal*. Bowers (Volume 46/1, 1992) suggests that there will be different levels of cultural engagement for English in the years ahead. Prodromou (Volume 46/1, 1992) investigates students' perceptions of the issues through a questionnaire survey. Adaskou *et al.* (Volume 44/1, 1990) explore the possible meanings of culture in relation to the foreign language cultural component of national textbooks.

## Standard English and other Englishes

WIDDOWSON (Volume 47/4, 1993) takes up what the author calls notions of 'property and propriety' and contributes perspectives on standard English to the debate on English as a world language. He takes the view that the standard must be sustained, else 'things fall apart', a strong view, but carefully justified in terms of the empowerment of first- and second-language learners and qualified by a respect for the purposes of other varieties and a disrespect for forms of linguistic chauvinism.

Other contributors to *ELT Journal* have also discussed the issues of
world Englishes. Interested readers will find comment on the role of
standard English as specific to the Nigerian context in articles by
Omodiaogbe (Volume 46/1, 1992) and Bisong (Volume 49/2, 1995),
which point to the need for understanding the complex nature of multilingual societies in relation to issues of English medium education and
the role of standard English.

Doubtless Widdowson's 'unanswerable case', as he describes it, for
the teaching of standard English will continue to be answered by those
concerned about the effect of English as a discourse of power on the
status of other varieties and other languages. As English continues to
respond to the pressures of internationalization, one suspects that the
debate will rage on with some intensity.

## Empowerment within projects

In her discussion of the effective management of ELT projects,
STEPHENSON (Volume 48/3, 1994) reflects a further dimension of ownership. An important focus of the textbook design project she describes
in São Tomé and Príncipe was the use of collaborative processes at a
local and grassroots level in order to involve teachers in the development of their own professional work and thereby to encourage a sense
of ownership over the new materials. Her discussion provides an example of the emphasis laid in recent years on ownership as the key to the
sustainability of innovation within projects.

Contemporary management theory has made much of how curriculum change implies other, more difficult, kinds of change among those
affected by it, particularly the teachers who are expected to put the new
curriculum into practice. For sponsors or managers, curriculum change
ostensibly involves identifying, defining, and resolving specific problems, for example, of course design, textbook design or in-service
teacher training. For the end users, the teachers, it involves new ways of
looking at their teaching, a transformation of perspective which
impinges on personal theories underlying classroom practice. These
may be deeply buried, strong, and resistant. If an innovation is to be
successfully adopted by teachers, it has now become a tenet of project
management that managers must be concerned not only with the substance of change but with strategies for initiating and implementing it.
Stephenson believes that those specific strategies should include the
benefits of participatory processes, especially in what are essentially
externally initiated, top-down frameworks.

Other contributors to *ELT Journal* have taken up the same theme over recent years. Woods (Volume 42/3, 1988) argues that local participants should be involved at all stages in the innovation process and describes how the new syllabus for a teacher training college in Sierra Leone was produced by staff in workshops so that the lecturers developed a sense of ownership and a commitment to promoting and developing it. Palmer (Volume 47/2, 1993) gives an account of how experienced teachers were found to be more willing to experiment with a government-initiated innovation in Norway when they were given the opportunity to make the idea their own. He points to a strong correlation between personal investment in a new idea and a commitment to trying it out. Waite (Volume 48/3, 1994), in a case study of setting up self-access learning facilities in Nicaragua, argues that success depended on decisions made within the teaching team during staff development sessions. And, giving the opposite experience, Tomlinson (Volume 44/1, 1990), in his case study of the PKG project in Indonesian secondary schools, comments on the difficulties engendered when some of the stakeholders in the innovation were insufficiently involved from the beginning and developed suspicion of the curriculum change as radical and subversive, not only of existing curriculum objectives, but also of the fundamental school culture.

These articles have in common a perception that managers cannot simply formulate aims and policies and implement them in what they see as a rational procedure. They suggest the need to build a sense of shared ownership of the change and support mechanisms during the process of change. They seem to suggest that centralized direction can be successfully integrated with local involvement and decision-making. As yet, no contributor has questioned whether notions of participation and ownership are being used, by those directing from the centre, as Hargreaves (1982: 254) puts it, 'as a legitimizing device for forms of social control'. It will be interesting to see whether project evaluators ten years from now will be discussing this essential tension between authority and autonomy which lies at the heart of many an ELT project.

## Gender and power

The theme of empowerment is also reflected in articles dealing with matters of a more local pedagogic nature. The article by SUNDERLAND (Volume 46/1, 1992) links gender and power. One of the questions she raises in her discussion of learner–teacher interaction in the classroom is that of 'more time for the boys'. She quotes studies which show the

unequal attention paid to male and female students in education and in
ELT and considers how this might reflect unequal power relationships
in the background culture. This is one of several questions addressed in
this article and those of other contributors to *ELT Journal* (Florent and
Walter, Volume 43/3, 1989 and two articles by Kaye, Volume 43/3,
1989a) concerning the role of women in TEFL: the importance of
avoiding sexism in EFL materials; the problems of dealing with linguistic sexism; the need for awareness of classroom gender differences; and
the danger of marginalizing female students.

Such articles demonstrate the increasing interest in the empowerment
of women and it is not insignificant that the last decade has seen the
establishment of the group 'Women in TEFL', which aims to improve
the status of women in TEFL, ensure equal opportunities, and improve
the portrayal of women in textbook materials.

Sunderland's article also indicates some fruitful areas for further
research, including for example, whether teachers employ double standards in error treatment or in their acceptance of classroom behaviour,
whether female learners are more proficient than male learners, and if
so, what that might imply.

## Learner empowerment

Perhaps that aspect of empowerment most frequently addressed in articles submitted to *ELT Journal* between 1988 and 1995 has been to do
with learner empowerment, although A. S. Hornby's editorial in
Volume 1/2 suggests that this is far from being a new concern. He wrote:

> It has been said that language study is becoming dehumanized and
> mechanical, that the pupil is caused to lose whatever he may have of
> initiative and that he becomes a mere automaton responding blindly
> to stimuli applied by his teachers ... In short, the learner is so hedged
> in that he may, with good reason, protest against so many restrictions
> on his freedom. (1946b: 31)

The freedoms implied by Hornby may well have been wider cognitive
and linguistic freedoms. The current concern is more specifically with
learner autonomy or, as some term it, self-direction in learners. This
concern with learner autonomy is well exemplified by the Talking Shop
interview with DICKINSON (Volume 47/4, 1993) and the article by
SPOLSKY (Volume 43/3, 1989).

## Aspects of autonomous learning

Leslie Dickinson is the author of several books on autonomy in language learning. In the interview in this collection he talks about autonomous learners as people who are aware of the teacher's objectives, who can formulate their own objectives for learning, can select and implement appropriate learning strategies, can decide which strategies are effective for them and can monitor their own learning. It is clear from this set of characteristics that one set of arguments for encouraging greater independence in learners comes from studies into the qualities of the 'good language learner'. Other contributors to *ELT Journal* have taken this perspective. Pearson (Volume 42/3, 1988), for example, describes how she came to appreciate the nature and importance of learner strategies through interviews with her students. Porte (Volume 42/3, 1988) gives insights into the strategies used by underachieving EFL learners in vocabulary acquisition and suggests how the teacher can help such learners to identify and refine their strategies. Dörnyei and Thurrell (Volume 45/1, 1991) look in particular at communication strategies and at classroom training activities for these. Fortune (Volume 46/2, 1992) describes a small-scale research study into learner preferences for inductive or deductive self-study grammar exercises and discusses how these fit with the characteristics of the good language learner. Schmitt and Schmitt (Volume 49/2, 1995) give a detailed discussion of the effective use of vocabulary notebooks as one metacognitive strategy which can be encouraged in leaners as part of their strategic investment in their own learning. All of these articles have a fundamental concern with whether it is possible to facilitate learning through the use of certain strategies and whether learners can modify their strategies and learn new, more effective ones.

Dickinson also highlights recent moves towards self-directed learning based on the belief that learners are capable of making judgements and decisions about their learning. This implies the need for structures within which learners *can* take on more responsibility for their own learning and some of these structures are considered in detail in Part Three. Other issues raised in the interview are the cultural appropriateness of autonomous learning as a concept and the need for further empirical work to investigate strategy training, a point echoed by Ellis (Volume 47/1, 1993) who discusses, in another Talking Shop interview, the need for a research agenda in this area. It is hoped that the next decade will see further discussion of both issues.

## Critical reading

Ellen Spolsky's article continues the theme of empowering learners. She examines the problems of selecting and interpreting texts in the teaching of literature. In doing so, she mirrors a current preoccupation with critical pedagogy and particularly with critical reading, an approach which seeks to help readers appreciate that texts are ideologically invested in various ways. There has been a good deal of debate in recent years about the degree to which learners are manipulated by the intended meaning of writers as communicated by their choice of language and image. Arguably, adult first-language readers can choose what stance they take towards the dominant discourse of a text though not all would agree that there is sufficient awareness even among these readers about the ways in which language can manipulate a response. The issue for English-language teachers, particularly those responsible for the maturing minds of secondary ESL readers with uncertain language competence, is whether awareness raising is a necessary procedure to ensure resistant reading.

Spolsky starts with sources in feminist literary criticism and their belief that women, in their education, are expected to submit to a value system which is essentially male and that they should be helped to resist that set of values. She draws a parallel between this and presenting literary texts to second-language readers whose acceptance of values in a culturally alien text might devalue their own culture and experience. Her examples are telling and make a strong case for training learners to be critical and resistant. The reflective reader will find many issues implicit within her article. What principles can define the pedagogic process when dealing with controversial texts in the secondary-school classroom? Is the mode of enquiry in critical reading methodology one of discussion or instruction? How do teachers use their authority? These issues are at the heart of current discussion.

The following articles have been chosen to reflect a variety of perspectives as discussion has proceeded on these issues of ownership and empowerment. Each article takes up a key issue and is representative of the professional debate of the last decade. The cogency of the debate remains unabated and will doubtless generate further arguments and counter-arguments in the coming years.

# I

## Displacing the 'native speaker': expertise, affiliation, and inheritance

M. B. H. RAMPTON

*The whole mystique of the native speaker and the mother tongue should probably be quietly dropped from the linguist's set of professional myths about language.[1]*

## Mystique and myth

Braj Kachru and Charles Ferguson are not alone in this observation, and dissatisfaction with the terms 'native speaker' and 'mother tongue' is now very widespread. At the same time, these terms seem to be very resilient, and efforts to modify them just end up testifying indirectly to their power. For example, a good deal of effort is now being made to show the independent legitimacy of Englishes worldwide, but when these are described as 'the other tongue' or 'nativized varieties', the English of the ethnic Anglos is still there in the background as the central reference point. There is a need for new terms and this article suggests some.

## The trouble with the native speaker

It is important first of all to be clear about what the problems actually are. Otherwise, alterations may be simply cosmetic. In an educational context, the idea of being the native speaker of a language and having it as your mother tongue tends to imply at least five things:

1 A particular language is inherited, either through genetic endowment or through birth into the social group stereotypically associated with it.

2  Inheriting a language means being able to speak it well.

3  People either are or are not native/mother-tongue speakers.

4  Being a native speaker involves the comprehensive grasp of a language.

5  Just as people are usually citizens of one country, people are native speakers of one mother tongue.

All these connotations are now strongly contested by many people. The capacity for language itself may be genetically endowed, but *particular* languages are acquired in social settings. It is sociolinguistically inaccurate to think of people belonging to only one social group, once and for all. People participate in many groups (the family, the peer group, and groups defined by class, region, age, ethnicity, gender, etc.): membership changes over time and so does language. Being born into a group does not mean that you automatically speak its language well—many native speakers of English can't write or tell stories, while many non-native speakers can. Nobody's functional command is total: users of a language are more proficient in some areas than others. And most countries are multilingual: from an early age children normally encounter two or more languages. Yet despite the criticisms, the terms native speaker and mother tongue remain in circulation, continuously insinuating their assumptions.

There are always ideological issues involved in discussions about who speaks what in education, and political interests often have a stake in maintaining the use of these concepts. Thus the supremacy of the native speaker keeps the UK and the US at the centre of ELT: at the opposite end of the scale, governments may use the notion of mother tongue to imply that certain languages are of interest only to particular minority groups, thereby denying either a language or its speakers full involvement in mainstream education.[2] On its own, altering terminology does little to change this state of affairs, but by inserting or removing particular assumptions, alteration can clarify or usefully redirect our understanding.

As concepts, mother tongue and native speaker link together several ideas which it is vital to separate. Summarizing the problem with these concepts, we can say that:

1  They spuriously emphasize the biological at the expense of the social. Biological factors doubtless do count in language learning, but they never make themselves felt in a direct and absolute way. Their influence is only ever interpreted in social context, and so to a considerable extent, they are only as important as society chooses to make them.[3]

2 They mix up language as an instrument of communication with language as a symbol of social identification.[4]

Recognition of the first difficulty helps to direct our search for alternative terms. Our selections must acknowledge the social nature of the processes which link people to particular languages. They must be able to connect productively with our wider understanding of society. With that requirement in mind, we can then begin to address the second difficulty.

## Language expertise

When educationalists have the communicative aspects of language in mind, they should speak of accomplished users as *expert* rather than as *native* speakers. Expertise has the following advantages over nativeness as a metaphor for considering language proficiency:

1 Although they often do, experts do not have to feel close to what they know a lot about. Expertise is different from identification.

2 Expertise is learnt, not fixed or innate.

3 Expertise is relative. One person's expert is another person's fool.

4 Expertise is partial. People can be expert in several fields, but they are never omniscient.

5 To achieve expertise, one goes through processes of certification, in which one is judged by other people. Their standards of assessment can be reviewed and disputed. There is also a healthy tradition of challenging 'experts'.

The notion of expertise overcomes at least some of the problems. It is also fairer to both learners and teachers. Firstly, if native-speaker competence is used to set targets and define proficiency, the learner is left playing a game in which the goal-posts are being perpetually moved by people they cannot often challenge. But if you talk about expertise, then you commit yourself to specifying much more closely the body of knowledge that students have to aim at. Learning and teaching become much more accountable. In addition, the notion of expert shifts the emphasis from 'who you are' to 'what you know', and this has to be a more just basis for the recruitment of teachers.

Expertise does not, however, cover the ways in which language can stand as a symbol of social group identification. This is a very important issue in education, and it is also strongly connoted in the terms native language and mother tongue. To emphasize that symbolic value, a term like 'language loyalty' (or 'language allegiance') needs to be added alongside language expertise.

## *Language loyalty*
### Inheritance and affiliation

In fact, two aspects of language loyalty are worth distinguishing: inheritance and affiliation. It is particularly important to use a specific term to stake out the claims of the second (language affiliation) in order to make sure that the shadowy authority of notions like native language don't lead us to give pride of place to the first (inheritance).

Both affiliation *and* inheritance are negotiated. This is fairly self-evident with affiliation, which we commonly think of in terms of the social processes that it involves (requesting, applying, granting, agreeing, breaking off, etc.). But it is also true in the case of inheritance. Governments make laws about it; people try to decide what cultural and material items to include in their legacies; while others accept, claim, reject, and contest them. The crucial difference between them is that affiliation refers to a connection between people and groups that are considered to be separate or different, whereas inheritance is concerned with the continuity between people and groups who are felt to be closely linked. Inheritance occurs *within* social boundaries, while affiliation takes place *across* them.

Because both inheritance and affiliation are matters of social negotiation and conflict, the relationship between them is always flexible, subtle, and responsive to the wider context. It would be very hard to assert definitively that X is a language of inheritance and Y is a language of affiliation—indeed in doing so, you would have to recognize that you were taking up a stance in social debate. People belong to many groups; feelings of group-belonging change, and so do the definitions of groups themselves. New but valued inheritances can emerge from powerful affiliations, while cherished inheritances can lose their value and be disowned. Wherever language inheritance is involved, there tends to be a sense of the permanent, ancient, or historic. It is important, however, to underline the fact that affiliation can involve a stronger sense of attachment, just as the bond between love partners may be more powerful than the link between parents and children.

## Inheritance and affiliation compared with other terms

There are a great many terms other than mother tongue and native
language which are used to describe the ties between speakers and languages. What is the particular value of thinking about language loyalty
in terms of inheritance and affiliation? The value of these terms lies in
the way they draw attention to language education as a social activity
in which efforts are made to manage continuity, change, and the relationship between social groups.

   There are, of course, many definitions of languages in terms of when,
where, and how much they are learnt and used—*first, second, primary,
home, school*, etc. But these do not go to the heart of language allegiance: it is perfectly possible for someone to regard a language learned
at age 35 in college as a part of his or her group inheritance. Other terms
focus more directly on group relations—for example, 'majority' and
'minority' language, or 'ethnic', 'national', and 'community' language.
But, for the three reasons below, these terms are not as incisive or as generally applicable as the notions of language inheritance and language
affiliation.

1  Whereas the terms mentioned can all be valuable concepts in *particular* settings, inheritance and affiliation point to aspects of loyalty that
   are relevant to *all* group situations, however they are defined (by family, class, gender, race, region, profession, etc.).

2  There is a tendency to think only of inheritance when terms like
   ethnic or community language are used, and as a result speakers may
   get fixed in language categories.

3  Affiliation and inheritance can be used to discuss the position of individuals as well as groups, and this is useful in discussion of education,
   which generally has to consider both.

## *Conclusion*

Sociolinguistic situations are always very complicated, and it is important to have a number of ways of thinking about the links between
people and language. For many purposes, the concepts 'expertise',
'inheritance', and 'affiliation' will be inappropriate, and they obviously
leave out certain issues that are relevant to language and inter-group
relations (for example, as they stand, they don't treat language enmity).
Nevertheless, they help us to think about individual cases and about
general situations more clearly than do the concepts 'native speaker'

and 'mother tongue'. They tell us to inspect each native speaker's credentials closely, and they insist that we do not assume that nationality and ethnicity are the same as language ability and language allegiance. They also remind us to keep our eyes on social affairs. It is not hard to think of governments which talk about reward according to expertise ('equality of opportunity'), require smaller groups to relinquish their inheritances, but then only concede them affiliate status. The 'native speaker' and the 'mother tongue' clutter our perception of these and other situations.

*Originally published in Volume 44/2, 1990*

## Acknowledgements

I would like to thank Jill Bourne and Dick Hudson for conversations relevant to this article.

## Notes

1  See Ferguson (1982) and Kachru (1982).

2  See, for example, Naysmith (1986/7) and Skutnabb-Kangas (1981)

3  For a full critique of the ways in which biological and 'natural' explanations of learning have been used to serve particular social ends in language education, see Bourne (1988).

4  On this distinction, see, for example, Weinreich (1953) and Edwards (1977).

# 2

## *ELT: the native speaker's burden?*

ROBERT PHILLIPSON

## *Inflated claims and a questionable assumption*

The current boom in the demand for English has been accompanied by inflated claims for what the *language* can do and for what the *language teaching profession* can do.

The assumption underlying such claims seems to be that more English or more ELT can only be for the good of the learners in question. But this is highly questionable as a general principle in educational language planning. It is a dubious assumption in relation to many specific issues, such as the current vogue in continental Europe to start foreign languages earlier in the primary school; or English being projected as a panacea for the ills of Eastern Europe (according to Douglas Hurd in the spring of 1990, it is British Government policy to replace Russian by English as the first foreign language throughout Eastern and Central Europe); or the continued dominant role of English in southern countries which are in educational and social crisis (Mateene 1985; Ngũgĩ 1986; Hawes and Coombe 1986).

When claims for English or ELT are put forward, the appropriate response would be to ask: 'What scientific evidence is there for them?' Analysis of such arguments, of who uses them and why, can illuminate the factors that determine decisions to promote a particular pedagogical approach, or one language rather than another, and the major social implications that such decisions entail. Analysis needs to place the arguments in their historical context if light is to be shed on the force of the arguments and their truth value. As Ansre has shown (1979) in relation to the advocacy of English in West Africa, the arguments may be false, or irrelevant to the planning of basic education, or both.

## Inflated claims about English

Inflated claims about *the English language* can be analysed as relating to three supposed attributes of the language. The arguments refer to the *intrinsic* nature of a language (e.g. English as 'well adapted for development and change', Strevens 1980: 85; English as 'tied to no particular social, political, economic or religious system, nor to a specific racial or cultural group', Wardhaugh 1987: 15); but these are matters which few linguists take seriously these days. Or they refer to the *extrinsic* resources associated with a language (e.g. availability of teaching materials or trained teachers); but these are arguments which tend to ignore the structural power which accounts for the privileged position of some languages. Or they refer to the *uses* to which a language may be put (English as leading to technological advance, prosperity, or national unity); but these are arguments which are in the nature of a promise, and which may turn out to be as unredeemable in Uganda or Nigeria as in Northern Ireland. Such special pleading for English has been analysed in depth elsewhere (Phillipson 1990a, and Phillipson 1992b), and will not be pursued further here.

## *Arguments used in marketing ELT*

This article will concentrate on claims of the second type: that is arguments used in marketing ELT, of which the following two are not untypical samples. The first comes from a policy statement on foreign language teaching in Europe after 1992, the second from an article on standard English published in *English Today*, and first delivered as a paper to the Japanese Association of Language Teachers.

> The native speaker should become the standard foreign-language teacher within the countries of the European Community. They know best what is important in the language teaching of tomorrow: the active and creative language use in everyday communication. (Freudenstein 1991)

> ... the latest ideas in English teaching. Where best, after all, to get the latest ideas on this than in the leading English-speaking countries? (Quirk 1990)

The progenitors of such arguments are eminent scholars who are well placed to influence the reshaping of the European and global linguistic maps.[1] Indeed, the notion that the ideal teacher is a native speaker of the language is a cornerstone of a monolingual pedagogy, this being 'the hallmark which set ELT apart from foreign language teaching in Britain' (Howatt 1984: 212). The British variant of ELT evolved in two main seedbeds, the adult education field (in which Palmer, Hornby, *et al.* worked), and colonial education systems, which in secondary and higher education attempted to reproduce globally the teaching of English as a mother tongue in the metropolis (Perren 1963). These strands came together when applied linguistics and ELT were actively expanded from the end of the 1950s, as a result of the British Government appreciating the connection between the promotion of English as a worldwide second language and the maintenance of British influence in the post-colonial era. American ESL started off by being contrastively orientated, but, under the influence of structuralism in linguistics and behaviourism in psychology, became almost equally monolingual in approach (the exception being the bilingual education programmes for particular minority group children).

## *The native-speaker ideal*

The native-speaker ideal dates from a time when language teaching was indistinguishable from culture teaching. All learners of English were assumed to be familiarizing themselves with the culture(s) that English originated from, for contact of some form with the culture(s). The ideal also predates tape-recordings, video, and other technical resources which now permit learners to be exposed to a wide range of native-speaker models as well as second language users of English. It equally predates any realization of the consequences of what Kachru (1986) refers to as 'nativization', the process by which English has indigenized in different parts of the world, and developed distinct local forms determined by local norms. In such countries, there may be controversy about norms, but the native-speaker norm has already been superseded by events, at least outside the classroom. (Nativization should not be confused with the native-speaker concept, and is invariably associated with bilingualism or multilingualism.)

In linguistics, the problematical theoretical status of the native-speaker concept is appreciated (Coulmas 1981b). In sociolinguistics, the native speaker has been unmasked, and proposals made for displacing him or her (Rampton 1990). In ELT, the native speaker has been sent worldwide to teach, train teachers, and advise. In the other direction, key language people have been funded by such bodies as the British Council and the Overseas Development Administration (ODA) to imbibe ELT at source. Official British conviction has been that 'University departments of applied linguistics in Britain lead the world in the research and practice of the teaching of language, and especially English as both a foreign and second language' (ODA 1990: 12), an ethnocentric claim which is cast in the same mould as those of Freudenstein and Quirk. It is intriguing to speculate on what evidence, scientific or otherwise, there might be for such a claim. Or are we to assume that it is merely academic jingoism, for the eyes of politicians and bureaucrats only?

Why should the native speaker be intrinsically better qualified than the non-native? This is presumably felt to be the case because of greater facility in demonstrating fluent, idiomatically appropriate language (the factor that Freudenstein highlights), in appreciating the cultural connotations of the language, and in assessing whether a given language form is acceptably correct or not.

None of these virtues is impervious to teacher training. Nor is any of them something that well trained non-natives cannot acquire. Teachers, whatever popular adages say, are made rather than born, many of them doubtless self-made, whether they are natives or non-natives. The insight that teachers have into language learning processes, and into the structure and usage of a language, and their capacity to analyse and explain language, definitely have to be learnt—which is not the same as saying that they have to be taught, though hopefully teaching can facilitate and foster these qualities.

The untrained or unqualified native speaker is in fact potentially a menace because of ignorance of the structure of the mother tongue, a point that Quirk makes convincingly in the article quoted above. There are indeed strong grounds for concern about the deficient metalinguistic awareness of any under-trained native speaker: many of the products of the British education system recruited into ELT apparently do not know much about their language (see the letter from an experienced ELT appointments officer in the *Guardian Weekly*, 23 July 1989). Nor is there anything new about awareness of the limitations of the native speaker: 'A teacher is not adequately qualified to teach a language merely because it is his mother tongue', warns the UNESCO monograph on the use of the vernacular languages in education (UNESCO 1953: 69).

But all this has not deterred the Anglo-American ELT world from operating with native-speaker-teacher competence as the ideal. This has occurred even though some influential ELT writers were aware of the nativization process in places to which the ideal had been transplanted, and suggested alternative norms for learners. A paper on 'Language and Communication in the Commonwealth', prepared for the third Commonwealth Education Conference (Ottawa, Canada, 1964) notes that in the African context 'English must be seen as an African language—albeit an acquired one—and must be ready to serve as the vehicle for distinctively African cultural values' (Perren and Holloway 1965: 20). Also in 1964, Halliday, McIntosh, and Strevens suggested a new realism in norms, when they described the emergence of 'educated West African English' and 'Indian English', labels which refer to a great number of varieties of English. They suggested that these could serve as acceptable local models, provided international intelligibility was maintained (1964: 296). This proposal to abandon a single, global norm was dubbed the 'British heresy in TESOL' by Prator (1968), whose arguments were unmasked as being ethnocentric and unscientific by Kachru (1976, republished in Kachru 1986).

The native-speaker-teacher ideal has remained as a central part of the conventional wisdom of the ELT profession. As with many hegemonic practices, there has been a tendency to accept it without question. The ideal can be seen in operation implicitly in the practices of the main ELT publishers, which for obvious reasons seek to market their products globally. The ideal can be seen explicitly in the reports of seminal conferences which nursed ELT into institutional existence and gave legitimation to a particular educational paradigm—for instance, the Makerere Conference on the Teaching of English as a Second Language, 1961, the key conference for 'Third World' ESL countries.

## Are non-native speakers better qualified?

In the European foreign language teaching tradition (teachers of French in Britain, of English in Scandinavia, etc.), which is highly successful in promoting some kinds of language learning, the ideal teacher has near-native-speaker proficiency in the foreign language, and comes from the same linguistic and cultural background as the learners. It is arguable, as a general principle, that non-native teachers may, in fact, be better qualified than native speakers, if they have gone through the complex process of acquiring English as a second or foreign language, have insight into the linguistic and cultural needs of their learners, a detailed awareness of how mother tongue and target language differ and what is difficult for learners, and first-hand experience of using a second or foreign language.

If this is so, it would seem to be a minimal requirement of teachers of English as a second or foreign language that they should have proven experience of and success in learning and using a second/foreign language themselves, and that they should have profound familiarity with the language and culture of the learners they are responsible for. Clearly, such teachers may or may not have English as their mother tongue.

Or is it enough if the ELT teacher, in addition to ideally being a native speaker (Freudenstein), has been through the best of British training (Quirk)? Quirk's claim seems to be that in places where English is used as a mother tongue there is the best expertise in the learning of English as a second or foreign language.

No one would dispute that there is considerable sophistication in British applied linguistics and ELT, in academic institutions in the public and private sectors, and in publishing houses, or that the scientific community worldwide should be familiar with this expertise. However, applied linguistics and English teaching circles in many other countries may have much more appropriate expertise for meeting the language learning needs of their country. British personnel may not fulfil the minimal requirements for a language teacher in such contexts. What is offensive in Quirk's argument is the apparent implication that there is less sophistication elsewhere, that Anglo-American monolingually-oriented experts are necessarily better qualified than their counterparts in countries where English is successfully learned as a second or foreign language.

One might posit as a general principle that scholars who regularly follow the scientific literature in several languages are in a better position than those who are limited to one; and it is interesting to speculate on what implications this might have for the anglophonic world.

## A dubious export

What is also highly dubious is how far British or American expertise is exportable to contexts with different cultural, linguistic, and pedagogic universes. Implementing educational innovation is an immensely complex undertaking, which presupposes control of a substantial number of variables. Monitoring educational change validly is an intrinsically difficult task. We are therefore frequently obliged to resort to more informal assessments. Among these there is abundant evidence of ELT not delivering the goods (see some of the critical papers from this journal collected in Rossner and Bolitho 1990). A recent example is Prodromou (1988), who wonders why 'a particular piece of "authentic" material may fall flat in the classroom; why the functional syllabus does not always function, why communicative methodology does not produce much communication, why Council of Europe Needs Analysis has not met the Greek learners' needs'. He concludes that the teaching material, ideological messages, and pedagogy, which are part of a globally marketed ELT, are culturally inappropriate.

The grave implications of this are drawn out pointedly by a scholar who is generally extremely sober and generous in his views. Writing not of Greece, but of Third World countries, Kachru says:

> The role of English in the sociolinguistic context of each English-using Third World country is not properly understood, or is conveniently ignored. The consequences of this attitude are that the Third World countries are slowly realizing that, given the present attitude of TESL specialists, it is difficult to expect from such specialists any theoretical insights and professional leadership in this field which would be contextually, attitudinally, and pragmatically useful to the Third World countries. (Kachru 1986: 101)

## Conclusion

Hopefully, those who are assessing the merits of claims about English or ELT are in a position to see through them when they are manifestly false. This may, however, be an unrealistic expectation when such claims are presented by 'experts' who represent a prestigious language or a dominant pedagogical paradigm. Such arguments, their role and functions, therefore raise serious ethical and professional issues. To pursue the analysis of such claims in more depth requires elaboration of a more substantial theoretical framework and more detailed study of specific instances of how arguments have influenced policy. There is a clear need for more study of the senses and contexts in which ELT can be considered the 'native speaker's burden' and what consequences follow for present and future policy.

*Originally published in Volume 46/1, 1992*

## Acknowledgements

I should like to thank Tove Skutnabb-Kangas for her non-native but informed comments on the first draft of this paper. Much of the argument of the paper is elaborated in more depth in Phillipson 1992b.

# *Note*

1   At the time of writing, Freudenstein directed an information centre
    on foreign language teaching. He was secretary of the worldwide
    Fédération Internationale des Professeurs de Langues Vivantes
    (FIPLV), for which he edited a journal which was subsidized by
    Unesco. Quirk is an influential grammarian, who has taken upon
    himself the role of guardian of the standard English language globally
    (Quirk 1990). See also the preface to the *Longman Dictionary of
    Contemporary English* (1987), in which Quirk makes strong and
    eminently disputable statements about the role of various types of
    dictionary in foreign language learning.

# 3

## Native or non-native: who's worth more?

### PÉTER MEDGYES

## The native speaker/non-native speaker dichotomy

John Trim, one of the originators of the Threshold Level, once said, 'Foreign language teachers are, for obvious reasons, among the most internationally-minded people' (Trim 1978: 4).

### An international perspective

International-mindedness or, to use an equivalent term, liberalism, entails the rejection of any kind of discrimination, whether on grounds of race, sex, religion, education, intelligence, or mother tongue. We all are equal, liberals contend. No one is more equal than anyone else. There are as many equal varieties of English as there are countries where English is spoken as a first or second language—and a lot more, if dialects and sociolects are also taken into account.

Some researchers go so far as to suggest that non-native varieties should also be proclaimed as equal. Ridjanovic, for example, asks (somewhat ironically, perhaps): 'If there is Pakistani English, why not have Yugoslav English?' (Ridjanovic 1983: 11). To be sure, native speakers of English, Kachru argues, 'seem to have lost the exclusive prerogative to control its standardization; in fact, if current statistics are any indication, they have become a minority' (Kachru 1985: 29–30).

## Who is a native speaker?

Now the question is: who *is* a native speaker of English? A Briton is. A Hungarian is not. An Australian is. A French national is not. So far, so good. But what about an Indian for whom English was the language of school instruction and has been the language of professional communication ever since? He does not fit snugly into either the native- or the non-native-speaker slot. Indeed, countries where English is a second language break the homogeneity of the native/non-native division. The trouble is that this division does not always apply in so-called native English-speaking countries either. Let us take Juan, for example, aged 9, who has been living in the United States for five years. His father is a Mexican immigrant, his mother comes from Norway. They both speak to Juan in their own mother tongue. Which is his native language, English, Spanish, or Norwegian? All three of them? None of them?

From a sociolinguistic perspective, then, the native/non-native issue is controversial. It is equally debatable from a purely linguistic point of view. Efforts to define native competence or native-like proficiency have yielded inconclusive results at best (see, for example: Stern 1983; Crystal 1985; Richards *et al.* 1985). This gives the progressively-minded applied linguist one more reason to claim not only that native and non-native speakers have equal rights in using (and abusing) the English language, but also that there is no use in setting up two separate categories. Ferguson (1982), for example, says: 'The whole mystique of the native speaker and the mother tongue should probably be quietly dropped from the linguist's set of professional myths about language' (Kachru 1982b: vii). A similar attitude is reflected in an article which was published in a recent issue of *ELT Journal*. Characteristically, the title is 'Displacing the "native speaker"' (Rampton 1990). An even more radical view is propounded by the lexicographer Paikeday in his book *The Native Speaker is Dead!* (Paikeday 1985).

Edge makes a similar point, though less vehemently:

> As far as the teaching of English is concerned, it seems more and more important that ... training and development should help us escape from the essentially nationalistic view of native speaker/non-native speaker and get us involved in furthering an internationalist perspective in which users of English are simply more or less accomplished communicators. (Edge 1988: 156)

## The interlanguage continuum

It stems from Edge's logic that all users of English are simultaneously learners of English. By virtue of speaking a more or less advanced degree of interlanguage (see Selinker 1972), they can, metaphorically, be placed on the interlanguage continuum at any stage of their learning process. Progress is determined by various factors of the learning situation, among which the country of birth and education is assumed to play a decisive role. Thus, if born and brought up in an English-speaking environment, a person would be likely to be a more accomplished user of English than if born and brought up in a non-English-speaking country. Hence native speakers are, potentially, more accomplished users of English than non-native speakers.

zero<br>
competence
        
native<br>
competence

FIGURE 1 *The interlanguage continuum*

## Some alternative concepts

Before I carry on with this line of argument, let me mention some terms recommended by liberally minded researchers to replace 'native' and 'non-native speaker'. As indicated, Edge suggests 'more or less accomplished users of English' (Edge 1988), which is similar to Paikeday's 'more or less proficient users of English' (Paikeday 1985). Rampton (1990) introduces the concepts of 'expert speakers' and 'affiliation', both resonant of Kachru's 'English-using speech fellowships' (Kachru 1985). A somewhat older, but persistent, term is 'educated English speaker'.

For lack of space, I shall not subject any of these alternatives to a critical analysis. Suffice it to say that their meanings tend to overlap and they are no less spurious than the concept of the native versus non-native speaker. Indeed, whereas several more or less successful attempts have been made to define native competence/native-like proficiency over the decades, these more recent concepts have been left largely unexplained. One cannot help feeling that their protagonists are tied by their allegiance to liberal ideas rather than to the rigour demanded by scientific investigation. As a consequence, they are all too eager to throw the baby out with the bathwater. Although I am also aware of the ambiguities inherent in the terms native and non-native speaker, I shall keep using them for want of more suitable ones.

## The interlanguage continuum revised

Returning to my earlier reasoning, few people would dispute that those who use English as their first language have an advantage over those for whom it is a foreign language. My claim is that this advantage is so substantial that it cannot be outweighed by other factors prevalent in the learning situation, whether it be motivation, aptitude, perseverance, experience, education, or anything else. In other words, for all their efforts, non-native speakers can never achieve a native speaker's competence. The two groups remain clearly distinguishable. In view of this assumption, let me suggest, in Figure 2, a modified version of the interlanguage continuum.

zero
competence

native
competence

FIGURE 2 *A modified version of the interlanguage continuum*

Figure 2 illustrates that non-native speakers constantly move along the continuum as long as they learn-to-use/use-to-learn English. A select few come quite close to native competence (cf. the nebulous 'near-native speaker') but sooner or later they are halted by a glass wall. Few have managed to climb over it. Joseph Conrad, alias Józef Teodor Konrad Korzeniowski, was one, but such immortals are exceptions to the rule.

The main reason why non-natives cannot turn into natives lies in the fact that they are, by their very nature, norm-dependent. Their use of English is but an imitation of some form of native use. Just as epigons never become genuine artists, non-native speakers can never be as creative and original as those whom they have learnt to copy.

Non-native speakers are ill at ease with using English accurately and appropriately, and their fluency does not come up to native levels, either. Their handicap is even more conspicuous when their English-language performance is compared to their mother-tongue performance. Few of us would deny that we are far more capable in our first language, implying, among other things, that we are capable of reaching our communicative goals more directly and with less effort (Medgyes 1990). However, the native/non-native distinction only makes sense if people with comparable variables, such as age, sex, education, intelligence, profession, and experience, are examined. For example, non-native-speaking English teachers should not match themselves against Scottish shepherds or twelve-year-old Australian schoolchildren but against their native counterparts, that is, against native-speaking English teachers. In which case, can anyone seriously wonder whose English language competence is better? In my experience, liberal-minded researchers often shut their eyes to the glaring differences between natives and non-natives. They insist that there are far more important issues to be reckoned with than the question of whether the teacher happens to speak English as a first, second, or foreign language.

So far I have dealt with the native/non-native division in a general sense. In the following section, my focus will be on how this division features within the framework of the ELT profession. I shall argue that the native/non-native distinction not only exists, but that it plays a key role in determining the teaching practice of all teachers.

## *The native speaker/non-native speaker dichotomy in ELT*

I presented this paper to a group of highly sophisticated ELT specialists at the *ELT Journal* 45th Anniversary Symposium in London, October 1991. I began by putting to them the following question.

'Suppose you were the principal of a commercial ELT school in Britain. Who would you employ?

a. I would employ only native speakers, even if they were not qualified EFL teachers.

b. I would prefer to employ native-speaking EFL teachers, but if hard pressed I would choose a qualified non-native rather than a native without EFL qualifications.

c. The native/non-native issue would not be a selection criterion (provided the non-native-speaking EFL teacher was a highly proficient speaker of English).'

Subsequently, I took a straw poll, which showed that about two-thirds of the sixty or so respondents chose (b), one-third chose (c), but nobody voted for (a). For lack of time, I did not ask for justification, but it is not difficult to suggest factors that may have influenced their decision. Those whose choice was (b) must have heeded both business and professional considerations. With regard to the former, presumably they were aware that international students studying in Britain preferred to be taught by native-speaking English teachers. This demand would have to be satisfied by the school principal—but not at all costs. On the other hand, their answers implied less homogeneity in terms of professional considerations. While they all agreed that native-speaking EFL teachers (NESTs) and non-native-speaking EFL teachers (non-NESTs) were better than native speakers without EFL qualifications, they may have had divergent views about who would be better, the NEST or the non-NEST.

Idealists, in contrast to pragmatists, in choosing (c) seem to have taken notice of professional considerations only—and so might run the risk of losing their clientele. The fact that no one selected (a) was a reassuring sign that principals who are led by short-term business interests, or by the delusion that native speakers are superior to non-native speakers under any terms are not welcome at distinguished professional gatherings!

A month later, I put the same question to a group of EFL teachers, most of whom were native speakers of French (IATEFL-France, Paris, 1991). The forty or so responses were surprising. While (a) again scored nil, two-thirds of the votes went to (c) and only one-third to (b). Afterwards I asked the audience a follow-up question: 'Suppose you were the principal of a commercial ELT school *in France*. Who would you employ?' The alternatives were the same as before. The proportion of responses was even more slanted towards (c); (a) still received no votes.

Incidentally, both in London and in Paris I had toyed with, then abandoned, the idea of asking one more question:

'Once you had decided to employ a non-NEST, would you:

a. ask the teacher to hide his or her non-native identity and pretend to be a native speaker of English?

b. leave it to the teacher to resolve this dilemma at his or her discretion?

c. insist that the teacher should reveal his or her "non-nativeness"?'

In the light of the results demonstrated above, I hope it is no exaggeration to state that:

1  the ELT profession acknowledges the native/non-native distinction, or at least uses it in everyday life;

2  the issue is controversial;

3  there are several categories of consideration involved in this context (business, professional, linguistic, moral, political, and others).

It is also clear that, once we accept the native/non-native dichotomy, the question 'Who's worth more: the NEST or the non-NEST?' is bound to arise.

## *The survey*

Before I risk an answer, let me briefly contrast NESTs and non-NESTs. I advance two hypotheses:

1 NESTs and non-NESTs differ in terms of their language competence and teaching practice.

2 The discrepancy in language competence accounts for most of the differences found in their teaching practice.

With respect to language competence, I regard it as axiomatic that all non-NESTs are deficient users of English. However, this is meant to be a relative statement insomuch as native speakers may well have gaps in their L1 competence or performance. (There is, in fact, an argument for saying that the native speaker is only *potentially* superior. Some non-natives do better in certain areas of language use.)

In spite of the fact that every non-NEST has his or her own idiosyncratic problems in the use of English, there are several common areas of difficulty. In order to validate this assumption and then specify the most typical difficulties, in collaboration with Thea Reves, I took advantage of a broader-based survey to circulate a questionnaire among some 220 NESTs and non-NESTs working in 10 countries.

One item in the questionnaire which related to non-native respondents only read as follows:

'If you feel you have difficulties in the use of English, what are they? Describe them briefly.'

The most frequently encountered difficulties covered virtually all areas of language use, but especially fluency, vocabulary, pronunciation, listening comprehension, grammar, and idiomatic English.

Another question aimed to reveal the divergences in the teaching practice of NESTs compared to non-NESTs:

'Do you see any differences between native and non-native speaker teachers of English in the way they teach the foreign language?

YES ☐      NO ☐

If YES, what are the differences?'

The results show that 68 per cent of the respondents did perceive differences between natives and non-natives and a mere 15 per cent gave a
negative answer. In this paper I will not specify these differences, but I
found that they were fundamental, and closely related to linguistic
issues.

Although the survey data seem to validate both above-mentioned
hypotheses, they should be treated with caution for at least two reasons.
The first is that the sample examined was rather limited in size; the second is that the study was not based on classroom observation but on
respondents' perceptions, the reliability of which cannot be assessed.

## The more proficient, the more efficient?

So far I have stated that NESTs and non-NESTs use English differently
and, therefore, teach English differently. Next, I would like to examine
whether or not these differences carry any value judgement. That is to
say, is it true that, by virtue of having a better command of English,
NESTs perform better in the classroom? Conversely, is it true that the
more deficient the teacher is in English, the less efficient he or she is
bound to be? Let me study this question in all three possible dimensions.

### The native/non-native dimension

If language competence were the only variable of teaching skill, a NEST
would by definition be superior to his or her non-native colleague. It
would also follow that any native speaker, with or without EFL
qualifications, would be more effective than any non-native speaker. As
this is in striking contradiction to everyday experience, I must assume
that there exist other variables of teaching skill that have a bearing on
teaching practice. It is certainly the case that variables such as experience, age, sex, aptitude, charisma, motivation, training, and so on play a
decisive role in the teaching/learning process. As non-language-specific
variables, they can apply to NESTs and non-NESTs in equal measure.
For example, the non-native's personality can be just as charismatic as
any native's; he or she may have undergone the same length and form of
training; and so forth.

It seems that language competence is the only variable in which the
non-NEST is inevitably handicapped. Can I conclude, then, that if all
the other variables of teaching skill were kept equal, natives would sur-
pass their non-native colleagues owing to their native proficiency in
English? Apart from the unfeasibility of keeping the entire gamut of

variables stable, or even identifying what they are, my answer is a definite no. In my experience, natives and non-natives stand an equal chance of achieving professional success.

Given this, one important factor accessible only to non-NESTs must have been overlooked. I would claim that this variable is capable of off-setting the advantage NESTs have over non-NESTs, thanks to their native command of English. My assumption is that, paradoxically, the missing link is to be found in the non-natives' deficient English language competence; it is precisely this relative deficit that enables them to compete with native speakers, particularly in a monolingual ELT setting.

What is a weakness on one side of the coin is an asset on the other, for the following reasons:

1 *Only non-NESTs can serve as imitable models of the successful learner of English.* Depending on the extent to which they are proficient as users of English, they are more or less trustworthy models, too. In contrast, though NESTs can act as perfect language models they cannot be learner models since they are not learners of English in the sense that non-NESTs are.

2 *Non-NESTs can teach learning strategies more effectively.* Non-NESTs have adopted language learning strategies during their own learning process. In spite of the considerable differences between them in degrees of consciousness, in theory they all know more about the employment of these strategies than native colleagues who have simply acquired the English language.

3 *Non-NESTs can provide learners with more information about the English language.* During their own learning process, non-NESTs have gained abundant knowledge about and insight into how the English language works, which might be presumed to make them better informants than their native colleagues.

4 *Non-NESTs are more able to anticipate language difficulties.* This anticipatory skill, which becomes more and more sophisticated with experience, enables non-NESTs to help learners overcome language difficulties and to avoid pitfalls.

5 *Non-NESTs can be more empathetic to the needs and problems of their learners.* Since they never cease to be learners of English, they encounter difficulties similar to those of their students, albeit at an obviously higher level. As a rule, this constant struggle makes non-natives more sensitive and understanding.

6 *Only non-NESTs can benefit from sharing the learners' mother*

*tongue*. In a monolingual setting, the mother tongue is an effective vehicle of communication in the language classroom, which can facilitate the teaching/learning process in countless ways.

In view of the above, I would argue that NESTs and non-NESTs can be equally effective, because in the final analysis their respective strengths and weaknesses balance each other out. From a native/non-native perspective, therefore, 'The more proficient in English, the more efficient in the classroom' is a false statement. By the same token, the question 'Who's worth more: a native or a non-native?' does not make sense, and may be conducive to forming wrong judgements about the differences found in their teaching practice.

## The non-native/non-native dimension

So far I have contrasted natives with non-natives. Now let me see whether the statement 'The more proficient, the more efficient' applies within the group of non-NESTs. All other variables being equal, a non-native's superiority over a fellow non-native can only be ascribed to his or her superior English-language competence. If we look through the list of arguments used to clarify the native/non-native contrast, it turns out that a more accomplished non-native user of English, who is implicitly a more successful language learner, can satisfy at least the first four of those criteria more fully than a less accomplished one. With regard to point 5, it has to be admitted that some of the most proficient speakers of English may in fact have picked up English so easily that they display insensitivity to their learners' problems. Nevertheless, in a purely non-native context, it looks as though 'The more proficient in English, the more efficient in the classroom' *is* a valid statement.

Given this, one of the most important professional duties non-NESTs have to perform is to improve their command of English. However, this continuous learning process, largely realized through self-study, is often impeded by several kinds of constraint. Objective factors such as the heavy teaching load imposed on many non-NESTs hinders their language development just as much as the lack of methodology dealing with advanced-level self-study, or possible ways of overcoming linguistic fossilization. Yet it seems to me that non-NESTs' progress is hampered most of all by a state of constant stress and insecurity caused by inadequate knowledge of the language they are paid to teach. This handicap is obvious in a native/non-native relationship, and can be even more painful in a homogeneously non-native context. The inferiority complexes of non-NESTs may be unfounded in some cases, but it hurts none the less, and manifests itself in various forms of contorted teaching practice (Medgyes 1983, 1986).

## The native/native dimension

Finally, in a native/native contrast, 'The more proficient, the more efficient' is an absurd assertion. In a linguistic sense, there can be no differences between native speakers in terms of their L1 competence, even though the differences in terms of their actual performance may be huge. The question, therefore, is whether or not NESTs can acquire the attributes of which non-NESTs are claimed to be the sole or, at least, the superior repositories.

My answer is yes—with certain reservations. With regard to all six points on the list, the NEST is a loser, just as the non-NEST is a loser with regard to his or her deficient English-language competence. However, neither statement should be regarded as absolute. On the one hand, as I pointed out earlier, some non-natives are nearly as accomplished users of English as natives. On the other hand, those natives who are successful learners of foreign languages can counterbalance some of their drawbacks. This applies with particular force to those who have reached a certain level of proficiency in the learners' mother tongue.

Thus, in a native/native relationship, the original statement 'The more proficient in English, the more efficient in the classroom' should be modified like this: 'The more proficient in the learners' mother tongue, the more efficient in the classroom.' In other words, all NESTs should take great pains to learn foreign languages, and those working in a monolingual setting should try to learn the vernacular of the host country. At the same time, they should strive to improve their knowledge of the grammar of the English language.

## *Conclusion: the ideal teacher*

As I have indicated, there are significant differences between NESTs and non-NESTs in terms of their teaching practice. These differences can all be attributed to their divergent language background. However, a teacher's effectiveness does not hinge upon whether he or she is a native or non-native speaker of English. The concept of 'the ideal teacher' is not one reserved for either category. Apart from a host of variables affecting teacher efficiency, in a native/non-native relation:

– the *ideal NEST* is the one who has achieved a high degree of proficiency in the learners' mother tongue;

– the *ideal non-NEST* is the one who has achieved near-native proficiency in English.

The ideal NEST and the ideal non-NEST arrive from different directions but eventually stand quite close to each other. Contrary to contemporary views, however, I contend that they will never become indistinguishable. Nor would it be desirable, either! Both groups of teachers serve equally useful purposes in their own terms. In an ideal school, there should be a good balance of NESTs and non-NESTs, who complement each other in their strengths and weaknesses. Given a favourable mix, various forms of collaboration are possible both in and outside the classroom—using each other as language consultants, for example, or teaching in tandem.

The central message of this paper is that the differences between NESTs and non-NESTs should not be blurred or ignored. On the contrary, we as ELT professionals should strive to highlight those divergences and place them under close scrutiny. We should sensitize teachers both to their limitations and potentials, and suggest ways they could make progress within their own constraints. This is what I would call a truly liberal attitude towards the native/non-native issue.

*Originally published in Volume 46/4, 1992*

## Acknowledgements

I would like to thank Zoltán Dörnyei, Joy Griffiths, Thea Reves, and Sarah Thurrell for their comments on earlier versions of this paper.

# 4

## *Development, education, and English language teaching*

GERRY ABBOTT

## *Introduction*

I read two things recently which reanimated a set of ideas that have been
at the back of my mind for a long time. They constitute no more than
a hunch; yet I have a feeling that even if the hunch is wrong, some
good will come out of pursuing it. The first text was a newspaper article
about a project to build a library in Alexandria, the Egyptian city
renowned more than two thousand years ago for its great library, a
resource which became an international centre of learning. What caught
my attention was a remark made by the director of the current project.
He said:

> Real civilisation always starts in the mind. It is ideas that make life
> grow green ... If we do not have them and cherish them we shall be
> tied forever to the wheel of circumstance.
> (The *Guardian*, 27 September 1990)

The second text was a new book (Hallak 1990) which deals, as the sub-
title says, with 'setting educational priorities in the developing world'.
Reviewing the parlous state of education in the Third World as it
emerges from its 'decade of crisis', this book provides a catalogue of
woes, from which the following is just one example:

> The lack of materials or equipment can be especially serious in pri-
> mary schools, where children from illiterate or bookless homes are
> being introduced to written figures and words—strange symbols to
> which very simple material could give concrete meaning. Generally

speaking ... it is especially in low-income countries that the availability of textbooks is critically low. (Hallak 1990: 35)

Though the first extract focuses on an abstraction ('civilization')
and the second on hard fact ('availability of textbooks'), both are
concerned with promoting 'development'. We label countries as 'developing' (some say 'underdeveloped') or 'developed' (some say 'overde-
veloped'); but the concept of 'development', like all the most important
things in life (e.g. love or happiness) seems to have defied definition.

## Perceptions of development

First, and perhaps still foremost in the public eye, is the view that development must be indicated by economic growth; the higher the GNP, the
greater the development. Confronted with an oil-rich state in which a
bloated élite benefit from the labour of an impoverished majority, most
people would reject that hypothesis; yet a great deal of Western aid has
been devoted simply to increasing the national wealth on the assumption that all would then benefit. One consequence was what could be
called 'the importation of modernity' by powerful and moneyed groups,
with high profits going to the rich local importer of non-essential goods
and the even richer Western exporter; and with no benefit accruing to
the urban poor and the rural impoverished masses, in spite of the fact
that it was and is this rural person-power (in Africa, largely woman-
power) that provides the agricultural produce for national export earn-
ings. A later view of development as a matter of distributing justice, of
spreading national services across social and geographical barriers,
seemed more appropriate than the mere transfer of technology from
outside. Education itself was one of these social services, and many
developing countries had, ever since their independence, devoted a far
higher proportion of their national budget to education than was spent
by any Western nation for that purpose. In the rapid expansion of provision for schooling, quality was sacrificed to quantity. In any case, these
education systems were, it seems to me, unlikely to serve their various
societies appropriately because they were in themselves copies of a foreign technology, a system of schooling developed in industrial Europe.
(Even the term 'development' itself, I might add, could be regarded as
embodying a foreign, First World concept.) None the less, schooling was
seen as a prerequisite of development.

# The relationship between education and development

There is, of course, far more to the relationship between education and development than I have touched upon, and in the last decade or so many books have been written on various aspects of the problem. (See Simmons 1980; Thompson 1981; Clarke 1985; and Hallak 1990, to mention just a few.) Development as a subject of study lies outside my own competence, and what I have said about it is intended merely to show how complex development is, and how difficult to achieve. The United Nations declared the 1960s 'The First Development Decade' and, as we enter the fourth decade since that optimistic proclamation, it is generally admitted that long-term successes in development policies and projects have been few and far between and that the forecast is rather gloomy. Education as currently practised, then, certainly has not cured the ills of underdevelopment and may even be said to have exacerbated some of them; witness the phenomena that led to 'the diploma disease' (Dore 1976), for instance.

## Reasons for the failure of education

If education can be said to have failed in this respect, we would expect writers on the subject of development to catalogue the possible causes of that failure; and so indeed they have. Hallak (1990: 33–9) lists such common shortcomings as overcentralization, overcrowding, underfunding, irrelevant curricula, teacher shortages, lack of textbooks, high pupil drop-out rates, drab and ill-equipped buildings, teaching in two or even three shifts, and so on. He also makes much of non-formal education, distance education, radio lessons, literacy, and the like; and yet, like all the other writers I have read on the subject, he omits any consideration of the linguistic medium of these activities. I find this omission puzzling, since it is well-known that a large proportion of the developing world's children are educated through the medium of languages that are not only not their mother tongues but are codes as exotic as mangoes in Manchester. In the context of sub-Saharan Africa, English, French, Afrikaans, and Portuguese readily come to mind. But we should also bear others in mind: Arabic in Berber regions of northern Africa and Kurdish areas of the Middle East; Indonesian in Java, Sulawesi, and elsewhere in the archipelago; Bahasa Malaysia in Sarawak and Sabah; and many more.

## ELT as 'cultural invasion'

Let us suppose at this point that the director of Alexandria's library project was right: that civilization does start in the mind. Of course, 'civilization' is a tricky word to deal with because earlier generations used it in contrast to cultures seen as 'primitive' and 'barbaric'. But if, in a more enlightened spirit of cultural relativity, we regard civilization as (say) 'the proud pursuit of one's own indigenous cultural systems', then I think we must agree that a staggering proportion of the world's young schoolchildren are victims of what Freire (1972: 121) calls 'cultural invasion', a state in which

> the invaders penetrate the cultural context of another group and, ignoring the potential of the latter, ... impose their own view of the world upon those they invade and inhibit the creativity of the invaded by curbing their expression.

For some decades now, English language teaching has been caught up in this process—more or less unwittingly, I like to think. The widely perceived need to promote technological development through teaching an international language such as English overshadows an arguably more basic need to transmit indigenous inherited cultures. Because development has been interpreted as 'becoming more like the West', western aid donors and cultural agencies have been accused of cultural imperialism. Perhaps the charge is at least partly justified; but the blame often lies closer to home. As Inayatullah (1967) has noted

> the goals of the élite in developing societies are generally in conformity with the technical assistance programs

and since these élites are seen as showing a concern to modernize their societies, for them

> the danger of being charged with cultural imperialism does not exist ...

## A love–hate relationship with English

The educated classes of developing countries may even practise a kind of double-think with regard to English, a love–hate relationship with a language which is resented yet whose great importance is acknowledged. It was, for instance, the English-using class in Pakistan that in 1979 proscribed the use of English as a medium of education and then proceeded to establish illegal but tolerated English-medium schools at a faster rate than before. Again, as I have noted elsewhere (Abbott 1984) a racial élite in Malaysia has established residential schools for selected Malays who are prepared for Cambridge English examinations and further education through the medium of English in other countries, while the normal schools must prepare students for exams not acceptable to universities in those countries. One irony about cultural imperialism, then, is that people inflict it upon others of the same nationality.

## ELT at the primary level

Another irony is that in many countries the teaching and use of English at primary school level is less a cultural invasion than an unnecessary invitation. Ministers of Education have concluded that since a command of English is an important product of the system, it is best to start teaching English from the very beginning. In most cases, this is a mistaken policy if only because of the catalogue of shortcomings in the system, some of which are mentioned above; children just cannot be expected to learn a second language efficiently in such conditions. Where English is used as the medium of education from the beginning of the schooling process, of the many who have dropped out before secondary level, most are either illiterate or will lapse into illiteracy; and one of the major causes of this must be the burden of having to learn an alien language as a prerequisite to literacy. Some will object, 'Ah, but there are no reading materials in the vernacular languages.' The answer is, 'Nor will there ever be any, at this rate!'

## Development starts in the mind

It is generally recognized that a society needs a certain level of literacy for development to take place. But in my view the main obstacle to development lies even deeper than the difficulty of first becoming literate in a strange language. My hunch is that development has nothing to do with wealth (GNP) or technology (industrialization), though these may accrue as a result of development or alongside it; nor with schooling or even literacy as such, though these are closer to the heart of the problem. True development, as opposed to the mere replica that lends itself easily to caricature, lies not 'out there' but 'in here'. It really does 'start in the mind' as our Egyptian project director said; and to the young mind written words really are, as Hallak says in the quotation above, 'strange symbols to which very simple material could give concrete meaning'. Teachers have to minimize the strangeness, the abstractness; and what words could be less strange than those of one's own spoken language? What meanings more concrete than those of one's own culture?

At this point, I must make it clear that I would not claim any great novelty for my hunch. Mabogunje (1980: 13) found a close relationship between poverty and ex-colonial status, which is almost the same as a correlation between underdevelopment and dependence on a non-indigenous language, or exoglossia. This was noted even in the case of Central and South American colonies that gained independence in the nineteenth century. If there is any truth in such observations, it also has to be admitted that there are exceptions (Singapore leaps to mind) and that conversely states such as Tanzania which abandoned exoglossia have not shown a startling increase in rate of development.

## Adopting a foreign language in education

It is true, of course, that in many countries sooner or later, for very sound practical reasons, the mother tongue must be abandoned for another tongue. But I am convinced that it should be later rather than sooner, if only because we have no way of knowing how much damage we may be doing (or, to be fair, how little) when we force very young, inexperienced, non-literate minds to adopt a foreign language in a schooling that has no place for their mother tongue, or even for a known vernacular. We are not yet able to prove or disprove the well-known hypothesis, expressed here by Whorf (1941) that

> the forms of a person's thought are controlled by inexorable laws of pattern of which he is unconscious. These patterns are the unperceived intricate systemizations of his own language ... His thinking itself is in a language ... in which are culturally ordained the forms and categories by which the personality not only communicates, but also analyzes nature, notices or neglects types of relationship and phenomena, channels his reasoning, and builds the house of his consciousness.

This hypothesis, seen here in its 'strong' form, is rejected by some authorities and treated with caution by all; but many would accept the 'weak' version, which simply states that language structures can influence cognitive categorization and processing. Even in its dilute form, the Sapir–Whorf hypothesis adds weight to my hunch that in attempting to account for underdevelopment one factor—only one, but a fundamental one if there is much truth in it—is the damaging psychosocial effect of having one's own culture (the main exponent of which is one's language) devalued in favour of an alien one, a phenomenon of which anthropologists have found dramatic examples among peoples as far apart as North American Indians, small African tribes, and Melanesian groups.

Culture shock, whatever the cause, can be horrific and even fatal. The Kaiadilt, a tiny group living on Bentinck Island off the northern coast of Queensland, were isolated even from their nearest Aborigine neighbours twenty miles away. When their fresh water was polluted by a tidal wave in 1948, groups were rounded up, transported to a nearby island, and crowded into a settlement supervised by missionaries. Calhoun (1972, in Whitten 1977: 117) described how psychiatrists visiting them in 1963 found a nightmarish state of affairs:

> The spiritual decay of the Kaiadilt was marked by withdrawal, depression, suicide and a tendency to engage in such self-mutilation as ripping out one's testes or chopping off one's nose. In their passiveness some of the anxiety-ridden children are accepting the new mould of life forced upon them by a benevolent culture they do not understand.

Such chilling accounts of culture-death are not rare, and the enforced learning of an alien language is often involved. Let us look at three cases that have involved the learning of English, starting with North American Indians.

## Case studies of learning English

### Case one

Cardinal, himself a Canadian Indian, describes what happened to him and his age-mates in the 1950s:

> The children were not allowed to speak in their own language. Their teachers ... made no attempt to understand the native tongue. They couldn't even be bothered to learn the children's names and gave them instead easier-to-pronounce Christian names. (Cardinal 1969: 86)

Residential schools such as the one he attended

> alienated the child from his own family; they alienated him from his own way of life ...; they alienated the child from his own religion ... (ibid.: 54)

Accounts of this sort are found wherever the medium of education is an exotic language. Cardinal concludes

As long as the Indian does not have a positive image of himself, … no human being will have a positive image of him and no one will ever respect him. (ibid.: 165)

Things have changed for the better in Canada since those days, but a widespread belief in the power of English still causes many to have a negative image of their own language.

## Case two

When I was living in Cameroon near a suburban village whose language was unwritten, I obtained the co-operation of a respected elder, and together, over about a year, we developed a draft Roman orthography that seemed to work. I transcribed and distributed one of the local folk-tales and began producing a picture-dictionary illustrated only with local objects, animals, and people. No one was interested. It was considered a waste of time to learn to read MoendaNkwe (my spelling) when one could be learning English.

## Case three

To this low-key but first-hand example can be added the more startling accounts cited by Swatridge (1985) of the cultural damage inflicted upon Melanesian societies by, *inter alia*, English-medium education. In the belief that white men were ancestors engaged in the fulfilment of an old myth by returning with 'cargo' (*kago*), local populations assumed that the white men's language must be learnt because it was a magic tongue for communicating with the dead, and consequently for obtaining more *kago*. (Anyone tempted to smile at this cargo cult might pause to reflect that the white man's literacy did indeed enable his ancestors to communicate with him (if not vice versa) and that a command of English did and does serve as a passport to lucrative employment.) Here, the local cultures degenerated into criminality.

Many more cases could be cited, but firm causal evidence is hard to find when it comes to language. Apocalyptic judgements would certainly be unwarranted, but, on the other hand, it cannot be denied that the teaching of English as a second language has played some part in cultural decay, social alienation, and psycholinguistic trauma. The questions to be addressed are:

1 To what extent and in what conditions may education through the

medium of a 'language of power' result in a lack of faith in one's own culture and therefore in the language that expresses it?

2 To what extent might such a lack of faith, when communally felt, hinder the process of development?

It is important to have precise data about the conditions necessary for the onset of such cultural despair, in order to find out why the effects are catastrophic in some cases and negligible in others. A little recent evidence from Eastern Europe may be relevant here.

## Political diglossia

In a recent BBC Radio 3 programme entitled 'Newspeak and Doublethink', some Eastern European politicians and academics described the Orwellian effects of being obliged for their own safety to use an official Stalinist language variety which 'glaringly contradicted their daily experience', so that in using it they 'produced a kind of irreal reality'. The effects were described as a sort of schizophrenia, a psychosis which presumably began to wear off as soon as the necessity to use the political gobbledygook was removed. It should be remembered that this language was a version of the mother tongue, warped to fit a certain world-view. How much more 'warped' might a foreign language of power seem to the powerless?

On the other hand, in conditions of greater social homogeneity and solidarity perhaps, the self-same Stalinist language may be rebuffed. Wierzbicka (1990) gives a detailed account of a phenomenon in Poland which she calls 'political diglossia'. This situation occurs when the few in power impose an official language on the many who, because this propaganda code fails to mirror reality as they see it, create an anti-propaganda in which to express their own values. The 'anti-language' in this case is (or perhaps *was*, so rapid are the political changes) a colloquial Polish with a distinctive robust political humour built into it.

## *Conclusion*

The 'ideas that make life grow green' *were* certainly stifled in Eastern Europe, language *was* used for the purpose, and development *is* now an urgent priority. But more evidence is needed. The Egyptian project director and I may both be wrong; but what is surely true is that development studies should take more account of language matters. There is, I suggest, a missing link between development studies and sociolinguistic studies, especially that part of sociolinguistics that deals with language planning. That link needs to be forged and fitted, to provide a coupling for the language-teaching profession to latch on to whenever and wherever necessary.

*Originally published in Volume 46/2, 1992*

# 5

# Target-language culture in EFL materials

CEM ALPTEKIN

## Introduction

Culture, aside from its reference to the artefacts of a given community, involves socially acquired knowledge. This knowledge is organized in culture-specific ways which normally frame our perception of reality such that we largely define the world through the filter of our world view. Put differently, schemas, which are cognitive structures through which we interpret information, evolve largely as part of a society's imposition of its own differential view of reality on its individual members. Culture, then, as 'socially acquired knowledge', can be said to play a central role in cognition.[1]

## Schematic and systemic knowledge

Widdowson (1990) refers to socially acquired knowledge as 'schematic knowledge', which he contrasts with 'systemic knowledge'. The latter, in his view, is the knowledge of the formal properties of language, involving both its semantic and syntactic systems. In native language learning, the child's schematic and systemic knowledge are said to develop concurrently, each supportive of the other. However, as Widdowson states, the *foreign* language learning experience is quite different: 'Here learners have already been socialized into the schematic knowledge associated with their mother tongue: they are initiated into their culture in the very process of language learning.' For example, while a child from the Anglo-American world will normally think of a

dog as 'man's best friend', Middle Eastern children are likely to perceive
it as dangerous and dirty. Similarly, whereas the image of the secondary-
school teacher in Japan is one of an intelligent, high-status, authoritarian, and humble male, the image of the typical Anglo-American teacher
does not necessarily match these traits. It follows that when learners
confront uses of the foreign language they are acquiring, 'their natural
inclination is to interpret them in reference to this established association' (Widdowson 1990: 110).

## The role of schematic knowledge in language acquisition

The 'fit', or consistency, between the culture-specific aspects of cognition and the native language undergoes a substantive degree of conflict
when one begins to learn a foreign language. The acquisition process
causes learners' schemas to be subjected to novel cultural data whose
organization for purposes of comprehension and retention becomes
difficult or even impossible to achieve. As a case in point, a learner of
English who has never resided in the target-language culture will most
likely experience problems in processing English systemic data if these
are presented through such unfamiliar contexts as, say, Halloween or
English pubs. Even if these are explained, the learner may still fail
to perceive Halloween or the pub in the same way in which they are normally evoked in the mind of the native speaker of English, as one's natural tendency is to assess a novel stimulus with respect to one's own
cultural system. As such, it is possible that the learner in question will
react to Halloween or the pub context with less than full comprehension, regardless of how much explanation is provided. And if one cannot fully access the schematic data, one can hardly be expected to learn
the systemic data with any ease.

One area where the violation of the 'fit' is shown to influence foreign
language learning negatively is that of reading comprehension. It is well-
established that readers make use of culture-specific schemas in relating
input to what they already know and, consequently, construct the
writer's intended meaning. When the relevant cultural background
assumptions and constructs are missing, however, reading tends to turn
into a time-consuming, laborious, and frustrating experience (Brown *et
al.* 1977; Steffensen *et al.* 1979; Reynolds *et al.* 1982; Nelson 1987). In
fact, familiarity with the dictionary definition of the lexical items and
knowledge of the sentence structures in a text do not seem to be enough
for learners to comprehend new information. Wallace (1988) attributes
this problem to the learners' lack of what she calls 'cultural compe-

tence', that is, 'a very complex package of beliefs, knowledge, feelings, attitudes and behaviour' (Wallace 1988: 33).

Given that culture plays a major role in cognition, which in turn significantly affects comprehension and interpretation, one of the salient issues in foreign language pedagogy is the determination of the type of schematic input to be presented to the learners. This article aims at discussing target-language culture elements learners often face in EFL materials, the practical and theoretical rationale for the use of such elements, and the social and psychological problems which ensue. Following the discussion, certain suggestions concerning the use of different types of schematic input in English language teaching are offered, with a view to facilitating the language learning process.

## Elements of the target-language culture in EFL materials

Writing operates in terms of schemas moulded by the social context in which the writer lives. Writers not only construct mental representations of their socially acquired knowledge, but such schematic knowledge also influences their writing in various areas such as the rhetorical organization of a text, audience awareness, topical priorities, etc. Numerous studies in contrastive rhetoric (e.g. Clyne 1981; Hinds 1983; Koch 1983; Kobayashi 1984; Norman 1984; Matalene 1985; Johnstone 1986; Nishimura 1986; Connor and Kaplan 1987; Alptekin 1988) demonstrate how thinking and writing operate in terms of culture-specific schemas. As a case in point, Clyne (1981) shows the fundamental contrasts between English rhetorical patterns—which are generally characterized by linearity in the presentation of ideas—and German rhetorical patterns—which are marked not only by digressions, but also digressions from digressions. Similarly, Koch (1983) points out that, unlike Western modes of argumentation, which are based on a syllogistic model of proof, Arabic argumentative prose makes use of repetition as a device for textual cohesion and rhetorical effectiveness. In the same vein, Jenkins and Hinds (1987), speaking of audience awareness skills, indicate that while American business letters are reader oriented, the French ones are writer oriented, and the Japanese ones are oriented to the space between the writer and the reader. Finally, it is no secret that topical priorities change from one culture to another. For example, while the White House seems to be a favourite topic with American EFL textbook writers, the British Royal Family appears to be a popular topic with British EFL writers.

Such examples show that EFL textbook writers, like everyone else, think and compose chiefly through culture-specific schemas. Because native speakers have face validity in EFL circles (Alptekin 1990; Phillipson 1990b), most textbook writers are native speakers who consciously or unconsciously transmit the views, values, beliefs, attitudes, and feelings of their own English-speaking society—usually the United States or United Kingdom. As such, when learners acquire a new set of English discourse as part of their evolving systemic knowledge, they partake of the cultural system which the set entails.

## Rationale for using elements of the target-language culture

### Commercial considerations

One reason for EFL textbooks focusing on elements about the American or British culture stems from the fact that it is generally not cost-effective for publishers to set materials in the learner's society, as such a decision would cause other learners from other societies not to make use of the materials in question on account of their irrelevance to their own cultures. Furthermore, the schematic focus on the target-language culture may offer a lucrative deal to the writer(s) as well as the publisher in those cases where the textbook is made use of in both EFL and ESL contexts.

### Author preference

Another reason is that native-speaker textbook writers, who normally reside in their own Anglo-American culture, find it hard to compose data that go beyond *their* 'fit'. By contrast, the presentation of the 'fit' through sets of discourse particular to the target language culture is relatively easy and practical. They write about their own culture and in tune with that culture's formal schemas, where they are 'at home' so to speak.

### Target language in its own culture

Apart from such mundane matters that affect the determination of the type of schematic input in EFL materials, one witnesses theoretical claims about the necessity of teaching the target language in relation to its own culture. In fact, various sources on the subject repeat the orthodox yet unsubstantiated notion that language and culture are inextricably tied together, and that it is impossible to teach a foreign language without its culture base. Stewart (1982), for instance, regards the target-language culture as an essential feature of every stage of foreign language learning, and asserts that teaching the formal aspects of the foreign language while referring to the native culture of the learner is virtually useless. Valdes (1986: 121) considers the use of the native culture in foreign language teaching a 'trap', leading to a 'gross misfit' or an 'impasse'. Besides, she claims that it is virtually impossible to teach the foreign language without its cultural content. Byram (1988) generally supports the belief that a language cannot be taught separately from its culture. If this is done, he says, it would lead to a denial of a purported fundamental purpose of language learning, namely, giving learners the opportunity to cope with experience in a different way.

## Problems with the rationale

### Lack of experience

Although practical advantages do exist in teaching and presenting the target language in relation to its own culture, there are several problems associated with this approach as well. To begin with, it forms part of the 'strange paradox' that, while in mother-tongue teaching the clarity of children's ability to express themselves is emphasized, in foreign language teaching learners are forced to express a culture of which they have scarcely any experience (Brumfit 1980: 95). Secondly, developing a new identity, or what Byram (1989: 57) calls 'otherness', as a result of one's sudden exposure to the target-language culture, is likely to cause a split between experience and thought which is conducive to serious socio-psychological problems affecting the learner's mental equilibrium negatively. Anomie (Alptekin 1981), regression (Green 1977), and schizophrenia (Clarke 1976; Meara 1977) are perhaps the worst of such problems in that, among other things, they are associated with reluctance or resistance to learning.

### Alien modes of behaviour

Of course, not all culture-specific schematic knowledge leads to such serious problems. Most often, the effects are more subtle. Edge (1987), for example, points to one such area. He says that the task-based and problem-solving activities which characterize communicative approaches and materials are not value-free modes of behaviour. Rather, they involve Western modes of communication which may not be in harmony with the traditions of some cultures—including learning conventions. Hence, argues Edge, learners from those cultures cannot learn English properly by behaving in ways which are both alien to their educational culture and proscribed in their daily life. Little wonder then that Chinese EFL teachers, for instance, seem to shy away from communicative procedures and materials (Burnaby and Sun 1989); Chinese EFL students prefer teacher-centred instruction over task-based learning involving the contribution of peers (Young 1987). After all, Chinese students are accustomed to simple transfer of information from the teacher and to retaining such data through rote learning.

## Ownership of language

Another problem concerning the use of target-language culture elements has to do with the fact that such a position equates a language with the combined uses and usages of its native speakers, thus making them not only its arbiters of well-formedness and appropriacy but, more importantly, its sole owners. Yet, as Paikeday (1985) notes, the notion that the native speaker is the arbiter of well-formedness and appropriacy is incorrect, as there are educated as well as naive native speakers. Differences among such native speakers in matters relating to well-formedness and appropriacy in a given language are only differences of degree. As such, some non-native speakers of the language may be more entitled to arbitrating well-formedness and appropriacy than some putative native speakers. In the case of English in particular, it is virtually impossible to think of its native speakers as the only arbiters of grammaticality and appropriacy and consequently as its sole owners, given the lingua franca status of the language. To cite Smith (1987: 3), 'English already represents many cultures and it can be used by anyone as a means to express any cultural heritage and any value system.' In fact, different norms of communicative competence have evolved for English, including those of indigenized varieties such as Indian English (Kachru 1985). Hence, rather than indulging in an over-simplification such as the inseparability of language and culture, it would be more realistic to speak of one language which is not always inextricably tied to one particular culture, as is the case with English.

## Acknowledgement of learners' needs

Finally, the position relating a language and its culture appears to ignore the positive effects of familiar schematic knowledge on foreign language learning. Familiarity with both content and formal schemas enables the learners to place more emphasis on systemic data, as their cognitive processing is not so much taken by the alien features of the target-language background.[2] Moreover, familiar schematic knowledge allows the learners to make efficient use of their top-down processing in helping their bottom-up processing in the handling of various language tasks.[3] Needless to say, familiarity in this context refers to schemas based chiefly on the learner's own culture.

Numerous examples exist in the literature, in fact, on how familiar schemas facilitate foreign language acquisition and, in particular, comprehension. Johnson (1982), for instance, shows that, in reading comprehension in the foreign language, syntactic and lexical simplification can be far less important than familiar content schemas. Similarly, Nunan (1985) suggests that more than the provision of systemic knowledge, what makes a foreign language text easier to process is the learner's degree of familiarity with its content schemas. Based on the findings of her own extensive research on the subject, Carrell (1987) concludes that good reading comprehension in the foreign language entails familiarity with both content and formal schemas. Winfield and Barnes-Felfeli (1982) stress the cognitive processing difficulties encountered by foreign language learners not only in reading but also in writing activities involving unfamiliar content schemata. In the same vein, Friedlander (1990) indicates that foreign language learners' planning and writing are enhanced when they are asked to write on topics related to their native language background. Hinds (1984) points to another interesting aspect of the positive role of familiar schematic knowledge in foreign language learning through his discovery of a relationship between the degree of the learners' familiarity with formal schemas in essays and the degree of their ability to retain information from such essays.

## Stereotyping

What further exacerbates the problem of presentation of the target language in relation to its own culture is the generally stereotypical representation of that culture in much instructional material. Hartman and Judd (1978), for example, show how many American EFL materials present stereotyped portrayals of men and women (often to the detriment of the latter), through one-sided role allocation, overt put-downs, or simple omissions. Likewise, Clarke and Clarke (1990) point to numerous instances of stereotyping in British EFL materials in areas of gender, race, class, and religion. In general, the authors argue, Britishness seems to be the standard, and cross-cultural perspectives in communication are de-emphasized or denied.[4]

## Pedagogic implications

Language has no function independently of the social contexts in which it is used. In the case of English, as a lingua franca, such contexts are as varied as they are numerous. Similarly, the schematic knowledge of the speakers of such contexts is quite diverse. Hence, to confine English to one of its native settings and, what is worse, to present that setting in a stereotypical manner is not only unrealistic and misleading, but also a disservice to EFL learners in that they are likely to find themselves in the undesirable position of tackling unfamiliar information unnecessarily while trying to cope with novel systemic data.

Instead of diving simplistically into the narrow confines of a given target-language culture, in a manner devoid of comparative insight and critical perspective, EFL writers should try to build conceptual bridges between the culturally familiar and the unfamiliar in order not to give rise to conflicts in the learner's 'fit' as he or she acquires English. Such bridges can be built, among other ways, through the use of comparisons as techniques of cross-cultural comprehension or the exploitation of universal concepts of human experience as reference points for the interpretation of unfamiliar data.

Finally, given that the traditional notion of the communicative competence of the native speaker is no longer adequate as a goal to be adopted in an EFL programme, the transition from familiar to unfamiliar schematic data should not necessarily be thought of as moving from the learner's native culture to the culture of the native speaker of English. Even though this still remains a strong option, other options may involve transitions from the learner's native culture to the international English of such areas as pop culture, travel culture, and scientific culture, or the culture of one of the indigenized varieties of English (e.g. Indian or Nigerian English).

*Originally published in Volume 47/2, 1993*

# Notes

1 Of course, not all knowledge is culturally determined. Cognition further involves 'shared non-cultural knowledge' as well as 'non-shared non-cultural knowledge' (Hudson 1980: 77).

2 Content schemas refer to a person's background knowledge of the content area of a piece of discourse. Formal schemas, on the other hand, refer to a person's background knowledge of the organizational structure of a given piece of discourse (Carrell and Eisterhold 1983).

3 Bottom-up or data driven processing involves activities derived from the nature of an incoming stimulus and nothing else. By contrast, top-down or cognitively driven processing involves activities influenced by factors not present in the stimulus itself. Such factors include the learner's general knowledge of the world or logic and inference competencies.

4 Even if textbook writers make serious efforts to eliminate stereotyping by striving for authenticity in the construction of teaching materials, it should not be forgotten that such efforts, in the final analysis, are normally based upon a selection process which is bound to be, at least, partially subjective. Thus, as Nostrand (1989: 50) indicates, the selected texts are not likely to present authentic reality but the writer's own artefact.

# 6

## *Proper words in proper places*

### H. G. WIDDOWSON

## *Introduction*

I feel honoured to be invited to give this, the first ELT lecture, and to be associated in so doing with the BBC and the Oxford University Press, two institutions which have done so much to further the cause of English language education in this country and abroad. Both institutions are still, I believe, inspired by motives other than the merely mercenary and have not, as others have, been reduced to the role of retailer by market forces. Of course they count the cost, but both recognize, I think, that this can never provide a complete account of the value of what they do. So I commend their enterprise—if that is the proper word to use, and if this is a proper place to use it.

Proper words in proper places. My title is taken from a letter written by Jonathan Swift in 1720 to a young clergyman of his acquaintance: 'Proper words in proper places, make the true definition of style.' But then what, we might ask, makes the true definition of 'proper'? And who is it that does the defining? And is it only style that can be defined in this way? These are questions I want to explore on this occasion with reference to the English language. And in the process we shall come across a number of current, and contentious issues in English language education: issues concerning linguistic propriety and linguistic property, standard English and standards of English, and standard bearers and native speakers. To be brisk, my theme is: what is proper English, and who says so?

## Proper places

Proper words in proper places. When, to begin with, is a word in its proper place? One answer is when it finds its niche in a grammatical pattern, when, suitably adjusted by morphological modification, it fits snugly into syntax. Propriety in this sense has to do with the *internal* relationships of words as determined by the linguistic code. In this case we can perhaps talk about the correct placement of words. But this is not the only answer. We can also think of words being in their proper place with reference to their communicative purpose. Here we are concerned with the *external* relationship of words with the context of their actual occurrence, and propriety is not now a matter of their correctness of form in a sentence, but of their appropriacy (or appropriateness) of function in an utterance.

Thus, if in the course of a routine interaction, a woman were to ask her husband:

Have you put out the small domesticated furry feline animal?

he would undoubtedly find the expression unusual, stylistically strange, an improper use of language. It would be out of place: *contextually* out of place. But it is a perfectly proper English sentence: the words all combine to make a correct syntactic fit. If, on the other hand, the wife were to utter:

Have you out the cat put?

there would be reason to suspect that she had not quite got a secure grip on the syntax of the language. This time the words are *grammatically* out of place. It is not that the words do not relate appropriately to the occasion, they do not relate to each other. They are just not English.

## Proper words

All this seems obvious and straightforward enough. Nothing contentious here, surely. Perhaps not so far. But as we shall see presently, things are not quite so simple when we consider them more closely. Meanwhile, we turn from proper places to proper words themselves.

### Context propriety

Again, the distinction between code and context propriety is relevant. It enables us to distinguish between the idea of *the* proper word and *a* proper word. Suppose (to take another scene from domestic life), at the funeral of an aged relative, I were to make the remark:

Well the old soak has finally snuffed it.

I might well be accused of a lapse in taste, a lapse in propriety indeed in failing to observe accepted decorum. But nobody would say that my words were not English ones. If, on the other hand, I were to come out with the utterance:

Well the old man has perspired at last.

this would be taken as a *linguistic* lapse, a malapropism, a miscue for 'expired', a slip of the tongue occasioned perhaps by an excess of grief, or finding too much solace in the sherry.

'Perspire' and 'snuff' are not the proper words to use: one is semantically mistaken and the other is pragmatically misplaced. But although they are not *the* proper words, they are nevertheless both proper words of English just as, for example, 'despire' and 'smuff' are not.

But they could be, of course. There is nothing in the formation of these words as such which is un-English. The language has the necessary phonological and morphological resources for their manufacture should the need ever arise. They are in this respect available as a potential in reserve, so to speak, ready for realization as and when required for service. So it is that Lewis Carroll can invent his portmanteau words like 'frabjous' and 'frumious' and 'chortle'. Of these, 'chortle' has been taken on as a proper English word and appears in the dictionary. The others have not.

They remain lexical curiosities, what might have been; an abstraction (as T. S. Eliot put it):

Remaining a perpetual possibility
Only in a world of speculation.
*Burnt Norton*

## Conventional usage

So we might define proper words as those which are sanctioned by conventional usage, and we might suppose that confirmation of this is to be found in the dictionary. But here we run into difficulties. Within the vast recesses of the *Oxford English Dictionary* (OED) in print and on disk are to be found large numbers of words which are historically attested, but now no longer in use: words, for example, like 'depertible', 'depredable', and 'deprehend'. Unlike the Lewis Carroll cases, these are has-beens, not might-have-beens. But although they are obsolete, and are marked as such, they do not seem to lose their status as proper words: history lends them prestige, and they are quite likely to appear in Philip Howard's word quiz in *The Times*. What greater prestige could there be?

## 'Has-beens' and 'might-have-beens'

But what actually is the difference between the has-beens and the might-have-beens? The has-beens are attested as having been used in the past. How often, though, and by whom? It must be on more than one occasion and by more than one person, otherwise the words remain in the perpetual possibility of the might-have-been. But then how do we explain the curious case of Shakespeare?

Shakespeare was, of course, a keen coiner of new words and a great number have become conventional and commonplace: 'assassination', for example, 'barefaced', 'laughable'. But he also came up with quite a few words which never took on. 'Appertainments' is one (from *Troilus and Cressida*) and 'exsufflicate' is another (from *Othello*). They are marked in the OED as 'rare', but they are not just rare they are non-existent, apart from a single idiosyncratic instance. They are, in fact, might-have-beens. So why do they take on the status of proper words in the dictionary? And apart from these words there are numerous others which have a record of more than a single occurrence—but only just.

So why does Shakespeare get this special treatment? Why are *all* his words counted as proper, whether they are taken on and made current or not? The reason in a word (another word from *Othello*, as it happens) is: reputation. He is, after all, the Bard, and as Aldous Huxley's character Mr Tillotson was fond of saying: 'The Bard is always right. He is always right; always right and proper.'

## Range of usage

It would appear, then, that we cannot establish whether words are proper or not simply by invoking the criteria of frequent usage or common currency. There are factors to do with the past and with prestige which come into play. And there is a further and related factor to take note of, one which is related to *range* of usage.

Consider the word 'deprehend', the has-been I mentioned earlier, and the word 'depurate'. The first is marked as obsolete in the OED and the second is not. But I personally do not recognize either or them: they are not proper words of English for me. If I did not have the OED to hand, I might suspect that both were fake coinages. They are both beyond my lexical range, one of them, 'deprehend', because it belongs to a remote domain of use in the past, the other because it belongs to a remote domain of use in the present—'depurate' is a specialist term in medicine.

It would seem, then, that what we identify as a proper word of the language depends on the necessary limitations of our own lexical knowledge. Propriety is relative. So for some people, for example, 'strake' and 'trunnion' are proper English words like 'steak' and 'onion', but for others they are not, because they do not have them as part of their vocabulary. The words are not proper because they are not possessed. Propriety is relative. And it is also closely related to a sense of property.

## A model for language learners

Proper English words, but proper *for* whom and *to* whom? The same considerations arise when determining proper *places* of words as well: different dialectal codes will have different rules of internal arrangement, and different communities will have different conventions of external use in context. A word which is properly placed as correct in one code or as appropriate to one social custom, is seen to be misplaced in others. All of this clearly raises the crucial pedagogic issue of whose usage we should take as the model for language learners to aspire to.

Those who make policy statements or plan language programmes often express objectives in terms of mastery of the language, or native speaker competence, as if these were coherent and well-defined concepts. But they are not. Which native speakers are we talking about, and what does mastery mean? As I have already indicated there are numerous English words that I have not myself mastered, and never can; and numerous possible placements I am ignorant of, and always will be. And I count myself as competent in the language. I am indeed a native speaker of English. So whose English do we try to get the student to master, if indeed 'master' is itself the proper word in this context.

### Lexical competence and dictionary design

This question is of obvious relevance for the design of learners' dictionaries. The selection of words to be included, and the manner of their treatment, should presumably be based on some notion of which lexical range constitutes an appropriate competence, and what explanations and examples are likely to assist the learner in its acquisition. This would be a very tricky matter for any language, but it is particularly so for English, given the extent and variety of its diaspora, so to speak, and its widespread use as an international means of communication within and across communities.

Consider the case of the *Collins COBUILD English Language* Dictionary (Sinclair 1987), for example. It claims on the dustcover, and in its publicity, that it is 'helping learners with *real* English' (with the emphasis on 'real'). Real English, Proper English. The dictionary does not include the words 'depurate', or 'strake' or 'trunnion'. The assumption is, reasonably enough, that as far as learners in general are concerned these are not real English words even though they are given that status in the *OED*. They might well be real, however, for students following certain courses of English for specific purposes (medicine or marine engineering, for example), and their omission is not helpful for these particular learners. Real (or proper) then, for what kind of communication?

Or for what kind of community? There are omissions of a rather different kind in the *Collins COBUILD English Language* Dictionary (Sinclair 1987). We find 'guitar' for example, but not 'sitar', 'warehouse' but not 'godown'. But these would be real enough for innumerable speakers of English in South East Asia and elsewhere and would figure in their daily discourse. They are, it might be suggested, part of the lexis of English as an international language. Or are they? What does it mean to talk about English as an international language anyway? I will return to this question a little later, but meanwhile there is a more delicate difficulty to deal with.

Consider the word 'prepone'. This does not occur in current British usage and never has occurred in the past. It is not, therefore, to be found either in *Collins COBUILD English Language Dictionary* or the *OED*. It does appear, however, in a handbook of Indian and British English published by Oxford University Press in New Delhi (Nihalani, Tongue, and Hosali 1979), and it is apparently quite commonly attested in India. Is it proper English?

In one sense it could not be more proper, for it is impeccably wellformed according to the standard rules of English morphology. It is indeed a good example of the productive use (or generative power) of grammar which is said to be a feature of linguistic competence, and this presumably applies as much to morphological formation of words as to the syntactic formation of sentences. 'Prepone', then, is properly formed. It is also semantically apt in that it contrasts neatly with 'postpone' to denote the advancing as distinct from the deferring of an event. A meeting can obviously be brought forward, preponed, just as it can be put back, postponed. The word neatly fills a lexical gap. All that standard British English has to offer instead is the rather cumbersome phrase 'bring forward'.

So is 'prepone' to be recognized as real English? It is, after all, coined to meet a communicative contingency just as are innumerable other lexical inventions which have been devised to deal with new technology over recent years, and which have been readily received into the language. Furthermore, it is, in its innovative use of linguistic resources, the kind of language which Shakespeare wrote, and this is usually highly commended and indeed, as we have seen, is considered proper by definition. But there is an obvious difficulty and this can, appropriately enough, be illustrated by reference to E. M. Forster's *Passage to India*.

## The issue of selection

The Nawab Bahadur is pondering on which of God's creatures might be admitted to the mansions of heaven. He has discussed the matter with the missionaries, the old Mr Graysford, the young Mr Sorley. What about monkeys, for example? Mr Graysford said no, but the progressive Mr Sorley 'saw no reason why monkeys should not have their collateral share of bliss'. And the jackals? He agreed, though with some hesitation, that, yes, jackals and indeed perhaps all mammals would be eligible. The Nawab continues to press him:

> And the wasps? he became uneasy during the descent to wasps, and was apt to change the conversation. And oranges, cactuses, crystals and mud? and the bacteria inside Mr Sorley? No, no, this is going too far. We must exclude someone from our gathering, or we shall be left with nothing.

Similarly, we must exclude *some* linguistic creations from the canon of proper English or we shall be left with nothing of the language. Creativity cannot itself be a qualification for inclusion. Indeed in a way it is a *dis*qualification, since what counts is conformity to some norm or other. Monkeys and perhaps all mammals are admitted to the divine presence because they are relatively close to the human norm, but wasps are altogether too remote. And similarly, one might say, some instances of language creation are considered close enough to conformity to be allowed the status of proper English, but others just go too far and must accordingly be excluded.

## The ownership of English

But excluded on whose authority? Who decides? In the case of the heavenly mansions, it is the missionary. The monkeys are not consulted. But in the case of proper English? Who is the authority here?

The English, perhaps. It is their language after all, or at least it is labelled with their name, so they should surely have a decisive say in the matter. If in doubt about proper usage, consult the native speakers: in this case the English. But not *any* of the English, of course: not indeed the majority of them, but a carefully selected sub-set of reliable sources of information. You are probably fairly safe with *The Times*, even though, at the time of writing, it is owned by an Australian, and edited by an Irishman, but less safe with the *Sun*. Stockbrokers from Surbiton are probably reliable informants, but avoid bricklayers from Burnley, whose English in many respects would be quite improper.

The sub-set of reliable informants is self-selected, and self-appointed, as the custodians of correct English, the real McCoy—no, let me rephrase that, the genuine article. What then of native speakers of English who, through no fault of their own, are not English at all: all those millions on the other side of the Atlantic, for example, getting up to all kinds of things with the language? It may be true that if you include everything in our gathering we are left with nothing, but if we exclude too drastically we are not left with much either. The Americans pose a problem, even those who are cognate with Surbiton stockbrokers and Bernard Levin of *The Times*. Is their English proper or not? More now, it would seem, than it used to be. More so than in 1946, for example. That was the year of the first appearance of *English Language Teaching* sponsored by the British Council. One of its features was a section about correct usage, and in response to a query from a reader about the expressions 'fry-pan' and 'frying-pan', we find the following judgement:

> *Fry-pan* is not accepted as standard English and is considered incorrect by most grammarians. It is probably an American form.

Not accepted by whom? The agent is conveniently deleted. Considered incorrect by which grammarians? Presumably American ones, like Charles Fries in Michigan and Leonard Bloomfield in Yale, have not been consulted. So who decides? The editor of *English Language Teaching* decides, assuming the authority as a representative of a particular group of native speakers of English. Nowadays, of course, it would not do to be so dismissive of American words like 'fry-pan', because we cannot afford to cause offence. We can still be dismissive of Indian words like 'prepone', because it does not matter if we cause offence in this case. And anyway the Indians are not native speakers, so they don't need to be consulted.

So the custodians of correctness have extended the threshold of their tolerance, but only so far, and no further. And their voice is still heard in the land, deploring the decline in standards, detecting abuses which defile the well of English—*their* English. A strong instinct of ownership still prevails: the language is to be protected against impropriety because it is their property, part of their heritage, part of their identity indeed. There is fundamental ambivalence here: on the one hand there is pride, complacency even, that English has become an international means of communication, but, on the other hand, there is grave concern that it might be misused, corrupted in the mouths of all these foreigners, many of whom are now actually living in this country. It was bad enough when we only had non-standard speakers among the English themselves to cope with.

## Standard English

The language must be protected and preserved. Proper English is standard English and unless there is conformity to its norms, chaos will come again, the language will disperse, and we shall indeed be left with nothing. If the centre cannot hold, things will fall apart, and standards of communication, indeed standards of social behaviour in general, will decline. The centre is the standard language, and so if that holds, standards will be maintained. Correctness is ultimately a matter of moral values.

You may think I exaggerate. Perhaps I do. But the attitude I have just described is still very much in evidence and although it may only be that of a minority, it is a powerful minority, and one which includes those in government whose decision is final, no matter how whimsical or misinformed it might be.

But there is surely a case for sustaining stability in language in some way, for otherwise things *do* fall apart, and we are left with nothing. It seems obvious, though, that proper English cannot be equated with the standard language, except by special pleading and capricious fiat. Propriety cannot be an absolute but only a relative matter. But relative to what? Relative, it seems reasonable to suggest, to the contexts of its use. Proper English is appropriate English. Proper words are not independently defined, but only in reference to the places in which they properly appear. Standard English is the kind of English which is to be found in certain places, and to the extent that its use is wide ranging and sanctioned by the conventions of institutionalized use, particularly in writing, its propriety is well established. But by the same token, there are places where it would be proper to use other forms of English.

## The case for teaching standard English

The case for the teaching of standard English, whether we are thinking of the teaching of English as a first or other language, rests on the fact that, especially in its written manifestation, it is the language of institutional communication, both within English-speaking countries and internationally, and if you are not competent in this language, then you are disqualified from entry into whole areas of social and professional life which are institutionally organized and not otherwise accessible.

In this respect, standard English is not essentially different from the established, institutionalized, indeed standard modes of thought and practice which define other subjects on the school curriculum. It seems generally to be accepted, for example, that it is the purpose of physics or geography as school subjects to initiate pupils into conceptual conventions which do not correspond with their untutored experience, and which in many ways directly challenge it. The justification for this is that these conventions have a more general currency which represents the values of a wider community. We do not usually hear arguments against physics on the grounds that it imposes values on pupils which run counter to ideas about the physical world which they have acquired through upbringing. Indeed, the basic rationale of schooling is based on the assumption that the primary socialization of upbringing is, in some respects, limited and limiting with regard to the requirements of the wider community. Standard physics meets those requirements. So does standard English. And indeed it seems clear that physics, and all other school subjects, can only be standard and so meet these requirements *in association with* standard English. The appropriate language in this case *is* the standard language.

## Issues of additive and subtractive bilingualism

The argument here represents the learning of standard English in this country as not essentially different from the learning of it as a second language: in both cases it is a means of extending people's verbal repertoire so that they can extend the range of their involvement in those areas of social and professional life which are served by the standard language. This leaves the language of upbringing, the mother tongue, or the first dialect of the closer and more immediate community intact, and available for other communal and communicative purposes *as appropriate*. It seems straightforward: you develop additive bilingualism. As the Cox Report, *English From Ages 5 to 16*, puts it, the aim is to 'add Standard English to the repertoire, not to replace other dialects or languages'.

But things are not so simple. Here, for example, is Norman Fairclough speaking out against this view:

> But there is an apparent paradox. How is it possible to add without replacing? Is it possible to teach pupils a variety of English so much more prestigious and powerful than their own dialects, or languages, without detriment to the latter? The Cox Report suggests that it is possible, and its argument rests upon the concept of appropriateness: different varieties of English, and different languages, are appropriate for different contexts and purposes, and all varieties have the legitimacy of being appropriate for some contexts and purposes. On the face of it, this resolves the paradox. But as soon as appropriate contexts and purposes for varieties other than Standard English are listed, it is clear just how fragile this resolution of the paradox is. For these are of course largely in the domain of the private and the quaint, and exclude those public, formal and written domains which have most social prestige. Will children not get the unspoken message that their varieties may be 'appropriate', but are pretty marginal and irrelevant? (Fairclough 1992: 35–6)

But there is, of course, nothing paradoxical at all in the idea that you can add without replacing. It is entirely possible. Indeed it is common, as is attested by the millions of additive bilinguals in the world who have no problem ranging over their extended repertoires and engaging them as appropriate. So why, one wonders, does Fairclough find a paradox here? One answer might be that although it may be possible in principle, and indeed attested in practice elsewhere, it is not so here in this country. And this is because there is a unique concentration of power in standard English, and this invests it with such prestige that all other languages and dialects dwindle in its presence.

Now it is true, of course, that standard English is used in 'public, formal and written domains' because it functions as the institutional language of a wider community, and it would be strange, paradoxical indeed, if it were not so. And it is also true, of course, that to the extent that power in any state resides in its institutions, then standard English is the language of power. But in that case you empower pupils by teaching it, thereby denying special privilege to those who happen to have acquired it by upbringing.

## Discourses of power and solidarity

Does this not mean, though, as Fairclough fears, that other varieties will be undervalued, seen as appropriate only to minor and marginal aspects of human life? This depends on what you believe is minor and marginal. Fairclough's assumption is that the only values which people will hold in esteem are those which attach to institutional authority and the public prestige which goes with it. His attention is fixed on the discourse of power. But what of the discourse of solidarity? People surely value the language of personal relationships, of peer groups and regional loyalties, whatever its public status. Indeed the very existence of prestigious institutional norms of behaviour will tend to encourage dissention from them in the interests of greater small group solidarity. Where is the evidence that people in general, or pupils in particular, are so deferential as to accept the 'unspoken message' about the inferiority of their language? I would have thought that what evidence there is points in just the opposite direction.

Fairclough's own message seems to be that power will always prevail over solidarity and that institutionalized values, which must of their nature be impersonalized to be effective, will always dominate the communal values of small group interaction. That being so, what must figure most prominently in educational thinking is the institutional function of language, so that pupils should be provided with the means of engaging in the 'public, formal and written domains' that Fairclough refers to, rather than being confined to 'the domain of the private and the quaint'.

The point is that these institutionalized domains are of their nature standardized and so need to be serviced by a standardized language. Other varieties have different conditions of appropriacy to meet and express different values: the essentially heterogeneous values of solidarity, communal identity and individual interpersonal relations. What one should seek to do, I would have thought, is to argue for the significance of such values rather than to dismiss them as quaint, or to try to invest them with a homogeneous function and a status based on institutional power which is both inappropriate and impossible. By giving priority to this function of language, Fairclough in effect himself marginalizes other functions, and the varieties of language which alone can discharge them. And at the same time, of course (and here *is* a paradox), lends support to the case for the only kind of language which can serve the institutional needs which he has recognized as primary in education: namely standard English.

## Standard English and educational objectives

It does not seem to me that there is any cogent or coherent case against the recognition of standard English as an appropriate educational objective, in first or second language situations, so long as education is seen as serving the institutional needs of the state. The real issue, I think, is how we can at the same time respect the propriety of other forms of English as proper to different needs and purposes. And these needs and purposes are also matters of educational concern. They have to do with objectives other than that of institutional support, and with the means whereby educational objectives in general are achieved.

Both the Kingman and the Cox Reports pay their respects to non-standard forms of speaking. Here is Kingman:

> When children go to school for the first time, their language may differ in many respects from Standard English, depending on where they live, their parents' speech habits and so on. This is natural and proper and a source or richness. However, one of the schools' duties is to enable children to acquire Standard English, which is their right.
> (Kingman Report 1988: Ch. 2 Para. 31)

### Standard English as an end of learning

Education reformulates and develops the experience of children by drawing on the resources of personality and perception which they bring to school. The children's resources, their culture, their very identity as people, are naturally and properly invested in their particular modes of speech. Now if these are indeed a source of richness of experience in the past and out of school, why then are they not a source of richness for learning in the present and in school? One can concede that one of the objectives of schooling is to provide students with the opportunity, otherwise deprived them, of learning the standard language for use where appropriate, but there seems to be no reason why other forms of speaking, whether these be varieties of English or other languages, should not be sanctioned, indeed encouraged, in the exploration of experience in the *process* of learning, precisely because of their richness or, as the Cox

Report puts it, 'since dialect is so closely related to children's individual identity'. (Cox Report 1989: Ch. 4 Para. 23). One can accept that the final edited version of language, so to speak, in certain domains of use, is required to take the form of standard English, but this is no reason for denying the value of interim drafts in a non-standard form which is the appropriate expression of the child's identity and experience. The language which is proper to the eventual product does not need to be the same as that which is proper to the interim process. I have argued that it is wrongheaded to suppose, as Fairclough seems to do, that non-standard forms can constitute the appropriate *ends* of English language education, but it is just as wrongheaded, I think, to suppose that the standard can serve as the appropriate *means*.

## Dialect as a means for learning

I realize that in proposing this argument, I run the risk of representing non-standard dialects as having the same sort of function as do the interlanguage forms in second language acquisition. These emerge as temporary, interim stages moving in gradual proximity to established forms of speaking. They are phases in language learning, not varieties of language use: they do not have the stable and communal character of dialects, but are unformed, unfinished, scarce half made up forms of speaking in embryonic state. In this sense they do not have the status of real language, and indeed their effectiveness depends on learners, and teachers, acknowledging the fact. They are appropriate for learning *because* they are unsettled and transitional. And the task of the teacher is to exploit their instability.

## Co-existence of standard and dialect

To suggest that dialects provide the means for learning might seem to imply that they have a similar ancillary and expedient character and do not have the status of the full-blown (standard) language, thereby undermining their integrity and diminishing their dignity in just the way that Fairclough complains about. But there is no such implication. Here is the crucial difference. Non-standard dialects, unlike interlanguages, are fully developed communal forms of speaking with their own domains of use, including those of classroom interaction, which co-exist with those for which standard English is appropriate. And an essential, and neglected, part of language education is to develop an awareness of this proper co-existence.

I have argued that non-standard language has for its speakers its own propriety as the expression of personal identity and communal solidarity, and for that very reason is appropriate as a means of learning, and inappropriate for institutional use. To seek to sustain its status by giving it responsibilities for which it is unsuited is actually to deny its real character and to support the idea that the sole objective of language education is to empower people to achieve institutional purposes.

## Countering linguistic chauvinism

But it is surely also the objective of language education to make people aware of the nature of language itself, and the different conditions of appropriacy in its use, to counteract Anglo-Saxon attitudes and the immense ignorance and intolerance which is everywhere apparent in opinion and policy in this country; and which are bred from the sense of exclusive pride in linguistic property which I referred to earlier. Let me quote an example of fairly typical linguistic chauvinism. When, a year or so ago, the Prince and Princess of Wales were visiting France, the following headline appeared in the *Sun* newspaper:

DI FOXED BY FROG LINGO

This was followed by a report of the Princess *sympathizing* with the children at the British School in Paris because of their difficulties in learning French. And this was not represented as in any way reprehensible on the part of the royal: on the contrary, the tone of the report, as the headline might suggest, was one of amused and indulgent tolerance. In view of such public and prestigious expressions of disdain for other languages, it is hardly surprising that children should adopt a negative attitude to learning them. Why should they get foxed by frog lingo, or kraut lingo, or dago lingo or any lingo other than their own, which all these frogs and krauts will learn anyway because everybody knows it is the language of international communication. Thus, just a year ago, the *Daily Mail* proclaimed in banner headlines that EUROPE NEEDS PLAIN ENGLISH (confusing, as is common, plain English with standard English). John Major, the article declared, must go on the offensive. 'English must become the sole official language for the Community.'

But these, it might be objected, are articles from the *Sun* and the *Daily Mail*: hardly the sources of serious or informed opinion. And anyway, they are about foreign languages, so what do they have to do with the theme of proper English? They illustrate, I think, a typical assertiveness of superiority, an intolerance of other people's language, whether this is considered a dialect or a different language altogether, whether this is French or Scouse or Geordie or Indian English. They are represented as limited in some way, a little lightweight, droll, quaint indeed, the stuff of comic soap opera. And of course it is in your interests to keep them quaint if you want to protect the special status of standard English as your own property, leased out for international use, but still account-able to you as custodian. It is these attitudes sustained by an unholy alliance of an ignorance about the social nature of language and a supe-rior sense of one's own property and propriety which it must surely be the business of language education to change.

## Endthoughts

I believe that there is an unanswerable case for the teaching of standard English, in first and second language situations, to meet the institutional objectives of language education as I have outlined them, and to provide the qualification for membership in a wider community, and the means for extending awareness through the written word beyond the bounds of immediate experience. The standard is indeed the language of power and hence people are empowered by acquiring it. The standard lan-guage is a proper language to learn, and school is the proper place to learn it. But it is only proper to the extent that it is appropriate, and it is not therefore *the* proper language, the one and only. And it is also a major objective of language education to make people aware of this, to school them in the sociolinguistic understanding of different conditions of appropriacy. The argument for the teaching of the standard language rests on a recognition of the different but equally valid propriety of other forms of speaking.

And let me be clear that I am not referring only to English in the con-text of domestic use in this country, but to English as an international language. English as an International Language: the phrase sounds grandly on the ear. But it is ambiguous in a way directly relevant to the points that I have been making. It can be taken, on the one hand, to refer to the language as a common denominator in communication within secondary superimposed cultures of business, technology, and other international, multinational domains of use and power where the stan-dard language is institutionally appropriate. But the phrase English as an international language can also refer to the *spread* of the language into small communal corners, the demotic diaspora which develops dif-ferent varieties and dialects to express the primary socio-cultural iden-tity of smaller communities all over the world. English for specific purposes, which serves the need for wider communication of the secondary superposed cultures, can never of its nature be specific to the social needs of these smaller communities.

My argument is that we need to recognize this distinction and to acknowledge that both kinds of international use have their proper place in the scheme of things and both are of crucial concern in English language education.

People in government in this country are fond of telling us that in education we should get back to basics. To them, much of what I have been saying this evening will no doubt sound crackpot, mere barmy theorizing: a talk (to use an appropriate Shakespearian phrase) full of 'exsufflicate and blown surmises'. Back to basics, I agree. But what is basic, to my mind, is not simply the mindless insistence on standard English, not simply the schooling in ability in *uses* of language, but the development of a corresponding *awareness* about the nature of language use in general—an awareness, indeed, about what it means to talk about what I have been talking about today: linguistic appropriacy, property, propriety, about proper words in proper places. If you deprehend my point. Or if, as Mrs Malaprop would have it 'if you reprehend the true meaning of what I have been saying'.

*Originally published in Volume 47/4, 1993*

# 7

## Management and participation in ELT projects

### HELEN STEPHENSON

## Introduction

In recent years there has been an explosion in ELT beyond traditional ESL situations in Anglophone and Commonwealth countries into private and aid-based ELT operations around the world. At the same time, theories on the teaching of English have proliferated, in an effort to develop effective ways of promoting learners' competence in using the *lingua franca* that English has become. In consequence, ELT projects are often involved in introducing new practices to ELT practitioners, particularly in Africa, Asia, and Eastern Europe.

Increasingly, funders and donors are demanding more accountability, more proof of 'value for money' from ELT projects. This in turn translates into an additional impetus to ensure that such projects and any innovations they implement are appropriate and sustainable in their given context.

Much emphasis has been laid on the value of the participation of the 'end users' or 'adopters' in the process of innovation, as a means of increasing the likelihood of that innovation being successfully adopted and incorporated into future practice. In other words, participation is seen as the key to sustainability. But participation is a feature of grass roots bottom-up processes of the Freirean school. (Freire 1972) and ELT projects are often rather more top-down in nature. To what extent is it possible to mix the two approaches?

## Top-down and bottom-up approaches

While the value of participation in innovation is not to be underestimated, it is simplistic to assume that it will bring automatic success. Innovations can fail where bottom-up approaches exist as well as when the approach is top-down. Institutional support for bottom-up innovation is as important as participant support for top-down approaches. Equally, it should not be assumed that participation is always welcomed by the practitioners involved. What is 'bottom-up participation' to the manager may simply be 'extra work' to a teacher who has not been consulted on any aspect of the proposed innovation. In order for this to be a useful strategy it is necessary to examine the broader picture and identify the aims, limitations, and modes of participation, as well as any other features of successful bottom-up innovation.

## Participatory approaches in development aid

Some areas of development aid have amassed a great deal of experience in participatory strategies and processes. I refer to the community-based work of the type often promoted by non-government organizations (NGOs) rather than capital investment aid targeted at government or infrastructure level. NGOs typically work at a grassroots level, their work often characterized by an emphasis on local, small scale, collaborative projects which mobilize the beneficiaries of the aid. Voluntary Service Overseas (VSO), for example, is involved in projects such as water source protection, community health, village wood plots, etc. Harrison (1987: 302) emphasizes the role of participatory approaches in this type of aid: 'The key is participation ... Almost every major survey of the ingredients for successful projects has pointed to the crucial importance of participation.' He summarizes nine 'keys to success' in development projects, of which six are specifically concerned with the individual's perspective and involvement.

## ELT and community-based development aid

A comparison of ELT with community-based development aid is valid because of the parallels which exist between the two.

## The 'culture gap'

Firstly, in both situations important cultural differences can exist between the innovator or agent of change and the implementer (if the two are separate entities). It may be thought that the 'ELT umbrella' brings teachers from around the world close together, but in fact there are often more differences than similarities to be found. The local culture of ELT is, at present, always likely to be different to that of the majority of English teachers in the world today. The vast majority of academic work, publications, and innovations in ELT derive from Britain, North America, and Australia (the notable exception being the work of N.S. Prabhu). The British Overseas Development Administration (ODA), too, shows awareness at management levels of cultural differences in ELT projects: 'There is a management gap between local project staff ... and expatriate staff (which is) widened by cross-cultural differences in the processes of consultation and communicating decisions' (Webb and Sinclair 1985: 7). It is worth quoting Kachru (quoted in Phillipson 1992b) to dispel any doubts about the existence of this cultural 'gap': 'given the present attitude of TESL specialists, it is difficult to expect from such specialists any theoretical insights and professional leadership in this field which would be contextually, attitudinally and pragmatically useful to the Third World countries.'

## The human factor

Secondly, both community-based development aid and ELT rely heavily on the so-called 'human factor', whereby it is the individual's behaviour which is both the mechanism for and the aim of the change. Although all innovation is principally concerned with changing human beliefs and behaviour, in aid and ELT the human factor is especially important. Both are concerned with changing human behaviour as the means *and* the end to the innovation, in ways in which commerce or industry is not. The qualitative changes that the innovations seek to stimulate are brought about by and for the individuals concerned, not, normally, for the good of any outside agent.

The sustainability of any changes relies on the willingness of the participants to continue with new practices long after the change agent has withdrawn. In commerce or industry, however, new working practices or new machinery become a part of the established routine, supervisors and managers do not withdraw but continue at post. The individual factory or office worker may never have been involved in the process of innovation and is unlikely to have the freedom to revert to previous practices. In aid and in ELT, the farmer, the health worker, and the teacher are the focus and embodiment of new practice.

## Lessons from community-based development aid

### Ten points for managers of innovation in ELT projects

Kennedy (1988: 341–2) has provided a list of useful questions for those involved in the management of change in ELT. In drawing up this list he makes reference to community-based development aid and the adopter's perspective of innovations. I suggest the following extension of Kennedy's list, drawing even further on the experiences of such aid, to provide more specific strategies to include the benefits of participatory processes in what are essentially top-down project frameworks.

### 1   Market the innovation

Ensure that there is institutional and political support for teacher involvement in the process of innovation. It is important to create a favourable image of the proposed changes with all the relevant parties, including professionals from outside the field of ELT. To do this it is necessary to give varying emphasis to the *how* and the *what* of the innovation at different stages in its life. In the early stages of the process, those likely to have an interest in the innovation may have limited knowledge of the nature of the innovation itself. Therefore *how* the process is being conducted will be important. (In bottom-up approaches relying on participants' contributions to shape the innovation, this is more obviously so.) Failure to 'market' the innovation successfully can have far-reaching implications. Tomlinson, for example, writing of change management in Indonesian high schools, acknowledges that a 'publicity and public relations exercise' is needed to assuage the critics (administrators and academics) who have labelled the programme as 'radical, subversive, and even neocolonial' (1990: 33). Tomlinson's project report brings into sharp focus the need for managers to foster communication between all sectors of the systems involved, and to have positive strategies for dealing with cross-cultural differences. It also offers evidence for the view that innovations cannot be sustainable if the 'powers that be' do not endorse the bottom-up styles of change.

## 2 Determine what the possibilities are for involving teachers in the innovation

Levels of involvement and strategies for involvement will depend on local cultural (including political, social, and economic) systems as well as the expertise of the participants. For instance, officials or administrators may be reluctant to allow teacher participation, as Kerr (1982: 232) points out with reference to developing countries. On the other hand, the political situation might be encouraging to grass roots level participation. Participants can have expertise in the local situation and in the focus of the project. For example, I was involved in a textbook production project in São Tomé and Príncipe, where the teachers were the best source of information on the feasibility of both the aims of the project and its methods in the local context. At the same time, the senior teachers had benefited from recent training in the USA and in São Tomé and Príncipe, and the potential for their involvement in the materials writing was also high.

## 3 Determine the mechanisms by which teachers will contribute to the innovation process

There must be functioning, not simply nominal, mechanisms whereby teachers can see that their contributions are valued, and the onus must be on the innovator to encourage involvement.

At the institutional level participation may be via 'special interest groups'—working parties, meetings, etc. In larger systems, surveys, school visits, teacher's centres, associations, INSET, or designated teacher representatives can provide structured input into the innovation process. In São Tomé and Príncipe we were fortunate to find a system-wide arrangement of weekly teachers' meetings, whose purpose was to prepare for the coming week's classes, prepare tests, etc. This was a ready-made forum for the exchange of ideas and for gathering input to new initiatives. Kouraogo (1987) also suggests mechanisms, such as teachers' groups, for participation in curriculum renewal even in 'difficult circumstances' like those in Burkina Faso.

## 4 Ensure that these contributions can be made in the design, implementation, and evaluation stages of the innovation

Kerr (1982) and Harrison (1987) both emphasize the need for participants to be involved at every stage of the change process, and this is equally true in an ELT project. If participation is to work it must begin from the earliest possible phases of a project. Teachers who are invited to comment on, for example, curricular or materials developments at a relatively late stage may, quite rightly, feel that they are simply being paid lip-service, and their contribution may lack commitment and effectiveness as a result. Ultimately, it is a teacher's commitment to materials that determine their use or otherwise in the classroom. This was illustrated by the storerooms full of boxes of English textbooks, the product of an earlier ELT project, in São Tomé and Príncipe, while teachers 'got by' with blackboard and chalk.

## 5  Determine what the role of the planner is to be compared to the other participants

When the innovator is an 'outsider', as is often the case in ELT projects, the post may not be a permanent one or one which existed prior to the life of the project. In such circumstances, the innovator can only be effective if the other participants know precisely where he or she fits in the organization and what they can expect of him or her. The innovator can be a manager, a facilitator, an observer, an inspirer in the change process. The choice of role will depend on the individual circumstances, but it should be clear to the teachers, head teachers, and administrators who are involved. Kouraogo (1987) describes how the secondary school inspectors in Burkina Faso fall victim to 'mistaken identity'. The inspectors are charged with providing in-service training to the English teachers, but the teachers have confused them with the primary school inspectors who have a more supervisory role, and a reputation for an autocratic approach. The teachers thus have a defensive attitude towards the inspectors. They expect the inspectors to be 'experts' whose function is to provide demonstration 'model' lessons, but, as a result of the defensive relationship, they often resist the pedagogical innovations introduced by the inspectors.

## 6  Investigate the historical factors which may have a bearing on the innovation

It is important for the manager to be aware of both the system's and the potential participants' previous experience of innovation per se. If there has been previous experience, the question must be 'Was it a positive or negative experience?'. Where people have had previous positive experiences of innovation the process will be easier, since participants are more likely to be flexible and to take risks. The innovator may be able to capitalize on earlier systems or channels of communication for the benefit of the current project.

Where people have had a negative experience, they are unlikely to look favourably on new ventures, as Harrison points out (1987: 308).

Similarly, countries in receipt of aid are often involved in several uncoordinated initiatives, all of which may demand a 'full contribution', from the individuals concerned, culminating in what can be termed 'recipient fatigue': (cf. 'donor fatigue', a term used to describe unwillingness on the part of the North to give increasing amounts of aid to the South). In 1987, for instance, The Gambia had 34 aid projects in the Education Sector funded by seven bilateral and six multilateral agencies (Bray 1991: 100). While it is unlikely that any one teacher would be involved in all 34 projects, there were several projects specific to ELT in which an individual might be expected to have a role. In São Tomé and Príncipe, secondary school English teachers were involved in Swedish, Portuguese, British, and American initiatives over the period 1983–90. Each new scheme was arranged at Ministry level and imposed on teachers, with the inevitable result of declining teacher enthusiasm and a lack of belief in the longevity of any innovations involved.

7   *Investigate factors which are outside the remit of the proposed changes but which may directly or indirectly influence success*

In other words, do the participants have any other perceived needs? In a supplementary materials project in São Tomé and Principe, teachers accepted the need for initiatives in these areas but initially were unable to make an effective contribution to the project, due to their overwhelming feeling that nothing could be done to improve English teaching while students lacked desks and schools lacked doors, windows, and electricity. In such a situation the innovator or entrepreneur has several options: to become involved in providing for these extra needs, to help participants find other sources of support, or to support alternatives which circumvent the problem. In São Tomé and Príncipe the project itself had minimal financial resources and so the first option was not possible. Examples of the second and third strategies which were followed are: first, the project tried to act as a link between schools and potential donors, and secondly, teachers were trained to act as listening models as an alternative to the tape recorder.

8   *Avoid pre-set goals where possible*

It is important to be flexible to the adjustments which will prove necessary during the process of innovation, particularly when the level of local participation is high. An initial statement of objectives will be based on an appraisal of the situation which by necessity cannot be as informed or as detailed as the process of innovation itself. Therefore it is inevitable that information will emerge, and situations will evolve, during the course of implementation, and hence modifications will be required. In the report of a textbook project in Cameroon (Wilson and Harrison 1983: 40), the authors describe how a range of activities from role play through to creative writing were dropped from their initial textbook design, as it became apparent during the trialling process that various aspects of the teaching situation meant that these activities were ineffective or unsuitable. Bowers (1983: 117) comments on the differences between planned and actual outcomes as follows: 'I believe that such variation is an essential and desirable part of curriculum development, created by the interaction between the innovation and the context into which it is planted.' Inflexibility and insistence on original plans is a strategy destined to fail since it is inevitable that as different practitioners implement the innovation so it will be modified and evolve. The manager's role then is to bridge any gap that might develop between donor or institution goals and the organic nature of an ELT project.

### 9 Pay attention to the pace of change

What may be a *feasible* timetable of change may not be an *acceptable* timetable to all the participants. Resistance to otherwise acceptable innovations is likely if people feel pressurized into changing too quickly. Forcing the pace can undermine teachers' own authority and their sense of ownership of the innovation. ELT projects may be influenced by the timetable of the academic year, but this does not necessarily reflect the way individuals adapt to change. In education, as in most things, the most enduring practices are often those which have evolved *in situ* over a period of time. Perhaps we should try to imitate this in ELT projects which are concerned, as most are, with changing classroom behaviour. By way of illustration, I offer my experience in trying to outlaw one of the more time consuming and pedagogically empty exercises, that of having the 'best' student write out all the answers to homework on the board, thus giving those students who have not done the homework ample opportunity to blindly copy the correct responses. Expecting this to be a quick and simple matter to remedy, I was not prepared for the six months of (stimulating) debate which followed before the practice began to decline.

### 10 Consider adapting existing practice rather than implanting something new and unfamiliar

Accounts of ELT projects often refer to the 'problem' of local practitioners reverting to previous practice. This seems to be a feature of projects which introduce major changes to existing systems and practices.

However, while progress involves change, not all change is necessarily progress. Building on what is familiar reduces resistance and is likely to produce a more favourable cost-benefit calculation. This is because risk-taking, which is viewed as a negative factor, is reduced. Adaptations can also be simpler and cheaper, and it is often simply a matter of approach—the how rather than the what. Harrison (1987: 311) gives the example of encouraging child spacing—a traditional African practice—to achieve family planning ends rather than introducing the new (Western) concept of limiting family size. An example from ELT (also referred to above) is to combine traditional teacher-centred styles of teaching with the use of the teacher as a listening model for active listening.

## Conclusion

I believe not only that real teacher participation is possible in ELT projects, but that it is an essential factor in establishing appropriate, feasible, and sustainable innovations. Where an ELT innovation is initiated at the national or institutional level its successful adoption will require the support and acceptance of both teachers and administrators. It is difficult for people to accept something they do not feel involved in, especially if it demands of them a change in their working practices or conditions. It follows that the participation of those affected by an innovation will enhance its chances of successful adoption. This article has been concerned with exploring some areas that managers in top-down project structures could usefully investigate if they wish to make the most of participant involvement.

*Originally published in Volume 48/3, 1994*

# 8

## Gender in the EFL classroom

JANE SUNDERLAND

### 'Gender' closely observed

'Gender in the EFL classroom' is a phrase which may conjure up in teachers' minds no more than complaints about the use of *he*, or about textbooks being sexist. Closer examination, however, suggests that gender operates at more than the level of materials. Other levels include the English language itself; and classroom processes, including learning processes, teacher–learner interaction, and learner–learner interaction. These levels interact, always within a particular political, sociolinguistic, and educational context (see Figure 1). One feature of the workforce in this context is that it tends to be characterized by 'gendered division', what Pennycook (1989: 610) describes as 'a hierarchically organized division between male conceptualizers and female practitioners'.

Also pertinent to gender is proficiency—does one gender have a superior ability to learn foreign languages?

The following, then, is an overview of the areas in which gender operates in the world of EFL, and of arguments and research associated with them. (In all except the section on 'The English language', I am using 'gender' to mean culturally (though not deterministically) influenced characteristics of each sex; 'sex' to mean whether a person is biologically female or male. And though I will be referring throughout to English as a foreign language, much may apply to the teaching and learning of other foreign, and second languages. It may also have implications for, *inter alia*, ethnicity and race in the language classroom.)

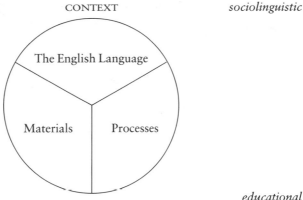

FIGURE 1 *Gender in the EFL classroom*


## *The English language*

Gender tends to be seen as unimportant in English, and as 'natural', i.e. corresponding to sex. Yet the traditional, prescriptive 'rule' of using *he*, *him*, etc., after sex-indefinite pronouns and to refer to a person of unknown sex illustrates that it can also be grammatical. That this may be changing is relevant to both learners and teachers of English.

Much has been written over the last two decades about sexism in the English language (e.g. Kramer 1975; Cameron 1985), and about non-sexist language change (e.g. Bate 1978; Cooper 1984). Linguistic sexism at code level has been identified in the pronoun system ('generic' *he*, *him, his, himself*); 'generic' *man*; masculine and feminine 'equivalents', which through 'semantic derogation' (Schulz 1975) are not so now, the feminine being often less prestigious and/or having sexual connotations (e.g. *master/mistress, manager/manageress*); under-lexicalization (**husband-swapping party*); over-lexicalization (e.g. the number of verbs used disparagingly for women talking and of nouns referring to sexually active women), and 'male firstness' (*men and women*). Discussions of change focus on, *inter alia*, the use of *s/he*, singular *they* (which is not new), *Ms, -person* words, and alternative, more familiar 'neutral' forms: e.g. *flight attendant*. There is evidence of change in written English: 'androcentric generics' may be disappearing, for example (Cooper 1984), and though there is less evidence for change in spoken English, personal observation indicates this is happening in some contexts.

What does this mean for the teacher, one of whose roles is promoting competence, overtly or otherwise, in English grammar, and who is often seen as a model of the target language her/himself?[1] Students living in an environment which includes little or no English may come across new 'gendered' items in school reading or listening texts; they may ask the teacher to explain and judge them. Yet the teacher may not be aware of the changes, or of the sociolinguistic context in which they have occurred. There are implications for both teacher education and materials here.

## Materials
### Pedagogic (and other) grammars

How do pedagogic grammars represent and evaluate 'gendered English', and its changes? I am referring particularly to the portrayal of alternatives to the 'generic' *he*, etc., nouns which are 'gender-neutral' (e.g. *chairperson, firefighter*), and *Ms*.

In my own study (Sunderland 1986) I looked at 22 recent English grammars, including 20 pedagogic grammars, to find out if the above items were included, and, if so, what was said about them. In principle, pedagogic grammars have an obligation to describe new forms which are in reasonably common usage and do not flout the rules of English syntax. However, they must also be selective, and whether a given item is selected, as well as what is said about it, will depend very much on the individual author.

Examples of 'generic' *he* still appear in grammars. However, even though it is no longer acceptable to many speakers in many contexts (Purnell 1978; Bate 1978; Cooper 1984; Cameron 1985), the alternatives of *his or her*, etc., and *s/he* are often deemed stylistically inferior, described variously as 'pedantic', 'unwieldly', 'cumbersome', 'heavy', and 'awkward.' *They* after an indefinite pronoun ('Everyone brought their own lunch') may be approved as an informal alternative in speaking, but students may be discouraged from using it in writing. For example:

> The use of plural pro-forms to refer to singular nouns premodified by *each* or *every* is not uncommon but often avoided by careful writers.
> (Van Ek and Robat 1984: 3.32)

The most recent of the 22 grammars, *An A–Z of English Grammar and Usage* (Leech 1989: 424–5), and *Using English Grammar: Meaning and Form* (Woods and McLeod 1990: 174) are, however, positive about *he* and *she* and singular *they*, the latter providing an accurate explanation and description, and useful advice:

> ... ['generic'] **his** is considered by many people to be offensive since it has a gender bias. There is a general tendency in English today to avoid sexist language. Two ways of avoiding it are either to use both the feminine and the masculine (**her or his,** or **his/her**) or to use the plural (**their**). In *informal* speech and writing, the second alternative, the use of **their,** is the most usual way to deal with the problem. In **formal** writing, the first alternative is more common.

The *-ess* decline (e.g. *poetess*) was mentioned only in *A Comprehensive Grammar of the English Language*  not a pedagogic grammar but a book often available to teachers:

> Some optional forms (*poetess, authoress*) are no longer in normal use, being replaced by the dual gender forms (*poet, author*, etc.). In order to avoid sexual bias in language, efforts have been made (esp. in AmE) to introduce sex-neutral forms ... (Quirk *et al.* 1985: 315)

*-person* words were mentioned more in the more recent of the 22 grammars, but were often portrayed as somewhat deviant. Illustrative here is the change over editions of *Practical English Grammar* (Thomson and Martinet 1980). In the third edition (p. 9) we read:

> *Recently* there has been an *attempt* to *desex* [salesman, saleswoman, chairman, chairwoman, etc.] by using *-person* instead of *-man*. This *fashion* may not last. (italics added)

The fourth edition (1986), however, referring to nouns which do not have the same form for masculine and feminine, includes the straightforward

> Also *salesman, saleswoman*, etc., but sometimes *-person* is used instead of *-man, -woman: salesperson, spokesperson*.
> (Thomson and Martinet 1986: 2)

*Ms* was likewise mentioned more in the newer grammars—though, again, some comments were not encouraging. *Practical English Usage* (Swan 1980: 212), reads

> *Ms* is used to refer to women who do not wish to have to say whether they are married or not.

One reading of this is that there is something a little strange about these women, even that they are being deliberately evasive or coy. Janet Holmes (personal communication) observes that the sentence is also misleading, since *Ms* is used at least as often to address women (especially in writing) as to refer to them.

Grammars also, of course, portray the two sexes—something normally associated with coursebooks (see below). The examples in
*University Grammar of English* (1973) have been found to under-
represent females numerically, to have females as the subject
of dynamic verbs only rarely, to use 'well-worn stereotypes' and to
present a 'disturbing and sometimes sinister picture of female
objectification and passivity' (Stephens 1990: 92, 98). The examples in
more recent grammars may be less stereotypical without improving
much as far as numbers of females are concerned.

## Dictionaries

Dictionaries are of interest not only for the extent to which, like grammars, they encode non-sexist changes, and how, but also for other
definitions and examples. Cameron (1985: 83) cites problematic
dictionary definitions of *woman, unfeminine,* and *clitoris*; Kaye
criticizes the examples in the otherwise praiseworthy *Collins
COBUILD English Dictionary* which 'build up a picture showing
women in a poor light' (1989b: 192)—that it is women rather than men
who are used in examples illustrating *muddle(d)*, for example. In particular, she notes:

> Perhaps the most amusing (or upsetting) portrayal is of woman as an
> alcoholic and a drug addict ... [This] emerges insidiously, often in
> extra information which could have been omitted, or in examples of
> words with little connection with drugs or alcohol.

A more general concern is that 'Dictionaries ... foster the illusion that
words have a limited number of meanings which can be listed out of
context'—which may hinder understanding of masculine and feminine
'pairs' and subtleties of connotation. This may be especially so for those
EFL learners who place great reliance on and trust in their dictionaries,
often very small ones!

Pedagogic grammars and dictionaries play an important role in language awareness as far as English gender is concerned. Non-sexist
reforms provide a reminder that language is constantly changing, as
well as an actual example of modern language change, and individuals'
and groups' use of new items and avoidance of others illustrates the
existence of language variation among native speakers of English. Also
important is understanding *why* 'gendered English' is changing. Class
discussion of the relevant sections of pedagogic grammars can promote
an understanding that there are relationships between language and

society, and that changes in gender in one are related to changes in gender in the other.

The actual items are also important. More advanced students need to understand that in some contexts male and female 'equivalents' are not equivalent at all—in number of meanings, status, connotation, or even denotation. And students need to recognize both *Ms* as a legitimate honorific, the denotative equivalent of *Mr*, and singular *they* as an alternative to *he* or *she*—because they are likely to encounter them. Productively, we do not want students who are coming to an English-speaking country speaking in a markedly old-fashioned way: 'generic' *he* can easily sound out of date; in some contexts (e.g. in *ELT Journal*) it is actually outlawed. New uses thus need to be reflected in grammars and dictionaries with their traditional variants in an accurate and helpful way.[2]

## Coursebooks

Discussion of coursebooks has focused not so much on 'sexist language' as on the more subtle image questions of relative invisibility of female characters; stereotypes in gender roles greater than stereotyping in society in occupations, relationships, actions, and age, shown by visuals as well as text; and language as discourse: What is the gender composition of the dialogues? Who speaks most in a mixed-sex dialogue? Who speaks first? What language functions do the males/the females exemplify? Females tend to be relatively rare, of lower-status occupations, younger, more often defined in relationship to the opposite sex, and relatively inactive, and quieter, speaking proportionately less, and being responders in rather than initiators of conversation (ETHEL 1980; Porecca 1984; Talansky 1986; Zografou 1990; Gupta and Yin 1990).[3]

Can these concerns be prioritized? In a recent international questionnaire study of male and female EFL teachers, in which respondents graded sexist features of EFL coursebooks according to their (non-) offensiveness, gender stereotyping was rated worse than both invisibility of female characters and 'exclusive vocabulary' in the form of masculine 'generics'—though coursebooks were criticized for the use of 'generic' *he* in the rubric, for example.[4] The prioritizing of coursebook stereotypes may be because stereotypes are seen by both sexes as restricting opportunities for both sexes. The most criticized books were *Streamline English* (the British more than the American series) and the *Kernel* series.[5]

Why does sexism in EFL materials matter? Convincing reasons must be offered to publishers, administrators, and teachers if change is to occur. Saying 'I and some other teachers don't like the sexism in these books' only invites the responses 'most teachers don't care' and 'the students are not complaining' and objections are likely to be perceived as trivial, irrelevant, and lacking in professionalism.[6]

The most convincing reason would be that coursebooks' (and dictionaries' and grammars') representations of gender potentially affect students as language learners and users. This could happen in three ways.

Firstly, if TV, films, videos, computer games, newspapers, and children's books can have an unconscious influence on audiences as agents of socialization, so presumably, can EFL materials. And any unconscious influence of female characters who play restricted social, behavioural, and linguistic roles does not suggest cognitive and communicative empowerment for female learners.

Secondly, if female learners are conscious of the female characters in their coursebook as relatively few, with limited roles, and are offended, alienated, or made to feel marginalized by this and subsequently demotivated, this is more likely to hinder than facilitate their learning. There is need and scope for research into such affective influences.

Thirdly, and perhaps most importantly, models of language can become classroom practice. *Functions of English* (Jones 1977), for example, was found to have a male initiating each mixed-sex dialogue (ETHEL 1980). Used in a mixed class, it is likely that both in any demonstration of the dialogue and in pairwork practice male students would speak first, not only giving them more practice in 'initiating a conversation', but also giving the whole class a model of conversational discourse characterized by 'male firstness'. Again, research might establish the extent to which coursebook models actually do become classroom practice.

These possibilities have to be addressed in relation to questions of credibility and cultural appropriacy, and I would also like to make three points here.

Firstly, Western coursebooks used by students coming to an English-speaking country should presumably be some sort of reflection of life in that country—however incredible and unpalatable this may be. Locally-produced coursebooks for students who are unlikely to work or study abroad are another matter. Secondly, a 'non-credible' text does not automatically hinder language learning—it depends what is done with it. Such a text can be used for discussion, for example, or as the stimulus for written argument. Thirdly, may there not be shades of racism in the claim that '[Group X] students wouldn't like this book'?[7]

It is noteworthy that gender *as a topic* has not been ignored in course-books, but has in the past rather been singled out for special treatment, for example, in the units 'A Woman's Place' in *Viewpoints* (O'Neill and Scott 1974) and 'Women's Lib' in *Communicate in Writing* (Johnson 1981). *Streamline English Directions* (Viney 1985) has a unit on equal opportunities, which includes a rather confusing exercise on non-sexist language change. These attempts to include the female sex and contemporary gender-related issues may be well-meaning, but they are no substitute for a realistic distribution and qualitatively fair representation of female characters throughout the book. The topic can, of course, be presented unselfconsciously, with warmth and humour—see, for example, the more recent *Writing Games* (Hadfield and Hadfield 1990) in which male and female perceptions of the same historical events are explored.

## Teacher's guides

It would be hard to make a case for teacher's guides being discriminatory. However, writers and publishers could perhaps aim not for a 'gender-blind' policy, but rather promote with due sensitivity equal male–female participation, raise awareness of the likelihood of teachers paying more attention to male students (see 'Processes' below) and, where the input of the coursebook reflects sexist practices or attitudes, if culturally appropriate, comment on this. Critical reading and listening may thus become a regular part of the suggested pedagogy. And if there is a picture of, say, a man changing a nappy (an image which some EFL teachers claim would be unsuitable in a book for students from certain cultures), this could be glossed for the benefit of the teacher.

## *Processes*

'Processes' here refers to what happens in the classroom because of *people's* gender. Here I look at learning processes, and teacher–learner and learner–learner interaction.

## Learning processes

There may be gender (or even sex) differences in language learning styles and strategies. When I asked 30 non-native-speaker teachers of English on an in-service course for their opinions about gender differences in language learning and teaching, 14 thought their male and female students had different styles and strategies. (Other gender differences were seen as less important.)[8]

Willing, (1988: 1) investigating learning style ('any individual learner's natural, habitual, and preferred way of learning') in adult migrants in Australia, found that liking to learn many new words, learning words by seeing, learning words by doing something, and learning by talking to friends in English were all rated highly by both sexes, but significantly more highly by women. And Oxford, Nyikos, and Ehrman, reviewing studies of strategies ('the steps or actions taken by students to improve their own language learning') found

> significant sex differences ... reflecting greater *use of language learning strategies by females* ... In three ... studies ... frequency and variety of strategy use was significantly greater for women ... In Study 1, the primary difference was in women's greater use of social behaviors for language learning ... In Study 3, women [showed] significantly more frequent use of conversation/input elicitation strategies ... Study 4, ... showed sex differences in authentic language use and in searching for and communicating meaning ...
> (1988: 321, 326)

If these results are generalizable, pedagogical questions are whether different styles and strategies are or can be catered for, and whether training in strategies is feasible and beneficial (see, e.g. Wenden and Rubin 1987; Skehan 1989).

## Teacher–learner interaction

Lesson transcripts made from tapes have shown secondary and tertiary level teachers of mixed classes to pay more attention to male students (Spender 1982: 56; Stanworth, 1983: 22)—*even when the teachers are committed not to doing so and even when they think that they are distributing their attention equally*. Insidiously, what seems like 'equal time for the girls', or even perceived as the girls getting more can actually be less:

> ... sometimes I have ... thought I have gone too far and have spent *more* time with the girls than the boys. But the tapes have proved otherwise. Out of ten taped lessons ... the maximum time I spent interacting with girls was 42 per cent and on average 38 per cent, and the minimum time with boys 58 per cent ... It is nothing short of a substantial shock to appreciate the discrepancy between what I *thought* I was doing and what I actually *was* doing (Spender 1982: 56).

This false perception is not only experienced by the teacher. One teacher who had spent 34 per cent of her time with the girls, reported that 'the boys ... were complaining about me talking to the girls all the time' (ibid.).

It is of considerable concern that 'more time for the boys' can become 'naturalized'. For though not all boys will get more attention than all girls, this tendency can cut down on the time available for all girls.

Applied to the EFL classroom, these findings might mean that males get more speaking practice and more feedback on their utterances—and this can be the case. Analysing data from ESL classrooms in Australia and New Zealand, Holmes (1989) found that the adult male students both responded more to the teachers' questions and asked more questions themselves—thus getting more speaking practice, presumably answers to their own questions (i.e. feedback), quite possibly feedback in response to their answers, and more practice in question-related language functions. Underlying all these lies a model of discourse of males both speaking and initiating more.

There are, of course, many further ways teachers can treat female and male students differently, including selection (who asks/answers a question? who demonstrates?), varying the level of difficulty of questions by gender, and employing double standards for, for example, error identification and treatment, presentation of written work, and acceptable classroom behaviour. These may be neither intentional nor recognized, by either teacher or students.

## Learner–learner interaction

'Learner–learner interaction' here refers to pair work or group work involving all the students in the class at the same time. It is intended to increase opportunities for classroom communication in general, spoken interaction in particular, and, hopefully, develop proficiency. Yet in pair and group work male students have been found to speak more frequently, and take longer turns than the females, who provide more feedback—echoing findings with mixed-sex groups of native speakers of English (Holmes 1989; Edelsky 1981). These female students were providing a good supportive environment for the males' language practice, but getting little conversational encouragement themselves.[9]

One message both teacher–learner and learner–learner interaction can carry, then, is that women and girls are discoursally if not socially marginal. Yet these classroom gender differences also beg questions. How much do they reflect gender roles in the students' background cultures? How much do they reflect power rather than gender? Does what seems like disadvantage perhaps represent female students letting the males do all the work, even encouraging them, and learning from it?—for we cannot assume that classroom oral production is the most effective path to proficiency. And what would a 'non-discriminating' classroom look like? Not one in which each student got an equal amount of teacher attention, surely, since *individual* needs and other differences must be catered for.

## Proficiency

I will conclude by returning to the question of foreign language learning proficiency and gender—how does this relate to gender in the English language, in materials and in learning processes? There is an apparent contradiction here: while some educational folklore claims that females are the better learners, and a little research supports this in some respects (e.g. Burstall 1974), research into classroom processes, materials, and the English language itself suggests females to be at least potentially *dis*advantaged.

There are, of course, other questions. What does the claim that females are better language learners really mean, and on what is it based? If 'correct', is this partly because of neurological differences (and thus a matter of sex rather than gender)? Reference must also be made to possible more general cognitive gender differences: do males and females learn differently? and to what extent is foreign language learning a special form of learning? This in turn raises the questions of the relationship between first and subsequent language learning, the roles of intelligence and aptitude, and formal (classroom) *versus* informal routes to proficiency. Any claims involving innate sex differences would have to be assessed against the different environmental influences on gender: attitudes, expectations, societal norms (Loulidi 1990), and career opportunities.

Attempts to assess the superiority of one gender over the other in foreign language learning proficiency may not be productive, and it may rather be the existence of possible gender *differences* in language learning styles and strategies which represents a more productive direction for research. Stemming as these differences are likely to do from configurations of factors, this would allow for the complexity anything to do with gender, in or out of foreign language learning, must have.

*Originally published in Volume 46/1, 1992*

# Notes

1 Teachers' own models of both gendered and non-gendered English may in fact not only vary with their accuracy and fluency, but also with their own gender. It has been suggested (Brend 1975) that female teachers' intonation may be inappropriate for their male students, but teachers' gender may also affect their choice of individual linguistic items. My own study, for example, found female native *and* non-native-speaker teachers of English more willing to use 'chairperson' than males from the same group (Sunderland 1986)—there may be variation in teachers' choice of other 'gendered' and 'non-gendered' items.

2 It is presumably because non-native speakers of English respect their grammars so much that they seem to take happily to 'his or her', but express horror and amazement at the discovery of singular 'they' which goes against all they have learned about number concord. My own questionnaire study suggests the preferences of native speakers of English to be the other way round (Sunderland 1986).

3 Possible reasons for this gender imbalance are: (a) the concept of 'male as norm' in conjunction with the fact that most textbook writers are male; (b) (an expectation that) male students are unwilling to read about female characters, whereas the reverse is not true; (c) male textbook writers are unaware of the phenomenon and are simply accepting a 'genre norm' (Gupta and Yin 1990: 41). It would be very valuable to have a study of (say) post-1985 ELT coursebooks to see if the situation of stereotyping and female invisibility has improved.

4 This survey was undertaken by 'Women in EFL Materials' (Convenor Annemarie Young, ELT Department, Cambridge University Press). The results were presented, with suggested 'Guidelines for Inclusive Language', to the Publishers' Association ELT Committee.

5 This must be partly—though not entirely—because these books are so widely used throughout the world.

6 Significantly, 'large classes' is also of concern to teachers rather than learners—and no one would claim it is not an important issue.

7 I am grateful to Jenny Glynn for this observation.

8 Eleven perceived gender differences in the proficiency of their learners, ten in the way they treated their male and female students,

and only five felt that being male or female had made any difference to their own foreign language learning.

9 They may of course have benefited from the larger amount of input thus available to them.

# Talking shop: aspects of autonomous learning

### LESLIE DICKINSON

## Characteristics of the autonomous learner

HEDGE: *In your own writings you focus on the autonomous learner. Can you give your understanding of an autonomous learner? What sorts of qualities and characteristics does an autonomous learner have?*

DICKINSON: I see autonomy very much as an attitude to language learning which may not necessarily have many external, observable features. But, in terms of that attitude, I think of autonomous learners as people who are characterized in a number of ways. I would list about five points. First of all, it seems to me that they are able to identify what's been taught. Now that point may seem simple and self-evident, but there's been a certain amount of research done which seems to indicate that quite a lot of learners actually don't know what is going on in their classes.

HEDGE: *Do you mean that they can pick out what a teacher is doing, what the aims and purposes are, can make them their own and work on them ...?*

DICKINSON: Yes, they can do that. More importantly, they see the importance of doing that, of being concerned about what they're trying to do. So, they are aware of the teacher's objectives. Secondly, they are able to formulate their own learning objectives, not necessarily in competition with the teacher, in fact, rarely so. But more often in collaboration with the teacher, or as something which is in addition to what the teacher is doing. They are people who can and do select and implement appropriate learning strategies, often consciously. That's a third characteristic. And they can monitor their own use of learning strategies. Then, and I think this one is very important, they are able to identify strategies that are not working for them, that are not appropriate, and use others. They have a relatively rich repertoire of strategies, and have the confidence to ditch those that are not effective and try something else.

HEDGE: *Can you give some examples of successful learning strategies you have observed in autonomous learners?*

DICKINSON: The sorts of things that come into my mind are relatively familiar to language teachers. For example, in approaching a piece of reading, effective autonomous learners will go through the sorts of processes that a teacher would go through with a class. So, rather than going straight in and trying to read it and understand it immediately, they will use whatever is available in the text, ... the pictures, title, subheadings, and so on. They may, without externalizing it, set up questions for themselves about the text, will draw on their own knowledge of the world and knowledge of the topic and, in that way, use all of that contextual information to help them to understand the text.

And the final characteristic, which is very important to me, is self-assessment, in other words, monitoring their own learning. I guess that all learners involve themselves in self-assessment to some degree, but I think effective autonomous learners are consciously involved with it and recognize its importance.

HEDGE: *Do you mean all learners are aware to the extent that they know whether or not they have understood a class, but an autonomous learner might make a more detailed analysis of successes and failures?*

DICKINSON: Yes, the realization might well be: 'My goodness, I didn't understand any of that. What went wrong?'

## Autonomy and age

HEDGE: *You've given a set of five characteristics. Do you see them as applying to some types of learner or some ages of learner, or is it possible to find autonomous learners at all levels and ages of learning?*

DICKINSON: Well, I think it applies across the range. It always seems to me that in relation to learning within formal educational institutions, the notion of autonomy is more easily attached to adults. Taking a much broader context, the notion of autonomy applies across the age range. The most autonomous learners that I'm aware of are small children, who are obviously learning about themselves and about the world. But I realize that this risks being a flip response. However, there is work going on in education which indicates that young children with learning difficulties can be trained to become better learners. And there is interesting work being undertaken by Dam in Denmark, where she is training secondary school children to become more autonomous. Of course, the approaches that one will take towards different ages as a teacher will be different.

## Learner training

HEDGE: *In fact, you've started giving examples of what is now commonly called learner training. Would you like to give a definition of learner training that would be helpful to English language teachers?*

DICKINSON: I think of learner training as learning how to learn. When I want a fuller definition, I use the Ellis and Sinclair statement. They make the point that it relates to the concept of learner autonomy, in that it aims to provide learners with the ability to take on more responsibility for their own learning. They make the useful point that 'ability' involves both strategies and confidence.

HEDGE: *Can you recount interesting experiences of working with learner training in your own teaching career?*

DICKINSON: My own interest has grown out of working with adult learners. In fact my interest and my articulation of it began way back in the mid-1970s when I was trying to negotiate useful approaches with adult learners who had various needs for learning. I was beginning to think about learning how to learn then. In fact I wrote a paper for a conference to which Philip Riley, who was in the audience, responded very positively. I made contact with the CRAPEL group at Nancy and my work really developed from that. Here, in Moray House, I have been concerned over the years with encouraging learners to work out their objectives, to think through a range of metacognitive strategies, to plan their learning, to give a time scale to it, to select materials to meet their objectives, and to undertake self-assessment.

HEDGE: *From what you are saying, it seems that you were already negotiating with learners and setting up learning contracts in the mid-1970s, a time when SLA studies were in their early days and the process syllabus was an unknown term.*

DICKINSON: It developed as what seemed to be a natural, common-sense approach to a group of relatively sophisticated adults who had different needs. When I came to formalize it, one strong influence was Knowles. He wasn't actually concerned with language learning but with general education. There was a movement in the States in the 1970s in this area of self-directed learning, and that was one source from which I gained a lot of ideas.

## Sources of influence

HEDGE: *Thinking about sources of insights and influences, there's obviously a good deal of deliberation in educational philosophy about the concept of autonomy, but there are also the insights from SLA studies into strategies. Have both of these sources played a part in your own thinking or has one been more influential than the other? Or have there been yet other sources of ideas?*

DICKINSON: Both have played a part, very much so, in a kind of progression over the years. The work on learner strategies was a much more recent source of ideas. Originally, the major source, as I said earlier, was the people working in CRAPEL at the University of Nancy, in France. Also Carl Rogers ... I was impressed by his ideas on adult learning. Another influence was Pirsig in a relatively short but significant passage in his book *Zen and the Art of Motorcycle Maintenance*. Another was Alan Tough in Canada, who did a book on adult learning projects. He looked at learning as part of living rather than as something that goes on only in educational institutions. Later came the work on learning strategies but, again, I was initially more interested in the early educational studies, as well as the later SLA studies.

HEDGE: *The sources and influences you've mentioned are Western, and ideas and practical approaches for learner training have been taken up in the West. I wonder to what extent they are seen as appropriate to other contexts around the world. I know that you travel quite a lot and that you are involved in various projects. What kind of response do you get when you present ideas about autonomous learning, and training for it?*

## Autonomous learning and educational context

DICKINSON: Well, as you were speaking, I was wondering whether it *was* a Western orientation. I came across some interesting work in Thailand. A Master's student there was quite excited about the link she saw between notions of autonomy and various precepts in Buddhism.

However, to answer your question, I'm aware of great interest in various parts of the world. I know that in Malaysia, for example, there has been a four-year-long project to establish self-access centres in all of the teacher training colleges: and there's a considerable level of excitement and interest in trainers and trainees. In Thailand there's a similar level of interest at the university level. One particular institution I've been connected with, King Mongkut Institution of Technology in Thonburi, has not only developed a self-access centre but has a module on the Master's degree in Learner Independence, and a Diploma course for managers of self-access centres. I know, too, that Philip Riley is helping to set up a self-access centre in the Chinese University of Hong Kong.

Self-access, of course, I see as being one means to practise autonomy. One problem with it, though, is that because it is very tangible, something concrete, people tend to focus on self-access rather than what seems to me to be the important underlying concept of autonomy.

HEDGE: *Yes, one often wonders, in fact, whether self-access centres are set up with a proper view to training the learners to use them successfully, and relating what happens in them to what happens in the classroom.*

DICKINSON: That is certainly an issue. The scheme I know in Malaysia is staffed by people who are well aware of the relationship between autonomy and self-access, and between self-access and learner training.

HEDGE: *You haven't mentioned activity at the school level around the world. I suppose innovation is much harder at that level as syllabuses and procedures are often prescribed.*

DICKINSON: Yes, I think that's the trouble. Problems at school level are often not so much the inappropriateness of the models or ideas to the children and their age group. It's because of the administrative rigidity of the system. But there is activity, for example, in Scandinavia, if we come back to the West.

HEDGE: *Obviously your interests have developed over the years. Is there any particular interest you have at the moment, any aspect of autonomous learning you're working on at the moment?*

## Researching learner training

DICKINSON: Two things really. Learner training is one. I'm currently working on an elaboration of my book, *Learner Training for Language Learning*, in order to investigate learner training in action. I have a research project running at the moment. We're trying to develop a procedure to focus learners' attention on metacognitive strategies. I have developed a framework for which we use the acronym GOAL. It's a checklist of things learners are invited to pay attention to in experiencing a lesson. So the first letter stands for Goal, in other words, what am I supposed to be learning from this? 'O' stands for Objective. What is the specific objective of the task I am about to do? 'A' is Act. How I am going to do it? What strategy is the best one? Is the obvious one the one I really want to use? Are there others? And 'L' stands for Look, in other words, looking at or monitoring the strategy in use and self-assessment. How have I done? Did I do okay? Do I need to do it again?

HEDGE: *Is this in various curriculum subjects, or in language learning?*

DICKINSON: We're concerned with language learning. As yet, we're in the initial stages. I've spent a while developing an appropriately simplified model. It's being used in a school in Malaysia at present, and we're trying to get access to schools in Edinburgh, but teachers are extremely busy people.

HEDGE: *Are the teachers your researchers? Are they observing their own classrooms?*

DICKINSON: That's the intention.

HEDGE: *So the research will raise the consciousness of the teachers?*

DICKINSON: That's right. The way I see it is that the teachers will train the learners over a period of time. It involves about ten minutes a lesson with the class. Were I to do it myself, I would have groups of learners telling each other how they tackled a piece of learning and, in that way, sharing strategies. And then they would report back to the others in the class in a plenary session, so that the class would gain an enriched set of strategies.

HEDGE: *And how would you collect the data? Have you designed a methodology for the research?*

DICKINSON: We would like to use learner diaries and teacher diaries. I don't think we can use any direct measures in terms of increase in competence. There are too many factors involved. But we thought that there might be indicators from children's more active involvement in their learning. It might be possible to measure this, for example, by the amount of questioning and by types of positive, helping sorts of question. These are the measures we can use.

HEDGE: *What kind of scale are you thinking of?*

DICKINSON: At the moment I'm hoping to get a couple of classrooms to pilot, and then expand.

HEDGE: *You mentioned two current interests?*

## Collaborative assessment

DICKINSON: Yes, the other is collaborative assessment. If I was asked to give one sentence about autonomy, I think of it as the learner being much more in control of his or her learning. One aspect of this control is the area of assessment. For a long time I have been concerned about how the learner can be involved in assessment, where assessment is for certification. I can see learner involvement very easily in formative assessment, but as soon as you move into formal certification, which is a feature of most educational situations, the learner traditionally has no control or involvement. The relationship between the teacher or tutor and the learner is one where virtually all of the power is with the tutor. Under those circumstances, to try to get learners to take responsibility for their learning is much more difficult, because they are obviously and demonstrably not in control of this important aspect. Someone else is holding all the cards.

I pondered for a long time about how one could share out the power. Here, we have developed and used for several years a scheme of collaborative assessment with teachers attending our Master's course in TESOL. This has been our test bed, as it were. Students are invited to assess themselves, that is, they have the option to assess their own coursework. The course is assessed through assignments. Students submit their self-assessed grade in a sealed envelope with the assignment. The tutor, having given a grade, then checks out the student's self-assessment. If the grades are different, though in fact they're often similar, the tutor invites the student to come along, talk about it, and negotiate an agreed grade according to the negotiating criteria that we use. And if the tutor is persuaded by the student's arguments for a higher grade, that grade goes forward. This gives the student real power.

HEDGE: *What happens if the tutor is not prepared to be persuaded?*

DICKINSON: They argue their respective cases according to the criteria. If they cannot reach agreement a referee marks the work, and the referee's grade is final. The student can choose the referee.

HEDGE: *How long has this procedure been in action? Have you been monitoring it? How would you judge its success?*

DICKINSON: Four to five years. I think it's very successful, but more at the learner training level than as an expression of autonomy. One of the things the students need to learn is the standard of the course, particularly where students arrive from outside the UK from different academic cultures and assessment procedures. This scheme is good for learning about standards and about what the academic culture is all about, in the sense of what is and isn't valued in academic writing.

HEDGE: *Presumably, as well, as your* MA TESOL *is for English language teachers, it goes a long way to encouraging them to reflect on assessment procedures in their own professional contexts?*

DICKINSON: Yes, it also makes them think very carefully about the content of their writing: they have to think through the criteria and reflect on their work in ways they might otherwise not have done. Yes, I think it's successful on many counts.

*Originally published in Volume 47/4, 1993*

# 10

# I come to bury Caesar, not to praise him: teaching resisting reading

## ELLEN SPOLSKY

## *Introduction*

I begin this article with the assumption that many teachers of English studied Shakespeare's *Julius Caesar* as school students. Many probably had to memorize Antony's funeral oration as well, and I further assume that they were less than delighted with the task. They were 'resisting readers'. As adults, however, those same students of Shakespeare might very well justify teaching that text within the English as a Foreign Language curriculum: 'Students of English language should also be familiar with English culture, and that means Shakespeare.' Or: 'Teaching a language means exposing students not just to everyday English, but to the literary language as well.' Some might even say that one of the major reasons for learning English is to have access to its literary culture.

The persistent presence of *Julius Caesar* in the EFL classroom, and my sense that EFL teachers share certain clichés about its value there, prompt some speculation on the relationship between literary texts and their students in the EFL curriculum, and particularly on the teacher's methodological responsibilities in bringing texts and students together. I am going to argue, via the example of some texts taught in the Israeli EFL high school curriculum, that in order to achieve their own assumed goals, teachers should encourage 'resisting reading'. Resisting reading is a kind of reading learned from recent feminist literary criticism, but, as I hope to convince you, it is not limited either to women readers or to texts written by women.

## A sense of the past

The reasons mentioned above for teaching *Julius Caesar*, are, I suggest, versions of the alterity principle in education: i.e. that learning is learning about undiscovered countries, about what one hadn't previously known. Learning is expanding one's sympathy to people and cultures which had previously been beyond one's horizons. If we ask, then, why English school children have to read *Julius Caesar*, we will see that the above answers apply as well in the classroom of native English speakers. It has been assumed that English school children also have to be educated into the local high culture, which means that they need to understand about Romans. The question can be pushed back even further: Why did Shakespeare, in England in the sixteenth century, write a play on the subject of the death of Julius Caesar in Rome in the first century BC?

The first answer to this last question is that the Renaissance was a neo-classical period, and one of the things it means to be a neo-classical period is to value a past culture. Neo-classicists feel that whatever culture they define as classical embodied eternal values which are worth preserving and imitating, even if the culture itself is dead. Educated people in Renaissance England, then, felt that the Greek and Latin classics taught permanently true lessons, for example, in public statecraft. Shakespeare, thus, in taking his text from North's 1579 translation of Plutarch's *Lives*, was bringing to his own society lessons about loyalty, honesty, and good government which he believed had not only been true in the past but were still true. Teachers of *Julius Caesar* in England today presumably share this belief, as do teachers of *Julius Caesar* all over the world.

A necessary condition of neo-classiscism, then, is a state of mind in which people value the remote past over their own experience, or over the experience and teachings of their more immediate predecessors. Thus, Renaissance thinkers ignored the ethical teachings of the Middle Ages, and prized the classical texts. In his book, *The Renaissance Sense of the Past* (1969), Peter Burke argues that one of the defining features of the English Renaissance, distinguishing it from the Middle Ages, was its sense of the alterity of the past. The past was different from the present, and from the recent past, and things have changed for the worse. Accompanying that sense of distance and of difference is a belief that aspects of that valued past, being eternally true, can be understood, recovered, relearned, and reintegrated into contemporary life for the benefit of the present.

The common thread, then, running from North's translation of Plutarch's *Lives*, to Shakespeare's writing of *Julius Caesar*, to teachers teaching *Julius Caesar* in English classes in England, and Israeli children memorizing Anthony's funeral oration, is the value placed on the recognition and understanding of alterity. Many EFL teachers have taken up this neo-classicist position, and assumed that what must be taught and what must be learned is, as Hamlet says condescendingly to Horatio: 'There are more things in heaven and earth, Horatio, than are dreamt of in your philosophy' (I.v.167–8).

## *A sense of the larger world*

It is hard to argue against such an ideal; surely all children, in order to be properly educated, must be given a sense of a larger world, a world with different values than the ones they learn in their own environment. They will be educated people only when they know how to get beyond themselves, to understand and deal with difference. Today in Israel we certainly want to teach our children to understand alterity; if not the Greek and Roman classics, then at least, the European Renaissance. We would like to teach them to understand and appreciate the Jews who live in another neighbourhood, and the other Arab cultures of the Middle East.

But we don't, any more, teach *Julius Caesar*. We teach Bernard Malamud's story, 'A Summer's Reading' and James Joyce's 'Eveline'. When I was in a position to influence the English curriculum a few years ago, I didn't suggest returning to Shakespeare. Instead, I suggested adding Tillie Olsen's story, 'I Stand Here Ironing'. This does not mean that I don't agree that understanding alterity is an important goal of education; today, however, we are more sceptical about how or even whether the gap between what is already familiar and what is distant, rich, and strange, can be bridged. How can people who differ learn to understand each other?

Theoretically, we are caught. We find the neo-classical epistemology naive in its assumption that we can have access to past cultures unmediated by our own frames of reference. We are thus sceptical about how much we can know about other cultures. We are not prepared, however, to abandon the goal of teaching alterity. We have a different idea of how to reach it. We assume that learning must take place not by confrontation with the unfamiliar, but by a motion from the familiar to the unfamiliar. Literary texts can contribute to this process. Not incidentally, this transfer has been described as a function of metaphor: 'metaphor enables one to transfer learning and understanding from what is well-known to what is less well-known in a vivid and memo-rable way, thus enhancing learning' (Petrie 1979: 439; see also Kuhn 1970 and Pavio 1971).

I am a literary theorist, however, not a cognitive psychologist, and what I know about the latest learning theory, I know second-hand. I will, then, tell you about something I know first-hand, that is, my own reading of texts, and, from what I have read about the experience of many others now reading and writing, I will try to explain the argu-ments for this alternative epistemology (alternative to the neo-classical, that is), for an epistemology of moving from the familiar to the less familiar, based on the experience of women readers, specifically of feminist readers.

## A feminist perspective

The most notable similarity between feminist critics of many different stripes is their appeal to their own experience of being taught to read texts from a point of view that was alien to them. In recent years, women readers have recounted stories of their literary educations which have marked parallels to the tales of students who have had to memorize passages from Shakespeare. They report having felt forced into an exer-cise which had little relevance to their own lives. Judith Fetterley in *The Resisting Reader* (1978) says that 'as readers and teachers and scholars, women are taught to think as men, to identify with a male point of view, and to accept as normal and legitimate a male system of values, one of those central principles is misogyny' (p.xx).

Fetterley provides a feminist reading of Hemingway's *A Farewell to Arms* as an example of how the male author requires a female reader to identify with his suspicion of women. The story tells of Frederic Henry, an American volunteer in the Italian army during the First World War who is wounded, then falls in love with his nurse, Catherine Barkley, and deserts with her to the safety of Switzerland. The two live an idyllic life until Catherine dies moments after their stillborn child. As she dies, she apologizes to the doctor and to Frederic Henry for giving so much trouble.

The usual interpretations of the book read it as a tragedy. The world fails the good and pure Frederic Henry—all his ideals about heroic war and pure love are shown to be misconceived. But Catherine dies—has to die, as Fetterley reads it—to allow Frederic to keep his high tragic view of himself. Fetterley herself, however, resists the tragic reading. Frederic Henry is, she reminds us, a deserter. His 'need to avoid responsibility is central to his character' (not very romantic, is it?). 'He is able to relate to [Catherine] precisely because and so long as their relationship has neither past nor future. He is spared complications by Catherine's death in childbirth ... Through Catherine's death Frederic Henry avoids having to face the responsibilities incumbent on a husband and father. Her death abets his desire to remain uncommitted and gives him a justification for it' (p. 60). Women mean death for Hemingway, in this as in other of his works. The hero of *For Whom the Bell Tolls* also dies to protect the woman he loves. Is this romantic, or is this simply blaming women for death? A female reader, Fetterley concludes, is led to identify against herself, unless she becomes a resisting reader—unless she is a suspicious reader, a reader who tests the text's moral system against her own experience before she accepts it.

Sandra M. Gilbert, another important feminist critic, has recounted in several articles (1979, 1984) how women students are educated to adopt a man's point of view in reading. By the time a woman finishes her undergraduate education in English, Gilbert says, she has:

> as Oedipus Rex ... interrogated and yet acquiesced in the fatality that causes a man to kill his father and marry his mother; as Pip, she had learned never to trust a fatal *femme* like Estella Havisham but rather to lower her expectations and make her own way in the world; as Huck Finn, she had lit out for the territories, escaping both the false gentility and the constricting domesticity of a slave-owning society ruled by fussy ladies like Aunt Polly; as J. Alfred Prufrock, she had worried about 'the overwhelming question' toward which flighty women who 'come and go/talking of Michelangelo' might paradoxically lead her; as Nick Carraway, she had admired the Faustian intensity of Jay Gatsby and deplored the selfish aplomb of Daisy Buchanan. (1984: 6)

The educated woman student of literature was, in the opinion of most feminist critics, schizophrenic. She learned to hate herself in order to read in a way that was acceptable to her teachers and to the literary establishment. The conclusion drawn from the experience of many women, then, is that the reading of literature is not free of gender bias. What has often passed for a 'neutral' or 'objective' reading has in fact been a male reading—worse, a male reading claiming to be a universal reading. But no reading can be universal. Everyone reads and interprets against the background of his or her own cultural and individual experience.

## Are there any 'universal truths'?

Hence the conflict with the neo-classic point of view. A classical epistemology assumes the existence of universal truths. The trouble, as femi-
nists have identified it, is that it seems always to be those in power,
usually men, who define what those universal truths are. It seems to
be a prerogative of power to declare one's own world view to be the
'natural' one, the right one. Thus the dominant patriarchy establishes
a set of gender alignments according to which men are assumed to be
'naturally' rational, serious, reflective, detached from social values, and
women are 'naturally' emotional, frivolous, spontaneous, and committed to the maintenance of social norms.

Feminist criticism, on the other hand, recognizes the inherent rela-
tivism of all reading and interpretation. This leads to a principle which
has been called 'the authority of experience'. Nina Auerbach expresses
it this way: 'Lives are our medium of exchange. Books are inseparable
from the private experiences that authorize them, while these experiences take on the semi-public and shared quality of our books. Finally,
this conjunction is the only gospel we trust' (1985: 231). Auerbach says,
further, that her 'own work [as a feminist critic] and the work of the
women I admire give their allegiance to the messiness of experience ... I
and my community are impurely human, and ... our diverse ideologies
have been soaked from the beginning in the impurities of experience'
(ibid.: 229).

A necessary condition of feminist criticism, then, is agreement that
education which forces the identification of the learner with alterity,
with the other, is not impossible (after all, so many of us did it), but it is
pathological. One is forced to devalue one's own self and culture in
order to achieve the desired identification. The feminist position thus
embodies the epistemology to which many in fact adhere today—and it
is this epistemology which kept me from recommending that *Julius
Caesar* be reintroduced into Israeli high schools as a required text.

Because we agree that lives and books must match, Israeli English
teachers have tried to choose texts for our students to read that will
allow them to see the identity of life experience and literature. Thus,
Israeli Jewish adolescents whose entire national history was turned to
catastrophe by the Roman conquest of their country, the destruction of
their temple, and the exile of their ancestors, are not asked to praise the
noblest Roman of them all (implication: they are all pretty noble). Their
current reading list asks of them only that they sympathize with adolescents who are, generally speaking, in conflict with their immediate envi-

ronments in the usual adolescent way. Is this healthier? Perhaps, but what about the value of understanding difference? How will we teach that?

## Getting angry with James Joyce

Let us take the teaching of James Joyce's 'Eveline' (from *Dubliners*) as a particularly interesting case. Joyce's heroine, virtually beaten into submission as housekeeper to her father, is given two alternatives within her culture. The first is to marry and be respected, although the example of her mother makes her suspect that there may be a darker side to marriage. The second is to remain a virtual slave to her father. Her third alternative, going away with Frank (we remember to point out that his name suggests freedom) who is 'manly and openhearted' and who will take her to Buenos Aires, a place of 'good air', is never really an alternative, and her failure to go in the end, as most Israeli teachers teach it, is predicted by the story until that point. Frank in the last sentence of the story is 'beyond the barrier', but she, Joyce tells us, is 'passive, like a helpless animal. Her eyes gave him no sign of love or farewell or recognition'.

Israeli students, no docile lot, find it hard to accept Eveline's passivity. They identify with her up to a point, but then become angry with her for not taking her chance to escape. Israeli teachers, hoping to teach them understanding of other cultures, argue that she was passive because her culture and education made her that way, and that Joyce means us to disapprove of the culture, but not to disapprove of the young woman who has no choice. These teachers, mostly women, collude, I would say, with Joyce in making their students, especially the women, agree that women have no choice but to accept what their culture demands of them. But why aren't they angry with Joyce? Why do they agree to let him, and the students, blame the culture, but yet insist on its inevitability? As the story ends, Eveline must give up her freedom, her Frank. Why? To prove Joyce's contention that women are passive and that they cannot escape the role which society assigns them. Frank, of course, a product of the same society, did manage to escape. Shouldn't teachers be teaching their students to resist Joyce's view of the relationship between women and cultural expectations?

A good way to teach resisting reading is to find a story in which environmental or cultural pressures are successfully resisted, such as Tillie Olsen's 'I Stand Here Ironing'. That is a story which, in the end, demonstrates a human being's independence of circumstances. In the end, the child who has indeed had some difficult times is not 'ironed' as a dress is ironed—is not flattened by life.

The narrative describes a mother's reminiscences of her 19-year-old daughter's life, prompted by a teacher's request that she should 'come in and talk about your daughter'. The mother does not share the teacher's faith that she can produce an explanation, an understanding of another person, even if that person is her daughter. She protests to herself: 'You think because I am her mother I have a key …? She had lived for nineteen years. There is all that life that has happened outside of me, beyond me.' But after the memories, the narrator-mother says: 'I will never total it all … Let her be.' And almost prays: 'Only help her to know—help make it so there is cause for her to know—that she is more than this dress on the ironing board, helpless before the iron.'

The proof Olsen offers that Emily is not helplessly subjected to environmental influences is her recently discovered talent for mime. Comedy, Emily's success in a talent show, is the metaphor Olsen sets against the ironing. 'Where does it come from, that comedy?' (p. 12). Emily's gift for comedy is unpredictable from her sad childhood—in direct contrast to the inevitability of Eveline's past and present. The story's immediate interest for adolescents is precisely in this subject of how much one's life is influenced by outside factors, especially by one's parents. This is equally true, of course, for students of both genders.

But I'm not finished with my argument yet. I may have convinced you that students should resist Joyce and might want to identify with the teenage girl in Olsen's story, and that we might want them to, but how does that satisfy the demand raised earlier that we help students learn to understand alterity, the other, that which is different from themselves?

Let's go back to 'Eveline' for a moment. By teaching the resisting reading, by letting the students get angry with Joyce for making Eveline so passive, we would teach not resignation, but the difference between how male and the female authors portray women's choices. Both stories are written by authors with personal familiarity with the culture of poverty, and both fictions reflect this reality. In one case, the author sees submission, in the other, freedom. And the important point would be that our students, both male and female, can understand both authors. They may not be able to identify with Eveline because they so thoroughly reject her choice, and they may have some difficulty identifying with Emily, the child in Olsen's story, because the story is told from the mother's point of view; but they can, if we help them, understand what the two authors are doing. They can be shown how each author makes the outcome seem inevitable, and this is the valuable lesson.

## A sense of ourselves

The lesson is that our students can read texts which they are not sympathetic with, precisely because understanding doesn't entail accepting. They are free to choose to accept or resist the morality of a text, just as they can accept or resist the social reality around them. They can and, we would probably say, must examine alternatives and choose for themselves. One of the ways we understand texts about people who are different from ourselves is precisely by resisting them. This, at any rate, is a first step. As teachers we should encourage, and not discourage, such resistance to texts.

When experience and texts conflict, the authority of experience must be allowed expression. If it isn't, students quite reasonably become angry with a teacher or an author who insists on their sympathy where they cannot give it. To be angry with Joyce over Eveline's fate is a legitimate response. From that response, based on life experience, the next step is recognizing that there are different cultures and that they have different values. But the third step must also be taken: we have to teach our students to understand and tolerate other cultures, without feeling the need to justify or agree with them all. A feminist can continue to read books in which the protagonists are male and can understand them; analogously, an understanding of alterity need not be synonymous with identifying with that culture's values. At some point, Israeli students have to learn that the western world and the Jewish world have different assessments of how noble the Romans were. They could learn this from a resisting reading of *Julius Caesar*. Maybe it should, after all, go back into the curriculum.

*Originally published in Volume 43/3, 1989*

# PART TWO

# PEDAGOGY

*Issues in the professional
development of teachers*

# PREVIEW

Pedagogy has been defined as 'the study of methods and styles of teaching' and 'the principles, practice or profession of teaching'. This section includes articles which have been concerned with how the study of those methods and styles, principles, and practices are instituted in the training of teachers, that is, how teaching is learned. Much discussion of the last decade has focused on how teachers can build an understanding of pedagogic principles and how they respond to them in terms of personal style and professional setting. Those responsible for training teachers have had a particular interest in how teachers make such principles their own and translate them effectively into classroom practice. The articles in this section relate to the three interlocking phases of a teacher's career, pre-service training, in-service training, and continuing professional development within institutional life. They are to do with the promotion of principles and development of procedures for these phases of teacher development.

## Developing the reflective practitioner

A substantial number of writers have contributed to clarifying the distinction between 'teacher training', a term which implies training in the skills and techniques of teaching, and 'teacher education', which implies a lifelong process of professional development. Current definitions of the latter would highlight the process whereby teachers refine and develop knowledge of their subject, enhance their skills in teaching it, and evolve a positive teaching style which is able to adapt as they judge changing circumstances and situations throughout their teaching career. The significance of 'process' as a concept in teacher education is that it holds the implication of development, that is, of the personal evolution of the teacher. Lange (1990: 250) has usefully described such development in this way:

> a process of continual intellectual, experiential and attitudinal growth, some of which is generated in preprofessional and professional in-service programs.

It is probably true to say that this concept of 'development' or 'process' has become the ideologically acceptable base of teachers' courses in the 1990s, at least in in-service education and at least with regard to Western contexts.

## Principles for in-service teacher education

Much recent discussion has centred on how to facilitate teacher development, particularly on in-service courses, and what principles might inform the design and methodology of such courses. One frequently quoted principle, for example, is to begin an in-service session at a point of access which is meaningful for teachers in terms of their previous experience, ask them to think about the way in which they approach some aspect of teaching, for instance, the development of reading ability in a second language and then build on their existing perceptions of what is valid and useful. Underlying this principle is the assumption that all teachers operate according to a set of beliefs about what constitutes good classroom practice, but some may never have made those beliefs explicit to themselves. Thus an essential part of in-service education is to encourage teachers to reflect on their own professional practice, to make explicit to themselves the assumptions that underlie what they do and then to review those assumptions in the light of new perspectives and practices. This key principle in contemporary approaches to teacher education builds on Schön's (1987) idea of the 'reflective practitioner'. It is taken up in the first three articles in this section.

NUNAN (Volume 43/2, 1991) presents principles for teacher development courses. He describes how the process of reflection was initiated in a teachers' workshop by asking the participants, several weeks in advance, to provide a description of a classroom task with which they had experienced success. In the workshop they discussed possible criteria for judging a good language learning task and applied these to their previously selected material. This procedure demonstrates several contemporary principles in action. The content of the workshop discussion developed in part from the teachers' own experience and enabled them to reflect on and review that experience. The 'theory' of the workshop, that is, the building of a critical framework for evaluating learning tasks, derived from the teachers' own professional practice as much as from the tutor's expert knowledge. The approach engaged teachers in a discussion of their work and could therefore be described as 'bottom-up' compared with the more traditional top-down lecture presentation by a specialist. Nunan presents an essentially process-oriented course in which the desired outcome is the reflective practitioner, a teacher able to review practice, explore alternatives, and come to an understanding of how personal improvement and development can be achieved.

## Issues in teacher education for innovation

It has been suggested that the process approach assumes even greater importance when the purpose of teacher education is to support curriculum innovation. The experienced teacher has built a teaching style, has developed a range of techniques based on personal beliefs about good teaching, and has made a personal investment in professional work. Taking on new approaches, acquiring new skills, and modifying routines may well be resisted if there is a feeling that previous, often long-standing approaches, skills and routines are somehow being judged as inadequate or inappropriate. This sense of devaluation, if unattended by those responsible for teachers' programmes, can seriously affect the potential for positive outcomes from in-service courses.

The article by LAMB (Volume 49/1, 1995) describes the sobering experience of meeting former trainees one year on and takes up a discussion on how to secure uptake of new ideas among in-service participants. In his view, take-up will depend on the extent to which teachers can accommodate new ideas within their own 'belief structures'. His article is a measure of how English language teacher education mirrors the movements in general teacher education towards reflective practice. It derives from a 'practical science' perspective on teacher development, one in which the practitioner

> reflects about the taken-for-granted beliefs and assumptions which underpin his/her practical interpretations of professional values ... (S)he begins to reconstruct his/her constructs of value and discovers that this opens up new understandings of the situation and new possibilities for intelligent action within it. (Elliot 1993: 69)

## The use of diaries on in-service courses

A primary concern in in-service teacher education has been to find procedures which will facilitate reflective practice. The article by JARVIS (Volume 46/2, 1992) exemplifies a popular procedure of recent years. She asked a group of teachers to keep diaries for each week of their course and encouraged them to record their learning as teachers. She describes how the diary writing was set up, her own role in the process, and some of the problems teachers experienced in being reflective. Her conclusions, that the teachers developed 'a heightened sense of their own responsibility ... for changing their teaching' and 'more confidence in their own ability to act' suggest that this procedure, if culturally appropriate, might be of the kind to help solve the problems described by Lamb.

Other contributors to *ELT Journal* have discussed similar procedures for encouraging reflection. Thornbury (Volume 45/2, 1991) describes the piloting of 'logs' to record self-assessment of teaching practice lessons. They proved to be a valuable consciousness-raising tool among the participants, developing perceptions of teachers' roles and tasks and learners' needs and, in this way, were instrumental in the 'development of personal theories of learning and teaching'. Ho (Volume 49/1, 1995) describes how trainees were encouraged to use their lesson plans, when the same lesson was taught to several classes in sequence, for progressively refining reflection on personal teaching performance. Such articles have added further procedures to the repertoire of those designed to facilitate reflective practice.

## *The needs of pre-service trainees*

As the field of teacher education has developed a new conceptual base for the design of in-service courses, one which places importance on critical self-awareness and self-evaluation, the question naturally arises as to whether current perspectives and practices in pre-service teacher training have gone through the same review and restructuring. Does 'process' have an equally significant role with initial trainees? There is a view that initial training should begin the process of helping teachers to work towards being reflective practitioners, the process Rosen (1983) once described as moving from 'tentative formulation, to formulation to reformulation'.

Thus, at the same time as they learn a variety of teaching techniques, they build understanding of the principles underlying those techniques and develop critical frameworks for evaluating them and their relevance and usefulness for different teaching situations.

BRITTEN (Volume 42/1, 1988) highlights the importance of attitude development when non-native teachers are trained, as they may bring strong perceptions of language teaching, based on the traditional methods they have experienced as learners. He suggests careful progression during training, for example, a gradual taking on of self-direction in lesson planning during teaching practice and in self-assessment. In this way, it is possible to guard against teachers reverting to the traditional teaching styles of the past when they enter their own classrooms in the first year of teaching. KENNEDY (Volume 47/2, 1993), however, sounds a note of caution about moves towards more autonomous approaches in pre-service teacher education. Her feedback exercise with trainees provides evidence to suggest that more guided approaches are appreciated by young trainees. She looks at the problems reported by trainees and concludes that, particularly with regard to teaching practice, there is a place for authority, for supervisors to articulate their own theories and to become partners-in-experience by teaching some sessions and reflecting on them with trainees. One major implication of Kennedy's study is the need for further studies of the kind to test out the effectiveness of different approaches. Although it may be true that English language teacher education has developed a clear set of principles in recent years to guide the design and methodology of courses, there is a lack of empirical work and a research agenda is needed.

## Training the trainers

Two articles in this selection deal with the training of trainers. It is often commented that trainers rarely receive training for their task of educating teachers but seem rather to be appointed on the basis of strong teacherly qualities, a reputation for effective classroom practice or simply seniority. Recent years have seen a growing literature on supervisory practice to which the article by SHEAL (Volume 43/2, 1989) and the Talking Shop interview with BODÓCZKY and MALDEREZ (Volume 48/1, 1994) contribute.

Sheal's article reflects current discussion on how to make supervision more trainee-centred, more constructive, and more supportive. He deals with the training of classroom observation as a key supervisory skill. His argument draws a parallel between the issues of classroom observation and those of performance review in the world of business where traditional, subjective methods of performance review fail to improve employee performance. He suggests strategies for setting goals, using carefully structured observation schedules, and for handling post-observation meetings. He gives an account of a workshop series intended to persuade supervisors of the need for observation procedures and comments on the possible reasons for resisting change to traditional, subjective, unsystematic, supervisor-dominated and judgemental approaches.

Other contributors have taken up discussion of principles for observation. For example, Williams (Volume 43/2, 1989), in describing a scheme of developmental classroom visits for primary teachers in Singapore, explores classroom observation as a 'mutual problem-solving experience' in which observation schedules took the form of questions to guide teachers' self-evaluation, trainers taking a supportive role as the teachers developed judgements about what was happening in their own classrooms.

Swan's article (Volume 47/3, 1993) takes the developmental aspect further in describing an experiment in which student teachers were given the opportunity to devise their own observation schedules, piloting and refining them with peers and supervisors through observation of video lessons. She argues that this procedure gave teachers the opportunity to develop critical awareness of what might constitute good teaching and had substantial advantages over the use of schedules prescribed by experts. The trainer, in this collaborative style of supervision, takes on the role of facilitator.

Wallace and Woolger (Volume 45/4, 1991) describe their attempt to improve the dialogue between supervisors and trainees. Their examples are drawn from a programme carried out in Sri Lanka. Their aim was to work from the teachers' inside experience of lessons, and to fulfil this aim they propose a four-stage post-lesson observation based on key questions: what happened? what were the objectives? what else could have been done? and what have you learned?

These articles attest to the hard work and sophistication that classroom observation, when properly conducted, entails. There is, however, a tension implicit in their discussions, and that is the tension between the use of observation schedules for teacher self-assessment and their use for external appraisal. It is a conflict between evaluation for development and evaluation for accountability and the issue is whether a supervisor can take on both roles simultaneously and successfully. Perhaps the next decade will bring studies of trainers' and trainees' perceptions of this problem and how it might be resolved.

Other contributors on the theme of training the trainers have been more generally concerned with appropriate structures to ensure that teaching practice is a productive experience and that novice teachers are properly supported. Representative of this concern is the Talking Shop interview with Bodóczky and Malderez. They discuss the design of a training course for selected school teachers who will become supervisors of trainees and novice teachers, and who will make classroom visits to support and counsel them. They describe a negotiated course content with a workshop base which enables teachers in Hungary with an authoritarian model behind them, to move towards a perception of the supervisor as guide and counsellor.

The same structure is described in a later article by Moon (Volume 48/4, 1994), who discusses a mentorship scheme in Bhutan, but her focus is on the benefit of the experience to the associate teachers in schools who were acting as mentors to the trainees on teaching practice. Her case study demonstrates the potential of mentorship for professional dialogue and development and the value of this in contexts where few resources exist for in-service provision.

Teaching practice is a time of intense reflection, and often of rapid and radical change in attitudes among trainees. They need to develop perceptions of the classroom and their own roles in it so that they can work successfully with learners. They also need to appreciate institutional ethos and find ways of working productively within it and with colleagues. The development of mentorship schemes pays testament to the current concern in teacher education to support novice teachers' transfer of skills from the training classroom to the real classroom and their development of self-reliance.

## Continuing professional development

In an ideal world, teachers would be working within institutions with coherent policies and programmes for professional development, to help them maintain and increase their effectiveness as teachers. At the moment, however, principles expounded in the literature on staff development, which aims to help teachers to 'measure their achievement' and 'open up opportunities for personal growth' (Everard and Morris 1985), are worthy in their intent but seldom explicitly formulated within institutions. The strategies suggested in the literature, such as the staff appraisal interview, counselling, or action planning within teams are relatively new or, indeed, rarely found across ELT contexts because funding, understanding, or will is lacking.

For many teachers, then, professional development is a matter of self-initiated growth. It is a do-it-yourself activity. Maintaining morale, sustaining vigour, increasing personal effectiveness and enhancing job satisfaction, are self-innovated and self-directed activities. The establishment of teacher development groups has been a feature of the ELT profession in recent years, one which has begun to generate a body of literature. The last article in this section is indicative of this. NAIDU *et al.* (Volume 46/3, 1992) give an account of a collaborative research project among members of a teacher development group. They record the way in which a group of teachers shared their experiences of teaching large classes, identified issues for exploration, observed each other's classes, evaluated their roles as teachers, and came to a better understanding of one aspect of their teaching lives. They reach a number of conclusions about the values of structured discussion among a small network of teachers. Not least among these is the benefit of reflective discussion as a means to 'recover our experience and frame it in ways that enhance our understanding and improve our practice'.

Their conclusions are reminiscent of a point made by Underhill (1987: 1) in one of the early issues of the Newsletter of the IATEFL Teacher Development Special Interest Group, an international group established during these years of burgeoning interest in the continuing professional development of teachers. He wrote:

> To what extent can we attend to the successful learning of our students if we are not successfully learning and changing ourselves?

It is a point reiterated in his own contribution to *ELT Journal* (Volume 46/1, 1992) on the facilitative role of groups in the development of a teacher's critical self-awareness.

All of the above themes can be seen to pivot on the central concept of the teacher as a personally and professionally aware, self-critical thinker, positively inclined to reflective practice and self-improvement. The following set of articles reflect the ways in which a coherence of thought and procedure has been developing with regard to reflective practice in the field of English language teacher education and continuing professional development. The articles are representative of the many different linguistic, sociopolitical and educational settings in which teacher education takes place. It is therefore perhaps not surprising that many of the articles also deal implicitly with the issue of empowering teachers in their professional work, the theme which connects the three parts of this book.

# 11

# A client-centred approach to teacher development

DAVID NUNAN

## Introduction

There are theoretical and practical reasons why the adoption of a client-centred approach should be considered in TESOL teacher-development programmes. In this article, a rationale for adopting such an approach is presented. Ways of making teacher-development workshops more client-centred are then presented and discussed.

## Trends in language-curriculum development

In language teaching, as in general education, there has been a gradual move away from a top-down approach to the planning, implementation, and evaluation of teaching programmes. The top-down approach is characterized by curriculum plans, syllabus outlines, and methodological procedures which are designed by 'experts' and delivered as a package to the teacher. In-service and professional development programmes are principally designed to train teachers how to use these externally developed syllabuses, materials, and methods. Top-down methods are fairly easily recognized. Despite their diversity, they have one thing in common: they assume that there is one best way of learning a second or foreign language, and they all provide a set of principles and procedures, which must be more or less faithfully followed by the classroom practitioner.

An alternative to top-down 'package-deal' teaching methods is to develop the content and methodology of language programmes through a process of consultation and negotiation with learners. Such learner-centred programmes attempt to incorporate into the classroom information by and from the learners themselves (Nunan 1988).

In a related development, the curriculum is being rediscovered, not as a set of prescriptive edicts, but as the documentation and systematization of classroom practice. Curriculum designers are becoming concerned with identifying principles of effective teaching from within the classroom itself. This is reflected in the current interest in classroom-oriented research. (See, for example, Chaudron 1988; van Lier 1987.)

## Principles for teacher development

If the ideas outlined in the preceding section are relevant for learners, they should also be relevant for teachers when they, in their turn, become learners. In order to test this notion, the National Curriculum Resource Centre in Adelaide, South Australia, which runs professional development programmes for teachers of ESL to adults, has attempted to build a number of 'client-centred' principles into its in-service workshops. These principles may be summarized as follows:

1 The content and methodology of workshops should be perceived as being personally relevant to participants. Following the principle that adults value their own experience as a resource for further learning and that they learn best when they have a personal investment in the programme, workshop content should, as far as possible, be derived from the participants themselves.

2 Theory should be derived from practice. In other words, teachers should be encouraged to derive theoretical principles from a study of classroom practices, rather than being exposed to a set of principles and being required to 'apply' these. (This issue is dealt with in some detail in Ramani 1987.) These practices need not (indeed, should not) be exemplary. Rather they should represent a range, including good, mediocre, and bad teaching. One can, in fact, learn as much from instances of poor practice as one can from instances of successful practice.

3 The approach should be bottom-up rather than top-down.

4 Teachers should be involved in the structuring of the professional development programme.

5 Teachers should be encouraged to observe, analyse, and evaluate their own teaching.

6 Professional development programmes should provide a model for teachers of the practices they wish to encourage, i.e. they should practise what they preach.

(For extended discussions on the principles of adult learning, see Brundage and MacKeracher 1980; Knowles 1983.)

I should also add that the professional development programmes conducted by the NCRC do not attempt to downplay or discredit theory. On the contrary, they seek to demonstrate the importance of theory by linking it to practice.

## *The principles in action*

With a little forethought, these principles can be realized in most teacher-development workshops. One way of doing this is by including data from and about the workshop participants in the design of the workshop itself. I should like to illustrate this by describing a workshop for teachers on classroom learning tasks. The workshop was run for thirty experienced teachers in the Australian Adult Migrant Education Program, a large English language programme for adult immigrants and refugees to Australia.

The workshop was the first in a series designed to introduce participants to language curriculum design. The concept of 'task' was selected as a point of entry area, as it seemed the most salient one for classroom practitioners and therefore more appropriate for introducing teachers to the field of curriculum design than the more conventional 'needs', 'goals', 'objectives', or 'content' (Shavelson and Stern 1981). The workshop in question was aimed at getting participants to identify those features which they felt typified 'good' learning tasks, to explore principles for grading and sequencing tasks, and to demonstrate how the selection and grading of tasks relate to other curriculum activities.

In order to give the workshop a client-centred bias, participants were asked several weeks in advance to provide a detailed description of a task which worked particularly well for them. Information was collected on the target audience for the task, the materials needed, steps in the task, learner groupings (whether individual, pairs, small groups or teacher-fronted), and rationale. Some of the tasks provided by teachers are set out in the Appendix.

The initial aim in the workshop was to get participants to explore and express their concept of the 'good' language task. To this end, they were asked to rate a series of statements from 0 to 4 according to whether these statements were characteristic of the 'good' task. The statements, which were derived from a variety of sources, are set out below.

## Questionnaire on the 'good' learning task

What do you believe? Circle the appropriate number following each of the criteria below according to the following scale:

0—This is not a characteristic of a good task.
1—This characteristic may be present, but is optional.
2—This characteristic is reasonably important.
3—This characteristic is extremely important.
4—This characteristic is essential.

*Good learning tasks should:*

|    |                                                                                      |         |
|----|--------------------------------------------------------------------------------------|---------|
| 1  | enable learners to manipulate and practice specific features of language              | 0/1/2/3/4 |
| 2  | allow learners to rehearse, in class, communication skills they will need in the real world | 0/1/2/3/4 |
| 3  | activate psychological/psycholinguistic processes of learning                         | 0/1/2/3/4 |
| 4  | be suitable for mixed-ability groups                                                  | 0/1/2/3/4 |
| 5  | involve learners in solving a problem, coming to a conclusion                         | 0/1/2/3/4 |
| 6  | be based on authentic or naturalistic source material                                | 0/1/2/3/4 |
| 7  | involve learners in sharing information                                               | 0/1/2/3/4 |
| 8  | require the use of more than one macro-skill                                          | 0/1/2/3/4 |
| 9  | allow learners to think and talk about language and learning                         | 0/1/2/3/4 |
| 10 | promote skills in learning how to learn                                              | 0/1/2/3/4 |
| 11 | have clear objectives, stating what learners will be able to do as a result of taking part in the task | 0/1/2/3/4 |
| 12 | utilize the community as a resource                                                   | 0/1/2/3/4 |
| 13 | give learners a choice in what they do and the order in which they do it             | 0/1/2/3/4 |
| 14 | involve learners in risk-taking                                                      | 0/1/2/3/4 |
| 15 | require learners to rehearse, rewrite, and polish initial efforts                    | 0/1/2/3/4 |
| 16 | enable learners to share in the planning and development of the task                 | 0/1/2/3/4 |
| 17 | have built into them a means of evaluating the success or otherwise of the task      | 0/1/2/3/4 |

Participants then worked in pairs to select the five characteristics which they considered to be essential to a good task. This step involved considerable negotiation for those participants who disagreed with their partner. When disagreements arose, participants were asked to provide evidence for their views, and to identify whether this evidence was empirical, speculative, or experiential. In several instances this led to a discussion on the nature of evidence and the status of knowledge. A convenient bridge was therefore established between practice and theory. At the conclusion of this step, a straw poll revealed that the most frequently selected criteria were 2, 3, 6, 10, and 11.

Once participants had established their criteria, they were given copies of the tasks they had provided before the workshop. The tasks were presented in a way which made it impossible for their authors to be identified. Participants were asked to rate each task from 0 to 3 according to how well each one encapsulated the criteria of a good task. This step had to be handled with some care. The principal aim of the exercise was not to evaluate the activities, but to encourage participants to validate the criteria they had selected against the sorts of tasks they had nominated as being 'good ones' before the workshop. At the end of the workshop, several participants said they had given low ratings to their own tasks, and that the exercise had prompted them to review their approach to task selection.

The second part of the workshop was devoted to the issue of task difficulty. Sets of criteria were provided to participants, who used these in deciding on the difficulty level of a range of tasks.

## Discussion

While the workshop was generally well received, there were a number of shortcomings. While some teachers quite rightly pointed out that their criteria for task selection would vary according to the target group of learners, all agreed that the workshop had achieved its aim of helping participants clarify and refine their criteria for task selection.

In the formal evaluation of the workshop, participants were asked, among other things, to indicate ways in which their ideas about tasks changed as a result of the workshop. They were also asked to comment on the idea of making the workshop more client-centred by basing it on their own learning tasks.

As the main point of this article is to make a case for such client-centred procedures in teacher-development programmes, it is worth setting out what the clients themselves thought. They were asked to respond to the question: What comments, if any, have you got on the idea of basing part of the workshop on your own ideas?

In analysing the feedback from the participants, I divided comments into those which were basically positive, and those which were negative. Participants giving positive feedback felt that the use of data from participants was good, in that it increased the relevance of the workshop. Most of the negative comments referred to the fact that providing one's own data was threatening, that there were too many tasks to analyse, and that there was a certain lack of balance in the tasks submitted by participants; in particular, that there were few tasks for low-level learners. This may say something about the difficulty of creating interesting tasks for beginners.

The sample comments which follow were typical:

*Positive:*

– 'It made the workshop relevant to what is actually done in the class-room by teachers. It was also interesting that there was compara-tively little for low-level learners.'
– 'It was extremely valuable. In fact, I got some good ideas from them. Being forced to apply the criteria to our own tasks made the work-shop very relevant.'
– 'Good. It enabled me to step back and reflect on my own teaching.'
– 'It was beneficial to look at tasks based on what teachers actually do.'
– 'It was interesting to see other classroom teachers' approaches.'
– 'A good idea, since these are the types of lessons given in our programme.'
– 'Good. It relates the workshop back to the classroom situation.'
– 'Very important as (a) we were working from relevant examples and (b) it was beneficial to teacher development to examine critically our own teaching and justify it.'

*Negative:*

– 'It was OK, although a little bit threatening, maybe.'
– 'Good, if you enjoy risk taking, but I would like to have seen more lessons for lower levels.'
– 'I prefer input. I can apply principles to my own work in my own time, not in valuable session time, such as this.'
– 'It was a good idea which made the workshop activities seem more rel-evant and realistic. However, there were too many tasks. It would have been better to look at about five in greater detail.'
– 'It was slightly invalidated by the lack of time for detailed analysis.'
– 'While I preferred it to using text/coursebook activities, a more engag-ing way of applying selection criteria would be by analysing our own activities in pairs.'
– 'It was good, but there were too many tasks and not enough feed-back.'
– 'Illuminating but slightly threatening.'

Overall, the feedback demonstrated that the majority of participants endorsed the idea of basing the workshop on data from their own teach-ing, although they did not do so uncritically. One particularly interest-ing aspect of the feedback was the number of participants who found the use of their own data threatening or unsettling, despite the steps which were taken to ensure anonymity. The anxiety was a result of the personal investment which participants had made in the workshop. This could, in fact, have been a virtue in that it prompted more awareness and commitment to workshop activities than to other types of in-service activities.

## Follow-up

The next time the workshop was offered, some major modifications were made. These were designed to obviate some of the shortcomings of the original workshop as revealed by the feedback from participants. I also wanted the evaluation of the tasks to be more closely tied to the classroom. As there is substantial evidence (Nunan 1987) to show that there is frequently a disparity between what teachers think they do and what they actually do, a preliminary step was to get teachers to teach their chosen task and record the lesson in which this occurred.

The modified format of the workshop was as follows:

### Preliminary activity

Participants were asked to select a 'good' task, to teach the task, and record that segment of their lesson when the task was taught. A transcription of the lesson segment was to be brought to the workshop.

*Step 1*: Whole group discussion and analysis of the 'good' language task. This step was similar to the one in the original workshop, and utilized the questionnaire set out above.

*Step 2*: Presentation and discussion of techniques for analysing and evaluating classroom interactions. Participants were provided with checklists and observation schedules for analysing learning tasks, classroom management, teacher–learner roles, grouping patterns, etc.

*Step 3*: Participants were divided into small groups, each of which was provided with one of the checklists. They viewed and analysed a video showing a range of tasks being taught.

*Step 4*: Each group then reported back to the group as a whole. This step demonstrated many different perspectives and ways of analysing classroom tasks.

*Step 5*: Participants were then given the choice of working individually or with one or more other participants to review and analyse the tasks which they themselves had taught, recorded, and transcribed.

*Step 6*: Feedback and discussion. Summarization of the 'good' task. Listing of insights derived from analysing tasks 'in action'.

The revised workshop took almost twice as long to present as the original. However, the revisions and the extra time were justified in that they obviated most of the criticisms stemming from the original format. Allowing participants to view and analyse some less-than-perfect tasks taught by others helped them to take a more objective stance towards their own teaching. It also served to reassure those who were disappointed with their own teaching. Providing participants with the opportunity of working alone when analysing their own tasks also removed a great deal of the threat felt by those taking part in the original workshop. It was gratifying, in fact, to find that there were participants who were prepared to work in pairs and small groups. The revised format also enabled participants to look in depth at one or two tasks, rather than trying to analyse many.

## Conclusion

In this article, I have made a case for the adoption of a client-centred approach to teacher-development programmes. One way of doing this is to use input from teachers themselves. The approach is illustrated with workshops which focused on classroom learning tasks. However, it could be used in workshops addressing any other curriculum issue, from needs analysis and objective setting, to the selection of experiential content, selecting and adapting materials, and assessment and evaluation.

*Originally published in Volume 43/2, 1989*

## Appendix

*A sample of the tasks provided by workshop participants*

The appendix has been included to indicate the range of tasks which can be used, to demonstrate the amount of detail required, and to illustrate the fact that the tasks should be representative of teachers' practice rather than outstanding examples of good practice. A collection of exemplary tasks would, in fact, defeat the purpose of the workshop.

SAMPLE TASK 1

1 *Type of student:* Low oral proficiency (3 classes, 4 teachers); mostly middle-aged learners in the case of my class.

2 *Materials:* A map of the city and a task sheet with very specific directions (street names, left, right, opposite).

3 *Grouping:* Small groups.

4 *Steps:*
   a. Teachers prepare a list of shopping and information-gathering tasks.
   b. Prior to sending students out, do lessons on understandingdirections.
   c. Teachers prepare direction sheets and task sheets (make phone calls where necessary to alert the general public) and warn students to wear comfortable clothes and shoes.
   d. Low-level students trace their route on their map before setting out. Students go out in small groups.
   e. Teachers meet students for coffee and debriefing at pre-arranged (large!) coffee shop.

5 *Rationale:* To increase learners' confidence, use the city as a resource for learning, and help learners become more mobile in the city.

### SAMPLE TASK 2

1 *Type of student:* This activity was designed for a multi-level group with basic literacy skills in their own language. Low oral proficiency. The more ethnic homogeneity in the group the better.

2 *Materials:* Articles from ethnic newspapers.

3 *Grouping:* Students are grouped according to ethnic background and proficiency level.

4 *Steps:*
   a. Buy or ask students to bring newspapers in their home language.
   b. Choose (an) article(s) that you would like to have translated.
   c. Divide students into pairs/small groups according to ethnic background/ level.
   d. Ask students to use any means they can to try and communicate to you what the message is about (e.g. speaking into cassette, sketch, mime, writing vocabulary items on paper).
   e. Bring groups back together. They as 'knowers' try to communicate to you what the article is about.
   f. Put what seems to be a skeleton of the text on the board and get the students to refine it.
   g. Either rub off translation and get students to tell you in English what the article was about, or pair students who worked on different articles and get them to tell each other what the article was about.

5 *Rationale:* Motivates students to express themselves in English; increases the status of L1; gives students confidence; empowers all learners, not just the stronger ones.

### SAMPLE TASK 3

1 *Type of student:* Upper-intermediate students who want access to tertiary education; literate in L1 and able to write in English with moderate ease.

2  *Materials:* Few: model essays probably written by teacher, and model diary
   entries.

3  *Grouping:* Essays and diaries are written individually; some writing time is
   allocated in class when students discuss their work in pairs or groups of
   three; correction sessions are sometimes done in small groups.

4  *Steps:* At the beginning of (20 week) term, students are told they must hand
   in two pieces of written work a week, a diary on any subject they like which
   will be read but not corrected by the teacher, and a set question related to the
   theme for the week which will be corrected. Occasionally the teacher writes
   a diary entry or essay which is read by students. As the course progresses,
   students reflect on and write about the English learning in their diary. Essay
   corrections become stricter and students are told to correct their mistakes
   and hand in the corrected version. Correction can sometimes be done in
   groups.

5  *Rationale:* To get students into the habit of writing. The uncorrected diary is
   to get them to express themselves as they choose, to take risks and to say
   something, even though they may be unsure of its correctness. The aim of the
   corrected essay is to get students to reflect on the accuracy of their written
   work.

# 12

## The consequences of INSET

### MARTIN LAMB

## Introduction

Short in-service teacher training (INSET) courses 'summer schools', 'refresher courses', 'professional upgrading programmes'—are familiar phenomena in many countries where English is taught. While they take various forms and are designed to fulfil many different functions, their popularity probably lies in what Widdowson calls the 'social and professional intensity of the event' (Widdowson 1987: 27): the break in routine, the chance to meet new colleagues and to discuss one's professional problems, the exposure to lots of stimulating new ideas, the novelty of being students again.

### The need for 'follow-up' courses

Yet how much good do they do? Brian Tomlinson asked the question of the short in-service courses he ran for Indonesian schoolteachers and concluded that without subsequent follow-up courses, their effect would have been 'disastrous', because the 'motivation and stimulus (the participants had) gained would soon have been negated by the confusion and frustration they would have suffered in trying to apply all that they had learnt ... within the existing parameters of syllabus, examinations, materials, official expectations, and class size' (Tomlinson 1988: 18). Too often, perhaps, the designers and tutors of INSET courses leave the country, or see off the participants, still glowing from the positive evaluations they received in the end-of-course questionnaires, and have little opportunity to discover the longer-term effects of their work.

I had the sobering experience of returning to face former INSET participants exactly one year after I had designed and co-tutored a two-week course in 'Teaching Reading Skills to Undergraduates'. I set out to discover, through interview and observation, how far the participants had taken up and implemented certain practical ideas promoted on the course. While warm greetings were expressed and fond memories averred, it was evident that many participants did feel confused and frustrated. These feelings were partly caused, as Tomlinson suggests, by inability to apply the new ideas 'within the existing parameters of syllabus, examinations', and other practical constraints.

## The individual teacher's theory

But even more significant, it seems to me, were the *mental* parameters within which they conceptualized the teaching and learning process, and which had determined how they had interpreted the ideas during and after the course. In short, what the tutors had said was not necessarily what participants had heard, or remembered later. The importance of teachers' conscious or unconscious beliefs has been recognized by several educationists in recent years. Ramani, for example, distinguished between 'research theory', the body of knowledge produced by academe, and the 'individual teacher's theory', which she described as 'a mix of vaguely perceived ideas and relationships, a primitive conceptual framework' which has a far more 'influential and determining effect on practice' (Ramani 1986: 117).

Analysing the words and actions of the participants, I found it possible to categorize the various reactions they had to the course and to particular ideas presented there. This analysis showed that the interaction of 'research theory'—the ideas presented on the course—and the personal theories of participants, sometimes had quite unexpected results. These may be of interest to designers of INSET courses in similar circumstances, and indeed to potential participants who, faced with the usual heady brew of new ideas, wish to avoid a subsequent hangover.

## *The INSET course*

The course took place in the Staff Language Centre of an Indonesian university.[1] It was designed and run by myself and two Indonesian colleagues in response to requests for help from several lecturers who

taught English to undergraduate students in various faculties. These lecturers were mostly untrained as language teachers, and had to work
with few materials in large classes of between 50 and 100 students,
whose level of proficiency on entry was very low. The course consisted
of twenty-five hours' tuition spread over ten morning sessions, and of
the 16 participants who attended, six taught at the university and the
rest at other tertiary institutions in the city.

On the basis of some class observations and our own background
knowledge, we decided to set four basic pedagogic objectives:

- to persuade the teachers to adopt a 'reading skills' approach, (as for
  example recommended in Nuttall 1982) instead of the prevailing
  general English grammar and vocabulary course.
- to encourage teachers to use ESP textbooks, or even authentic
  subject-area texts that their students might have to read, instead of
  rather old-fashioned general English textbooks.
- to use group work to alleviate some of the problems of large classes,
  by enabling small groups of students to share and discuss texts, and
  work on learning tasks together.
- to use communicative oral activities as a way of adding variety to
  lessons and motivating students, since we saw that lessons were bor-
  ing for students and teachers alike.

The approach adopted to encourage the teachers to change their practice
was essentially rational-empirical (Kennedy 1987). In the belief 'that
people are rational beings and that a change will be adopted once evidence has been produced to show that it will benefit those whom it
affects' (ibid.: 164), we assumed that a clear explanation of the rationale
behind the teaching approach we favoured would convince. Further
explanation would be given about how to implement the approach in the
classroom. We recognized that participants needed to see (in the case of
materials) or even experience (in the case of activities) the practical manifestation of many ideas before they could fully understand, and so accept
them. In the second week teachers produced their own lesson plans or
materials adopting the new principles, and discussed them in detail with
course tutors. We assumed that after the course the teachers would
replace some of their current practices—which had been mentioned only
anecdotally during the course—with those we recommended.

The initial evaluation of the course carried out on the final day was
very positive. All participants said that they had enjoyed the course and
found most of the sessions useful, and the majority said that they would
try to implement some of our suggestions in their classrooms.

## The effects of the course

Evaluating the course a year later, I realized that without any baseline description of teachers' views and behaviour from the time of the course, I would not be able to make unequivocal assertions about the way the participants had changed or not. Instead, I hoped to build up a partial, impressionistic picture of the effects of the course by listening to the participants' own accounts of their last year's work, and tracing the survival and evolution of ideas they might have picked up on the course.

I interviewed 12 of the original 16 participants about how their teaching had progressed since the INSET course, and observed four of them performing in class. The interviews lasted an average of thirty minutes and were, as far as possible, non-directive, in that I let the participants direct the discussion. They talked about the ideas from the course that still held some meaning for them and occasionally I offered prompts concerning some of the major themes of the course (such as 'what about group work?'). Where participants claimed to have adopted ideas from the course in their teaching, I tried to elicit as much practical detail as possible, to guard against the understandable tendency to assure me, their former course tutor, that my work had had considerable impact and benefit. In the case of the four participants I observed teaching, it was possible to check directly whether their words corresponded to their practice.

It was possible to identify seven different ways in which participants had reacted, consciously or unconsciously, to ideas presented on the course.

### No uptake

The brute fact of the matter is that all the participants had forgotten most of the information and ideas that they had previously been exposed to. On average, each participant mentioned only four ideas from the course that had impressed them in some way. Some ideas were not mentioned at all, including particular reading skills we had recommended them to develop in students (increasing reading speed, taking notes, and utilizing non-text information), as well as songs, and information-gap activities. Presumably they were so far removed from the teachers' current preoccupations and practices that they made no impact on their cognitions.

## Confusion

In contrast to those ideas that had been lost altogether, there were also cases where teachers mentioned ideas that had been remembered but never well enough understood to affect their teaching in any way. For example, one teacher remembered the game 'Snakes and Ladders', and was aware that it was intended to 'stimulate the students', but could not understand how to use it (and took the opportunity of my visit to try to clarify the matter[2]). Thus, after one year this teacher still had a lingering sense that 'modern' methods of teaching exist which could be of help to her. This game, however, was so different from her normal classroom routine that she could not conceive of how to put it to good use.

## Labelling

Some teachers had clearly just applied a term they had picked up on the course to an activity they were already doing. For example, one teacher described her standard procedure of teaching reading as follows: '[I] let them read silently, and after finishing [the] reading materials I ask them what does the writer in the first paragraph tell us. It's just what you call skimming … getting the main point of each paragraph.' The two terms picked up on the course ('skimming' and 'getting the main idea') are used synonymously to describe a text-summarizing activity common in Indonesian classrooms.

Another example of 'labelling' will be familiar to many teacher trainers. This teacher claimed to be 'using the communicative approach … to increase the courage of the students to speak, for example, I ask them to read the text, "stand up please" or "just sit in your seat", and so on'. It appears that she considered her long-standing practice of having students read texts aloud to be 'communicative', an interpretation of the term quite different from that put forward on the INSET course.

## Appropriation

Sometimes participants had appropriated an idea from the course in order to justify a change in their teaching which was not anticipated by the tutors—illustrating the essential unpredictability of teacher interpretation of new ideas. At one point during the course, for instance, it was suggested that it was quite valid to use the mother tongue at times, such as when explaining the instructions to a complicated learning task. One teacher explained in her interview that one of the major changes in her teaching since the course was that she 'didn't ask them in English any more but ... in Bahasa Indonesia, and I allow them to answer in Bahasa Indonesia'. She said that when she had used English in the past, those students who did not understand her tended to get out of control; this 'enraged' her, and threatened to disrupt the social harmony of her class, which she saw as extremely important. As a subsequent visit to her class confirmed, this fear of ill-discipline restricted not only her use of English, but *all* oral work in the class, since even in Bahasa Indonesia she tended to answer her own questions quickly to avoid several students calling out the answer at once, or making unruly responses.

Another example involved teaching materials. While five of the teachers took our advice of trying to motivate students by using more subject-specific materials, one teacher claimed to use more *general* English texts now, for exactly the same reason. It seems that the message she picked up was not 'use subject-specific texts' but 'materials are important—changing them can have a positive impact'.

## Assimilation[3]

Particular techniques introduced on the course seemed to have been transferred wholesale into the teachers' pre-existing classroom routine, without them necessarily understanding the rationale for the techniques. They seemed to work well because the techniques did not compromise in practice any of the teachers' (or students') basic beliefs.

This was the case, for instance, with the reading skills that many teachers claimed to be teaching, such as 'guessing the meaning of unknown words', 'interpreting discourse markers', and 'interpreting reference words'. All these skills are easily understood as tests of students' knowledge of grammar and vocabulary, and could equally easily fit into a traditional reading lesson format of text plus long list of comprehension questions and grammar exercises. As one teacher put it, 'When I check them about the grammar I just ask them what does it refer to, like that ... so I apply the [INSET] course ...' Her words suggest that the 'new teaching technique' was a slight elaboration of her existing routine, rather than a change in approach to teaching reading; it was certainly the case that other essential aspects of a 'reading skills approach' we had promoted on the course (such as making students aware that they already apply these skills when reading in Indonesian, and giving students plenty of time to read the text silently on their own) were quite absent from the lesson I observed her teach.

## Adaptation and rejection

Other new ideas that teachers put into practice had not worked so well, and in many cases were rejected by them. This is because, when implemented, they did not satisfy teachers' basic concerns. Often ideas had been implemented in a way designed to satisfy those concerns rather than the ones assumed by the INSET instructors, with the result that new and unexpected problems were created. One teacher, for instance, had been initially enthusiastic about communicative language teaching: 'Once I tried it with the students of the Faculty of Law but they just laugh and laugh you know!' She never 'risked' it again. Evidently the communicative activity, however it was actually implemented, came close to creating discipline problems—a much more serious matter to this teacher than whether the students were enjoying the class, or using their English 'communicatively'.

Pair and group work offered another example of a novel idea which many teachers tried out but adapted so that it served their own concerns. On the INSET course the instructors had seen group work as a possible solution to some of the problems teachers had in large classes—it could provide opportunities for oral practice, for example, increase students' sense of responsibility for their own learning, encourage cooperation and exchange of ideas, and make aspects of classroom management more efficient.

Yet the fact is that the teachers simply did not perceive the same problems in large classes as we instructors had done. For them, large classes were problematic because it was difficult to evaluate students and give them individual attention, and because they couldn't control the class comfortably. Group work didn't help solve these problems, and sometimes actually seems to have exacerbated them. Thus, one teacher complained that when using group work 'it's rather hard to govern them in a satisfactory way'. Another said that 'the lesser students unfortunately feel safe with this group work ... they just give the answer made by their group'. Many teachers complained that group work took up too much time because of all the 'checking' they had to do: 'I have fifty students or sixty, and if I group them into fifteen and each group consists of five students then I have to check from one group to another, one group to another, and I have only 100 minutes. So 100 minutes divided by fifteen, how many minutes [does] each group have my attention?'

The way many teachers implemented group work was inevitably different from how the INSET instructors envisaged it, because they adapted it to try and solve *their* problems. Thus, one teacher created groups of between nine and eleven students each so that she wouldn't have too many groups to check on—but this meant that there were far too many students in each of the groups to function coherently. Another teacher created smaller groups, with students sitting in circles, while actually continuing to teach in traditional lecture style, using the blackboard as a prop. It is not surprising then that both these teachers said that they found group work unsuitable for their classes, and rejected it.

## Engagement

Of the various ways in which teachers reacted to new ideas described so far, none is likely to have had a significant positive effect on the learning of their students. The last category of reaction, however, may in the long run prove more beneficial. This is where teachers engage with new ideas and gradually accommodate them within their own belief structures by making adjustments in their own thinking. It may be a long process, having little immediate practical effect in their teaching, and with the tension between previous and recent ideas taking years perhaps to find a resolution. There may even be a temporary decline in performance as the teacher tries out new procedures in an uncertain way, just as students' language production may falter as they struggle to accommodate a new grammatical rule into their interlanguage.

The first stage on this long road to accommodation involves doubting aspects of one's current practice or beliefs. Several of the teachers said they felt the need to make their classes 'more lively, more vivid, make them more interested in the ... subject'. They had come to realize that many of the activities they did in the class were dull. But they satisfied other basic concerns, such as keeping discipline and imparting sufficient quantities of knowledge about the language, so most teachers persisted with them.

This internal conflict between new and older beliefs may only gradually have practical effects. The teacher quoted above, for instance, whose lesson I had observed, certainly tried hard to project an informal image, sharing occasional jokes with her students. Yet, at the same time, she retained the dull text and the formidable battery of exercises which made up the core of the lesson. It may be some time before her new concern with motivation leads her to experiment with new texts and tasks.

Practices representing contradictory approaches may temporarily co-exist in a teacher's classroom routine. Another teacher reported having introduced silent reading of texts into his classes after the INSET course 'because as a matter of fact the main objective of English teaching [in my faculty] is … not for oral skill I think but just for comprehension'. Yet he continues to have the students read the text aloud one by one for the first part of the lesson, apparently because he still believes it is important for students to know how to pronounce the words in the text, and because he feels confident of controlling the class when there is one dominant voice focusing students' attention.

A few teachers argued persuasively that the INSET course had prompted a fundamental change in their approach to teaching. One teacher, for example, claimed that he now realized 'that the most important or main point in my teaching is language, not the knowledge' and that 'I'm not giving a speech but I'm teaching.' He mentioned two behavioural consequences of this change in his beliefs: he has realized the value of homework for increasing the amount of language practice his students get, and he focuses his teaching more purposefully on their expressed needs. At the same time, though, he retains former practices and concerns that seem to contradict these new beliefs. For instance, he claimed that the most important thing for a teacher in his circumstances was to appear knowledgeable, and that teachers must avoid at all costs the risk of being asked questions they don't know how to answer.

## Conclusion

Whilst stopping short of applying Tomlinson's term 'disastrous', I was forced to acknowledge that the course had had effects quite unanticipated by the instructors. A great deal of our original 'input' had simply been lost, and what was taken up was reinterpreted by teachers to fit their own beliefs and their own concerns about what was important to them and their students. One may speculate that the limited practical changes which resulted were rarely likely to promote student learning.

But Tomlinson's (1988) suggested remedy of follow-up sessions is surely not enough. True, after a course such as this, they might be useful as first aid for teachers painfully trying to understand and apply the advice they have been given. For a hangover-free INSET, though, it will be necessary to moderate the input itself, especially that distilled wisdom—'research theory' or 'received knowledge'—of a culture alien to many classroom teachers in the UK as well as overseas. As Freeman (1991: 19) has pointed out:

> Models of teacher education which depend on knowledge transmission, or 'input-output' models of teacher education, are essentially ineffective. This is because they depend on received knowledge to

influence behaviour and do not acknowledge—much less encour-age—teacher–learners to construct their own versions of teaching.

The focus of the short INSET course, where experienced teachers already have well-developed mental constructs of teaching, should be the teachers' beliefs themselves. These need first to be articulated, and then analysed for potential contradictions with each other, the teaching circumstances, and the beliefs of learners. Only then will teachers be able to accommodate new ideas—to appreciate the theory underlying them, understand their practical realization, and evaluate their usefulness.

## Initial awareness-raising

This being the case, there is a strong argument for beginning INSET with awareness-raising activities, where participants confront their own routine practice and the values it is intended to serve. This can be done, for example, through examination of video-taped lessons (Ramani 1987), analysis of classroom tasks (Nunan 1989a), or the completion of questionnaires on teacher and learner roles (Wright 1990). And, finally, instead of tutors recommending ready-made solutions for predeter-mined problems, it should be the participants themselves who, on the basis of this expanded awareness of their own practice, determine the specific areas of their teaching that they wish to develop, and formulate their own agenda for change in the classroom. In this way, the short INSET course could serve not only as an intense learning experience in itself, but could also enhance the learning value of all the many occa-sions when teachers are exposed to new ideas—in the classroom, at con-ferences, during staffroom conversations, and when reading journals like this.

*Originally published in Volume 49/1, 1994*

## *Notes*

1  I was working as a British Council Teacher/Specialist on an ODA-funded project aimed at development of the Staff Language Centre at Gajah Mada University, Yogyakarta. I am grateful to the ODA for the grant that enabled me to carry out this research.

2  This and all subsequent quotations by teachers are taken from Lamb (1991).

3  'Assimilation' here deliberately echoes Piaget's use of the term to describe superficial learning, in which new knowledge is added to old

without any significant reordering of underlying knowledge structures or beliefs. By contrast, I saw much less evidence of Piaget's
'accommodation', where new ideas force fundamental readjustments
in thinking—though the process of 'engagement', discussed below,
may lead gradually to accommodation.

# 13

## Using diaries for teacher reflection on in-service courses

### JENNIFER JARVIS

## Introduction

In the last ten years, many teachers have asked learners to keep diaries of their learning, perhaps as a means of helping the learners become more aware of how to learn; or as a means of evaluating the learners' reactions to the courses they are giving. However, in searching the literature on the results of these uses of diaries, I have not yet found anyone who has used diaries for the same purposes as mine, Howell-Richardson and Parkinson (1988), suggests 16 separate uses for learner diaries, but mine did not seem to be among them. This article is an attempt to share with readers the use to which I put learner diaries, and some implications of using them with trained professionals.

## The training context

In recent years, I have run specialized in-service teacher training courses for small groups of experienced English teachers. The courses are short (of three or four months' duration), intensive, and oriented round a particular need. One of these courses has been for secondary English teachers, with a special focus on teaching reading. The 15 teachers are all non-native speakers of English, and all from the same country. The course includes a preliminary language-improvement component, followed by work on methodology related to the participants' context.

I have asked each group of teachers to keep a learning diary of each week of their course; a diary which records their learning as teachers.

I shall first give some brief excerpts from the diaries, then discuss issues in using them.

> The task provided me a fundamental experience on what to do if given an assignment as per my profession in future. (A Week 5)

> I learnt much from this visit. (A Week 6)

> Comprehension lessons have been misled by most teachers back home. In most cases left to the learner to find his way through. This I have discovered here after this topic to have been a grave mistake on the side of the teacher. I've also noted that if the comprehension strategies are laid down for our learners at their first year in secondary education, they will grow up to be very good in facing comprehension tasks. ... It is very difficult for the learner to attempt a comprehension task if they lack the background knowledge. (B Week 7)

I was, of course, happiest to read comments such as the third one above, and I will now explain why, and suggest my purpose in using the diaries.

## Use of the diaries in teacher training

My main aim in asking the teachers to keep a learning diary of their course was to provide an opportunity for them to *reflect on their teaching* in the light of the work we were doing. Schön, in his influential book, *The Reflective Practitioner* (1983), has suggested that professionals' understandings are theoretic *and* rooted in action. Changes in professional awareness come if the awareness is situated in practice, a kind of reflection-in-action. The practitioner moves from a real-life problem, to reframing the theory which accounts for the problem, to new action. For some time now, this has seemed to me to be a useful way of perceiving professional development: I therefore sought to use the diaries to help the teachers be aware of the importance of their own reflection, and to provide a spur towards their creating a meaning for new ideas which was rooted in their own practice.

Huberman (1985) calls a very similar perception of teachers' needs a 'knowledge–use perspective'. He says teachers gain knowledge which they relate to the 'surround in which they operate', because their needs are 'situationally created and situationally resolved; they cannot be context-stripped'. The task of in-service professional training is therefore to help the professional reframe the familiar, and I sought to use the diaries to do this.

Gunstone *et al.* (1988) similarly suggest teachers are 'constructivists' who construct their own meanings from experience. In teacher training, they suggest we aim at improvement in 'specific, task-related competencies', development in teachers' beliefs about effective teaching, their self-confidence, and their perceptions of inter-personal relations. Reflection helps the achievement of these aims.

In the intensity of a short course, a teacher can often feel quite battered by the amount of 'new' or different or even familiar information he or she is meeting. I felt that the diaries might provide a space in which there was at least an opportunity for reflection, for reframing and constructing personal meanings, perhaps as in excerpt 'B Week 7' above. However, using diaries, or as we began to call them 'learning records', raised many issues; both of how to manage their use in a course, and of learning records themselves as a teaching/learning instrument.

## Setting the task and giving a meaning for reflection

The idea of writing a record of what has been learnt on a course was a new one to the teachers. Individuals had written personal diaries at different times in their lives, but to be asked by a tutor to write a record as an 'official' course requirement was very different. The first priority, it seemed to me, was to seek to explain *why* I wanted them to do this. I therefore explained what I believed about reflecting on what they were doing, and talked about the chance the record could give them to relate the work of the course to their own teaching. We discussed how the diary might contain a putting-into-words of what they had thought was happening in a class, their comments on its personal usefulness, and any questions or doubts they might have. The focus would be on selecting what they thought they had learnt from what we were doing.

### Change of name

In early courses, I used the label 'learning diary', but changed to 'learning record' in subsequent ones. This was because the word 'diary' seems to have associations in many people's minds with 'confessions' or 'bearing the soul', and to highlight the unavoidable tension between writing a record of personal relevance and having it read by a tutor. Changing the name did not remove the tension (see below). But the change of name did perhaps lessen the tension, because 'record' has more associations with 'public' than does 'diary'. In early courses, too, the teachers handed in their diary every week. In subsequent ones, we changed to every two or three weeks, so that the records were more aligned to topic blocks; and the turnaround was just more manageable by writers and

reader. Writing and reading the record involves a large time commitment, and it is important to ensure that this does not get so burdensome
that the task is resented or becomes tokenized. I found that the longer
time-span led to the task being taken more seriously, and to more
reflective comments.

## Getting started

A full explanation of the purpose of the learning record is an essential
preliminary, but not nearly enough. The learning record is a new genre
to the teachers, and so they need to gain a sense of what it can be like.
After one has used records with teachers, one has, of course, a source of
models, and it is possible to use excerpts from previous groups to illustrate what can be done. However, I have found it more motivating to let
the group try the first instalment in whatever way they can, saying that
we will then share ideas of how to do it based on their work. After the
first instalment, I copy excerpts from their records onto overhead transparencies and we discuss which ones seem to help the writers think
about what we are doing. One route to this is to discuss which might
provide a record that will be useful when they return home, and why.
We then get a variety of styles from within the group, and these begin to
provide graspable models.

## My role at this stage

As the course proceeds, I may show particularly interesting excerpts on
other occasions, as reflecting in writing is a very difficult process, and
takes time to learn to do successfully. I also comment on the records in as
varied a way as I can. These may include reactions like 'Yes, I agree',
'Good idea'; or questions like 'How would you use this with your
class?', 'Where might this fit in your work on the class reader?'; or suggestions like 'Could you put down one thing you didn't like about the
visit, and say why?'. If an idea seems to have been misunderstood, I
either explain it in my comments on the record (useful, for example, if
the meaning of a term has been wrongly perceived), or give an explanation in class if it seems possible that this will help several participants.
Showing that I am really interested in what is said, in these varied ways,
is important in motivating the group to reflect.

## Being reflective: some problems

I should like to suggest some of the problems participants have in moving towards reflection in the records.

## Listing

The main type of problem I could call reliance on 'listing'. An example from the first week of the course reads:

> *Day 1*
> Introduction to the programme
> —Self introductions
> —Timetable distribution
> —General information about the University life and Leeds City.
>     (A Week 1)

While this is not at all a surprising response for the first attempt, a few writers keep to this for most of their course, only modifying it in directions which do not seem to encourage reflection. Being asked to reflect 'publicly' is, of course, seen as threatening by some teachers. Some in the group may fear loss of 'face' before their tutor if they appear less professionally knowledgeable than they would like. A list of things done provides a way of fulfilling the task without the danger of offering one's own opinion. So, variations on listing seem to me to be used to cope with this threat. Perhaps for some, previous experience of classrooms where 'ignorance' is mocked proved too powerful an expectation to be overridden during their four-month in-service course. I feel I am dealing here with an aspect of educational culture which is not necessarily country-specific but very widespread.

## General summaries

However, as the course goes on, listing may undergo interesting modifications. The first is to present general summaries, with no clear sense of developing a new frame, as no detail or justification for the generalization is given. For the same part of the course as quoted from teacher 'B Week 7', above, one teacher wrote:

> We looked at close range at what we are doing when we are comprehending a passage. We noted that we are filling in meaning by making connections, and at the same time making relationships between words or using meaning-markers. (C Week 7)

At first sight, this looks like a competent summary, but it differs from B7 in having no other supporting detail (B7 notes several actual teaching techniques in support of her observations) and, primarily, in having no created link to the teacher's work practice. It is therefore hard to see any sense of reflection on practice emerging. Possibly the generalities were seen as 'safe'—the task was fulfilled creditably, but without revealing anything of the teacher's own views. It is, of course, possible that the writer gained a great deal from putting topics of the course into his own words, and I am not assuming that lack of overt written reflection means no learning was going on. Barnes once commented (1976) that some people prefer to 'flow into a mould', and imitate a role, rather than change their role by self-exposure or introspection. The trainer, however, is faced with real difficulty in judging what kind of comment to make in response to the writer. On the whole, I found a mixture of praise for the summary and suggestions that the writer should think about how this understanding might be used in his teaching helped some to try to make connections.

## 'Pleasing the teacher'

A second modification of listing in the teachers' records was when some writers appended evaluative comments after the list of things done. It can perhaps be equated to the 'pleasing teacher' response quoted by Bailey (1983). With my group of teachers, it led to comments such as 'I learnt much from this visit', or 'A very useful lesson'. When used without any justification for the evaluation, the result seems enthusiastic but leaves a sense of lack of questioning of self or of the course. My reaction here was to ask for reasons why.

## A sense of competitiveness

The third modification of listing seen in the records involved comments which do relate to teaching, but none the less do not reveal positive reflection on practice. In one of her articles on her own learner diaries, Bailey (1983) comments on the sense of competitiveness she felt with regard to the other members of the class. This often prevented her from learning. A few members of one of the groups of teachers showed similar competitiveness, particularly in comments on teaching/presentations by their peers. The need to feel better than others was very strong in a few individuals, and could lead to unreflective judgements. One teacher, for example, seemed to misunderstand totally a presentation by a leading member of the group. The comment was:

... in my opinion, the work on reading presented by one of us ... left
some of us wondering if the designer carefully considered the level of
the pupils for whom the task is set. The entire task is suitable for the
vocational department in a trade school printing department. Long
and wordy instructions have been avoided in the setting of examinations. This task does exactly the opposite. (D Week 11)

The task in question was a carefully planned activity designed to help
learners use layout features, but the record-writer did not perceive
the purpose. It is possible that negative competitiveness influenced the
writer's judgement here, so that although thought was being given to
the teacher's practice, no change of action was likely. Negative competitiveness, then, is another effect of classroom experience which prevents
reflection in some individuals. In the relatively few examples of this
which occur, I feel it most useful to talk privately to the individual concerned about possible purposes for their colleague's lesson, to try to help
them see alternative interpretations.

## *Being reflective: some solutions*

But there were, of course, record-writers who managed to overcome the
understandable pressures to save face, please the tutor, or to compete.
I have found it illuminating to try to work out what they did.

### Reordering notes

An important step in helping the writers move towards using the records
for reflection, was when they moved from chronology to reordering
notes made during class sessions. The record then became a means of
organizing the understanding of a period of work because it highlighted
what was personally significant. As Barnes (1976) suggests: 'by formulating knowledge for oneself one gains access to the principles upon
which it is based'. One sign of this was when the writers summarized or
highlighted aspects of the course, then added a statement of the principle or background understanding they had worked out. Sometimes this
was expressed formally, as in: 'Important principle to remember: The
learner is capable of helping himself as much as possible' (E Week 10).

Others generalized the principle, as in this comment following a
record of work on setting writing tasks: 'We teachers should always
know that a purpose must link or relate to the reader therefore this question should always be asked: "Who's this story for", so as to have a purpose in writing.' The record goes on to identify a purposeful task in the

students' textbook, and suggests how the teacher could create purpose through 'a class exercise book in which the best students write their exercise' for others to read (F Week 6). This excerpt comes from a group of three teachers who decided to write a group record. It proved very valuable for them, as they pooled understandings of the class sessions, and issues of meaning and interpretation came up in the task of writing, and were reflected in the record.

## Exemplification

A writer's use of an example or anecdote of his or her own seemed to me to be sign of an attempt to relate ideas to practice. One teacher pondered on some of our work on introducing class library books to pupils:

> In the first place how have I myself been choosing the books I read/have?
>
> Either:
>
> 1 Someone told me about it; sometimes I see them advertised—I read the advertisements; sometimes they are recommended by the teacher.
>
> Or:
>
> 2 It is the title which attracts me. I look through the book: the pictures, chapter titles, the blurb (if any), author's introduction; the Foreword (if any).
>
> I have read other books written by the author. I see how this one is recommended by others. I buy it.
>
> So I should tell my students to more or less do the same when choosing a book. (G Week 5)

## Commenting

Some teachers added a section called 'Comment', where they specifically tried to give their thoughts on the teaching applications of the ideas they had noted. Others, without using the heading, ended each section of notes with a comment, such as these reflections on teaching items of grammar:

> In the past I've been allowing comparatively limited practice in my teaching because I believed I needed as much time as possible to set out the rules for the learners, for I could never fancy learners making out any grammatical rules for themselves. Thus, I would try my best

to give long explanations on what the rules meant. This would be accompanied by several examples though; and then exercises would follow. The number of wrong answers used to disappoint me much and they left me wondering as to why at all these learners could not refer to the given rules and give the correct answers! It's now then, that I have discovered that we teachers sometimes try to force learners to understand by our long and dominant talk. I have also realised that I will need to spend much more time on my lesson preparation so as to come out with as many and as much interesting practical activities as possible. This will build in success and challenge in my learners. It will also ease tension in myself (less talk) as well as reduce the number of exercises I've had to mark in the past. (H Week 4)

Teachers, therefore, seemed to move towards using the record for reflection when they used it to reorganize notes and underline the principle behind their reorganization; add examples or anecdotes; or overtly discuss their thoughts on the experience they were having.

## Types of reflection

In rereading the records and trying to understand what the writers were doing, I have found it useful to try to categorize the types of reflection in them in other ways too. A comment by Huberman (1985) has been helpful here. He says:

... teachers will reach outside the classroom for information and expertise that can explain or alleviate the problems they confront in getting their work done satisfactorily. Teachers also reach outside to make the most of the instructional opportunities they can open up within the constraints of the classroom. Or they may reach outside to justify and legitimize their own convictions and routines.

In the records of my groups of teachers, I have found examples of each type of reflective search Huberman mentions: solving problems, seeking new teaching ideas, and justifying what is already done.

### 1 Solving problems

Several teachers made reference to things they found difficult at home, and sought to relate new ideas to these problems. One gave a very clear summary of work we did on writing with beginners, and commented:

I have always thought of teaching writing for beginners as almost impossible but the technique which we learnt this week has made me feel that it's not as tough as I thought. (E Week 11)

Excerpt H, above, reveals a similar sense of new awareness. Perhaps one essential step in problem-solving reflection-on-action is a sense of new possibilities which, of course, await trial back in the work situation.

## 2  Seeing new teaching ideas

Most of the teachers saw gaining new teaching ideas as their prime reason for coming on the course, so that they were already predisposed to look for these. The records for them became a chance to focus on personal specifics and to work out why the new idea was useful. One wrote:

> Frankly, the purpose of comprehension is to have skilled readers. In the comprehension lessons we need to better or improve the ability of our learners to use clues in the text by trying the following … (B Week 7)

She then summarized various techniques. What is interesting here is the writer's shift in perception of the purpose of a 'comprehension lesson', which was a necessary prerequisite of her understanding the value of the techniques. The necessity to explain her ideas in the record seemed to help this writer move to working out the theory behind the techniques, as well as seeing relevance in the techniques themselves. Another showed how a non-competitive (or positively competitive) approach to peers could also stimulate reflection. The teachers designed lessons, then discussed each other's lessons in small groups, before peer-teaching them. One wrote of the discussions:

> I found this exercise very useful as I chanced to see the useful technique which my colleagues had designed for comprehension. It's really interesting how creative some people are in designing things which I, personally, wouldn't have ever thought of. Through this very exercise my colleagues helped me modify some parts of my lesson plan to make it more practical. (E Week 11)

Here again, I get a sense of the writer reflecting on new possibilities in her own teaching.

## 3  Legitimize own practice

A very necessary form of understanding for an experienced professional is a renewed sense that one is on the right lines, through understanding more fully why something works. Several teachers showed this kind of awareness in their records. After work on context-guessing, one wrote:

I've been using this method for quite a long time without knowing that it was so useful (it wasn't exactly the same as this). I have now discovered which parts I have been omitting in the whole procedure. When I go back it will be as successful as ever, I believe. (E Week 6)

This kind of awareness can be seen as a form of reframing the familiar, while confirming current practice. I felt that the need to write the record helped this teacher to articulate for herself her new understanding, and so make it more firmly understood.

## Teacher evaluation of the records

As part of the evaluation of the course, we asked the teachers to comment on the 'value' or 'usefulness' of writing the learning records. (The different terms were used in different years.) These are some of the reactions:

Writing my learning record is the storage for future reference and revision of what I have done.

This process helped in making us revise and internalise more ideas.

Writing my learning record was the most difficult homework I had. Though difficult I became so much impressed with the comments the teacher put in my work and I found that the notes will be very much useful to me when I go back home.

Though it was a bit tough to write what I learned, I found very useful because I've come up with very helpful notes and other valuable pieces of information.

Writing my own learning record is an activity that cannot be surpassed. It enabled me master all topics that we saw in session besides having them in a nutshell. It was a hard work which was of great importance and utility for later use.

Useful, because new thing written down before its details are forgotten.

It was very useful because I was able to arrange well all what I have learned here and go back home with them. It also by writing helped me revise.

Extremely useful and satisfying.

These reactions seem to me to suggest that the teachers did perceive a value in the record, and it is interesting to see their stress on the usefulness of the writing in helping them to make sense of their course; to get a grip on it. Perhaps 'making sense' is another way of viewing 'reflection'. The majority of the responses were of this type, but individuals did feel confident enough to express a negative view if they felt it. One, for example, wrote:

> ... perhaps the writing of our learning records were exaggerated because we already were taking notes during classes. So there was little need to write these since it was like rewriting the notes.

It seems inevitable to me that there will be teachers for whom this particular form of supporting learning does not work, and it is not necessary or sensible to claim universal benefit for it.

## Conclusion

For the tutor, obviously, the record is not only a means of stimulating learner reflection, it also functions as feedback about learning, about attitudes to the course and anxieties about the course. I have found the records give me a necessary sense of being in contact with my learners' learning, and, in Bruner's terms (1985), help me understand when 'scaffolding' learning may help, and what form it may take. A sense of tutor interest and of dialogue with the tutor is welcomed by many writers, and perhaps gives teachers a new awareness of how learning may emerge from an interaction between teacher and taught.

Despite the real pitfalls of using learning records to encourage reflection on practice, I shall use them again with in-service teachers, as I have been convinced that they can help deepen many teachers' understanding. In an article in ELT Journal, Ramani (1987) speaks of the importance in INSET of 'raising the theoretical awareness of teachers by encouraging them to conceptualize their practice'.

She was speaking of training practices in the classroom, but I think that records can be used to extend the range of opportunities to outside class work too, and so gain more chances to achieve the aims of the training. An additional value is that those who succeed in reflecting on practice, seem also to reveal a heightened sense of their own responsibility for their learning and for changing their teaching. They seem to have more confidence in their own ability to act. Obviously, this can only find expression in action, and all I have been able to do so far is to observe a few of the teachers working with colleagues in in-country seminars, and get reports on them from in-country personnel. The impression I get is that there is some relation between those who were able to use the record for reflection, and positively changed practice. Their enthusiasm for change and action is also greater than most of those whose records were mainly of the listing kind. My survey is far too limited to come to any reliable conclusions, but the impressions are sufficiently positive for me to wish to continue to use learning records as a means of supporting the learning of teachers.

*Originally published in Volume 46/2, 1992*

# 14

## Three stages in teacher training

### DONARD BRITTEN

## Introduction

Accounts of pre-service (P/S) teacher training often give a static view of
the relationships involved, regardless of the point in the training process
that is being considered. The aim of this article is to present a picture of
the P/S trainee—and more especially of the non-native-speaking EFL
trainee—as a person in movement, with a particular starting point at the
outset of training and a more or less clearly specified destination. The
distance to be covered is great, so if we can break it up into stages, we
can help to resolve certain apparent conflicts between different desider-
ata in P/S training. Such a procedure can also tackle the problem of
transfer (or rather non-transfer) of what has been learnt from the training context to the later working situation. I will make some suggestions
as to how the design of a training programme can best take account of
the trainees' evolution and therefore maximize transfer of training.
Finally, I will raise a problem about training people in autonomous
self-evaluation.

## The non-native speaker as P/S trainee

Most people would agree that EFL teacher trainees for whom English is
a foreign language are learning to do something very much harder than
native-speaking trainees, as is well brought out in Medgyes (1986).
Firstly, they need to establish communication in a foreign language
(English) with students who very likely share their own mother tongue.

Secondly, such trainees must master a set of professional skills which will probably have to be performed in the foreign language. But thirdly, and above all, non-native trainees have to outgrow not only ideas about teaching and learning foreign languages which were acquired as pupils in school only a few years earlier, but also perhaps previous ideas about the nature of language and what it means to know a language. Models of teaching and learning picked up in childhood can be durable influences, particularly when associated with admired or respected former teachers. Influences of this kind no doubt affect pupils whose favourite subject is English and who decide to become English teachers themselves. And all this is in addition to the enormous task of mastering the foreign language itself and maintaining that mystery.

Non-native trainees, then, know both more and less than native speakers; but the main problems arise in areas where they know *more*, particularly as regards their previous experience of EFL. Previous EFL exposure would generally be counted on the credit side (even if it contained some bad teaching models) *provided* that the aim of teacher training was to reproduce the teaching of a decade earlier. But it hardly ever is. EFL moves fast, and yesterday's orthodoxy is today's training heresy. Indeed, a recent interview in *ELT Journal* (Corder 1986) suggests that there may soon be more big changes in EFL teacher-training syllabuses.

For most native-speaker trainees, on the other hand, deep-rooted ideas about how the language should be taught and learnt come only after teaching for some time. So for them conscious or unconscious resistance to new teaching models arises only in in-service (I/S) training, whereas for their non-native-speaking colleagues it may be an important factor in P/S training too. The inclusion of various theoretical components in the I/S training syllabus has been justified as teacher education for flexibility—preparing people to be receptive to *future* changes of method. That is perhaps a good reason. But for non-native trainees the biggest change may be the *present* one: the change from the method they experienced as learners to the method they are being trained to use themselves. So the main justification—if justification it is—for having theoretical subjects, including the theoretical treatment of methodology, in P/S training syllabuses, is that they foster and underpin attitude change during training itself and minimize reversion, once training is over, to older teaching models.

## Conflicting desiderata in training

In the planning of a P/S training programme, there are several pairs of apparently contradictory requirements that have to be reconciled (see Table 1). Thus, in their observation of other people's teaching, one requirement is that trainees should focus on clearly observable, even countable, behaviours (teacher smiled; teacher repeated response, etc.). This yields non-contentious data and clear prescriptions for changes in the trainees' teaching. Yet it is also desirable that they should discern in others and develop in themselves less easily observed teaching qualities such as enthusiasm, good organization, and sensitivity to students' feelings. This latter requirement calls for a different, much more interpretive kind of observation and more open discussion afterwards.

| Topic in training | First desideratum vs. Second desideratum | |
|---|---|---|
| Guided observation | Directly observable behaviours | More significant categories |
| Skills training | Prescriptive approach to basic skills (lockstep training) | Exploratory approach to develop individual teacher's potential |
| ELT approach | Focus on the teacher (for training purposes) | Learner-centred teaching (for better learning) |
| Evaluation of teaching performance | Assessments made or checked by trainers | Practice in self-assessment |
| Methodology component | Need to impart knowledge (lectures) | Reflexive principle: practise what you preach |
| Working mode | Small groups for attitude development | Individual for self-reliance |

TABLE 1 *Contradictory requirements in P/S training programme*

By the same token, in skills training, there are standard teaching tactics and procedures that all trainees should master, which it makes sense to present and practise prescriptively. On the other hand, trainees are not nowadays expected to converge on the same faceless model of good teaching: training should explore and build on each trainee's strengths and should buttress individual weaknesses.

Teacher training necessarily focuses on the behaviour of the trainee. Any piece of practice teaching may thus have pedagogical objectives in terms of teaching behaviour which assume more importance than its didactic objectives in terms of pupil learning. To this extent the training is teacher-centred. But at the same time the type of teaching aimed at—the ELT approach promoted by training—is likely to be learner-centred, seeking to adapt to the needs of students and subordinating means to ends.

Or again, for the reliable assessment of trainees' teaching performance, evaluations by teacher trainers are needed. But realistic practice in self-assessment requires uncorroborated self-reports by the trainees. The lecture format is used for much of the theoretical part of training, yet this is incompatible with the principle (if adopted) that training should reflect and illustrate only those methods that the trainees will be expected to use.

Finally, the trainees' attitude development is favoured by working in small groups, to study lesson planning or evaluation, problem-solving, discussion tasks in methodology, and so on. But in practice working teachers will not have this sort of peer-group support very often, and so training should prepare the teachers, as trainees, to make their own decisions and judgements.

## *The incremental approach*

The opposition between the items in the columns called 'first desideratum' and 'second desideratum' in Table 1 comes from seeing them as simultaneous training requirements, rather than as needs at different stages in training. In fact the items in the 'first desideratum' column are generally appropriate at earlier stages in training, or at earlier stages in dealing with a particular content, and those in the 'second desideratum' column are appropriate at later stages.

The sort of incremental approach to P/S training that has become widespread in EFL in the last ten or fifteen years does to some extent move from the first to the second column. Such an approach can be analysed in terms of certain progressions (summarized in Table 2). It is no surprise that there are parallels between incremental teacher training and a three-stage view of language teaching and learning: both are based on a skills-learning model.

The first progression—that of scale—is a matter of controlling the risk level in practice teaching. Starting with short encounters with small classes makes for easier planning, simpler class management, and low stress, so that the trainee can devote more attention to content and procedure. Secondly, a progression of integration involves practising new skills or procedures in isolation at first, concentrating and receiving feedback only on the skill in focus. The trainee progresses from

| Progression of | From | To |
|---|---|---|
| Scale | Small learner groups. Short teaching encounters. | Full classes. Whole lessons and lesson sequences. |
| Integration | Isolated skills or lesson segments. Skills objectives. | Skills integrated to achieve learning objectives. |
| Autonomy | Lesson planning and evaluation by trainer or group. | Individual planning and self-assessment. |

TABLE 2 *Progressions in P/S training*

this initial stage of skill-getting (the *what* of a teaching skill) to that of skill-using (the *why*, *when*, and *with whom*). Micro-teaching in its standard form starts off right at the beginning of these two progressions.

The third progression—in autonomy—concerns attitude development and the individualization of the trainee's teaching style. The planning, execution, and evaluation of practice teaching early in training is usually based on the teacher trainer's authority or the trainee-group consensus. Later on in training, however, most lessons should be planned by the trainee alone; much practice teaching should be observed; and the lesson evaluation, I would maintain, should often take the form of trainee self-assessment, reported orally or in writing to the teacher trainer (who was not present at the lesson).

## The three stages and the problem of transfer

Transfer of training is probably a very serious problem for the P/S training of non-native language teachers in many countries. There is a transfer problem whenever teachers, once they are fully qualified, adopt patterns of teaching behaviour that were stigmatized during their training, but which the teachers had earlier seen used year after year by their own language teachers at school, and which may still be used by many of their older colleagues now they are teachers themselves. This problem can be dealt with only if, during training, the acquisition of skills goes hand in hand with the acquisition of appropriate attitudes to teacher development. This is necessary because attitudes command skills. You may *know* how and when something ought to be done, but you still may never actually *do* it if you do not feel inclined to, if you feel no personal commitment to working that way.

The initial commitment, during P/S training, to the use of the officially approved skills and procedures is based, firstly, on the authority of the trainer as the presumed 'representative of the profession', and later, perhaps, on the authority of the peer-group. Conformity is also a necessity for the examinations in methodology and practical teaching. But the methodology exam can be mere recitation; and self-reporting of attitudes, for instance in an oral exam, is no test of subsequent commitment—especially after the trainee peer-group has been replaced, in service, by a colleague peer-group much less likely to favour innovation. If trainees are not sincerely committed to the recommended method before the end of training, they will probably become less, not more, committed later.

The logic of this, it seems to me, is that the centre of authority should shift in training, first from the teacher trainer to the small peer-group, and later, well before the end of training, from the peer-group to the individual trainee. In the initial period of heavy input, it is the teacher trainer who draws the conceptual map of the terrain: this is the stage of trainer-dependence. In the second stage, group planning and evaluation and discussion are the vehicles for collective, public endorsement of this conceptual map and the various routes for travelling about it: this is the stage of group-dependence. And what should then follow is a stage of self-reliance, when the trainee travels the terrain under his or her own power and becomes personally committed to the map while still, to some extent, professionally answerable to teacher trainer and peer-group.

## Implications for programme design

The practical consequences of this analysis can be listed, following Ellis (1986: 91), as features of either awareness-raising components or experiential components of the training syllabus.

### Awareness-raising components

1 Reduce lecturing as training progresses.

2 Discovery learning whenever possible.

3 Trainee-mediated presentation when practicable (Rinvolucri 1981: 49). Individual trainees prepare topics for presentation to the others.

4 A steady increase in the amount of self-access work.

5 Case studies for problem solving in the later stages of training. Rather than reciting the approved methodology, trainees should consider how to apply it in specific difficult situations.

6 Regular samples or elicitations of trainee's attitudes, from the start of training, with questionnaires for self-report and discussion.

7 Maximum small-group discussion in earlier parts of the pro-gramme—with serious consideration given to their outcomes. Little or no group work later.

8 Less theoretical coverage of background disciplines, to allow more time for the above.

## Experiential components

1 Practice teaching distributed, not massed. Or, if there has to be block teaching practice, there should also be part-time observation and teaching before and after. It is in practice teaching that attitude change occurs fastest during P/S training (Wragg 1982: 68). So for the fullest development of new attitudes to teaching and learning lan-guages, and for the best integration of those attitudes into the general value-system of the individual (which is certainly part of what we mean by personal commitment), the period of practice teaching should be as extended as circumstances allow.

2 The inclusion of increasing amounts of unobserved practice teaching.

3 More and more self-assessment reported to the teacher trainer with-out supervisory or peer feedback.

4 Deferred practical assessment. If the final practical exam or inspec-tion takes place while the trainee is still in training, there is much less incentive later to apply the approved methods rigorously in the work-ing situation, especially if they are new to the students. The longer the probationary period leading up to the practical exam, the better the chances that the teacher will apply the lessons of training.

## *A final problem: unmonitored self-assessment*

There remains the problem of how to train people for unconstrained self-assessment. In the early days of practice teaching, we want to guide people's self-assessment and check the quality of the product. Formally or informally, its accuracy is a factor in the teacher trainer's evaluation of the trainee, and the trainee knows this. For self-assessment to con-tinue to be monitored and evaluated until the end of training is, how-ever, one way of hindering the trainee's attainment of self-reliance. On the other hand, we want to ensure that it is done, and done seriously.

The question is, how? Teacher self-assessment is an important but neglected area in TEFL.

*Originally published in Volume 42/1, 1988*

# 15

## *Meeting the needs of teacher trainees on teaching practice*

JUDITH KENNEDY

## *Introduction*

Writing about the future of teacher education within the UK, Lawton (1989) points out that the way we think about the relationship between educational theory and pedagogical practice has changed substantially during the last ten years. He sees teaching as moving towards the 'practice-based' professions in that educational theory now tends to arise from educational practice—a focus realized in the concept of the 'reflective practitioner' first elucidated by Schön (1987) and elaborated by many others (Soloman 1987; Fish 1989). Practice is the pivot of this approach. It is when trainees start to evaluate critically and seek to understand their own classroom experiences that they will develop the kind of intuitive professional 'know-how' that Schön (1987) refers to. These ideas, which now inform many current teacher education programmes, stem in part from a reaction against the 'apprentice' model of teacher education and from the belief that it is very difficult to describe effective teaching skills and strategies in behavioural terms. But does such an approach actually help trainees to cope with their teaching-practice experiences? If the priorities of the trainers and trainees are radically different, then tensions can be set up. More importantly, young novice teachers can become cynical about the value of any institutional training—'well it certainly didn't help me much'. Only by persuading trainees that we do, in fact, speak the same language can we foster the kind of mutual confidence that is needed to enable reflective programmes to succeed.

## Background to the study

In order to see how far trainers and trainees shared the same perceptions of what are important and relevant areas of concern on teaching practices, a feedback exercise was carried out with young EFL trainees following an initial teacher training course at the Centre for English Language Teaching (CELT), University of Warwick. The trainees, who were all from overseas, had completed a final assessed teaching practice in their home countries, supervised by staff from the Centre. Forty trainees were given extensive questionnaires to complete following the teaching practice and selected students had participated in structured follow-up interviews about issues which seemed a common concern of the whole group. The returns from the student teachers revealed a variety of concerns within the three areas of lesson planning and preparation; the classroom and pupils; self-evaluation, supervision, and assessment. Some questions received an overwhelmingly positive response from the trainees, and it is these questions and the response to them that form the framework of this article—in particular, the implications that such commonly shared concerns have for our conceptualizations of the process of teacher education.

## The teacher as decision maker

Teaching is a decision-making process, perhaps particularly so at the planning and preparation stage. The ability to make the right decisions depends on many factors, including not only knowledge but also experience and judgement as to which decisions are relatively unimportant and can be made quickly.

### The format of the lesson plan

As trainers, we would probably consider the content of a lesson plan to be of more importance than the way in which it was set out. Yet these trainees' overwhelming concern was in fact with the form of the plan rather than its substance. In the question shown in Figure 1, 98 per cent of these trainees, for example, allocated 5 points (i.e. a great deal of concern) to the items d, e, and f. The other choices, and the percentage of students allocating 5 points, are given in Figure 1.

Q. How much concern did the following aspects of writing your lesson plans cause you?

Answer on a scale from 'very little' (1) to 'a great deal' (5)

a. Selection of aims and objectives
b. Choice of activites
c. Allocation of time to task
d. Deciding on a format
e. Amount of detail to put in
f. Making it look good
g. Making it easy for me to use
h. Organization of headings and subheadings

Percentage allocating 5 points to choices a–h

| | | |
|---|---|---|
| a 85% | b 35% | c 45% |
| d 95% | e 95% | f 90% |
| g 18% | h 65% | |

FIGURE I

As trainers, we had adopted an approach which attempted to focus on a lesson plan as a statement of each teacher's individual objectives and intended strategies. The important issue is what they are, not how they are set out on a page. But trainees worried over these surface manifestations, and the anxiety deflected them from the plan itself.

## Objectives for lesson plans

In addition, deciding on objectives for their lesson plans was universally difficult—though often they were not short of ideas on what the lesson itself would consist of. It was easy for them to decide on activities or tasks, but much more difficult to work out exactly what the learning outcomes of these tasks were supposed to be as expressed in aims and objectives. In many cases, trainees would work backwards, choosing what they thought would be a 'good' interactive activity and then seeing what kind of aims and objectives they could derive from it. In other cases, they said they used textbook chapter headings, or specified such a vague objective that it would fit every occasion (e.g. Obj: 'To be able to read a text'). The number of objectives was also a cause for trainee concern with all the students saying it was hard to find 'enough'. The difficulty with formulating objectives is more serious perhaps than the problems students had with the surface features of a lesson plan because it suggests that for inexperienced teachers the reason behind many language activities and tasks is not always very clear. However, the difficulties these trainees had with formulating aims and objectives are not unusual. John (1991), writing about teachers of Maths and Geography in the UK, shows that neither novice teachers nor experienced teachers planned lessons according to the traditional rational model with its emphasis on aims and objectives.

Yet the context of a teaching practice generally demands this of them, thus adding to their problems as decision makers. For trainees, or even novice teachers, few decisions at the pre-lesson stage are automatic: the trainees' lack of experience and knowledge mean that what might seem straightforward decisions to trainers, are problematic to the trainee faced with the competing expectations of the school, the pupils, and the supervising tutors. As trainers, we need to create a delicate balance between taking minor decisions out of the trainees' hands—by, for example, setting out explicitly a pro-forma lesson plan, giving clearly written objectives for tasks, and so on—and yet allowing trainees to develop their own strategies which harmonize with their teaching situation.

## The hidden messages of the trainer

Part of the preparation is deciding what materials will be used for any task or activity. The question below received a 100 per cent positive response.

Answer on a scale from 'disagree' (1) to 'strongly agree' (5)

It was very hard to find enough materials for a lesson other than a textbook.

(100 per cent answered 'strongly agree')

It was not the writing of materials that proved problematic for many trainees, but rather the finding of materials other than a textbook. On further discussion it emerged that even where they felt the book was adequate, they did not 'dare' use it alone. Being a 'good' teacher, they felt, meant providing interesting and stimulating materials outside the book. This was something that we had obviously signalled, if not explicitly advised. Questions asked of trainees during training, such as 'Is the material lively and interesting?', may give the impression that a lesson stands or falls by the quality of the materials. The way in which method classes are implemented can also convey messages about what is valued by trainers in teaching. Thus, these students at an early stage in their teaching career were spending too much preparation time trying to amass supportive materials, when in reality it would have been better to

have given more thought and time not only to using the book compe-
tently but also to the classroom activities themselves. In fact, many
trainees chose activities not from a position of conviction concerning
their efficacy but rather because they wanted to 'please the supervisor'.
Training courses may claim to want to encourage trainees to develop
their own theories of professional action through, for example, experimental learning, but for young trainees it may be preferable if, as trainers, we make explicit our own philosophies and beliefs.

## Reflective teaching and metacognition

One of the areas we were particularly concerned to investigate was that
of student self-evaluation. In addition to questions asked of the trainees,
and their own written lesson evaluations, supervisors were also asked
for confidential comments on how trainees coped with this area. Most
teacher training courses are concerned with self-evaluation because as
Calderhead (1989) says 'reflective teaching is generally understood to
concern more than the cognition involved in teaching; it concerns
metacognitive processes of comparison, evaluation and self-direction'.
So we get trainees to reflect upon their own performance because
teacher training is ultimately about the development of professional
knowledge and understanding. It is hoped that students will not only
acquire effective teaching skills, but also that they will develop professional autonomy through an emphasis on an analysis of their teaching
experience. Trainees' responses to questions in this area revealed two
issues which need to be addressed. Firstly, the kind of self-evaluation
that they seemed to want and need may not agree with our desire for
them to become professionally reflective. Secondly, there was a very
wide gap between how trainees saw their own performance and how
observers saw it.

### Unstructured versus structured evaluations

Some writers have suggested that trainees can be helped to self-reflect
more effectively if the process is structured in some way: for example,
Williams (1989) suggests students choosing a focus area prior to the
lesson; Thornbury (1991) discusses the keeping of structured logs as a
means of developing 'craft knowledge'. However, these trainees were
universal in their dislike of such 'forms', seeing them as yet another
thing to be 'done'. What they did find valuable, however, was the opportunity to express their feelings in an unstructured way. When they did

this, their evaluations were more descriptive and affective than analytic, and concerned more with the failings of the pupils than pedagogic aspects. They revealed the often defensive feelings of young teacher trainees, for example:

1   Some of the students were not even interested in the lesson. So when I spoke they lost interest. Some of them even think of school as a place to gather and meet friends and chat!

2   There are boys who are just not interested. I try to attract their attention but they don't bother. In fact, they just show their sour faces to me. This is why they have such a poor command of English.

3   The major problem is that 60 per cent of the students are too lazy to bother about learning English. Some of the students were disturbing their friends. I managed to keep them quiet by threatening that I would send them to the headmaster. They started to make noises again …

One solution is to ask trainees to evaluate their lessons in two ways. Initially, at the start of the practice, trainees would be free to respond in their evaluation to the feeling of the moment. The next stage is to review with individual trainees any recurring areas that these open evaluations revealed, and build up from them a more structured evaluation sheet. This has the virtue that it recognizes that every classroom situation is different and every trainee has particular strengths and weaknesses—for example, one student was particularly concerned with his pupils' unwillingness to participate in oral lessons: 'They just won't say anything. They whisper. They aren't interested.' These comments can then form the basis of a more structured evaluation sheet for later use which focuses on this particular aspect: for example, asking the trainee to watch particularly whether any activities promoted oral interactions.

## Realistic self-appraisal

Trainees' perceptions of their own performance often differed markedly from those of the observer or supervisor, for example:

TRAINEE: The lesson went OK. Students are more co-operative but raising hands are not heeded. I think they have reached their objectives.

SUPERVISOR: No plan and very chaotic approach to the materials. Has not reviewed the exercises. Extremely weak trainee—the lesson showed little understanding of the aim or language level of the class, questioning techniques or organization. Trainee's own English needs attention.

TRAINEE: Students found lesson dull. The grammar bit was too simple for them. Difficult to maintain their attention. Students found passage on QE2 not interesting.

SUPERVISOR: Lively and clear presentation. Children responded well to open and friendly manner. Lesson on s/v agreement was one X found difficult to make interesting—very much revision for the children so need to move quickly to production.

Some trainees seemed to feel that analysis of their own performance required a kind of self-denigration, for example:

I must follow my plan next time. I spent too much time on comparatives. There must not be any activity out of lesson plans. Must allocate time for every section skill so that the lesson will go as planned.

Some trainees, on the other hand, could find little to say about their own performance:

The lesson went well. Objectives achieved.

Feiman-Nemser and Buchmann (1987) similarly found that student teachers' ability to self-reflect remained at a fairly superficial level. Many trainees are so involved in the actual teaching process that they find it almost impossible to detach themselves from the crisis of the moment, and in many cases they lack the knowledge of teaching alternatives which might help them examine their practice. In addition, of course, young inexperienced trainees are often defensive and feel under threat from supervisors. It may be that in the early stages of learning to teach, trainees need to concentrate on acquiring a confident grasp of classroom routines and that critical analysis develops at a much later stage.

## *Supervision as development or evaluation*
### Models of supervision

In looking at the supervisory problems that the trainees said they experienced, I would like to reiterate the distinction between training and development. Training can be seen as reflecting a view of teaching as a skill which has finite components which can be learnt. Development focuses much more on the individual teacher's own development of a 'theory' through personal reflection, examination, and intelligent analysis. These have often been presented as being in conflict—but perhaps this reflects the fact that much of ELT is concerned with practising teachers or postgraduate students and not so much with younger students who are at the start of higher education. With students on pre-service training courses, it seems to me we are concerned primarily with training but also with some elements of teacher development.

Related to this distinction between teacher training and teacher development are different types of supervision practices—thus we have the most traditional role of supervisor: he or she checks briefly with the trainees before the lesson, observes, and then after the lesson talks to the trainees about what has been seen. The overtones are prescriptive, and the ways in which these supervisions are carried out can be variously helpful, ineffective, or positively damaging to trainees. This type of supervision tends to go with the initial stages of teacher training and may be 'pure' or 'impure'. By 'impure', I mean essentially a prescriptive type of supervision but one in which the trainees are offered a series of alternative practices rather than the one right answer. The move towards teacher development as a reflective process necessarily entails a different sort of supervision—clinical supervision. The wealth of literature on clinical supervision (e.g. Goldhammer 1969; Schön 1983, 1987; Gitlin and Smyth 1989) is testimony to its popularity with trainers. The original intentions of clinical supervision as envisaged by Goldhammer in the USA in the late 1960s and 1970s placed a high value on 'intellectual engagement', and stressed equality between the participants. It is the trainee teacher, not the supervisor/tutor, who, before the lesson, sets out the agenda for observation. The supervisor collects information, as agreed, objectively and neutrally. The supervisor's role is more that of a neutral arbiter whose contribution has nothing to do with judgement or evaluation.

This concern with styles of supervision has arisen partly because research shows that traditional supervision seemed to have little direct effect on trainees' performance. I would suggest that this is not because the traditional approach is intrinsically bad, but because it can be implemented inappropriately. For example, some supervisors may be not only authoritative but over-critical and personally judgemental, never listening to the trainees, blaming them, ignorant of the context. But, equally, the traditional model of supervision can accommodate a supervisor who is warm and caring, who listens sympathetically to the trainees' problems, who is not prescriptive but helps with problems the trainees raise; all qualities which are often regarded as only characteristic of more collaborative 'clinical' supervision (see Gebhard (1990) in Richards and Nunan (1990)). The development of models of supervision has sometimes been based on trainees' reactions to supervision rather than any examination of classroom effect. To ask trainee teachers on teaching practice if supervisors make them feel anxious or if they are worried about assessment naturally brings positive answers.

## Trainees' feelings about supervisors

These trainees most liked close supervision by someone they knew and who was a practitioner in the field. What they most disliked was supervision by someone they hardly knew whose visits, whilst supportive and kindly, were unhelpful. By unhelpful 'they didn't seem to have any ideas'. The commonest remark tended to be 'He/she was very kind and nice but ...'. At this stage, many problems present themselves for which trainees require prescriptive advice delivered in the right way. At times, they seemed to want quick answers from someone who was strongly supportive and confident on their behalf, who could reassure them and say 'It's alright—I know where you want to go and I can help you get there'.

## The supervisor as assessor

Trainees were naturally anxious about assessment, but on an initial training course this is an issue that cannot be avoided. Assessment often lurks in the background of supervision. Supervisors who try to move away from a more judgemental role into a pseudo-clinical supervision role may not realize that for clinical supervision to be really successful the roles of assessor and counsellor cannot realistically be combined. However much we tell the students that it is their lesson, their pupils, their agenda, we, the tutors, usually have clear ideas about what we want. In our feedback exercise, the students clearly told us: 'We like you to involve us in the process and we like to be treated like adults—we want to know what criteria we will be judged by and we want your honest opinion.' A traditional model of supervision recognizes the authority relationship and demands that supervisors be more transparent in their dealings with trainees. In a sense, failing to confront trainee teachers honestly may be treating them like children. Challenge which leads to debate can be effective if offered in an atmosphere of emotional and social support.

## Fostering reflection in young trainees

Self-evaluation and intelligent reflection are not easy skills to develop. Both require a strong knowledge and experience base which young trainees may not have.

One of the ways in which it could be developed is by removing the focus from the trainees to the supervisor. One question which drew 100 per cent positive response from all trainees was 'Would you like to see your supervisor teach'. There may be many reasons for this—some trainees have had little opportunity to watch whole-class teaching, some are curious about how their supervisors would put their theories into practice. Trainers certainly tend to be rather shy about teaching in front of their trainees, fearful perhaps of giving the so-called 'demonstration' lesson, the dangers of which are well described by Bolitho (1979). While the once-only, staged demonstration lesson on a short in-service training course may not be of value, there are stronger arguments on an extended school practice for supervisors to drop the role of supervisor and try to develop the role of partner-in-experience by teaching some sessions.

Certainly this was essential to the original intention of clinical supervision '... a preparedness on the part of *both parties* to have their teaching observed, critiqued and reconstructed if necessary' (Gitlin and Smyth 1989: 102, my italics). For young trainee teachers, the first stage to self-reflection might be to develop the power of sensitive critique (not criticism), and to see how their supervisors not only teach but themselves self-reflect afterwards.

## *Conclusion*

The above discussion warns against applying principles of teacher education too rigidly. What we as trainers might want—a theoretical underpinning to practice—may not meet the needs of our trainees in the best way at certain stages in their careers. We should avoid making too complex the tasks trainee teachers have to undertake on their practices. The age and maturity of trainees are important factors to be considered when thinking about ways of developing reflective practitioners. At some point, teacher trainers must articulate to their trainee teachers their own philosophies and theories. Supervisors must together be absolutely clear how they are to evaluate and assess practice and they must make that explicit to trainees.

Methods of supervision derived from therapeutic counselling may not be appropriate at this stage. So-called traditional supervision does not exclude argument and debate, nor does it necessarily mean that the supervisor always has the answers. But it does mean that the relationship is an honest one, with supervisors accepting that they are in reality the more powerful partners because they have the sanction to pass or fail trainees.

*Originally published in Volume 47/2, 1993*

# 16

## *Classroom observation: training the observers*

### PETER SHEAL

In an article entitled 'English in the world: aims and achievements in English language teaching', Bowers refers to a drifting apart of language teaching theory and practice. He comments, however, that:

> This is where I take substantial comfort from the growing interest in observational research. For perhaps in the argument between theory and practice, it is observational research which is the intermediary. In twenty years' time the major advances in our understanding of ELT will ... be seen as coming not from the psycholinguistic end of our profession ... but from this sociologically inspired sphere of investigation—the scientific study of what actually and beneficially happens in classrooms. (1986: 393)

Clearly the kind of scientific observational research Bowers refers to can provide researchers and teacher trainers with valuable information. But what about the practising teacher? Generally he or she doesn't read the research literature, and may have already dismissed much of what comes from teacher trainers as too theoretical and impractical. Observational research, then, may be very useful, but will have little impact on the way individual teachers teach.

What would have a significant impact, however, would be the involvement of teachers themselves in observational research. Such classroom-oriented research would provide a valuable resource for new teachers, and stimulate more experienced teachers to try out fresh approaches. A critical element for in-service staff development would have been established.

Several important obstacles, however, stand in the way of such research:

1 Most classroom observations are conducted by administrators rather than by practising teachers. Peer observations are not very common. Consequently, observation tends to be seen as judgemental, and one more aspect of administrator 'power'.

2 Much of the observation that goes on is unsystematic and subjective. Administrators and teachers generally have not been trained in observation or the use of systematic observation tools. Consequently, they tend to use themselves as a standard, and they observe impressionistically.

3 Most observation is for teacher-evaluation purposes, with the result that teachers generally regard observation as a threat. This leads to tension in the classroom, and tension between teacher and observer at any pre- or post-observation meetings.

4 Post-observation meetings tend to focus on the teacher's behaviour—what he or she did well, what he or she might do better—rather than on developing the teacher's skills. As feedback from observers is often subjective, impressionist, and evaluative, teachers tend to react in defensive ways, and given this atmosphere, even useful feedback is often 'not heard'.

If classroom observation is to be used for staff development and to improve the quality of instruction, some of these problems need to be overcome. The focus needs to shift more towards colleagues working together, and towards teacher development rather than teacher evaluation.

This article describes a series of three workshops designed to train classroom observers and overcome the obstacles that stand in the way of observation for staff-development purposes. The target population for these workshops was administrators and senior teachers responsible for English language training in our company training centres. The majority of these administrators and senior teachers are from the Middle East, but about 25 per cent come from the US or UK. Among the classroom teachers, the same approximate percentages apply.

## Needs assessment

Before developing our observer training workshops, we conducted a needs assessment. There were three major elements in this assessment—a survey of the literature, a series of structured interviews, and a variety of classroom observations in our training centres. First, we surveyed the 'state of the art' in classroom observation procedures and forms. We reviewed a variety of textbooks, magazine articles, and existing observation forms, mainly from the US and UK. Then we interviewed administrators and senior teachers in our training centres. In this way, we built up a data base on observation procedures and forms. These structured interviews, following a standard questionnaire, also established face-to-face contact with our target population, provided them with an opportunity to give input into the workshop programme, and obliged them to reconsider their own procedures and forms. Most important of all, these interviews encouraged administrators and senior teachers to recognize the need for observer training and the need to 'buy into' the workshop programme.

In conjunction with these interviews, we conducted a series of classroom observations. Some of these were co-observations with administrators and senior teachers, and the purpose was to assess with them their own procedures and observation forms. Some were our own observations where a colleague and I focused on the applicability of a particular observation form, tested our own observer reliability in using the form, and considered how effectively it could be used by an individual observer. Above all, the purpose of these observations was to ensure that we kept our feet firmly anchored to the ground—the real needs of classroom observers and the teachers they supervise.

Based on our needs assessment, we identified three phases and three potential workshops for observer training:

1  Classroom observation for staff-development purposes.
2  Classroom observation forms.
3  Classroom observation meetings.

## Classroom observation for staff-development purposes

This four-hour workshop was designed primarily to 'break the ground' on classroom observation issues. The specific objectives were that participants would be able to:

– Identify problems facing classroom observers.
– Outline ways of dealing with these problems.
– Assess their own reliability as observers.

# Workshop elements

## Introduction

This focused on classroom observation as a potential staff-development tool and as a means of improving instruction. We established right at the beginning that we were not dealing at this point with the evaluation of teachers. Our experience has shown that establishing this point is necessary because participants often want to focus immediately on teacher evaluation.

## Discussion of pre-workshop readings

A week before the workshop two reading passages on classroom observation (from Cooper 1984 and Zuck 1984) were distributed, together with some questions which linked the passages to the situation in our training centres. These questions on the problems facing a classroom observer immediately established a vital link between the literature and our own training situation. They also provided a structure for discussion. A final product of this discussion was a list of what the participants identified as the main problems facing them in classroom observation— for example, disagreements between observer and teacher, differences between observers, the danger of subjectivity, tendency to generalize (*he or she is a good/bad teacher*) based on one observation, and the need for adequate observer preparation.

## Classroom observation videotape

A specially produced videotape presented a model approach to observation with a pre-observation meeting, an observation where a form was used, and a post-observation meeting.

## Observation exercise

Part of an elementary English lesson was included on the videotape, and we devised an observation exercise to be used with it. The exercise proved to be critical. It made watching the videotape into an active rather than a passive experience, and it highlighted the problems of subjectivity and observer reliability that were identified in the readings and discussion. Participants were given the following feedback form before they observed the lesson. They were told to complete the form, and that the post-observation meeting mentioned was for staff-development purposes.

---

*Classroom observation feedback*
Write down three things you would tell this teacher at a post-observation meeting:
1.
2.
3.
Rate this teacher on a scale of 1–10. 1 is very poor and 10 is outstanding.
Circle the appropriate rating: 1 2 3 4 5 6 7 8 9 10.

---

After watching the videotaped lesson, observers completed the form and took a ten-minute break outside the workshop room. We collected the feedback forms and listed participants' comments on a flipchart. Then, on another page of the flipchart, we noted the range of evaluations.

## Discussion of exercise

In many ways this discussion became the pivotal point of the workshop. When the participants returned, we went through their list of comments. We discussed whether the points that were mentioned several times were critical, and how the contradictions between observers had come about. The importance or triviality of particular comments were discussed (there were no names on feedback forms, so the 'trivial' could remain anonymous), and we kept a score of the negative and the positive points.

Although we had emphasized that the post-observation meeting was for staff-development purposes, observers generally made negative and evaluative comments. The ratio of negative to positive comments shocked participants. We pointed out that some of the negatives could have been eliminated, if there had been an adequate pre-observation meeting to discuss the class and ensure that the observer and teacher were on the same wavelength. This served as a neat response to those participants who had claimed earlier that pre-observation meetings weren't necessary. We then compared the comments to the evaluation ratings: generally they did not match. Participants would often list three negative comments about the teacher's performance but then give a high rating. Indeed, they seemed to be asking themselves two separate questions:

1 In writing down comments, they were asking, 'What's wrong with this teacher's performance?' 'What could I do better?' Here, observers tended to be negative and use themselves as standards. Even though we emphasized that the post-observation meeting was for staff-development purposes, they tended to see staff development in terms of telling the teacher what he or she had done wrong.

2 In making an evaluation, they were asking 'How does this teacher compare to the others I've seen?' Again, however, the standard was shown to be very subjective. Observers' ratings for the same teacher and the same lesson ranged from 2–8 on the 10-point scale. This exercise confronted workshop participants with their own subjectivity and the lack of consistency among observers. Certainly the exercise reinforced what had been said earlier in the workshop and made the need for observer training tangible.

## Further reading and administrator's self-check exercise

Some principles of classroom observation were explained in the reading (National Center for Research in Vocational Education 1980). These were principles of purposefulness, co-operation between observer and teacher, objectivity, completeness (observe a complete lesson), and 'influenceability' (only make suggestions about things a teacher can change). The exercise described a series of situations involving observers and teachers. Workshop participants were required to identify the observation principles that were being neglected in these situations and to add their own comments.

## Discussion

Participants discussed their responses to the situations, and this provided one more opportunity to review basic principles and to relate the literature to the situations which observers faced in their training centres.

## Workshop summary

We reviewed the workshop objectives and discussed what had been accomplished. Problems related to classroom observation had been identified through both the literature and the videotape exercise. We had outlined some ways of dealing with these problems. In particular, we had recommended that observers should follow the same observation guidelines, and that pre-observation meetings should be held to ensure that observers and teachers were on the same wavelength before the observation. We had only begun to touch upon the critical issues of observer subjectivity and consistency, however. In our next workshop we promised to concentrate on these issues and deal with observation forms.

## Classroom observation forms

During our first workshop, the videotape exercise exposed a high degree of subjectivity among observers. The workshop revealed the problems that arise when observers observe without an observation form and without a degree of co-ordination. We had distributed feedback forms at the end of the workshop and participants suggested that there was a need for future workshops on observation forms and teacher evaluation. This feedback provided additional justification for us going on to the next phase of observer training—a workshop on classroom observation forms and how to use them. The specific objectives of this workshop were that participants would be able to:

- Explain the principles of clinical supervision/classroom observation.
- Outline the features and limitations of four types of observation form.
- Describe a lesson by using a standard observation form.
- Produce classroom observation notes to guide a post-observation meeting.

This second workshop was a full-day session, so that not only could concepts be introduced and discussed, but participants could gain more extensive practice in systematic observation.

## Workshop elements

### Introduction

This focused on the differences between traditional teacher supervision/observation and 'clinical' supervision/observation. A week before the workshop two readings on this topic (Harris 1975 and Lucero 1983) were distributed, together with questions which linked the ideas in the passages to the situation in our training centres. Again, we discussed the readings and established a link between the literature and the participants' classroom observation responsibilities.

### Observation forms

Here, I gave a presentation explaining the purposes of observation forms. These were:

1 To provide guidance for pre-observation and post-observation meetings.

2 To provide a structure for the observation.

3 To increase observer objectivity and act as a control on subjectivity.

4 To generate specific observation data/feedback for the observer and teacher.

5 To increase consistency among observers.

6 To provide a record of the lesson and teacher development. Comparison of observation forms over a period of time should illustrate a teacher's development.

I then described the four main types of observation form:

1 *Frequency tabulation*: a form indicating the frequency of specific teacher and student behaviour. We used the American COKER (Classroom Observation Keyed for Effective Research) form as an example because it seemed to us the most ambitious attempt to describe objectively teacher/student behaviours in the classroom (for a description of this form see Medley, Coker, and Soar 1984).

2 *Structured description*: a narrative of what occurs in the classroom. Various sub-headings are often given in this type of form, to provide some focus and structure to the narrative.

3 *Checklist*: an attempt to record the presence or absence of particular types of behaviour. Like the frequency tabulation, this is an attempt to provide a comprehensive, systematic, and objective approach to observation.

4 *Rating scale*: a form which focuses on evaluation rather than on describing behaviour. This is the most subjective type of form, the most open to bias and the type which creates most disagreement between observer and teacher. The rating scale, however, is relatively easy to use and complete. As a result it is the most popular type of form.

The features of each type of form were described and examples of these forms given. The advantages and limitations of each type were then discussed, with particular reference to the examples.

## A standard form

Here, we introduced an observation form which we had developed for the purposes of the workshop. This form combines the features of the frequency tabulation, structured description, and checklist and had been tested out and modified through the observation of a variety of classes at different levels. We introduced and explained the use of the form. Then we used a ten-minute videotaped classroom activity to give participants a chance to practise using the form. Any problems in its use were then discussed.

## Classroom observation

We showed a videotape of an English language class and required participants to complete their observation forms individually.

## Group activity

We divided participants into groups of three or four and gave them the following task: *Compare your marking of the Classroom Activity Frequency categories on your observation form. Use the overhead transparency provided to produce an agreed marking of these categories. Then identify three main things that you would discuss with this teacher at the post-observation meeting.*

This twenty-minute activity enabled participants to discuss the video tape and compare their findings in the relative privacy of the small group. In this way, they could learn from each other and have an opportunity to modify their subjectivity. Finally, the group representatives reported their findings on an overhead transparency. As in the first workshop there were important discrepancies, with the main disagreements arising between those who preferred a teacher-centred approach and those who preferred more learner-centred activities. Although the observation form moderated observer biases, clearly more practice was required in recording specific teacher behaviours and thereby providing useful feedback at a post-observation meeting. We discussed the reasons for the observers' disagreements and pointed out how these would produce different post-observation meetings.

## Workshop summary

We reviewed the objectives and reinforced once more the idea that classroom observation should focus first of all on describing what occurs. This detailed description should be directed to staff development and the improvement of instruction. Over a period of time, however, a series of these observations and forms could justifiably be used as the basis for teacher evaluations.

# Classroom observation meetings

In our final workshop we intended that participants should apply what they had learnt to the conduct of pre- and post-observation meetings. A recurring theme of the workshops had been the importance of good interpersonal communication between observer and teacher if classroom observations were to be effective. In our final workshop we addressed this issue directly. The specific objectives were that participants would be able to

- identify strategies for effective classroom observation;
- outline a systematic approach to teacher observation/evaluation;
- provide specific feedback on a lesson by using an observation form;
- conduct more effective post-observation meetings.

# Workshop elements

## Pre-workshop reading

Before the workshop we sent participants a task sheet consisting of three case studies. The case studies described situations where disagreement and conflict had arisen between a teacher and an observer. For each case study the participant was asked, 'What mistakes did the observer make?' and 'What should the observer do now?'

## Observation case studies

After reviewing the progress of the classroom observation workshop series and this workshop's specific objectives, we referred participants to the pre-workshop task sheet. We discussed the case studies, the mistakes that had contributed to conflict, and what the observer should do to try to remedy the situation. The case studies had been deliberately written to represent the circumstances and the problems that our participants face in conducting observations and post-observation meetings. They had also been written so as to provide a review of some of the important points and issues we had dealt with in the earlier workshops. As a result the discussion was lively, and the observation principles and strategies that we elicited and wrote up on the flipchart provided a reminder of what had been covered in the first two workshops. These principles and strategies included: providing an orientation to observation purposes and procedures, observing professional courtesies and involving the teacher in the choice of class to be observed, using a standard observation form to record data, acknowledging and respecting the teacher's experience, discussing alternative approaches, and the need to avoid being too negative.

## The One-Minute Manager and supervising teachers

Here we introduced a well-known supervisory and management training videotape, 'The One-Minute Manager', taken from Blanchard and Johnson's (1983) course of the same name. The tape shows how a supervisor can use goal-setting, praising, and reprimands to improve employee motivation, work relationships, and productivity. In particular, it shows how the supervisor can serve as an on-the-job trainer and develop his or her staff. After introducing the tape we distributed a task sheet (below) to participants. The questions on the task sheet obliged participants to consider how they could apply the principles of the 'One-Minute Manager' to their own behaviour and classroom observations and observation meetings.

---

TASK SHEET: *The One-Minute Manager and Teacher Supervision*

As you watch the One-Minute Manager videotape, consider the following questions. We will discuss them at several stop points during the tape.

1　Why is goal-setting important?

2　How can you use goal-setting in pre-observation and post-observation meetings?

3　What are the main points to remember about praising?

4　How can you use praise in observation meetings?

5　Why are reprimands not used with new or untrained employees?

---

The tape is divided into three sections, with each section approximately 15 minutes long. We stopped the tape at the end of each section so that participants could answer the appropriate task-sheet questions and discuss them. The questions once more emphasized the importance of setting clear and mutually agreed goals, recording specific behaviour in an observation and giving specific feedback, and the senior teacher's role in developing teaching staff. The whole activity took over an hour. It provided participants with a fresh perspective on classroom observation and on their own role as supervisors.

## Diagnostic, formative, and summative observation

Here I made a brief presentation outlining a systematic approach to teacher observation and evaluation. The approach consists of three observation phases: diagnostic, formative, and summative observation. Features of the three phases were identified on overhead transparencies:

### Diagnostic observations
– New teachers/beginning of academic year
　Pre-observation meetings held
– General observation for staff-development purposes
– Post-observation meetings identify specific development goals

### Formative observations
– Conducted throughout the year
– Follow-up on diagnostic observations
– Observations focus on development goals
– Post-observation meetings discuss development

## Summative observations

- Towards end of academic year
- General observation of teacher performance
- Input provided for teacher performance review

The overhead transparencies provided a structure for the presentation and, as we came to each feature, I amplified. For example, when I presented the diagnostic observation phase, I gave participants a checklist of points that might be covered in a pre-observation meeting. This checklist included orienting the teacher to the classroom observation form and procedures, eliciting the teacher's lesson objectives and the background of the class, discussing what the teacher had done with the class, and identifying what had worked well and what difficulties there had been.

## Classroom observation

We then observed on videotape an English language teacher teaching an advanced class. Workshop participants completed the observation forms they had been introduced to in the second workshop. They were asked to note down at the end of the form three things they would like to discuss with the teacher—two positive points for 'praising', and one suggestion for improvement/development.

## Post-observation meetings

Workshop participants were divided into pairs. One person would be the teacher we saw in the observation videotape and was given Role Play 1; the other would be the observer/supervisor and was given Role Play 2.

We gave the pairs ten minutes' preparation time and then took what we considered to be the best prepared pair to role-play the post-observation meeting in front of the others. Participants discussed the first role play and then a second pair were required to role-play. In this way, based on the completed observation forms and the role-play sheets, post-observation meetings were held. Each meeting lasted about ten minutes, with another ten minutes at the end for a discussion on the meeting's effectiveness. We provided an hour and a half for this activity and ensured that everyone participated in at least one meeting. The role plays, as we anticipated, proved to be the 'heart' of the workshop—the activity where the principles and strategies we had discussed came alive. Role Play 2 provided a solid structure for the observer, but the 'disruptive' elements of Role Play 1 helped replicate the tensions of a real post-observation meeting. Those who merely paid lip-service to staff

POST-OBSERVATION MEETING: *Role Play 1*

You were the teacher shown on the videotape. You now need to prepare for the post-observation meeting with your supervisor. Using your completed observation form,

1 Note particularly some of the good things that you did.
2 Prepare to explain some of the things that did not go well.

At the post-observation meeting you also wish to discuss *one* of the following issues with your supervisor.

1 You are concerned about the fact that there are some students in this class who are much slower than the others.
2 The textbook you are using is not very good.
3 You are hoping for a promotion.

Select one appropriate issue and prepare to discuss that and the classroom observation at the meeting with your supervisor.

---

POST-OBSERVATION MEETING: *Role Play 2*

You have observed a videotaped lesson and completed the observation form. Now you need to prepare for the post-observation meeting.

1 Read through the model below, which outlines a step-by-step procedure for conducting the post-observation meeting. Indicate the questions/statements you would like to use for your meeting.
2 Working with the observation form and the model, prepare to role-play the post-observation meeting.

---

development were revealed in their authoritarian role, and those who wanted to try a new approach were given some guidance and rehearsal in doing that. In particular, we ensured that observers went through the four stages of climate-setting, review, problem-solving, and goal-setting. Too often post-observation meetings tend to halt after the review, and no positive arrangements are made for the future. When appropriate, and in some cases necessary, we also referred back to the 'One-Minute Manager' principles, and the need for both the observation and post-observation meetings to refer to specific behaviour and be positive in nature—'catch people doing something right', rather than always trying to 'catch people doing something wrong'.

## Workshop summary

Here, we reviewed the workshop objectives and discussed how close we had come to achieving them. As this was the last of the three workshops, we also necessarily reviewed the workshop programme and how effective it had been. Our emphasis was on positive achievements:

- The identification of observation problems—subjectivity, inconsistency among observers, lack of observer preparation, and lack of effectiveness in producing improved teaching.

---

*Model for conducting a post-observation meeting*

| OBSERVER ROLE | SAMPLE STATEMENTS/QUESTIONS |
|---|---|
| Climate-setting | How do you feel it went? |
| | What do you think about the class you were teaching? |
| Review | What were your objectives? |
| | How successful do you think you were in achieving them? |
| | What do you think about the suitability of the materials you were using? |
| | Talk me through the lesson … |
| | Here's some of the data I collected … |
| | I liked the way you … |
| | That was nicely handled. |
| | The class seemed to have a difficulty with this … |
| Problem-solving | Looking back, what might you have done differently? |
| | What do you think are the areas we should work on/develop? |
| Goal-setting | What are you going to do when you teach this class again? |
| | What should we focus on in the next observation? |

---

- The presentation of some solutions—pre-observation meetings, systematic observations with a form which focuses on specific behaviour, and more effective post-observation meetings.
- The identification and practice of strategies for conducting more effective pre- and post-observation meetings.

We could not ignore the slow progress, however, and recommended that workshop participants practise more with the observation form, joint observations to improve their reliability, and with the pre- and post-observation meeting strategies.

## Conclusions

A great amount of research, time, and effort had gone into developing the classroom observation workshops. Undoubtedly participant knowledge and awareness of the issues had been raised. In particular, participants had been made more aware of their own biases and subjectivity, the need for observation procedures, and an observation form to control these. Finally, they had practised some post-observation meeting techniques. Two and a half days of observer training, however, were clearly insufficient to change attitudes and improve observer objectivity and reliability. Some of the reasons for this lack of progress may relate only to our own teaching situation, but others, I suspect, have a more general relevance.

First, a systematic and objective approach to observation requires a level of expertise, effort, and time which many supervisors of teachers really do not feel is necessary. They pay lip-service to staff development and to the 'improving' aspects of observation. But 'drop-in' observations and subjective 'rating scales' are much easier for them to work with.

Secondly, supervisors of teachers tend to be more resistant to training than other groups of supervisors. They have university degrees and teaching qualifications—haven't they received enough training? Moreover, the world of education tends to be a 'world unto itself' and teachers and their supervisors often fail to realize that they may learn something from other worlds. Indeed, the issue of classroom observation is remarkably similar to the issue of performance review in the world of business and industry. Just as traditionally subjective classroom observations and meetings fail to improve teacher performance, so traditionally subjective methods of performance review fail to improve employee performance. The strategies for improving performance review—goal-setting, more specific and objective review forms, and the training of supervisors—can certainly be used to improve classroom observation.

Thirdly, supervisors of teachers tend to see themselves as administrators rather than as senior staff with important training responsibilities. A study of over a hundred ESL administrators (Reasor 1986) showed that the predominant style was a 'separated' style, oriented towards rules and procedures. Such a style is not characterized by good interpersonal skills: as classroom observers, administrators often sit in judgement on teachers, and lack the skills or confidence to assist and play a staff-development role. This is particularly detrimental in terms of the orientation and training of new teachers. Too often new staff are left to sink or swim, and the classroom observer behaves as a judge and a threat rather than as a guide or mentor.

Fourthly, supervisors question the feasibility of systematic observation, in particular, the amount of time it might take. Systematic observation, however, need not take more time—in most cases a large number of short, subjective, and unproductive observations would be replaced by a smaller number of quality observations.

At the conclusion of this series of workshops we felt that not only a lot more work needed to be done in training classroom observers, but that much more needed to be done in training senior teachers. In particular, they would benefit from the type of supervisory-skills training courses provided for other supervisors. Courses in time management, oral presentation skills, and supervisory techniques like 'coaching' (particularly important in the observation process) certainly seem as relevant to supervisors of teachers as they are to supervisors elsewhere. Indeed, to a large extent, improvements in education and training are dependent on improvements in the quality and effectiveness of teacher supervision. Our workshops on classroom observation were, we hope, a step in that direction.

*Originally published in Volume 43/2, 1989*

## Acknowledgements

I wish to acknowledge the invaluable assistance of my colleague, Michel Bekhazi, in the development and implementation of the classroom observation workshops.

# 17

# Talking shop: pre-service teaching experience and the training of supervisors

## CAROLINE BODÓCZKY
## & ANGI MALDEREZ

HEDGE: *Yesterday you had a training day. What was it for? What was the training?*

MALDEREZ: It was a special day in many ways as we had both last year's group of COTs and this year's group. Each of us worked with one of the groups.

HEDGE: *Perhaps you could explain what exactly a* COT *is?*

BODÓCZKY: Yes, it's a word we use for co-trainer because we didn't like the word 'supervisor'. We wanted to get away from the idea of hierarchy so we tried to find a new word and we called them co-trainers. That became COT, which is a very convenient little word.

HEDGE: *So a* COT *is a supervisor of teaching practice but rather different from a traditional supervisor?*

BODÓCZKY: Yes, the reason we started to train the COTs is that our teacher training scheme is new and the whole idea of teaching practice … we call it teaching experience … is different from what has happened before, at least in Hungary. Our trainee teachers take a class in a school, working in pairs, and they teach the class for the whole school year, not just individual lessons, which was the traditional model.

HEDGE: *So the trainees are actually responsible for a class for the whole year?*

BODÓCZKY: Yes, the number of hours depends on the particular school. We stipulate a maximum of five contact hours, an hour being a forty-five minute teaching session, every week. In some schools it's actually six, depending on how they block their lessons. We had to go along with what the school wanted on that.

HEDGE: *But, basically, the trainees deal with the reality of being with a class and teaching a programme through several lessons a week?*

BODÓCZKY: Yes, in practice it's three times a week and they are the only people teaching the class. They are totally responsible for it. That's why we call it teaching experience rather than teaching practice. It's not a trial-run practice where the class teacher is always on hand should difficulties arise. It's an authentic experience where the full responsibility lies with the trainees. The COT stays in the background as a support and as a trainer.

HEDGE: *Presumably the COT is somebody who is in the school and knows the school?*

BODÓCZKY: Yes, the COTs are school teachers and we decided it probably wasn't enough to expect them to supervise without some form of training. Previously in Hungary the universities had particular schools designated as training schools. The better teachers got jobs there and, as they became more experienced, they took on trainees for the supervisory work. However, they were not actually trained themselves in supervisory responsibilities. We felt, as our scheme is both new and much longer, that training was desirable, particularly because the COTs don't act as models. We've moved away from the craft model of teacher training.

MALDEREZ: Our new teaching experience scheme had to be responsible towards the schools, the pupils, and the parents. We needed to ensure that the children were learning.

BODÓCZKY: There had to be enough support for the trainees.

MALDEREZ: That's right. Also, I think we felt that the nature of the training we were giving to our teacher trainees was different from the type of training the COTs themselves had undergone. They had probably experienced the authoritarian supervisor, the one who tells you: That was right, that was wrong, and so on. With our teacher trainees we were trying to develop something different and we felt that our model of a supervisor and the traditional model would clash. So we needed to train the COTs.

HEDGE: *So are you really going for someone who is more of a guide, a counsellor, an adviser?*

MALDEREZ: Yes, exactly.

HEDGE: *What about the assessment element though? Isn't there a tension between the role of counsellor and the role of assessor? How do you resolve this?*

BODÓCZKY: Well, yes, there is an assessment element. Trainees have to be evaluated. The university requires it.

MALDEREZ: And that task is divided among the university-based classroom studies tutor, the COT, and the trainee. The tutor's duties fall into two categories. One is to help the trainee with ideas and preparation with teaching practice. And then we go into schools and visit a number of lessons over the whole year and act as an arbiter of standards. We give both the COTs and the trainees feedback on where they are with regard to the standard.

HEDGE: *That creates quite a useful distinction, then, between the two roles of counsellor and assessor.*

MALDEREZ: It does. It does, very much.

HEDGE: *The* COT *can be seen much more as a friend.*

MALDEREZ: As an ally, yes, but we've only resolved the tension between the two roles gradually.

BODÓCZKY: Yes, we've also had to revise the traditional model of the assessing role. We didn't want 'exam lessons' when the tutor from the university comes in as God and sits in judgement. So we devised the idea of having a series of lessons over the year to assess and we worked out an assessment sheet, so the whole process becomes more gradual.

MALDEREZ: And we used criteria to assist the process of development.

BODÓCZKY: Sets of criteria. But we don't call ourselves examiners any longer. In fact, what happened was that in our classroom studies sessions at the university we would troubleshoot about the trainees problems in the classroom, and inevitably developed a supportive relationship with them. When we actually visited them in their classrooms to act as evaluators and standard-bearers we couldn't cope with the tension between roles. What we do now is to go into lessons, be as supportive as we can and discuss what needs to be done.

MALDEREZ: And we leave it to the COT and the trainees to work together to devise strategies for bringing up to scratch whatever aspect of the teaching is not yet standard.

HEDGE: *Do you do follow-up sessions with the trainees after the class?*

BODÓCZKY: The COT leads them and we sit in, and at the end we discuss together our perceptions of where the trainee is in relation to the standards. Incidentally, the COTs developed the criteria with us so that we have a common understanding of those issues.

MALDEREZ: I think the selection of COTs is an important issue here. We set about the selection process by advertizing for interested teachers. We visited applicants, watched them in class, and in interviewing them we were looking for qualities such as openness, flexibility, and so on.

BODÓCZKY: We got a good response but we needed an awful lot of people. We have about one hundred trainees a year. So we hit on the idea of creating pairs because pairing would, in any case, provide each trainee with a partner's support. And each COT would work with two pairs so we needed twenty-five COTs.

MALDEREZ: We ended with something like thirty-four and took twenty-eight. We expected a drop-out rate and, as we predicted, some people were surprised they were expected to read articles, do tasks and observe peers. They were expecting something more like a traditional lecture series.

HEDGE: *Are the COTs paid and is it a reasonable enhancement of salary?*

BODÓCZKY: They are now. It could be more but it's a lot better than nothing. And they have a reduction in teaching hours but are paid full salaries.

HEDGE: *So yesterday was a training day for COTs, old and new?*

MALDEREZ: Yes. The COTs we trained last year, who are carrying out support roles in school this year, come in about every six weeks.

BODÓCZKY: We do some input, we discuss business. Yesterday we did a general evaluation of the whole COT project. We didn't want to structure the feedback too much so we asked them to write a questionnaire themselves. Yesterday's session was spent doing that. They wrote a questionnaire about the role of COTs and the COT training, which will be administered on themselves.

HEDGE: *What exactly were the aims of the COT training course? What were the duties you were training them for?*

MALDEREZ: Well, apart from what you might call day-to-day comfort and support, they would introduce the trainees to the school and the staff, help with lesson planning, choice of materials and so on, observe lessons and give feedback, troubleshoot when necessary, organize remedial work, and write progress reports for the university. During the course we also had to make sure they knew about the course their trainees had followed and about current EFL methods and materials.

HEDGE: *And how would you characterize the course you designed for the* COT*s?*

BODÓCZKY: Well, we planned that a significant part of the course would be negotiated. We used a questionnaire to decide on which methodology topics to update in our weekly sessions. And feedback was an important element in the course. At the end of every session the COTs gave us written feedback sheets and at the beginning of every session we responded to the feedback.

MALDEREZ: So they could bring out issues, make comments and requests, and we could do the same. We shaped the course in that way, through a constant feedback dialogue.

HEDGE: *So the* COT *course has an element of awareness-raising about contemporary approaches.*

BODÓCZKY: But the chief component was the development of trainer skills: observation, feedback, counselling, and evaluation. This is a really useful element because it gives us a shared metalanguage for thinking and talking about classroom and supervisory work. We also use video-based role plays and have compiled a workbook with selected readings and think sheets (see Appendix). These referred COTs to three articles by Bamber, Bowers, and Gebhard which had helped us to shape the principles of the course.

MALDEREZ: We assigned the core readings at different stages of the course and asked participants to work through the think sheets with a work partner. Then, at the following session, the COTs would work in groups to discuss, share insights, raise issues, and formulate action plans. For example, we chose the Bamber article to encourage the COTs to think about the profile of a teacher trainer. Having read the article, feedback from COTs contained questions like: If self evaluation is the most valuable form of evaluation, how can I help my trainees to do this? They began to realize that evaluation is a skill which needs time and practice to develop. The Bowers article introduced COTs to the HORACE framework for beginner supervisors: Hear (H) Observe (O) Record (R) Analyse (A) Consider (C) and Evaluate (E). The article by Gebhard expands the range of interaction possible at different stages of HORACE and after HORACE.

After reading this and watching a video of a variety of supervisors at work, our COTs requested time to work out the categories of questions you might use in different styles before carrying them out in role play.

BODÓCZKY: However, the course is not reading based. The readings simply provide support for the active workshops. Also, these were our original think sheets. As our ideas develop we're moving away from the HORACE model to one that fits our own needs more closely. So our workbook restructures as we go along.

HEDGE: *The course for COTs aims at providing them with the skills to assist trainee teachers during teaching experience. But how does the teaching experience fit into the degree scheme as a whole? Is it in the final year?*

MALDEREZ: Yes, it is.

HEDGE: *Do the trainees have any classroom visits early on? Or any experience to help them find out if they are going to feel at home in a classroom?*

MALDEREZ: Yes, in the second year there is a methodology block that includes micro-teaching. There is also a component called Classroom Studies I. This takes them into schools to observe classes and try out observation techniques which they will use in a classroom research project in their third year. They can also be involved with a class and perhaps take over a class. In fact, they all get a chance to micro-teach, at both primary and secondary levels. They get a taste of both. We train for both Hungarian primary schools, which go up to fourteen years of age, and for the secondary school level. So our methodology component has to address both levels.

HEDGE: *I asked because one of the criticisms frequently made of pre-service teacher training courses is that you don't actually find out whether you are going to be able to stand on your own feet in a classroom right until the end of the course ... by which time you have invested years of your life in something you may not be suited to.*

BODÓCZKY: Yes, I think we are incredibly lucky. Because CETT is a new institute and there are no precedents we've had great autonomy and flexibility. It's very much a pilot project, this three-year course and the COT training that goes with it, inspired by our head Péter Medgyes. Obviously, there are some Ministry constraints but we've been able to build on our own ideas. So, as far as the methodology training is concerned, we're able to provide trainees with an opportunity to do a bit of training in school—enough to get a taste.

HEDGE: *You explained that trainees work in pairs on the actual teaching experience in their final year and that the pairing can be very supportive. Are the trainees self-selecting in the pairs or do you think long and hard about how to pair people up?*

BODÓCZKY: We send a form to trainees asking them to choose their partner from among the colleagues they have got to know during the first two years of the course. One problem is that at the end of the second year there is a very stiff language exam and we lose a number of trainees along the way. This means that some people get partners they have not chosen. Partner selection, in fact, is one of the developing aspects of the project. Some of the current trainees are doing work on pair planning and teaching for their research project and, in future, we might be able to use their work to guide selection more precisely.

HEDGE: *The classroom research projects seem to be one of the innovative aspects of the training. Would you like to say more about them?*

MALDEREZ: Well, one of our objectives in having the longer teaching experience is to build up to the initial year of teaching. Research has shown that the first year is a survival year and there's a substantial drop-out from the teaching profession. We don't want our teachers to drop out. So one of our aims is that they develop a sense of professionalism and the knowledge, the skills, and the confidence to be able to teach and stand on their own feet at the end of the year. We want them to be able to continue their own development. So we thought an extended study involving research and reflection would be a useful part of that development process.

BODÓCZKY: Yes, and it was a productive way of using the university regulation that a degree must have a thesis. Our teachers receive a degree at the end of the course.

HEDGE: *Can you give some examples of the topics they have chosen to research?*

MALDEREZ: One of the trainees has been trying to find out why it is that she and her partner … who is actually her boyfriend … can't teach together. The other pair of trainees in the same school are planning and teaching extremely well together so there is a marked contrast. She has decided to focus on the planning process and is considering factors like fundamental beliefs, interpersonal skills, and so on.

HEDGE: *Is she studying the other pair as well?*

MALDEREZ: Yes, she has tapescripts of their planning sessions and her own with her partner and is very excited about the data. There is all this information about how successful planning takes place and we don't normally see this because it's usually inside the individual teacher's head. She has some fascinating data.

BODÓCZKY: We want to publish the good ones eventually in order to share ideas with other teachers and trainers.

MALDEREZ: Another trainee is using story-telling as a teaching technique, getting her students to participate in a series of story-telling activities. She records the sessions, takes field notes, and collates feedback from her notes with feedback from the students.

BODÓCZKY: Some are focusing on particular activities and evaluating how effective they are. For example, using games as a testing device.

HEDGE: *And will there be a chance for trainees to read each other's projects?*

BODÓCZKY: Yes, they'll be in the library.

HEDGE: *You said earlier that you were asking COTs to evaluate their role in the programme. Have you been monitoring trainees' responses as well, for example, to the teaching experience component?*

MALDEREZ: Yes, on the whole we've had very positive feedback about the COTs. Their role is seen as valuable and supportive. It's also interesting to see a change in perception about the length of the teaching experience. In the first semester, when the scheme first started, the trainees thought a year was too long. Now they can see the reasons for the length. In fact, at one point, we started to question whether trainees should teach a primary class in one semester and a secondary class in the other. This is something of an issue. For example, a headmaster in a secondary school might ask: Where did you do your training practice? And if the applicant teacher says: In a primary school, he may well say: Well, no thank you very much.

BODÓCZKY: But when we asked trainees about this possibility they said: Oh no, we couldn't leave our students. We don't want to do that.

HEDGE: *So they've clearly got the feel of teaching a class. They want to see the students through the whole year to the end. That's the professionalism coming out.*

BODÓCZKY: That's right. And the other thing ... some of them are making contracts with the school and agreeing to go on teaching the class the next year because they don't want to leave them, which is lovely.

HEDGE: *What have you, as trainers, particularly enjoyed about your involvement with an innovatory scheme?*

MALDEREZ: Oh, the people. The amazing dedication of the teachers in Budapest, with no money and already doing another three jobs in this multiple-job economy. That has been both incredible and humbling for me.

BODÓCZKY: Yes, I think that is what I would say. And the fact that we actually have a say in what we do, which has been very challenging. We can bring ideas in front of colleagues and say: Look, would you agree? Do you think this is a good idea?

MALDEREZ: And I have learned so many skills during the COT course.

BODÓCZKY: Yes. I think for Angi and I the cream of it has been the COT course. It's something new for us, not ordinary teacher training. We are going into areas which are to do with counselling, how to give non-judgemental feedback. And we've been able to watch people ... people with an authoritarian model behind them, gradually changing in front of our eyes. They write development reports during the course and there are times when these are so moving. And a bit frightening, actually, to know the training is having this effect on them. It gives us a huge responsibility, bigger than I have ever felt before, towards what we are doing, how effective we are being, and how careful we need to be.

*Originally published in Volume 48/1, 1994*

## Note

In this interview the authors develop points raised in 'New style teaching experience and the training of supervisors in Hungary'. IATEFL Teacher Trainers SIG Newsletter. No. 8/9: Spring/Summer 1993.

# *Appendix 1*

## *Supervision: COT Core Reading 1*
Training the trainers (Bamber 1987)

### THINK SHEET

*Before you read*

What are some of the differences between a teacher and a teacher trainer?

*Introduction*
Bamber divides supervision into three main skills. What are they?

| Name of skill | Knowledge needed |
| --- | --- |
| 1 | |
| 2 | |
| 3 | |

He considers _____ the most difficult because it requires s_____, s_____, and

s_____.

Which do you think *you* will find the most difficult?

*Five 'musts' for teacher training*

1 Language teacher competence.

   Two components: _____

   _____

2 Adopt a flexible approach.
   Skim this section. (Don't worry about different kinds of supervision, we'll return to that in another article.) Note some key words/concepts in this section. We'll start:
   open-minded

3 Be sympathetic (to trainees' problems).
   What ways can you think of to become more sympathetic to a trainee's problems?
   What do you understand by 'diplomatic language'?

4 Establish relationship of mutual trust between themselves and trainee.
   How?
   Is it feasible? (see next section)

5 Be aware of what is feasible.
   What is the caution in this section?
   Is this relevant to you/us?

*Three underlying principles*

1  The ultimate aim of a training programme is the continual professional growth of the teacher.
   Any ideas on how you will make yourselves 'redundant', that is, enable your trainees to continue their professional development without your help?

2  The most valuable form of evaluation is self evaluation.
   Do you agree? What do you think you could do to help your trainees self evaluate?

3  There is no substitute for hands-on experience.
   Hence the whole concept of the year-long teaching experience for our students, your role, and the reason we are asking you to do this 'theory-reading' in your own time, so that we can practise in valuable session time! (Incidentally, you have all had recent experience of being on the receiving end of one very specific kind of observation. We will reflect more on this later.)

NOTES

*What I want to know now:* _____

*What I want to do now:* _____

## Supervision: COT *Core Reading 2*
Developing perceptions of the classroom: observation and evaluation, training and counselling (Bowers 1987)

THINK SHEET

*Introduction: The nature of counselling*

What do you understand by 'counselling' in our context? (Try to define it.)
How important do you think this will be for your future COT role?

*The need for a paradigm*

Make notes on the three recurrent pitfalls for the new counsellor, and the lessons to be learnt from them (criteria).

| Pitfalls | Criteria |
| --- | --- |
| 1 | |
| 2 | |
| 3 | |

*Step One: H and O*

Who are you 'hearing and observing'?
What is 'ACME'?

List the questions you can ask yourself as you listen to the trainee before the lesson.

A: _____

C: _____

M:_____

E: _____

How can these 'thought questions' be used?

*Step Two: R and A*

Rank these methods for recording your observations in order, according to which methods you think most useful with trainees:

    Diary studies
    Structured narrative and case studies
    Count-coding
    Time-lapse coding
    Rating systems
    Transcript systems.

Which system(s) would you use:
– to give a trainee feedback on TTT (Teacher Talking Time)?
– as a trial run before an exam lesson?

*Step Three: C and E*

Considering the evidence:
What is the first question the observer should ask the teacher before offering advice?

Evaluation means measuring against a standard. On which of the three levels: *individual, system,* or *professional* will we (COTs, Budapest) most need to establish a standard?

*After HORACE*

Consultation: The importance of the four SSSSs.
Make notes for yourself.

S  _____

S  _____

S  _____

S  _____

Remediation: The three TTTs

T  _____

T  _____

T _____

Which will you use most? Why? How?

NOTES

*What I want to know now:*_____

*What I want to do now:* _____

## Supervision: COT *Core Reading 3*
Models of supervision: choices (Gebhard 1990)

THINK SHEET

*Before you read*

Discuss/describe/make notes on the kinds of supervision you have experienced. What were they for? How did you feel? Were they useful to you? Why/why not?

*Introduction*

List the six models Gebhard is going to describe.

1 _____    3 _____    5 _____

2 _____    4 _____    6 _____

Can you guess already which was/were the model(s) you experienced?

*Directive supervision*

What does the supervisor do?

1 _____    2 _____    3 _____

Gebhard lists three problems with this kind of supervision. What are they?

1 _____    2 _____    3 _____

Any more? _____

_____

_____

_____

*Notions of good teaching*

'It nevertheless appears that most people, including teachers, supervisors, school administrators, the owner of the neighbourhood hang-out, and the person on the street believe they can identify good teaching when they see it.'

Why? _____

What are the implications for us? _____

*Alternative supervision*

Why do beginning teachers feel the need to be told what to do?

1 _____ 2 _____

What effect does giving a variety of alternatives have?

1 _____ 2 _____

Which three techniques that Fanselow uses to generate alternatives are mentioned?

1 _____ 2 _____ 3 _____

'If teachers are provided with strategies that give a way to understand the consequences of what they do, teachers can gradually rely on themselves to make teaching decisions.'

What evidence can/do teachers use to 'understand the consequences of what they do'?

What strategies can you think of to provide trainees with?

*Collaborative supervision*

Cogan believes teaching is mostly _____

Who identifies the problem?
In the series of events:

a. problem identification
b. hypothesis formation
c. experiment solution x
d. consider effects
e. evaluation solution x
f. repeat (if necessary) from c

Which stages are not mentioned here?

What do you think about the focus on problems only? Realistic? Unfortunate?

*Non-directive supervision*

How can non-directive supervision help the relationship between the supervisor and the supervised?

What does the supervisor actually do?

Which techniques from this approach at which stage of HORACE might be useful with our trainees?

*Creative supervision*

Make your own notes on this section.

*Self-help*

What is the aim of this kind of supervision?

Which of the following reasons for lesson observation do you think best suit(s) this model?

| | |
|---|---|
| initial *training* | of trainee by 'expert' |
| | of 'expert' by trainee |
| in-service *development* | of and by peers |
| | of teacher by 'expert' |
| | of 'expert' by teacher |
| assessment/*evaluation* | of teacher/trainee by 'expert' |

*Conclusions*

Which model(s) can you envisage using with trainees? When? Why? If you think 'it depends', what will it depend on?

At what stage(s) of HORACE would your choice of model make a difference?

NOTES

*What I want to know now:*_____

*What I want to do now:* _____

# 18

## Researching heterogeneity: an account of teacher-initiated research into large classes

B. NAIDU, K. NEERAJA,
J. SHIVAKUMAR, & V. VISWANATHA[1]

## Introduction

We are a group of teachers involved in teaching English at tertiary-level institutions in Bangalore, South India. We belong to a network of teachers who have come together to advance our professional development. In this paper we discuss a collective research project undertaken between July 1989 and February 1990. The process of sharing our individually substantive teaching experience and retrospectively interpreting it proved to be an exciting phase in our group's life. We intuitively knew that the process we had gone through was rich and complex, and productive both in cognitive and social terms. We thought it might be worthwhile to share this experience with teachers in other parts of the world.

## The background

All of us are members of the Classroom Interaction Group (CIG) which is a special interest group of the English Language Teaching Community (ELTC), Bangalore. The ELTC is a loose network of three small special interest groups. In addition to the CIG, there are the Grammar Group and the Literature Group. The ELTC has thirty members and is committed to staying small and locally manageable. It is based on the principles of decentralization and rotating leadership.[2]

Though the CIG had been meeting desultorily since June 1987, it was only in July 1989 that the group stabilized with the decision to work on a collective research project, based on our common teaching experiences. As large classes (of over a hundred students) constitute a daily reality for four members of the group, we decided to focus on our experience of teaching large classes. Earlier, members of the group had responded to two questionnaires on large classes for the Lancaster–Leeds Research Project (Coleman 1987; Allwright 1988) and this served to heighten awareness of our problems.

## Our research process

In the following sections of our paper we aim to reconstruct the collective process we went through over 18 meetings in eight months. We are keenly aware that we are retrospectively making sense of an experience which, at various points, was not very clear to us. As we see it now, the process was an amalgam of clear plans and spontaneous digressions, a collage of structured and unstructured activity. Our collective introspection and consolidation yielded the following stages.

## Stage one: Individual articulation of our experience

In this first stage, which involved four meetings, each of roughly two hours, we talked about our experiences, both positive and negative, of teaching large classes. Though the accounts were largely anecdotal, they were shaped by two questions which we had identified at our first meeting. These questions were:

1 What problems do I face in large classes?
2 What strategies have I evolved to cope with these problems?

We found that we needed to give details to each other on the classes we taught. We referred, for example, to the mixed cultural milieu of our students, the largely apathetic attitudes of teachers and learners, the differences we perceived in teaching 'general' English to Science versus Arts students, and the widespread lack of motivation among our students.

The problems we articulated were diverse: the feeling that many students in our lessons were under-involved, our inability to plan and cope with written work, the issue of relating some of the prescribed literary texts to the students' life experiences, and our inability to handle a wide range of student responses to our questions in class. Our 'solutions', too, were varied, and probably motivated by differing preoccupations. We talked of 'converting textbook tasks into processes', 'giving clear instructions', 'keeping questions open-ended', 'writing up new ideas on the blackboard', 'encouraging students to work in pairs and triads', 'separating comprehension from written production'.

We were struck by the spontaneity of our articulation. Individual presentations and ensuing discussion often exceeded the time allocated. We realized that our tendency to abandon time-keeping revealed the value of this kind of experiential sharing in building up the necessary background knowledge for a group research project.

## Stage two: Identification of topics for research

In this stage of our exploration we decided to identify topics for deeper discussion. This was done by consolidating issues that had persistently come up or had been extensively discussed at stage one. We identified three such areas:

1  Handling the 'heterogeneity' of our classes.
2  Developing our students' writing skills.
3  Handling our students' responses to our questions in class.

One member (BN) was then asked to consolidate from her notes all the interesting points and telling episodes related to the areas we had identified. (We need to state here that all of us kept detailed notes of our meetings, a practice already part of the ELTC's way of functioning.) BN's presentation stressed her perceptions of the dominant concerns for each member of the group, as well as shared preoccupations. For example, on the issue of 'handling our students' responses', she noted our anxiety about not tapping all the responses pertinent to a specific question, rejecting a student's response either by ignoring or dismissing it out of hand, imposing our views on the learners, and consolidating diverse responses within the class.

The value of this stage of our project was the retrospective structure we were forced to bring to our first anecdotal accounts of classroom experiences. In this way, we recovered a set of priorities from the rich preliminary discussions. This delimitation was, we believe, a crucial early step in our research process.

## Stage three: Planning the project

After identifying the central issues for our research, we began to consider the design features of our project. One of our members (ER), who had collected data from teachers in Bangalore for the Lancaster–Leeds

Large Classes Project, presented her perceptions of how we should go about our research. Her view that we should take a qualitative, ethnographic approach was supported by the rest of the group.

We discussed in great depth what it meant for us to do ethnographic classroom-centred research. These are some of the major decisions we took:

1  We would concern ourselves with recovering the 'pedagogic hypotheses' that lay below our teaching practices.

2  We were clear that we were looking not merely at some phenomena of large classes, but more specifically at our own problems and solutions.

3  We were not specifically interested in the 'spectacular' events of our classrooms, but the recurring patterns that would enable us to describe and comprehend our everyday reality.

We also decided that we would observe each other's lessons, but postponed discussing the logistics of observation until we had a clearer idea of what we wanted to observe and why.

## Stage four: Refining our understanding of one issue

By consensus, we agreed to take up first the question of heterogeneity. All of us considered it to be a central problem, but we had not so far sustained a discussion of the exact nature of the problem.

We began our discussions with the hazy notion that large classes are always heterogeneous. We realized, consequently, that what we needed to consider was how heterogeneity was manifested in our classes. To facilitate this exploration we decided to spell out our positive and negative experience of heterogeneous classes, using concrete examples and generalizing, on the basis of these experiences, the constraints that each of us faced in handling our classes.

### Isolating one manifestation of heterogeneity

This round of presentations revealed that one recurring problem was the presence of students with varied abilities and attitudes, which resulted in our feeling that we did not 'reach out' to all our learners in the course of our teaching. We experienced an acute sense of inadequacy in handling in real time the varied responses of our learners in whole-class discussion. Our dissatisfaction led us logically to consider the factors that determine the heterogeneous responses of our students.

## Understanding the factors contributing to heterogeneity

For the first time we engaged in a serious discussion of the causes of heterogeneity. (This part of our paper draws substantively from KN's informal write-up on the causes of heterogeneity.) We discovered that heterogeneity is the manifestation of several complex forces at work, both external (socio-economic, familial, and cultural) and internal (motivation, aptitude, attitude, proficiency, and life experience).

We also discovered that several factors within the classroom contribute to heterogeneity. We wondered why the same learner responds so differently to different teachers. We speculated on the effect that we have on our learners. We accepted the possibility that our own competence, our attitude to particular students, our state of preparedness and frame of mind in specific lessons could also shape our learners' differing responses in class.

To the influence of the teacher, we added factors relating to teaching content. As most of our teaching is based on prescribed literary texts, we reflected on the effect of theme, genre, task-type, and task-level, on student responses. For instance, we commented on how a poetry lesson often lends itself to a greater range of responses than an essay. The questions we ask also influence the patterns of responses. For instance, while teaching a prose lesson, we found that the kinds of questions we asked ('information-seeking' or 'evaluative') determined which students volunteered to respond, and the probing questions we directed at each other during this phase, and our analysis, turned us for a time into amateur sociologists of our own classrooms, a role that we had never systematically engaged in or even envisaged before.

The 'outcome' of this phase of our discussion was a heightened awareness that teaching/learning is an extremely complex process, highly differentiated in terms of teacher and learner inputs and expectations, and teaching and learning 'styles'.

## Our classroom practices

Having explored the factors leading to heterogeneity, we began to talk about what we actually do when we teach English using the prescribed texts.

We discovered that rather than paraphrase the texts (a pervasive practice among teachers) we asked questions and invited responses from our students. By reflecting on what we actually did with these responses we discovered that we had widened the range of our talk. In our classroom

efforts to consolidate, we were forced to repeat student responses, reformulate, illustrate, and relate them to other ideas, thus making them
available to a wider spectrum of learners at their own level. This process
of negotiation aimed at bridging the gap between the heterogeneous
levels in the class without attempting to banish heterogeneity.

Our discussions moved into another related area of discovery. All of
us realized that we had been using a methodology in our classes which
we called the 'interactive mode'. In addition, we recognized that our
classrooms were teacher-fronted. This led us to an ethnographic
description of the teacher-fronted lecture classroom. The ability to
describe the differences between these two types of classroom and our
personal awareness of what they were actually like yielded perhaps the
most valuable generalizations about our classroom procedures.

## Differences between the teacher-fronted lecture mode and the teacher-fronted interactive mode

In the teacher-fronted lecture classroom, one-way communication from
teacher to learners is the norm. The teacher is primarily engaged in
transmitting content without much of an attempt to negotiate with
learners. Sometimes the input might be beyond and outside student
grasp or need. This approach, we discovered, is convergent: the version
of the text is the teacher's version, which is presented as an authoritative
view of the text. Such a classroom process may be desirable for two reasons—it solves the problem of discipline by keeping learners 'occupied'
and it imposes 'homogeneity' on what is really a heterogeneous group of
learners.

The assumptions underlying this mode of classroom activity are that
input becomes intake and that all learners learn in the same way, at the
same pace. We discovered that though such a classroom can be
described as successful because it keeps learners 'quiet', it ignores the
individuality of learners, their knowledge of their world, their level of
competence, and their learning styles.

We described the teacher-fronted interactive classroom in terms of
our own practices. We had unconsciously evolved strategies that did not
seek to 'homogenize' the class but which were concerned with enriching
the learning process. The learners' negotiation at three levels—with the
text, with peers, and with the teacher—converts classroom activities to
communicative processes. These processes acknowledge learners' interests, knowledge, levels of competence and limitations, and thus extends
the scope of interaction.

We saw that our activities are not geared merely to the subject (content) but also to learning. Divergent responses are valued as positive and enriching. Our strategies do not aim at keeping learners quiet, but at involving them in cognitively challenging activities which also call for affective involvement. We had chosen to operate as facilitators/challengers, rather than as transmitters/compilers. Though the management of learning is predominantly in our hands, the classroom environment is more democratic and fluid.

We realized later that all these generalizations were made possible through our disciplined effort to research our past teaching experience through talk. At this stage, we did not observe lessons or discuss future plans for improving our teaching. We were concerned with seeing the recurring patterns in our teaching and linking them to our assumptions about the relationship between teaching and learning. These assumptions were what we came to call our 'pedagogic hypotheses'.

## Stage five: Peer observation

Around October 1989, three months after we had started on our project we felt ready to sit in on each other's lessons. Our main purpose was to get a sense of how heterogeneity really 'looked' in practice, but we decided to focus on two areas:

1 How we used techniques to convert text into 'process'.

2 How we consolidated diverse oral responses in whole-class discussion.

We intended to note down our impressions both in real-time, and retrospectively, and to tape-record the lessons we observed. However, our plans could not be carried out fully due to various contingencies. We managed eventually to observe only two lessons. Both teachers (BN and JS) had described their classes as problematic, and gave us their perception of what made the interactive mode difficult to use in their classes.

### Class A

BN described her class as heterogeneous, in which half the students could be termed 'weak' in their use of English, a quarter average, and the rest articulate in degrees. It was a problematic class because its composition created an unusual mode of communication. The articulate learners were not willing to invest sustainedly in the interactive mode, feeling the pressure of so many 'wills' that remained quiet but became a powerful, silent majority. The interactive mode was successful in patches depending on the text (greater success with drama, very little success with essays).

BN felt that perhaps learners' perceptions of what the teacher is traditionally supposed to do (that is, transmit knowledge of content) unconsciously shaped the course of her lessons. Several learners may have seen the interactive mode as superfluous, that is, the teacher was not doing what she was supposed to do—explain chronologically, gloss all the difficult words, and dictate notes.

Perhaps they were looking for an authoritative view of the content (the teacher's) without the interruption of other learners' perceptions of the content. The divergence in views expressed might have confused them.

## Class B

JS described her 'problem class' as a batch of ninety students, mostly intelligent, motivated, quite insightful, keen on participating in group work, and other interactive activities. However, she found this class 'difficult to handle' for the following reasons:

1 She was unable to consolidate the responses of the enthusiastic students in a way that was beneficial to the other students.

2 Some students articulated their views clearly and precisely, but were unwilling to accommodate the views of less articulate students. This led to JS feeling that there were 'fixed boundaries of argumentation' beyond which the class could not move.

3 JS felt unable to evolve a framework within which she and her students could satisfactorily reconcile differing points of view.

4 She was concerned that several negative processes might be occurring in her lessons: domination by the more vocal students; feelings of insecurity among the less confident ones; her own attempts to placate some of the students leading to intolerance or submission.

When we went in to observe the lessons of BN and JS, therefore, we were already equipped with a picture in our minds of what to expect, and what particular mismatches worried these two teachers. The actual experience of teaching and observing was exciting and we all made copious notes. But again, due to our inability to stay on for detailed discussion after each lesson, we could not use our notes for feedback and analysis. Also, we could not analyse our taped data. In the near future we plan to transcribe and study some of this data. But even from this fragmentary experience we realized that every classroom observation is potentially revealing. In our later attempts to consolidate our first impressions, many interesting insights emerged.

## Insights gained

Some of the insights gained were:

1 Both lessons confirmed our view that these classes were widely heterogeneous, and had students with a range of abilities.

2 Both the teachers were indeed trying to use an interactive mode of teaching. They urged students to respond and tried to give value to their articulations (by writing up points on the blackboard, for example).

3 One of the teachers (JS) did seem to experience difficulty in consolidating learners' responses.

4 For reasons we have still to explore, BN's lesson turned out better than she herself had anticipated. She thought it was unusually 'patterned', a view that the observers concurred with.

5 On some points, there were differences in the teacher's and observers' impressions of the same episodes.

Our subsequent discussions of the observations always seemed to throw up further insights and issues. We believe that in peer observation the self-reflective and critical assessment made by each teacher prior to the collective discussion is valuable in its own right. It serves to heighten the teacher's awareness of her own practice. For the observer, seeing a colleague teach in a context similar to her own confirms her own experience and serves to legitimize her own understanding.

Our conclusion from this phase is that having made one attempt to conduct non-evaluative and supportive peer observation, we are now ready to go into it more systematically and realistically in the future.

## *Stage six: Moving from facilitative talk to writing*

We were so struck by our characterization of our own teaching that we decided to write it up as a first draft for a paper on heterogeneity. We collectively evolved a format to capture our insights. This format was no more than the outline of headings, given below:

Our definitions of heterogeneity
Nature of heterogeneity

Evidence of heterogeneity
Positive aspects of heterogeneity
Problematic aspects of heterogeneity
Personal comments.

We decided that we would each write a draft based on this outline, and anticipating our resistance to writing, we fixed a time (10 p.m.) at which we would all begin writing, each in our own home. This pressure was most constructive, and the outline initially facilitating. But we discovered that, after a point, the format was extremely constraining, and we each found our own ways of digressing from the agreed outline.

On examining the drafts we had produced, we discovered that there were several new insights that we had not articulated during our discussions or had only been peripherally aware of. It seemed as if the act of writing had enabled us to tap more fully our faintly-held perceptions so that they achieved a deeper level of conviction.

One of the drafts (VV's) made the most explicit attempt to spell out our new understanding which we then collectively formulated as a set of insights. While our discussions at stage four had brought us to a detailed description of our actual classroom practices, and a complex formulation of the differences between the teacher-fronted lecture mode and the teacher-fronted interactive mode, the act of writing recovered our reasons for using the interactive mode. We found ourselves talking about our beliefs and values as teachers.

## Our beliefs about heterogeneity

We discovered that for us heterogeneity is a positive phenomenon, rooted in reality. It reflects the uniqueness and individuality of each of our learners. By allowing heterogeneity to manifest itself (for example, in the divergent responses to our questions) we were actually fostering learner individuality. We realized that heterogeneity is the natural result when many minds are trying to come to grips with an idea through dialogue. Given the uniqueness of our learners (and of human beings, in general) any expectation of homogeneity would be unreasonable.

More importantly, we recognized that learning is personally meaningful only when individual frames of reference are involved in the learning. If our aim is not to produce unthinking learners who 'accept' everything the teacher says, then we must make the development of individuality an active goal of teaching. In other words, we found ourselves affirming that heterogeneity is not a necessary evil as we had thought it to be, but a desirable condition, immensely challenging to our pedagogic creativity.

## The need for a different notion of homogeneity to sustain heterogeneity

Our discovery about our changed attitude to heterogeneity, captured aphoristically in a statement we often repeated (Heterogeneity is a challenge to be faced, not a problem to be wished away!), did not blind us to the problematic nature of our situation.

The lecture mode (which we had all used but outgrown) did provide, we realized, an external 'discipline', within which the act of teaching could take place. At the least, the students maintained silence and appeared to be attentive. In our mode of interactive teaching, we could not guarantee this 'discipline'. We had to actively evolve a disciplined framework, which could foster learner individuality. We redefined our challenging problem more rigorously: How can we enable different learners to bring their own ways of understanding to the lesson within the real-time pressures of a large class? We realized that we needed a common framework within which to nurture learner individuality. In our teaching, several factors contributed to the establishment of this framework: minimally these were the common text, the tasks we set, our instructions, and the time-frame in which to accomplish the tasks. We therefore had created homogeneous learning contexts. In addition, we had to evolve over time, with each particular class, a discipline of a different kind. This requires that students:

1 truly listen to our questions and instructions;
2 listen to each other attentively;
3 accept our turn-allocating role;
4 express their ideas audibly.

We believe that it is possible to enable our students to see the value of this physical discipline. In our experience, most students submit willingly enough to these requirements, once they realize their value. There is also another kind of discipline that we felt we were fostering. We called this 'mental' discipline, and it required that students:

1 focus on the given task;

2 attempt to present their thoughts clearly;

3 react to other, especially, opposing views;

4 attempt to see the relation between the original question and various responses.

We thought that by enforcing this discipline we were developing our students' ability to think and analyse issues.

These two kinds of 'discipline', we believed, enabled the teaching–learning activity to proceed as a collective enterprise, in which a culture of dialogue could slowly evolve. We think that we have managed to establish this culture, in different degrees, in our own classes. The framework that enforces the need for physical and mental discipline constitutes the homogeneity that we believe draws out and supports heterogeneity.

## Our role as teachers

We realized that our role in sustaining both kinds of discipline and in ensuring a homogeneous framework is crucial. We catalogued the knowledge and skills we possessed (in varying degrees) and used in this central pedagogic role. These were:

1 an intimate knowledge of our students;
2 sound teaching instincts (which we glossed as 'ability to recognize and exploit learning opportunities');
3 skills of questioning (including range, appropriacy, and timing);
4 skills of moderating a discussion (involving stating, restating, reformulating, elaborating, reacting, highlighting, rejecting politely, and consolidating).

This articulation makes the teacher's role seem stupendous. It is. We also see that we are but identifying what we already do intuitively. By naming what we do we have recovered our practice, which otherwise might have been lost irretrievably (a fate we believe that many teachers have suffered). Further, we can now identify for ourselves what aspects of our practice we are confident of and what we need to strengthen. We can also account for our more satisfying lessons in terms of our appropriate and timely use of some of these skills. What for us has been most valuable is the awareness-raising exercise that we collectively experienced by articulating our unacknowledged repertoire of skills as teachers.

## Some clarifications

We have attempted to convey in this account a sense of homogeneity in *our* practice as teachers. To claim that all aspects of our individual practice are uniform would simply not be true. We recognized even as we shared our thoughts, and observed each other's lessons, that there were many points of difference in both perception and practice. For example, some of us use pair and group work as a supplement to teacher-fronted lessons, and many details of our practice even here are divergent. We have also intuitively recognized that the value we attach to 'affective' factors varies among ourselves. We plan to explore these differences systematically in the future.

What has united us in the account we have provided is one small area of our classroom experience, and one perceived problem. Our researching enabled us to see how much of this experience was indeed shared and how pervasive was our dissatisfaction with this one aspect of our teaching. As a result of our joint exploration we have a surer understanding of at least this area of our teaching lives.

Another issue we have worried about is the absence in our account of references to other research on heterogeneity and on large classes. At several points during our research we talked of the need for professional updating. Some of us studied some of the Lancaster–Leeds Large Classes Project reports, as well as other papers, but we intuitively felt that giving priority to a scholarly literature search would have diverted us from the pursuit of our faintly held ideas, a pursuit we consider more worthwhile at this stage of our research. Confident of our perceptions we now feel ready to share with, to confront, and dialogue with the insights of other researchers.

## Conclusion

In this concluding section of our paper, we would like to make explicit some propositions which we believe are generalizable across teaching contexts. We believe that:

1 As teachers, we possess a vast repository of classroom experience, which when shared with other teachers can lead to a body of theoretical insights and practical procedures.

2 As teachers, we can generate systematic knowledge about teaching in a collective research process.

3 Teacher research can often be purely reflective, involving a search for

one's pedagogic principles, and an interpretation of one's classroom experience in the light of one's past and current beliefs.

4 As teachers, we can set up our own research agendas, by identifying questions rooted in the problematicity of our teaching situations.

5 A small, supportive network of teachers facilitates teacher-initiated research.

6 By using talk deliberately and in a disciplined way, we can both recover our experience and 'frame' it in ways that enhance our understanding and improve our practice.

Finally, we end with the most general statement we have derived from our project: small-group talk and writing yield cognitive and social gains that far outweigh the difficulties of setting up and maintaining teacher groups.

Further, while groups that are committed to their own long-term survival will evolve forms of talk that sustain initial enthusiasm and ensure ongoing renewal, we believe that even transient groups (such as teachers on time-bound MA programmes, or those attending short-term workshops) can use disciplined talk creatively and productively.

*Originally published in Volume 46/3, 1992*

## Acknowledgements

Vanamala Viswanatha would like to acknowledge the influence of the Discourse Analysis Group (Bangalore 1981–86) and in particular, of Dr Michael Joseph in evolving the explanatory modes of talk and writing used in our project.

## Notes

1 Esther Ramani, one of the original authors of this article, has withdrawn her name from this republished version. She, and Michael Joseph, whose ideas are acknowledged in this paper, believe that the institutional pressure to publish has led to the overproduction (and reproduction) of 'expert knowledge', and to the disempowerment of teachers.

2 Further details about the ELTC are available in a report in the IATEFL TD Newsletter (1990) No. 12:13.

# PART THREE

# PRACTICE

*Issues in curriculum design
and development*

# PREVIEW

The word 'curriculum' means different things to different people. For some it has the relatively simple definition of a course of study, in other words, the programme presented to students. In this section, the wider reference is to various dimensions of curriculum practice: investigating learners' needs, setting learning goals, managing classroom activities, designing materials, facilitating a range of teachers' and learners' roles, and formulating procedures for evaluation of programmes.

The value of this wider concept of curriculum is that it suggests a model for the responsible planning of ELT programmes. Firstly, there is the need to formulate clear objectives which hold in view the desired outcomes of classroom learning, in other words, the knowledge, competencies, values, or qualities which a group of learners need or wish to acquire. Then a practical programme of activities is required to work towards the objectives. And, as an accompaniment to these two processes, teachers need to look for ways to evaluate and improve the learning experiences offered by the programme so that learners arrive at successful outcomes.

These aspects of professional practice are examined in the articles in this section. That the articles display a strong link between needs, aims and content is perhaps not remarkable. They are examples of principles and practice in a profession where a needs-based, student-centred approach has been well established for some time. However, what is perhaps noteworthy, and what reflects the main criterion for selection, is that they represent teachers reviewing, questioning, and appraising aspects of their work. Good language teachers have always taken the perspective of researchers, acknowledging that language teaching is a complex task and needs constant analysis of problems and experimentation with solutions.

These articles demonstrate reflective practice in relation to a range of problems. How can teachers ensure the development of communicative competence? Does a particular classroom activity work? What does learner centredness imply for the teachers' roles and for the learners' contribution? How can process models of second-language pedagogy be effectively implemented? What are the roles of teaching materials and how does the representation of language in them relate to language in the real world? How best can programmes be evaluated and revised?

## Characteristics of the communicative classroom

The 'communicative revolution' occurred many years ago in English language teaching but the debate about what constitutes a communicative classroom or a communicative task continues, informed in its progress by increasing insights from second-language acquisition studies.

KUMARAVADIVELU (Volume 47/1, 1993) addresses the problem of how to create genuine communication in the classroom. He suggests that teachers need a set of strategies, that is, plans for classroom activity derived from theoretical, empirical, and pedagogic knowledge about second-language learning which will help them to prepare classes. He goes on to present such a framework of strategies and then applies it in the analysis of two classroom episodes. Some of his strategies would be recognized by teachers as principles which have underpinned good practice for a long time but others have clearly derived from more recent insights into the way in which learners acquire languages. For example, his strategy to 'facilitate negotiated interaction between participants' links strongly to the notion of communication strategies and the need to give learners the opportunity to develop strategic competence through participating in meaningful interaction.

The article by GERBER (Volume 44/3, 1990b) on using role play in literature classes contains a transcript which demonstrates some of Kumaravadivelu's principles in practice. Here, the teacher provides learning opportunities by asking students to take on the roles of characters in the literature they have just read and to imagine that characters are reviewing their lives with each other. Language is practised in a contextualized fluency activity, students initiate interaction and become involved in such discourse features as clarification, confirmation, requesting, repairing, and so on. This is the stuff of the interaction hypothesis, that learners acquire new forms when input is made comprehensible through negotiating for meaning.

NOBUYOSHI and ELLIS (Volume 47/3, 1993) also set out a framework of characteristics, in their case for focused communication tasks, which they believe can facilitate learning as the teacher 'pushes' learners to produce more accurate output. They discuss a small-scale experiment which provides some evidence to suggest that pushing learners in this way can contribute to acquisition, as claimed by the comprehensible output theory. The methodology employed to 'push' students, through requests for clarification rather than through more traditional forms of error correction, holds implications for classroom procedures within the communicative approach.

All three articles have the same fundamental orientation, that of providing the means in the classroom for learners to practise language under 'real operating conditions'.

As well as an interest in communicative methodology, these articles also have in common a research perspective, an endeavour to observe and analyse the curriculum in action. This is a form of educational enquiry which has received much attention and support in recent years. It is one in which teachers test out their ideas in action and evaluate the outcomes. They thereby become 'participants' in research not just 'recipients' of research (Stern 1983).

Various terms have been used to describe the approach exemplified in the studies carried out by Gerber and Nobuyoshi and Ellis: 'reflective practice' as discussed in Part Two is one of them; 'action research' is another. Elliot (1991: 53) usefully describes the aims of action research in this way:

> A felt need, on the part of practitioners to initiate change, to innovate, is a necessary precondition of action research. It is the feeling that some aspect(s) of a practice needs to be changed if its aims and values are to be more fully understood, which activates this form of enquiry and reflection.

The explorations described by Gerber and Nobuyoshi and Ellis show typical features of action research: the process was initiated by teachers concerned to explore what they perceived as a problem in their own teaching situation; their interest is in improving the quality of experience for learners in the classroom; and the aim is improved practice. They are good examples of how motivated teachers can 'increase the richness, and therefore the relevance, of the body of knowledge we have of language teaching' (McDonough and McDonough, Volume 44/2: 108, 1990).

## Teacher and learner roles

### Learner-centred methodology

A trend in recent years, which has derived in part from the communicative approach in ELT and in part from notions of learner self-determination in education, has been the development of learner-centred approaches. One definition of learner centred has been Nunan's (1989c: 19):

> information by and from learners is used in planning, implementing and evaluating language programmes.

This implies the participation of learners in all aspects of the curriculum. But the concept of 'learner-centredness' is much debated.

A recent exchange of views in *ELT Journal* is representative of the debate. O'Neill (Volume 45/4, 1991) questions the new orthodoxy, that learner-centred methods are superior to teacher-fronted ones, in an article that commented on the 'worrying lack of evidence' from SLA studies which might support one over the other. TUDOR (Volume 47/1, 1993) replies to some of O'Neill's points. He approaches the term 'learner centred' from the four different perspectives of activity organization, of resource-based learning, of curriculum design and of a humanistic concern for affectively based methodology. He goes on to look at the teacher's role as learning counsellor and the responsibilities that role assumes.

The concept of role has, in fact, been one of the most pervasive in ELT literature in recent years. Learner-based methodology has substantially increased the range of roles that teachers and learners can play and it is common now to hear the terms 'guide', 'facilitator', 'informant', and 'resource', as well as 'instructor', 'presenter', and 'assessor'.

### Moves towards self-access learning

These new roles take on particular significance with moves towards resource-based learning in ELT contexts worldwide. One current view of learners is of people who can take on more responsibility for their own learning, who are capable of developing successful strategies for independent learning. Institutions which have acknowledged this capacity have created opportunities for independent learning through setting up self-access centres. The precise design and functioning of such centres has exercised the minds of many contributors to *ELT Journal*.

ASTON (Volume 47/3, 1993) discusses the involvement of learners in creating an effective self-access centre. He describes an experiment in which students, as part of project work, evaluated the resources of their university self-access centre and produced information leaflets for potential users. His emphasis is on learners' active contribution to rather than passive consumption of self-access resources.

Other contributors have provided practical suggestions from their own experience to inform colleagues in the profession. Miller and Rogerson-Revell (Volume 47/3, 1993) describe four systems for self-access centres and argue that the system chosen must fit the purpose and context. Lin and Brown (Volume 48/2, 1994) provide practical insights for teachers involved in producing self-access materials. Barnett and Jordan (Volume 45/4, 1991) give a case study of the self-access centre in their institution and argue the need for learner training. O'Dell (Volume 46/2, 1992) turns her attention to the problems faced by teachers when their organization introduces a self-access centre and proposes four solutions: induction material for teachers; ideas for lessons based on the self-access resources; counselling materials and staff seminars.

These articles represent the issues of self-access learning centres; the establishing of principles for their operation; the varying resource bases on which such centres can rest; the involvement of learners and the preparation of teachers. What the profession needs now is evaluation of this mode of learning: its effectiveness compared with classroom learning; the strategies used by learners working with self-access materials; whether or not self-access learning is culturally appropriate in all contexts; and what kind of resources work best. These are the questions which need to be addressed in the future.

## *Process approaches to writing*

Another focus of interest in recent years has been on process models of second-language pedagogy. Articles on the practicalities of teaching the language skills have always been a feature of *ELT Journal* but in recent years there has been clear concern to explore insights from research into the processes of comprehension, speaking, and writing and to formulate effective classroom procedures which build on these insights. Nowhere is this more evident than in the number of articles submitted to *ELT Journal* in recent years on the pedagogy of second-language writing. This has been substantial and pays testament to continuing interest in the topic. Such interest is indicative of the value accorded to writing, particularly for learning purposes in education. It is also indicative of the problems experienced by writers in expressing themselves successfully in a second language, and therefore of the issues for teachers in helping learners with the process of writing.

The concern to develop an effective pedagogy for second-language writing has been especially strong in educational contexts where the second language is the language of the classroom and of examinations, through which it performs a gate-keeping function. Learners able to perform successfully on written tests are able to pass through the gate to greater opportunities in learning and in life. KEH (Volume 44/4, 1990) focuses on writing in this context. Here, writing is an instrument in the process of learning and effective writing instruction at the college level has the crucial function of facilitating learning through the preparation of coursework. The emphasis of the article is on feedback in the writing process as the means of generating revision. Research studies of the last twenty years have built a strong picture of the successful writer as one who takes a recursive approach, drafting and redrafting the product. It is not surprising, then, that teachers are concerned to encourage a multiple draft approach in second-language writers. Feedback of various kinds creates an incentive for revision and Keh discusses three options; peer feedback, conferencing, and written comments. Her use of questionnaires to discover students' reactions to these options and their preferences among them is further evidence of the teacher as researcher, investigating a particular aspect of writing methodology and trying to improve on it.

Other contributors to *ELT Journal* have taken up the role of feedback or other elements in a process approach to writing. Hyland (Volume 44/4, 1990) describes two techniques for giving feedback to students: minimal marking and taped commentaries. Charles (Volume 44/4, 1990) discusses a four-step self-monitoring technique. Mangelsdorf (Volume 46/3, 1992) investigates the benefits and problems of peer reviews, where students read drafts of their fellow students' essays in order to make suggestions for revisions and she proposes a set of principles for undertaking the activity successfully. Perhaps the article by Dheram (Volume 49/2, 1995) sums up the contemporary view of second-language writing pedagogy. She uses an old Telegu saying about a two-bullock cart to characterize the need for mutual understanding of teachers and learners about the role of feedback in keeping the writing process moving in the right direction.

# The roles of teaching materials

In the early 1980s *ELT Journal* readers enjoyed a debate between Allwright (Volume 36/1, 1981) and O'Neill (Volume 36/2, 1982) whose articles, respectively entitled 'What do we want teaching materials for?' and 'Why use textbooks?' discuss the role of published materials in the management of language learning. Do materials dominate and direct or do they serve and support? Their arguments encompass both the potential and the limitations of such materials for 'guiding' students through the learning process and both writers reflect on teachers' needs and preferences in using textbooks. Such issues are still part of current debate on the role of materials in ELT. Other issues have arisen in the intervening years, among them the role of textbooks in innovation, the authenticity of materials in their representation of language, and the setting of contextually appropriate criteria for the evaluation of materials.

# Textbooks and innovation

HUTCHINSON and HUTCHINSON (Volume 48/4, 1994) take up the issue of what role textbooks might play in innovation. It is interesting to note how their perspective has been influenced by the kind of management theories discussed in Part One. Textbooks, they argue, can support teachers through the potentially disturbing and threatening change process. They demonstrate new methodology through 'on the page' materials; they can introduce change gradually and create a scaffolding upon which teachers can climb to a more creative methodology of their own. Only the textbook, they suggest,

> can really provide the level of structure that appears to be necessary for teachers to fully understand and 'routinize' change. (ibid.: 323)

In this way, they counter what might be perceived as an anti-textbook stance in some quarters of the ELT profession. It remains to be seen how the textbook will fare if process approaches to course design, with a fundamental characteristic of ongoing negotiation of content between teachers and learners, assume greater significance in mainstream ELT than at present.

If one accepts the value of textbooks, it must surely be with the qualification that they are of an acceptable level of quality and appropriate to the learners with whom they are being used. An article by Sheldon (Volume 42/4, 1988) deals with the problems of evaluating coursebooks. His criteria touch on a whole range of factors including design, practicality, subject matter, cultural appropriateness, educational validity, sexism and racism. The range involves more than just language on the one hand and methodology on the other and, in these days, many students and teachers are looking for something more. Cunningsworth and Kusel (Volume 45/2, 1991) take a similar view towards teachers' guides. They consider the functions of these, develop a set of model criteria for appraisal, and provide useful comment on a neglected area.

Two other articles have been concerned with materials design involving students. Assinder (Volume 45/3, 1991) states a case for using materials developed by students. Wessels (Volume 45/3, 1991) takes the case for student-made materials one stage further and describes a process in which, with the use of drama techniques, students created and produced materials which eventually appeared in published form.

## The authenticity of materials

The article by BARDOVI-HARLIG *et al.* (Volume 45/1, 1991) addresses another aspect of the role materials play in language learning, that of presenting samples of authentic language. Candlin and Edelhoff (1982: x) have commented on this role:

> Materials should have twin aims: on the one hand they offer information and data about the language being studied, and in particular about the social context and the culture within which communication takes place and derives much of its meaning and value. They need, in this sense, to be authentic to communication and to the world outside the classroom.

Bardovi-Harlig and her colleagues claim that 'many commercially available English language materials do not provide natural or even pragmatically appropriate conversation models for learners'. They demonstrate their point with reference to one phenomenon: leave-taking in American English. They state their case not only with reference to theoretical considerations but also with reference to a telling analysis of 'Saying goodbye' in textbooks. They also give some suggestions for a more pragmatically oriented approach to teaching students how to cope with goodbyes.

Yule *et al.* (Volume 46/3, 1992) present a similar argument, offering a range of examples from written and spoken English to illustrate how speakers and writers report what was said using structures which do not seem to appear in textbooks. They suggest that this might well hinder learners in their attempts to understand and interpret reported discourse. In a similar way, Crystal (Volume 49/2, 1995) takes readers on a journey to discover some features of contemporary English, particularly the nature of conversational English, with the intention of pointing out some implications for materials. White (Volume 47/3, 1993) demonstrates, through examples of Japanese speakers' difficulties in using 'please', the need learners have to make connections between language form, pragmatic use, and the conditions governing that use in cultural contexts. His discussion also holds clear implications for the careful contextualization of such items as politeness markers in materials and methodology.

These articles show the complex nature of language use and the dissonance that can occur between the way language is used in real discourse data from the world outside the classroom and the way in which language is presented and described in textbooks. They demonstrate how interest in issues of discourse and the pragmatic features of language have persuaded the ELT profession to explore the extent to which communicative textbooks represent communication in the real world.

Other contributors to *ELT Journal* have been concerned with sharpening teachers' insights into the structure and use of the English language they teach and with the implications of new or refined descriptive frameworks for methodology and materials design. Maule (Volume 42/2, 1988) gives a re-assessment of conditionals, a topic later revisited by Fulcher (Volume 45/2, 1991). Pociecha (Volume 42/4, 1988) proposes a distinction between action and condition verbs which could help post-elementary learners. Brown (Volume 43/4, 1989) questions the usual distinction made between clear and dark /l/ and discusses other significant allophones. Side (Volume 44/2, 1990) suggests a new treatment for phrasal verbs. Harman (Volume 44/3, 1990) helps teachers to rethink indirect speech. Crewe (Volume 44/4, 1990) takes a hard look at the teaching of logical connectives. Taylor (Volume 45/1, 1991) investigates the principles of word stress and accent placement in relation to the information structure of compound words. Berry (Volume 45/3, 1991) describes a range of complex problems to do with the teaching of articles and suggests some practical solutions. Bahns (Volume 47/1, 1993) makes significant distinctions among collocations and suggests principles for deciding which might be included in language programmes for learners with specific first languages. In all of these discussions, the suggestion is strongly implicit that teachers and textbook materials need to present these aspects of language in ways that make more sense than the ones with which we are most familiar.

# Evaluation

MACKAY (Volume 48/2, 1994) discusses the practice of evaluation, which is fast becoming a topic of concern among ELT professionals. The approach that he proposes and illustrates with a case study from Indonesia provides insights from experience into the process of course review. Mackay makes a distinction between the 'bureaucratic approach' to programme review, which looks at outcomes such as students' performance in tests or resource utilization and an approach concerned with improvement which focuses on specific issues within the curriculum. In doing so he reflects wider professional debate on evaluation for accountability and development and the need to integrate the two approaches. Weir and Roberts (1994: 5), for example, usefully compare accountability-oriented evaluation 'intended to assess the degree to which staff have met contractual or professional accountability demands' with development-oriented evaluation, 'intended to bring about programme improvement' and these are the two aims which Mackay synthesizes in a model which will be of interest to those responsible for programme evaluation and review.

Other contributors to *ELT Journal* have given further case studies of evaluation in practice. Sharp (Volume 44/2, 1990) describes how summative evaluation of a pre-sessional course provided tutors with useful insights for the planning of future courses. Of particular interest is the list of constraints he provides on this kind of activity. An article by Morrow and Schocker (Volume 47/1, 1993) focuses on formative evaluation and describes a range of procedures for engaging course participants in a continuous evaluation of course content and methodology: daily individual feedback through structured interviews; an end of week open poster forum, and pyramid discussion for end-of-course evaluation. They report evidence that the process of evaluation, in inviting participants to reflect on how the course was made, created a higher level of tolerance and rapport among group members than they or their tutors had previously experienced. Williams and Burden (Volume 48/1, 1994) give a case study of illuminative evaluation in which two evaluators worked to facilitate innovation of a sheltered immersion programme in a school in Switzerland.

These examples of evaluation in action show its potential in teaching and learning if it is perceived as something explicit and structured according to carefully defined criteria. If systematicity and principle are ensured, then it can, in the words of Rea-Dickins and Germaine (1992: 3) 'provide a wealth of information to use for the future direction of classroom practice, for the planning of courses and for the management of learning tasks and students'.

Each article in this section is a snapshot in a collage of current thought and practice. In that sense, they reflect the aim of a professional journal to offer its readers case studies, practical examples and classroom data. These are intended to give teachers the opportunity to appraise critically ideas about the professional practice of English language teaching and to make informed judgements about the applicability of those ideas to their own classrooms.

# 19

# Maximizing learning potential in the communicative classroom

## B. KUMARAVADIVELU

## Introduction

Communicative language teaching (CLT) which started in the early 1970s has become the driving force that shapes the planning, implementation, and evaluation of English language teaching (ELT) programmes in most parts of the world. Curriculum planners are preoccupied with communicative syllabus design. Materials producers have flooded the textbook market with books carrying the label 'communicative'. Testing experts have come out with batteries of communicative performance tests. Teachers invariably describe themselves as communicative teachers. Thus, theorists and practitioners alike almost unanimously emphasize communication of one kind or another.

## The communicative classroom

The emphasis on communication seems to slacken, however, where it matters most: in the classroom. In theory, a communicative classroom seeks to promote interpretation, expression, and negotiation of meaning. This means learners ought to be active, not just reactive, in class. They should be encouraged to ask for information, seek clarification, express an opinion, agree and/or disagree with peers and teachers. More importantly, they should be guided to go beyond memorized patterns and monitored repetitions in order to initiate and participate in meaningful interaction. In reality, however, such a communicative classroom seems to be a rarity. Research studies (Guthrie 1984; Nunan 1987; Walz 1989) show that even teachers who are committed to

CLT can fail to create opportunities for genuine interaction in their classrooms.

What prevents a communicative classroom from becoming genuinely communicative? There may be myriad reasons. An earlier article in this journal (Kumaravadivelu 1991) proposed the mismatch between teacher intention and learner interpretation as one possible reason. Another possibility is that teacher educators appear to have been less than successful in providing classroom teachers with strategies minimally required to cope with the challenges of a communicative classroom. As Savignon (1991: 272) rightly argues, 'in our effort to improve language teaching, we have overlooked the language teacher'. While considerable attention has been directed to designing communicative syllabuses, producing communicative materials, and formulating communicative methodologies, very little systematic inquiry has been conducted into identifying strategies that will help teachers prepare themselves to be communicative teachers.

This article is based on one such inquiry which resulted in a framework of macrostrategies for L2 teacher development (Kumaravadivelu 1992). I present here a follow-up study that seeks to assess how far the framework will help the CLT teacher become genuinely communicative.

## Macrostrategies

The idea of macrostrategies is based on a rather self-evident hypothesis: L2 learning/teaching needs, wants, and situations are unpredictably numerous. We can therefore only help teachers to develop a capacity to generate varied and situation-specific ideas within a framework that makes theoretical and pedagogic sense. Such a framework is here conceptualized in terms of macrostrategies which are general plans derived from theoretical, empirical, and pedagogical knowledge related to L2 learning and teaching. Each *macro*strategy can generate several situation-specific classroom techniques or *micro*strategies. There are five macrostrategies, which are briefly described below:

### Macrostrategy 1: Create learning opportunities in class

The first strategy—create learning opportunities in class—is based on the popular belief that we cannot really teach a language: we can only create conditions under which it will develop in its own way. The creation of learning opportunities is not entirely constrained by a predeter-mined syllabus or a prescribed textbook because it is the result of a joint production by participants engaged in the classroom event. Thus, learning opportunities can be created by the teacher as well as the learner.

## Macrostrategy 2: Utilize learning opportunities created by learners

The second strategy—utilize learning opportunities created by learners—is closely linked to the first, and is based on the premise that teachers and learners are co-participants in the generation of classroom discourse. The teacher is one of the participants—one with greater competence and authority, of course, but only *a* participant—and as such cannot afford to ignore any contributory discourse from other partners engaged in a joint venture to accomplish classroom lessons. It is therefore imperative for the teacher to show a willingness to utilize learning opportunities created by the learner.

## Macrostrategy 3: Facilitate negotiated interaction between participants

The third strategy—facilitate negotiated interaction between participants—refers to meaningful learner–learner and learner–teacher interaction in class. Negotiated interaction entails the learner's active involvement in such discourse features as clarification, confirmation, comprehension, requesting, repairing, and reacting. Above all, the term 'negotiated' means that the learner should have the freedom to initiate interaction, not just react and respond to what the teacher says. This macrostrategy is the most important of all and is premised on theoretical insights and empirical results which overwhelmingly stress the significance of meaningful interaction in the learner's comprehension of classroom input and in L2 development.

## Macrostrategy 4: Activate the intuitive heuristics of the learner

The fourth strategy—activate the intuitive heuristics of the leaner—is based on the premise that all normal human beings automatically possess intuitive heuristics, that is, conscious and unconscious cognitive processes of inquiry that help them discover and assimilate patterns and rules of linguistic behaviour. One way to activate the intuitive heuristics is to provide enough data so that the leaners can infer and internalize underlying rules from their use in varied communicative contexts.

## Macrostrategy 5: Contextualize linguistic input

The fifth strategy—contextualize linguistic input—is based on the psycholinguistic insight that comprehension and production involve rapid and simultaneous integration of syntactic, semantic, and discourse phenomena. Pedagogically, it means that linguistic input should be presented to learners in units of discourse so that they can benefit from the interactive effects of various linguistic components. Introducing isolated sentences will deprive learners of necessary pragmatic cues, thereby rendering the process of meaning-making harder.

## *The study*

As stated earlier, the primary objective of this classroom observational study is to assess whether the macrostrategies framework will help CLT teachers become more communicative and thus maximize learning potential in their classrooms. For the purpose of this study, I selected two teachers (T1 and T2) who described themselves as 'believers' in the CLT movement, T1 and T2 each have a Master's degree in teaching English as a Second Language (ESL). T1 (male) has been teaching for 3.2 years, and T2 (female) has been teaching for 4.1 years. At the time of data collection, they were teaching an intermediate-level class consisting of international students. T1 taught a 'speaking' class, and T2 taught a 'grammar' class. Since the study was conducted in the middle of an eight-week term, the learners were familiar with their teachers and their teaching styles.

The teachers were told that the objective of the study was to assess the communicative nature of classroom input and interaction. T1 was fully briefed on the theoretical and pedagogic aspects of macrostrategies and was asked to design classroom techniques using as many macrostrategies as possible. T2 was not aware of the macrostrategies framework and was told to use whatever communicative techniques she would have normally used. The classroom activities were videotaped and transcribed. During the analysis, I talked with the teachers and a random group of learners to seek necessary clarifications.

Excerpts of classroom interaction are given in the Appendix. Episode 1 is from the class taught by T1 and episode 2 is from the class taught by

T2. What follows is a discussion of classroom input and interaction in relation to the use or non-use of the macrostrategies framework.

## *Episode 1*

The purpose of the speaking course was to develop conversational skills, and the specific objective for the day was to highlight the role of certain linguistic and paralinguistic features that contribute to successful conversation. T1 tries to impart this knowledge by presenting a role play and by asking a series of questions. He succeeds in eliciting from the learners some of the features he wants to focus on. For instance, in turn 5, student 5 (S5) points out the role of back channelling to get the conversation going; in turn 11, S1 highlights the importance of facial expressions; in turn 35, S5 talks about paying attention to what one's conversation partner is saying; in turn 37, S9 identifies eye contact as an important feature of successful conversation. By following the fourth and fifth macrostrategies—activate the intuitive heuristics of the learner, and contextualize linguistic input—the teacher has been able to provide enough contextualized data for the learners so that they can infer certain underlying principles governing dyadic conversation. This has been done without long explanations and explicit instructions on those conventional features.

What about promoting negotiated interaction in class? Generally, the type of questions asked by the teacher will determine whether negotiated interaction is promoted in the class or not. Mehan (1979) proposed four major types of elicitation techniques. The first is *choice* elicitation which calls upon the learners only to agree or disagree with the teacher's statement and/or choose a yes or no response from a list provided by the teacher. The second is *product* elicitation which asks them to provide a factual response such as a name, a place, etc. The third is *process* elicitation which asks for the learners' opinions or interpretations. The last is *metaprocess* which asks them to formulate the grounds of their reasoning, or to explain the procedure by which they arrived at the answers. Though choice and product elicitations do have a place in language teaching, process and metaprocess elicitations, by their nature, facilitate greater negotiated interaction in class.

An analysis of classroom interaction in episode 1 indicates that T1 has predominantly used process and metaprocess elicitation techniques. Consider some of the questions asked by T1: What do you think about the conversations? (turn 1); Why does she need to do that? (turn 6); How do you know that she is not interested? (turn 8); What makes you say she doesn't like me? (turn 10); and, What do you know about paying attention? (turn 36). For every question, the teacher gets a very enthusiastic response.

What we have here is negotiated interaction, in the sense that the teacher and the learners were jointly engaged in creating meaningful classroom discourse. The teacher's questions were aimed at eliciting the learners' opinions and interpretations of conversational skills rather than getting linguistic samples that could be mechanically lifted from the text or recalled from memory. The teacher facilitated such an interaction by asking a series of process and metaprocess questions and by focusing entirely on the flow of information. He achieved this by providing linguistic as well as paralinguistic cues which helped the learners in their effort to structure their participation.

The teacher also followed classroom procedures which create learning opportunities successfully. One such procedure was to role play certain communicative situations. Another procedure was to ask a series of questions in order to create an opportunity for learners to think about the topic in hand. For example, in turn 1 he asked: What do you think about the conversations? Later on, in turn 40 he asked the learners themselves to suggest certain situations that might make a person worried.

The teacher also made effective use of learning opportunities created by learners. For instance, in turn 5, S5 suggests that in a conversation one is supposed to say *good, all right.* The teacher does not ignore this learning opportunity created by the learner; instead, he pursues the same line of argument to ask them why we need to do that. Towards the end of this episode, the teacher gathers from the class several situations that might make a person worried. In the portion that I have not included for analysis, he designs group work based on two of the situations suggested by the learners themselves.

## Episode 2

The purpose of the grammar course was to develop functional abilities in the use of selected grammatical structures. The specific focus for the day was the use of comparatives and superlatives. During the pre-observation conversation, the teacher (T2) informed me that she makes her class communicative by encouraging learner participation and by introducing grammatical items within a communicative context. As the transcript of episode 2 reveals, she successfully contextualizes her linguistic input and discusses the grammatical usage in a communicative context by attempting to draw from the learners' experience.

The communicative nature of episode 2, however, is strikingly different from that of episode 1, particularly with regard to learner response. First of all, T2 attempts a deductive mode of presentation of the grammatical usage chosen for the day. She starts with a long period of explanation and instruction. At the end of her explanation, the learners are expected to have learnt the grammatical usage well enough to produce sentences of their own. The fact that her approach has not yielded the expected result is shown in the exchanges in turns 14 to 26. Her specific objective is to elicit samples with superlatives like *the worst, the least*, etc. After listening to her fairly long explanation, S7 comes out with the sentence (turn 15): Japan has a lot of earthquakes. This sentence is grammatical and meaningful, but the teacher's stated objective was to help the learners to learn and use superlative forms, and the learner did not do that. Ironically, it is this model provided by S7, not the one provided by the teacher, that was imitated by another learner (S1) later in turn 25: We have a lot of typhoons.

Secondly, there is very little negotiated interaction in the class. In fact, in the first part of the episode, the teacher's monologue constitutes nearly 90 per cent of the classroom discourse. Furthermore, even when a learner attempts to negotiate, he is immediately rebuffed by the teacher. Consider turn sequences 4 to 8. In order to elicit a sentence with an *as ... as* comparative structure, T2 starts a sentence *I am ...* expecting the learners to complete it. S5 (turn 4) responds to the cue and completes the sentence: *... as tall as you.* Even though the response is grammatically correct and communicatively appropriate, T2 admonishes him: You don't understand what I want, and a puzzled S5 seeks confirmation by saying: *the same?* and T2 confirms it: *the same, yah.* S5 is confused. He does not know what is wrong with his answer and, in a state of confusion, gives up.

The confusion is compounded when another learner (S1) in turn 8 says *I am as tall as you are* and T2 approves it. The learners are left wondering why the sentence *I am as tall as you* is wrong and why *I am as tall as you are* is right. They are also left to wonder what the teacher meant when she said in turn 5: You don't understand what I want. Because of a lack of negotiated interaction, T2 achieves only a less than optimal success in making her class communicative.

Thirdly, the teacher fails to utilize learning opportunities created by learners. In turn 25, a learner makes a reference to typhoons. T2 picks up the response and asks the class: What is a typhoon? This is a good strategy on the part of T2 since the class had students from countries where typhoons are unknown and typhoon is not a frequently occurring word. However, without utilizing this learner-created opportunity and without waiting to hear a response to her own question, T2 decides to move on. Another example is to be found in turn sequences 28 to 30. T2 says if a country has many different dialects, communication problems will occur. A learner disagrees with the teacher and says that although there are several dialects in her country, there is no problem. T2 ignores the learner's challenge and repeats her point without substantiating it. Here is yet another learning opportunity created by a learner which the teacher fails to utilize.

## Comparing the two episodes

In sum, the two communicative classroom episodes analysed here show substantially different kinds of classroom input and interaction. Even though both the episodes feature the same group of learners, their classroom behaviour varies considerably across the episodes. Episode 1 shows a group of learners who are highly motivated, enthusiastic, and very active. Episode 2 shows the same group of learners less motivated, less enthusiastic and much less active. Correspondingly, an analysis of teacher input shows that episode 1 has a roughly equal distribution of teacher-talk and learner-talk, while in episode 2, the teacher-talk predominates. Besides, T1 uses process and metaprocess questions to promote interaction, a strategy not used at all by T2. The use and non-use of macrostrategies appears to have contributed to this remarkable variation in the communicative nature of the two episodes.

## *Conclusion*

I started this article with the assumption that if CLT teachers have not been able to make their classes as communicative as they desire, it is probably because teacher educators have not given them the necessary tools to succeed. I proposed a framework of macrostrategies which might offer a possible tool to make CLT classes genuinely communicative.

   An analysis of two classroom episodes taught by two teachers committed to CLT and featuring the same group of learners revealed that episode 1 was remarkably more communicative than episode 2. The relative success in maximizing learning potential witnessed in episode 1 and the relative failure witnessed in episode 2 can be attributed to the use and non-use of the macrostrategies framework. In addition to improving the chances for maximizing learning potential in the communicative classroom, the framework also helps to create and sustain a high degree of motivation among learners. This classroom observational study lends credence to the belief that given appropriate tools CLT teachers will succeed in making their classes genuinely communicative.

*Originally published in Volume 47/1, 1993*

# Appendix: transcripts of episodes 1 and 2

## Note

I have given only a broad transcription sufficient for the above discussion. The transcription conventions are given below.

| | |
|---|---|
| T | teacher |
| S1 | an identified student. (The class had 15 students, numbered according to the alphabetical order of their names, S1 to S15.) |
| S | an unidentified student |
| Ss | group of unidentified students |
| x | indicates a missing word |
| xx | indicates a missing phrase |
| [ ] | *my interpolations, intended to make the context clear* |
| ... | indicates a pause |
| 1, 2 | the serial numbers in each episode indicate sequence of turn-taking and not line numbers. |

## Episode 1: (intermediate—speaking)

*[The class begins with a role play by T1 and a colleague—not included in the transcript.]*

1 T   Now, the purpose of that was to see what you think about conversations. What do you think about the conversations we've just had? Were they good conversations?

2 Ss   No ... *(laughs.)*

3 J   No, not the acting ... not the acting ... we know that. *[J is the colleague who participated in the role play.]*

4 T   Yah, we know we are good actors. *(Ss laugh.)* But what about the situation? Did you notice anything about it?

5 S5   You speak with her but she is not giving you any ... you know ... xxx she goes yah ... I like this you know ... she must say all right, good, I think ... the University of Georgia is best ... or something like this.

6 T   Why does she need to do that? Does anyone have an idea? Why didn't she do that?

7 S7   She is not interesting about ... your conversation ...

8 T   How do you know that she is not interested?

9 S1   She doesn't like you. *(Ss laugh.)*

10 T   Maybe she doesn't like me. But what makes you say that? What makes you say she doesn't like ...?

11   S1   Her face … the emotions … it seems she is not xx.
12   T    Ah … O K, so, she doesn't talk to me. That's one thing that maybe we
          could improve. What's another thing in … the other situations that you
          noticed?
13   S3   Mmm … she might be Japanese … *(Ss laugh.)*
14   T    She might be Japanese. What makes you say that?
15   S3   She doesn't understand …
16   T    She doesn't understand. *(Ss laugh.)* All right. Why do you say she
          doesn't understand? … Any idea?
17   S3   Maybe she is shy … she is afraid to talk to you because her English is no
          good.
18   T    OK, what about the first situation … you remember what I was talking
          to her …?
19   S8   You don't understand what to talk about …
20   T    Maybe I did understand …
21   S8   You don't care … you said … you said that's good. I don't want to … I
          want to …
22   T    Was there something wrong with what I said to her?
23   Ss   Yah …
24   T    Why?
25   S8   Oh … that's great. Her car is broken and you said 'Oh that's great …'
26   T    So that's not a good conversation?
27   Ss   No …
28   T    What about the … mmm?
29   S2   She misunderstood what you said.
30   T    She misunderstood what I said?
31   S6   You misunderstood what she said.
32   T    OK. Right. Maybe there's a misunderstanding. Good. What about …
          when I was going to be the editor of the school newspaper …?
33   S7   She didn't interest you … xxx
34   T    She is not interested … What makes you say that she wasn't interested?
35   S7   Because she's not paying attention to you … she's facing the wrong …
36   T    Not paying attention … what do we know about paying attention …
          when you are paying attention to someone …
37   S9   Eye … straight … xxx
38   T    Eye contact … very good. So when we had these conversations, have
          you ever felt like in one of these situations?
39   Ss   Yah … *(Ss laugh.)*
40   T    OK, that's what we are hoping to do in this class is to give you some
          opportunity to interact with each other and … ah … respond in an
          appropriate way. You know sometimes there may be situations like
          Julia's car is broken and she is worried about this. She needs to … she
          needs some help from a friend. Can you think of some other situations
          that might make a person worried? What situations can you think
          about … that might make a person worried?
41   S    Fire in the apartment …

42 T  Fire in the apartment ... *(writes on blackboard)* good ...

43 S11 Car accident.

44 T  Car accident ... right ...

45 S2 Sick ...

46 T  Sick ... in what way would you be sick ... can you ...?

47 S  xx

48 T  You are sick ... and ...

49 S  xx *(Ss laugh.)*

50 S2 Sick ... xx ... mind ...

51 T  *(laughs.)* Maybe a mental sickness ... but ... maybe you're sick and ...
need a doctor fast ... OK. What else?

52 S12 Your wife ... baby ... xx *(gestures.)*

53 T  Your wife is having a baby.

54 S  She's having a baby xx *(Ss laugh.)*

55 T  Oh ... yes ... there's a movie called 'She's having a baby'. So what else
might ... ah, these are situations that might mean an emergency. What
if you are just worried about something?

56 S  xx future.

57 T  Your future. OK.

58 Ss xxx *(laugh.)*

59 T  Future plans.

60 S10 Homework ...

61 T  Worried about your homework ... All right ...

62 S  xx *(Ss laugh.)*

63 T  You are worried about me?

64 S2 Grade ... grade ...

65 T  Oh, worried about grade ... OK. That's good. Now ...

## Episode 2: *(intermediate—grammar)*

1 T  There are different ways of comparing things, you know. We can
compare things ... and one is just as the other. You know what a scale
is? A scale: when you weigh things on it. You know I weigh myself ...
(pretends to weigh herself on a scale) I am ... woo, a hundred and fifty
pounds. I weigh a hundred and fifty pounds. You know what a scale is?
... Sometimes it is easier for you to understand what it is if it's written,
is that correct? *(writes 'scale' on blackboard.)* Do you know what a
scale is?

2 Ss Yah.

3 T  All right you weigh things ... OK? You weigh things on a scale. OK.
And ... s ... when we have a scale ... and we put two things on a scale
they are the same. It will not go up or down, right? It will be like this, all
right? When one is heavier than the other, what happens? *(gestures.)*
Boop ... goes down, all right? Or, the other one goes down, right? And
in between the two extremes, there is a variety, right? We can express
that in language, right? We can express the idea in language, right? We
can say you are as tall as I am, right? You are ... eh ... taller than I am.

What happens here? We are the same, right? Everybody ... he is as tall as I am. He is taller than I am, right? You are ... nothing personal, I am just playing right now ... you are smaller than I am, right? And, Mr X *[referring to the colleague operating the camera]* is the tallest ... of all, right? Eh ... but then we can also say *(writes on blackboard)* OK ... Mr Wallace is the tallest ... of what ... the tallest. Sometimes you don't have to use all of it because we know what we are talking about, right? In a conversation if we don't know sometimes we may just have to say yes or no, you know, and sometimes we have to make give more information, O K? *(writes on blackboard)* is the tallest of the class, right? All right? Eh ... x let's see ... Let's make a sentence with eh the same, O K? I am ...

4   S5   ... as tall as you.
5   T   You don't understand what I am what I want.
6   S5   The same?
7   T   The same, yah ... give me a sentence with the same.
8   S3   I am as tall as you are.
9   T   O K. *(writes on blackboard)* I am as tall as you are. O K. Eh ... most of the time ... most of the time ... or, let me put it this way ... there are probably more things that are different, right, than the same. Would you agree with me? Yah? *[break in interactional sequence]*
10  T   Let's see if we can talk about the worst ... the coldest ... you know the most the most negative ... O K. All right, the most negative ... O K. All right, the most negative. What's the worst for you? The worst experience ... or something something that you really ... now we've talked about tornado and earthquakes, right?
11  S9   We xx Tuscaloosa is the worst thing xxx tornado ...
12  T   Tornado?
13  S9   Yes.
14  T   The worst thing that they have in ... O K. What about your country? What is the worst thing in your country? We've talked about some good things ... Let's see the ... we have also to talk about bad ... right? What's the worst you can think about your country? If you have to say one thing really bad, what would you say? ... *(long pause)* ... you have to think ... all right? That's good. You know ... think ... xx one thing about country xx ... I can tell you one bad thing about the Midwest ... Midwest has very bad weather ... It has perhaps the worst weather of all ... states that I have lived in. It's not true ... but it seems ... It's very cold. It's much colder than here ... much much colder than here ... and the sun does not shine very often ... O K, the sun doesn't shine enough. You understand what I mean ... doesn't shine enough, all right. Now, what about your country?
15  S7   Japan has a lot of xxx.
16  T   A lot of ...?
17  S7   Earthquakes.
18  T   Earthquakes ... earthquakes.

19 S7 Earthquakes.

20 T Mmm yah, that sounds ... eh ... that sounds scary ... does it does it interfere with your daily life?

21 Ss Mm

22 T Yes. Everywhere in Japan? Are there earthquake dangers everywhere in Japan?

23 S7 Almost everywhere.

24 T Almost everywhere. H ... hm ... all right. O K. What about your country?

25 S1 We have a lot of typhoons.

26 T What is a typhoon? Does everybody know what a typhoon is? Right, if we all know we don't have to waste our time, right? That's good. Do you agree? I mean. Yah?

27 S1 I agree.

28 T Hmm, I would think that ... what about language? Some of you ... not Japan ... but ... Taiwan ... is a problem of language, right, because there are so many different dialects ... right ... of China ... Chinese? Isn't there a problem? When there are ... communication problems, right?

29 S9 xxx xxx we have the same ... so many xxx that's no problem.

30 T But, Chinese language ... has many different dialects right?

31 S9 Yes.

32 T And that's a that is a most serious problem if you want to ... be able to communicate ... There is another country that has the same problem. Which is that? Which country?

33 S5 India? Problems of xxx

34 T India ... too many languages ... the most languages of all countries ... I don't know what the number of languages ... O K ... All right.

# 20

# Literary role play

ULRICH GERBER

## My teaching context

Swiss pupils at pre-university level will have read a number of English or American plays and novels by the time they go to university, whatever subject they may intend to study there. Reading 'good' literature, is still considered to be an integral part of any demanding English syllabus which tries to capture the learner's attention and offer them meaningful and authentic reading material. Literature in this context is frequently taught not only for its own sake but also as a sort of prompt to encourage students to think and speak in English.

## A standard approach

Most teachers try to depart from question-and-answer techniques, because it is hard for them to keep asking genuinely open-ended questions, and students can easily feel that the teacher is directly or indirectly imposing his or her view of the text in question.

One variation of this standard approach has, however, proved very successful. In this variation, teachers get students themselves to ask questions about the text they have read. This not only gives them practice in asking relevant questions—which they will have to learn for their university studies in any case—but also enables them to take their own interest as the starting point for working their way into the text. The questions are then discussed in groups, with an exchange of findings towards the end of the lesson.

When this variation of the standard approach works well, it can be very satisfying for teachers, who are always pleased to hear busy classes actually speaking the foreign language. The language arising from such work can include asking for and expressing opinions, agreeing and disagreeing, expressing personal insights, giving examples, and so on. At best, the approach does help students to deal with texts sensitively.

On the other hand, teachers who watch and listen to group work carefully will be aware that in this situation some students do much more talking than others: indeed some students, though diligent, may appear to be somewhat passive. I have also noted that simply asking students to ask questions about the text favours a rather intellectual approach, which does not necessarily tap the energies dormant in all my students. I wanted to give all my students opportunities for a more total and less detached response, especially in those parts of a lesson where we had a final, overall discussion of a text.

## A different approach

What are the alternatives open to the teacher in search of more variety? In the case of plays, solutions are relatively accessible, because they can be acted out. When it comes to novels, though, eliciting a complete and enthusiastic response can be more difficult. In the following, I am going to describe an activity I have tried out recently with a class at my school[1]—an activity in which I tried to solve the problem of teaching a novel.

The class was a mixed group of 17 students towards the end of their fourth year of English, aged 18 to 19. Having read and discussed four-fifths of Kingsley Amis's *Lucky Jim*, we felt that it was time to adopt a different approach. I wanted the pupils to become more involved emotionally, to look at the novel from within the story, so to speak. Ideally, they should identify themselves with the characters of the novel and at the same time experience something about its inner structure (plot, point of view, etc.). The starting point for my activity was Klippel's 'fishbowl' (1983: 10), which I developed further to suit my purposes.

## Method

### Setting up the activity

*Step 1:* An empty space is provided in the centre of the classroom.

*Step 2:* An (inner) circle with nine chairs is formed.

*Step 3:* Eight chairs are each marked (with a big name tag) with an important character from the novel (Dixon, Margaret, Christine, Professor Welch, Mrs Welch, Bertrand, Carol Goldsmith *and* Kingsley Amis); the ninth chair is left empty—this represents the 'Joker'.

*Step 4:* Eight pupils are assigned one of these roles and take a seat in the 'inner circle'. The rest of the class stand around these chairs in an outer circle.

### Instructions to the students

*Number 1:* The pupils on the chairs are told that for the purpose of this game they have to take the roles of these characters. They are in 'Heaven', looking back on the events they experienced while living through the novel. They are expected to talk about their lives with each other.

*Number 2:* The pupils standing around this inner circle are informed that they can also take part in the ensuing discussion at any given moment by simply tapping on the shoulder of one of the characters and taking his or her seat. They can also sit on the empty chair—the Joker— and take on the role of any other character in the novel.

The activity then starts. Once the seated pupils begin, there is no more need for the teacher to intervene or interfere with the inner circle. It may be necessary, however, to encourage pupils in the outer circle to relieve one of their colleagues. More passive students can be assigned a role and sent into the inner circle. In this way, the teacher can indirectly steer and influence the course of the talk in the inner circle.

## Results

Here are transcripts of three typical extracts:
*Extract one:*

> TEACHER: I would like you to start anywhere. You're just sitting there, together, in Heaven.
> BERTRAND: Well, Kingsley Amis, why did you let Christine go out from the ball with that bloody Dixon?
> KINGSLEY AMIS: Well, my intention in that was to give Dixon like another woman next to Margaret to make the story somehow interesting (*general laughter*) and Christine, I wanted to get some, get Dixon really into women, er, get some conflict. That's why.
> CHRISTINE: And Dixon, why did you seduce me? (*general laughter*)

DIXON: Well, I just felt I had to. (*pause*)

CHRISTINE: But do you think it was fair?

DIXON: What was fair? (*general laughter*)

CHRISTINE: To seduce me. I mean my boyfriend's Bertrand.

DIXON: So what? Look at this bearded art maniac. (*general laughter*) He doesn't deserve you, or you don't deserve him, whatever you want to put it. I felt that I was just kind of the right guy for you. (*general laughter*)

PROF. WELCH: You weren't very fair against Margaret. You were the boyfriend of Margaret.

DIXON: Well, she didn't want to sleep with me in the first place. (*general laughter*)

*Extract two:*

MRS WELCH (boy imitates old woman's voice): But Dixon, what did you make with my blankets, my sheets?

DIXON: You see, I was in the pub till eleven, twelve o'clock, and then I went home and Mr Welch was in the bathroom so I went to bed and smoked a cigarette. Then I slept and ... *eingeschlafen* (*prompt by other pupil: fell asleep*) ... fell asleep. And in the morning I saw ...

MRS WELCH: Didn't you lit off your cigarette?

DIXON: No, I didn't. I was pissed, you see. And in the morning I saw the table, burnt edge, and blankets, the hole, and, well, didn't know what to do.

*Extract three:*

CAROL GOLDSMITH (to Mrs Welch): You aren't so important in the story.

MRS WELCH: I'm very important in the story. But the problem is (*general laughter*) if ... er, what?

DIXON: You're the brain of Mr Welch. (*laughter*)

JOKER: Professor Welch, I'm the car of you. (*general laughter*) Why did you treat me so miserable?

PROF. WELCH: Well, I think it's quite hard to drive a car and ...

CAR: (*protesting*) I had to suffer!

DIXON: Me, too. I got two holes in the trousers because of your car. It was the spring.

PROF. WELCH: Yes, well, I think it's your fault when you sit on the spring.

## Evaluation of the role play

In the following, I shall point out some of the advantages of this activity, referring to the evidence in the transcript where possible.

### Methodological advantages

- There is no direct teacher intervention. Once the pupils grasp the idea, the activity keeps going 'automatically' for a whole lesson. Students help each other to formulate what they want to say.
- The atmosphere is merry and relaxed with frequent laughter.
- There is genuine interaction among the pupils.
- Student participation is extremely high. With the exception of one pupil, everybody took part. Even normally very passive pupils were prepared to put themselves forward spontaneously. There was a high turnover of pupils adopting the same role.
- The characters ask each other about the motivations behind their actions in the story and pupils discuss the importance and the functions of the characters in the story. The presence of the author is also very stimulating.
- The Joker (empty seat) is important. It is a means of ensuring the constant influx of new and unforeseen ideas to which pupils have to respond spontaneously. It allows for creativity and inventiveness (for example, Professor Welch's car) and calls for even more rotation among the participants.

### Linguistic advantages

- The English used is more natural and more real than can normally be heard in a classroom. Pupils ask follow-up questions for clarification.
- The whole style is closer to colloquial English. There is variety in the registers used, from formal, standard English to 'bloody Dixon' right through to 'I was pissed' (i.e. I was drunk).
- The students speak fluently and actively use words learnt from the text ('bearded art maniac', 'blankets', 'sheets', 'spring', etc.).
- A number of different speech acts occur, similar to the ones observed in the 'standard' approach above; the students (all of them) express opinions, agree and disagree, give examples, and so on.

It proved important that I had chosen some of the more fluent pupils to start with, because they had to trigger off the discussion. The pupils in the role of 'Kingsley Amis' (the author) sometimes had a hard time, because he was not spared any tricky questions. The participants increasingly seemed to realize through taking part in this role play that they were actually talking about and virtually experiencing the special effects resulting from the plot and the point of view of the narrative.

## Dealing with mistakes

Of course, the students made mistakes ('Didn't you lit off your cigarette?' etc.) and I was able to note these down for further language practice. But I feel that a discussion of a literary work is not the time for systematically insisting on linguistic accuracy. What counts is the quality and quantity of the communication between the pupils, and these are what this activity has helped them to practise.

## Students' reactions

In the class discussion afterwards, students unanimously said that it was a most enjoyable activity. They liked the completely different approach and the fact that it gave them a framework within which they were able to respond as they pleased. In particular, less talented actors were able to make a contribution because they could choose whether they just wanted to speak the role or to act it out with mime and gesture.

## Conclusion

In selecting Lucky Jim for a class reader, I opted for a novel that is linguistically complex. It is only appropriate that such a text should be scrutinized thoroughly. The standard approach of questioning and discussion, as described at the beginning of this article, serves this purpose well, yet this method of intellectual analysis clearly has its deficiencies. That is where literary role play can add a new dimension to the foreign language classroom. It involves the pupils emotionally, prompts them to use more natural language, and is particularly effective in that it facilitates fluency. It does not replace other ways of dealing with literature in the language classroom (see Collie and Slater 1987) but forms a useful addition to the repertory of the foreign language teacher.

To sum up the basic idea, there is an 'inner circle' of pupils who are performing a linguistic task without any direct intervention by the teacher. The pupils in the 'outer circle' replace or relieve the participants in the inner circle. It is clear that this kind of set-up can be applied to other areas of teaching English literature, such as teaching plays (Gerber 1990a) and poems.

*Originally published in Volume 44/3, 1990*

## Note

1 My school is a gymnasium: a selective state school at which students have to take at least eleven subjects up to the final exam, the matura, which entitles them to study any of these eleven subjects at university.

# Focused communication tasks and second language acquisition

## JUNKO NOBUYOSHI & ROD ELLIS

## Introduction

Communication tasks have been defined as tasks that 'involve the learner in comprehending, manipulating, producing, or interacting in the target language while their attention is principally focused on meaning rather than form' (Nunan 1989b: 10). They contrast with other, more traditional language tasks, that require learners to pay attention to specific linguistic properties (phonological, lexical, or grammatical) in order to learn them or to practise using them more accurately.

The pedagogic rationale for the use of communication tasks rests in part on the claim that they will help to develop learners' communicative skills and in part on the claim that they will contribute to their linguistic development. In other words, communication tasks are important for both 'fluency' and 'accuracy' (Brumfit 1984). They aid fluency by enabling learners to activate their linguistic knowledge for use in natural and spontaneous language, such as when taking part in a conversation. One way in which this is achieved is by developing strategic competence, defined by Canale (1983) as the verbal and non-verbal strategies used to compensate for breakdowns in communication and to enhance the effectiveness of communication. They contribute to accuracy (i.e. linguistic competence) by enabling learners to discover new linguistic forms during the course of communicating, and also by increasing their control over already-acquired forms.

Second language acquisition researchers have suggested a number of ways in which communicating can lead to acquisition. According to the interaction hypothesis (Long 1983), learners acquire new forms when input is made comprehensible through negotiating for meaning, as in this example (Young and Doughty 1987: 213):

NS:   Do you wear them every day?
NNS:  Huh?
NS:   Do you put them on every day?

Here the native speaker (NS) asks a question which the non-native speaker (NNS) does not understand. This leads the NNS to negotiate for meaning by means of a clarification request, which in turn causes the NS to paraphrase her initial question. Such negotiation may help to make new forms and their meanings transparent in the input, with the result that they can be more easily acquired. According to the comprehensible output hypothesis (Swain 1985), acquisition takes place when learners are 'pushed' into producing output that is more grammatical, as in this example:

NNS:  He pass his house.
NS:   Sorry?
NNS:  He passed, he passed, ah, his sign.

Here the NS negotiates for meaning—by means of a clarification request—when she fails to understand the non-native speaker's initial utterance, causing the learner to reformulate the utterance.

The purpose of this article is twofold. It aims to report a small-scale study that provides some evidence to suggest that 'pushing' learners to produce more accurate output does indeed contribute to acquisition—as claimed by the comprehensible output hypothesis. It also claims to illustrate how this can be achieved by means of focused communication tasks and to consider the place of such tasks in language pedagogy.

## Focused and unfocused communication tasks

Communication tasks have the following characteristics (Ellis 1982):

1  There must be a communicative purpose (i.e. not just a linguistic goal).
2  There must be a focus on message rather than on the linguistic code.
3  There must be some kind of 'gap' (e.g. an information or opinion gap).
4  There must be opportunity for negotiation when performing the task.
5  The participants must choose the resources—verbal and non-

verbal—required for performing the task (i.e. they are not supplied with the means for performing the task).

Individual tasks can be more or less 'communicative', depending on whether all or just some of these characteristics are present.

## Unfocused communication tasks

A distinction can be drawn between focused and unfocused communication tasks. In the case of the latter, no effort is made in the design or the execution of a task to give prominence to any particular linguistic feature. The language used to perform the task is 'natural' and only very broadly determined by the content of the task. For example, a one-way picture description task that requires a learner to recount the information shown in a series of pictures to the teacher or another learner and, ultimately, to work out the story is an unfocused communication task, because there is nothing in the task that requires the participants to attend to or use specific linguistic features.

## Focused communication tasks

A focused communication task, in contrast, does result in some linguistic feature being made prominent, although not in a way that causes the learner to pay more attention to form than to meaning. Communication tasks can become focused either through design or through methodology. Loschky and Bley-Vroman (1990) observe that 'different tasks can put different requirements on particular grammatical knowledge, and it is correspondingly possible to construct tasks which involve grammatical knowledge in various ways and to varying degrees'. They distinguish tasks in which the use of a particular grammatical structure is 'natural', those in which it is 'useful', and those in which it is 'essential'. In a communicative task that is fully focused, the grammatical structure must be essential (i.e. its use is required by the task), but as Loschky and Bley-Vroman acknowledge, such tasks are difficult to construct, especially if the aim of the task is learner production.[1]

The inherent redundancy of language and the availability of rich contextual clues in many tasks obviate the need for learners to use any particular grammatical structure. For this reason, most production tasks are focused only to the extent that a particular structure is 'useful' or 'natural' and, as a consequence, may not actually result in its use.

It may be possible, however, to bring about a substantial degree of focus in the performance of a communication task through the manner in which it is carried out—that is, through methodology rather than design. Consider the one-way picture description task outlined above. Let us imagine that a learner is performing the task with a teacher and is given these instructions after receiving the pictures: 'The pictures tell a story about what happened last weekend. Tell me about your pictures'. These instructions make the use of the past tense 'natural', but by no means 'essential'. If, however, the teacher deliberately requests clarification of any utterance the learner produces containing a past tense error—irrespective of whether the teacher has or has not understood the utterance—the use of the past tense becomes a focus of the task. From the teacher's perspective, the task is not a truly communicative one, as the focus has shifted from message to code (see characteristic 2 of communication tasks above). However, from the learners' perspective the task remains communicative providing, of course, that they treat the teacher's request for clarification as a demand to improve the quality of the message rather than to display correct language.

The two examples below were taken from an actual performance of a one-way picture description task by a teacher and a learner. Although we cannot be sure that the learner did not become 'conscious' of the need to pay attention to the past tense, there was nothing in the actual discourse—or indeed, in the overall performance of the task—to suggest that this was the case. The learner appears to be focused on conveying meaning. However, when faced with a request for clarification, she responds by correcting her past tense error:

1 LEARNER: Last weekend, a man painting, painting 'Beware of the dog'.
  TEACHER: Sorry?
  LEARNER: A man painted, painted, painted on the wall 'Beware of the dog'.
2 LEARNER: He pass his house.
  TEACHER: Uh?
  LEARNER: He passed, he passed, ah, his sign.

In effect, the learner is being 'pushed', in the course of trying to communicate, to produce utterances that employ correct use of the grammatical feature (i.e. past tense) which the teacher, unknown to the learner, has elected to focus on.

Focused communication tasks, in particular those where the focus is achieved methodologically, offer the teacher a means of 'teaching' grammar communicatively. Such tasks provide a means of encouraging learners to produce output that is comprehensible and, at the same time, grammatically correct. The question that arises is 'Do such tasks contribute to acquisition?'.

## The study

The purpose of the study was to undertake a preliminary investigation of whether methodologically focused communication tasks lead to more accurate learner production that is sustained over time. Two research questions were addressed:

1  Does 'pushing' learners by means of requests for clarification result in more accurate use of past tense verb forms in communication?

2  Do learners continue to show improved accuracy in the use of past tense verb forms in subsequent communication when there is no attempt to 'push' them?

## Subjects

Six subjects participated in the study. They were all adult learners of L2 English enrolled in weekly-held conversational classes at Kanda Institute of Foreign Languages in Tokyo. They were of fairly low-level proficiency, but all of them were capable of using at least some past tense verb forms correctly.

## Tasks and procedure

The subjects performed two picture jigsaw communication tasks of the kind described in the previous section. The subjects were told that the pictures they held described events that happened the previous weekend (for task 1) and the day before at the office (for task 2). They performed the tasks individually with their regular teacher.

Three of the subjects comprised the experimental group and the other three the control group. All the subjects performed the two tasks twice. On the first occasion the experimental group received requests for clarification every time they produced an utterance in which the verb was not in the past tense, or the past tense was incorrectly formed. On the second occasion, however, they received only general requests for clarification (i.e. when the teacher genuinely failed to understand something they had said) and never when an utterance contained an incorrect verb form. The subjects in the control group received general requests for clarification, none of which followed an utterance containing a verb incorrectly marked for past tense, on both occasions. There was a one-week interval between the two occasions for both groups. To ensure that the subjects did not practise performing the task in the intervening week, they were not told that they would be asked to repeat them.

To confirm that the tasks did provide a natural context for the use of the past tense, baseline data from two native speakers were collected. These showed that except when background information (e.g. concerning the personality of one of the characters shown in the picture) was being provided, the task did indeed result in use of the past tense.

## Analysis

The oral interactions between the teacher and the individual learners were recorded and transcribed in normal orthography. Obligatory occasions for the use of the past tense were then identified.[2] This led to some of the learners' utterances being excluded from the analysis, as when the sequence of events was interrupted by background information (e.g. 'Last weekend a man was painting a sign. He *has* a dog. The dog *is* dangerous. So he painted 'Beware of the Dog'.). For each obligatory occasion a learner was scored as supplying or not supplying the correct past tense verb form. If a learner successfully self-corrected in the course of producing an initial utterance, he or she was credited as supplying the past tense form. In the case of the experimental group on the first occasion, all utterances that were subsequently reformulated as a result of the teacher's focused requests for clarification were examined to determine whether the learner had corrected the original past tense error.

## Results

Table 1 gives the total number of obligatory occasions for the use of the past tense by each learner together with the number of occasions it was used correctly and incorrectly and the percentage of correct and incorrect use on both occasions. In the case of the experimental group, the number of times the learners correctly reformulated initially incorrect past tense verbs during the first administration of the task is also given, together with a revised percentage of correct forms.

Most of the learners produced a substantial number of errors in the use of the past tense during the first administration of the task. In the case of the experimental learners the teacher's requests for clarification led to two of the learners reformulating their utterances in a way that corrected their past tense errors. However, the third learner paid less attention to past tense verb forms in his reformulations, correcting hardly any of his original errors.

The two experimental learners who had successfully reformulated their utterances to increase the use of correct past tense verb forms during the first administration of the task sustained the gain in accuracy during the second administration, even though on this occasion the teacher made no attempt to 'push' them into correct use. Both learners improved on their initial level of accuracy, learner 1 moving from 31 per cent to 89 per cent, and learner 2 from 45 per cent to 62 per cent. The third learner, however, showed no overall gain in accuracy. Neither did any of the learners in the control group.

| | Experimental | | Learners | | Control | |
|---|---|---|---|---|---|---|
| | 1 | 2 | 3 | 1 | 2 | 3 |
| *First administration:* | | | | | | |
| Obligatory occasions | 13 | 20 | 24 | 14 | 19 | 17 |
| Correct | 4 | 9 | 3 | 7 | 9 | 0 |
| Incorrect | 9 | 11 | 21 | 7 | 10 | 17 |
| % correct | 31 | 45 | 13 | 50 | 48 | 0 |
| Correctly reformulated | 4 | 7 | 2 | – | – | – |
| % correct after reformulation | 44 | 64 | 10 | – | – | – |
| *Second administration:* | | | | | | |
| Obligatory occasions | 9 | 26 | 24 | 15 | 12 | 16 |
| Correct | 8 | 16 | 1 | 7 | 6 | 1 |
| Incorrect | 1 | 10 | 23 | 8 | 6 | 15 |
| % correct | 89 | 62 | 4 | 47 | 50 | 6 |

TABLE 1 *Correct and incorrect use of the past tense in two administrations of communication tasks*

## Discussion

This study provides some support for the claim that 'pushing' learners to improve the accuracy of their production results not only in immediate improved performance but also in gains in accuracy over time. Two of the learners in the experimental group showed significant gains in accuracy, whereas none of the learners in the control group did so. This augurs well for the comprehensible output hypothesis. However, one of the experimental learners failed to show any immediate or long-term improvement in the use of past tense verb forms. His level of accuracy remained essentially the same in his initial and reformulated utterances produced during the first administration and in the utterances he produced during the second administration. In other words, this learner did not seem to benefit from being 'pushed'.

One possible interpretation of the results is that 'pushing' learners to make their output more comprehensible leads to linguistic development only in some learners, while others do not benefit. A number of researchers (e.g. Meisel *et al.* 1981; Clyne 1985) have distinguished functionally- and structurally-oriented learners. The former tend to display good comprehension skills and have well-developed communication strategies. The latter have more interest in how language works, take greater efforts to keep the first and second languages separate, and are more inclined to engage in self-correction. It is possible that the first two learners in the experimental group were structurally oriented, while the third was functionally oriented. Thus, whereas the first two made efforts to improve the linguistic accuracy of their output when 'pushed', the third was content to simply get the message across. Such an interpretation is supported by an examination of the kinds of reformulations the third learner produced when the teacher requested clarification. These typically consisted of partial or complete repetitions of previous utterances, as shown in this example:

LEARNER:  But he sleep. He becomes a sleep.
TEACHER:  Sorry?
LEARNER:  But he sleep. He become asleep.

In other words, this learner was more concerned with general fluency than with accuracy. If this explanation is right, it suggests that the comprehensible output hypothesis will need to be modified to take account of the type of learner.

This study was based on an extremely small number of learners and for this reason can only be considered exploratory. It will need to be replicated with a larger sample and with different linguistic features before any definite conclusions can be arrived at. The results it has provided, however, are intriguing.

## Conclusion

One of the purposes of this article was to explain and illustrate what a focused communication task consists of. It is extremely difficult to bring about a focus on a specific linguistic feature while at the same time maintaining true 'communicativeness'. Once learners realize that the task is intended to provide such a focus, they are likely to stop treating it as an opportunity to communicate and switch into a 'learning' mode. One way in which this can be prevented is if the focus is induced methodologically by means of requests for clarification directed at utterances containing errors in the feature that has been targeted. The data from the study reported above indicate that focusing in this way need not disturb the communicativeness of a task.

Methodologically-focused communication tasks, however, will only be of practical use if they can be used to 'teach' a range of different structures. It is not clear, yet, how possible this is. It is fairly easy to design a task that encourages the use of the past simple tense. It may also be possible, with ingenuity, to design tasks that afford opportunities for using such structures as present perfect, future forms, relative clauses and conditionals. But it is less clear whether they can be designed to 'teach' morphological features such as articles and third persons that are largely redundant, contributing little to the meaning of a message, or syntactic structures such as adjectival order and adverbial position, where, again, adherence to native speaker norms contributes little to message conveyance. As a number of second language researchers have suggested, it may be that certain types of grammatical features cannot easily be acquired through interaction (White 1987).

It is also possible, as the study indicated, that some learners will not benefit much from being 'pushed' while interacting. This raises the question as to how these learners are to succeed in developing acceptable levels of grammatical accuracy. One answer might be to argue that it does not really matter if they remain grammatically incompetent, as long as they are communicatively competent. If there has to be a choice between the two, it is surely better to go for communicative skill. However, this might not satisfy some teachers. The alternative is to provide 'formal' instruction consisting of tasks designed to focus the learners' conscious attention on specific linguistic features. Indeed, it is not the purpose of this article to suggest that focused communicative activities should *replace* traditional grammar work, only that, for some learners at least, it can serve as a way of helping them to acquire interactively.

Finally, it is necessary to consider in what way focused communication activities can aid 'acquisition'. In this respect, it is useful to distinguish two meanings of acquisition—(1) acquisition as the internalization of new forms, and (2) acquisition as the increase in control over forms that have already been internalized. Arguably, the first occurs as the product of comprehending input, as claimed by the interaction hypothesis, while the second is aided by 'pushing' learners to improve their output, as claimed by the comprehensible output hypothesis. Focused communication tasks would seem better suited to increasing control than to 'teaching' new forms.[3] They provide a means for encouraging learners to maximize their linguistic competence under real operating conditions.

*Originally published in Volume 47/3, 1993*

## Notes

1  It is much easier to construct communicative listening tasks in which attention to a specific linguistic property is essential. This is because in listening tasks the designer rather than the learner has control over the linguistic content.

2  An obligatory occasion consists of an occasion when a learner creates a context that requires the use of a specific linguistic feature—irrespective of whether the feature is or is not actually used. For example, both the following constitute obligatory occasions for the use of the past simple tense:

Yesterday we visit the Tate Gallery.
Yesterday we visited the Tate Gallery.

3  It is interesting to speculate that different pedagogic techniques may be needed for (a) teaching new forms and for (b) helping learners acquire greater control over forms that they have already learnt, as the pyscholinguistic processes involved in these two aspects of acquisition appear to be different. To some extent, this is already acknowledged in language pedagogy, as in the distinction commonly made between 'skill developing' and 'skill using' activities.

# 22

# Teacher roles in the learner-centred classroom

IAN TUDOR

## Background

The recent interest shown in learner-centredness in language teaching, apparent in concepts such as learner autonomy, self-directed learning, or syllabus negotiation, revolves around a redefinition of the role students can play in their learning of a language. In a learner-centred approach, students are seen as being able to assume a more active and participatory role than is usual in traditional approaches. Logically, however, student roles cannot be redefined without a parallel redefinition of teacher roles. It is this aspect of learner-centredness that will be considered in this article, that is, the roles and responsibilities of the teacher within a learner-centred approach to language teaching.

## Did you say 'learner-centredness'?

Discussions of learner-centredness are often complicated by the fact that the term is used to express at least the following four related, but none the less distinct, perspectives on language teaching.

### An approach to activity organization

In this use of the term, learner-centredness relates to a way of organizing classroom activities. The basic idea is that learning activities will be more relevant if it is the students, as opposed to the teacher, who decide on the conceptual and linguistic content of these activities. It also assumes that students' involvement and motivation will be greater if they can decide how activities are structured. O'Neill's (1991) article in this journal deals in the main with this type of learner-centredness.

## The humanistic perspective

The humanistic movement stresses the importance of qualities such as understanding, personal assumption of responsibility, and self-realization (see Stevick 1990). From this perspective, language learning is seen as an activity which involves students as complex human beings, not 'simply' as language learners. Language teaching should therefore exploit students' affective and intellectual resources as fully as possible, and be linked into their continuing experience of life. Despite certain reservations that have been voiced about various humanistic methods (Atkinson 1989; Brumfit 1982), the humanistic movement has had an undeniable impact on language teaching practice. This can be seen, for example, in the increasing popularity of affectively-based communicative activities and of drama.

## Practical necessity

In recent years, there has been considerable interest in learner autonomy (Brookes and Grundy 1988; Holec 1979) and self-direction (Dickinson, 1987) in language teaching. In part at least, this arises from the need to cater for language teaching in situations where a traditional classroom-based approach is not feasible. There can be a variety of reasons for this: students may not have sufficient free time to follow a traditional course; there may be insufficient demand for a given language to justify setting up a standard teacher-led course, or budgetary restrictions may place limits on staff–student contact time. Faced with real-world constraints of this nature, the teaching profession has looked for new approaches to teaching which allow students to attain their goals with less direct teacher support. This has involved a re-examination of what students can contribute to their learning of a language, and experimentation with teaching methods designed to exploit students' 'autonomous' learning potential.

## The curriculum design perspective

Writers such as Brindley (1984) and Nunan (1988) have suggested that curriculum design can be seen as a negotiative process between teachers and students. In this view, decisions regarding the content and form of teaching can be made at classroom level via consultation between teachers and learners. This differs from traditional approaches to curriculum design where these decisions are made by 'outside' experts such as needs analysts or course planners. Nunan (1989b: 19) expresses this in the following terms:

> While a learner-centred curriculum will contain similar elements and processes to traditional curricula, a key difference will be that information by and from learners will be built into every phase of the curriculum process. Curriculum development becomes a collaborative effort between teachers and learners, since learners will be involved in decisions on content selection, methodology and evaluation.

This represents the strongest and most coherent view of what learner-centredness can mean in language teaching terms. However, most work on the practical application of this approach has been conducted in Australia—and thought needs to be given to the way in which these principles can be applied in other teaching contexts.

Moving away from these different uses of the term learner-centredness, and the perspectives on language teaching they reflect, there would seem to be a number of basic ideas which, in one form or another, underlie most discussions of learner-centredness. These are:

- goal-setting can be made more relevant if students can contribute to the process on the basis of their own experience;
- learning is more effective if methodology and study mode are geared around student preferences;
- students get more out of learning activities if they have a say in deciding their content and in organizing the activities;
- learning will, in a general sense, benefit if students feel involved in shaping their study programme.

In the rest of the article, the term learner-centredness will be used to refer to this set of tenets.

## Learner-centredness and the teacher

At the price of a certain oversimplification, there would seem to be two main roles which teachers perform in most traditional modes of teaching. The first is that of *knower*: the teacher is a source of knowledge in terms of both the target language and the choice of methodology. In other words, the teacher is a figure of authority who decides on what should be learnt and how this should best be learnt. The second role is that of *activity organizer*: the teacher sets up and steers learning activities in the right direction, motivates and encourages students, and provides authoritative feedback on students' performance. Both of these roles will persist in a learner-centred approach, but teachers will need to assume a further role, that of *learning counsellor*.

Oskarsson (1978: xi) expresses one of the principles of the Council of Europe's Modern Languages Project in the following, very learner-centred terms:

> ... the intentions and resources of the learner should be the controlling factors for reaching proper decisions as to what he should learn and how he should learn it.

Gearing language teaching around students' intentions and resources in this way has a number of implications for the teacher, who will need to

- get to know students well enough to be able to understand both their intentions (what they need and would like to do) and their resources (what they are able to do);
- help students clarify their intentions and develop their resources;
- channel student participation in a pedagogically useful direction.

It is here that the extra responsibilities of the teacher as learning counsellor arise. In a learner-centred approach, the teacher may be seen as performing the five main functions discussed in the following sections.

## Preparing learners

If language teaching is to be geared around students' intentions and resources, then both the teacher and the students themselves need to understand what these intentions and resources are. From the students' point of view this involves the development of awareness in at least the following areas:

*Self-awareness as a language learner* This relates to students' motivation to learn the language, the amount of effort they are willing to put in, and their attitudes both to the target language (TL) and to the process of learning itself.

*Awareness of learning goals* Here, students need to develop an understanding of why they are studying the TL, of their communicative goals and of their current abilities in the language—together with the ability to analyse and discuss their goals.

*Awareness of learning options* This involves students acquiring an understanding of what language learning entails, of the various learning strategies, study options, and resources they can use, and of how different activities can advance learning—in both in-class and self-study contexts.

*Language awareness* Without having to become linguists, students need at least a basic idea of how language is structured and used—e.g. certain grammatical or functional categories, the ability to recognize formulaic expressions, some notions of register and appropriacy.

Helping students develop awareness in these areas, a process often referred to as learner training, is a crucial part of the teacher's role in a learner-centred approach. This will generally involve the teacher making suggestions and providing students with information (on alternative learning strategies or study options, for example). More importantly, however, the teacher has to help students to look at themselves and at language learning in an open and constructive manner. This calls for skills which have little to do with language teaching in a narrow sense: the skills involved are essentially educational—skills designed to develop understanding and human potential.

There are a variety of options available to teachers. If time and resources allow, individual interviews and regular consultation with students can be arranged. Alternatively, a course may begin with a learner training programme along the lines suggested by Ellis and Sinclair (1989). If time is limited, however, awareness development may essentially revolve around ongoing discussion and consultation between teacher and students on the basis of day-to-day teaching activities.

## Analysing learner needs

Holec (1980: 33) suggests that:

> ... it seems unlikely, to say the least, that needs analysis can be successfully carried out by anyone other than the learner himself.

As it is the students who will be using the language they are learning, it does not seem unreasonable to assume that they might have something sensible to say about what they should learn. In fact, they may well have a closer insight into their communicative needs than the teacher. Content selection is thus an area where there would seem to be good reason for listening carefully to what students have to say.

A learner-centred approach to needs analysis and goal-setting asks two main things of the teacher. The first is to assess how much students have to contribute, as this varies a lot between students. Let us take, at one end of the scale, the case of a German businessman who requires English to perform functions parallel to those he performs daily in German. This student should be able to provide information on the situations in which he will need to use the language, the ideas he will wish to express, and the communicative functions he will wish to perform. He may also be able to specify the performance criteria which are crucial for him—fluency, good pronunciation, the ability to establish social contacts, or whatever. It would clearly be wasteful *not* to take advantage of what such a student had to say. At the other end of the scale, a British secondary school pupil studying German together with ten or more other subjects is likely to have a rather different set of priorities, and could make a much less direct contribution to goal-setting. At the risk of stating the obvious, what students can contribute to goal-setting depends largely on how clear their learning goals are.

Once the teacher has identified a potential for contribution the next task is to help students to formulate their insights in a pedagogically useful form, which may not be as easy as one might imagine. Even if students have thought objectively about their communicative needs, they may lack the analytical categories to express them, or they may perceive their needs in terms of their prior learning experience—which may or may not be helpful. In most cases, the teacher will need to provide some basic terminology and a few guidelines to get students thinking along useful lines. Depending on the type of student, a variety of other techniques can be used. Questionnaires can elicit information useful to the teacher as well as helping students structure their experience. Learner diaries, where students record their language use over a period of time, can be extremely useful, though they demand a fair degree of commitment and training. Other techniques include the pooling of experiences among students, teacher–student consultation, and student-based simulations.

## Selecting methodology

A good deal of what has been written about language teaching over the last two decades (if not longer) seems to have been concerned with finding better, or ideally, *the best* teaching method. This has undoubtedly improved many aspects of language teaching practice and has enriched the range of methodological options from which teachers can choose. However, teaching method, although important, is just one aspect of language teaching. Every teaching situation involves the interaction between a given teaching method, the students, and the wider socio-cultural context of learning. If this interaction is not a happy one, learning is unlikely to be effective, no matter how good the credentials of the teaching method may be in theoretical terms. Teaching method needs therefore to be chosen not only on the basis of what seems theoretically plausible, but also in the light of the experience, personality, and expectations of the students involved.

Learner-centredness in choice of methodology is more complex than in goal-setting. Some students certainly do have greater familiarity with their communicative needs than their teachers, whereas relatively few will know more about language teaching methodology. Adopting a learner-centred approach to choice of methodology will thus generally operate in two stages. In the first, the teacher must get to know students on a number of counts, though in particular with respect to their preferred learning style and their attitudes to or experience of language learning. On this basis, the teacher must use his or her professional judgement to select a teaching–learning mode that seems likely to hit the right chord with students.

The second stage involves students participating actively in the planning of their learning programme. This, however, needs preparation. To begin with, the teacher has to encourage students to think critically about their learning experiences and about themselves as learners. This is best done on the basis of concrete learning activities: what did students get out of a given task? what can they learn from intensive text study? or from going to the cinema? what do they mean by 'grammar'? how can they organize their vocabulary lists? why do they not enjoy the language laboratory/pair work? and what can they learn from these activities? Nor will all students show the same ability or willingness to think critically about their learning. None the less, with good will and give-and-take on both sides, negotiating methodology can be fun and can give students a valuable bonus—the ability to learn for themselves.

## Transferring responsibility

Learner-centredness represents what could be called a 'partnership model' (see Eisler 1987) of language teaching, decisions regarding the content and form of teaching being shared between teachers and students. This does not, however, mean that responsibility is wholly transferred to the students. In a learner-centred mode of teaching, as in any other, the teacher remains ultimately responsible for ensuring that effective learning takes place. Assessing how much, and which areas of responsibility to transfer to students is thus a key aspect of the teacher's role. Essentially, this involves the teacher evaluating three main points:

- what students have to contribute;
- how this can make learning more effective;
- how capable students are of assuming a constructive and responsible role in shaping their learning programme.

We have already looked at this in terms of goal-setting and choice of methodology, but there is a lot more involved.

Language teaching is a complex social and cultural activity. The teacher therefore needs to understand students within their socio-cultural context, quite apart from accepting them as psychologically complex individuals. A wide range of factors merit consideration in this respect (Tudor 1992), though the teacher should think of at least the following questions:

1 *How motivated are my students?*
Involvement in course development requires students to invest thought and effort additional to what is called for in a traditional mode of teaching. The teacher should therefore be prudent, and not place demands on students which they may not wish or be able to fulfil.

2 *How mature are my students?*
Sharing knowledge and experience, and negotiating study mode, require mutual respect between teacher and students, a willingness to see the other person's point of view, and a fair degree of give-and-take. Personal maturity (which is not, of course, synonymous with age) is essential: the less confident the teacher is of finding this among the students involved, the more prudence is called for.

3 *What are my students' cultural attitudes to (language) study and to the roles of teachers and learners?*
No teaching approach will work unless it is accepted by both teachers and students. If, for example, students come from a culture where the teacher is seen as a figure of authority, the attempt to share decision-making with students (however well-intentioned) may be seen as an abdication of responsibility—and may thus forfeit students' commitment to the course as a whole.

4 *Are there any external constraints that place limits on learner direction?*
Allowing students to develop their own path in learning a language can have a number of very real advantages. At the same time, there

may be constraints, most obviously perhaps in the form of an external examination, which place limits on how far students can deviate from a given study path without encountering difficulties. Such factors need not rule out learner direction, but they may restrict how far the teacher can responsibly allow learners to go.

## Involving learners

Once the basic decision has been made to adopt a learner-centred approach, two questions soon arise: where to start? and how to start?

Regarding where to start, it needs to be borne in mind that learner involvement is not an all-or-nothing affair. Course planning is a very complex process, one to which different types of students can contribute to varying degrees. Students with clear learning goals and a responsible attitude to their learning can potentially become involved in most levels of decision-making; in the case of students who are less mature, less motivated, or who have poorly defined learning goals, involvement may be limited to just one or two sub-parts of the process. Teachers need to make choices on the basis of their initial assessment of the students. Teachers may find it helpful to draw up a list of the decisions *they* have to make, and then select from this list the areas where their students seem most likely to be able to make a sensible contribution to decision-making. Such a list might include the following points:

1 course structure (e.g. the mix of in-class, self-access, and independent study components);

2 goal-setting;

3 choice of methodology;

4 activity selection and organization;

5 linguistic syllabus (e.g. will the teacher decide on the language points to be covered, or will these arise out of students' observed performance in communicative tasks?);

6 choice of materials (e.g. can students provide materials directly relevant to their learning goals?);

7 topic selection;

8 evaluation;

9 independent study.

Two points need to be borne in mind in terms of how to start. The first is that student involvement will generally be a gradual process. The second is that self-direction is best learnt in a hands-on manner. Once the teacher has selected those aspects of course planning where there seems most scope for student involvement, the next task is to get students participating actively in the choices and decisions which arise in these areas. To begin with, this may simply involve students thinking critically about what the teacher proposes: how relevant are the materials? what did students get out of them? how else could they be exploited? could the students supply better or more relevant materials?

In this area, it is important to distinguish between the substance and the form of student involvement. The rather painful 'learner-centred' lesson described by O'Neill (1991) has the external forms of learner-centredness. However, it was patently ineffective because the students had not *really* been involved: the teacher had, it seems, imposed her ideas on the students without adequately preparing them or sharing her ideas with them. In other words, under the guise of learner-centredness, the result was a classic 'teacher-knows-best-so-do-as-you're-told' type of lesson, which probably left the students feeling both frustrated and confused. In this respect, much can be learnt from Underhill's (1989: 260) suggestion that 'doing the same things with a different awareness seems to make a bigger difference than doing different things with the same awareness'.

## The teacher's perspective: a cautionary note

There can be little doubt that opting for a learner-centred approach adds to the responsibilities of the teacher. The teacher, in the role of learning counsellor, needs at least three main sets of skills in addition to those required in traditional modes of teaching:

*Personal skills* Evaluating students' potential and negotiating their involvement in a sensitive manner calls for an array of human and inter-personal skills. Maturity and human intuition are key qualities.

*Educational skills* In a learner-centred mode of teaching, the teacher has to develop students' awareness and shape their ability to make the most of their knowledge and experience. Language teaching thus becomes an educational endeavour far more than a matter of skills training.

*Course planning skills* Being open to student input and participation can make advance planning more difficult, and requires the teacher to live with more uncertainty than is usual in traditional approaches. Furthermore, co-ordinating goal-setting and choice of methodology assumes a solid familiarity with course design and with the various methodological options available.

Learner-centred teaching is anything but an easy option. Few teachers who have tried out a learner-centred approach will not, at one time or another, have ground their teeth and wished they had stuck to a more predictable mode of teaching. Inevitably, the more open teaching is to students' participation, the more dependent it is upon their co-operation—which can put the teacher in an awkward situation if students decide not to play the game.

Probably the main risk is going too far too quickly. Both the degree and the form of student involvement need to be geared round the realities of the teaching situation. In the first instance, this relates to the students themselves, but also includes factors such as availability of resources, cultural attitudes, or class size. One also needs to be realistic about oneself as a teacher. Adopting a learner-centred approach makes extra demands on the teacher's time and energy, makes advance planning more difficult, and, as a result of the developmental nature of course structure, can add stress. Furthermore, non-native-speaker teachers may feel less at ease in situations where language content can be unpredictable. The teacher, just as much as the students, must feel good about an approach for it to work well.

## Conclusion

This article has looked at the implications of a learner-centred approach from the perspective of the teacher. Learner-centred teaching adds a number of responsibilities not normally found in traditional approaches—these responsibilities relating to the development and channelling of students' human and experiential potential. It has been suggested that teachers who envisage adopting a learner-centred approach should think carefully of the implications of this choice in terms of the extra work and responsibilities it entails. The same applies to department heads or educational bodies who might wish to experiment with a learner-centred mode of teaching on a larger scale: appropriate teacher preparation and ongoing support are essential.

All this having been said, however, it would be wrong to view learner-centred teaching as something intimidating. To begin with, as has already been pointed out, learner-centredness is not an all-or-nothing affair: the teacher need never feel obliged to go further in involving learners in decision-making than his or her professional judgement says is appropriate. Learner-centredness is not a method, nor can it be reduced to a set of techniques. In the first instance, it involves a recognition of students' potential to contribute meaningfully to the shaping of their learning programme, and then a willingness to accommodate this potential as far as the situation will realistically allow. To repeat a point that was made earlier, one needs to distinguish between the form and the substance of learner-centredness. Learner-centred teaching is essentially very simple. Primarily, it boils down to responding to students' in-built needs as both language users and language learners: the means by which this is achieved are secondary, and can vary quite considerably from one learner group to another. Furthermore, for a learner-centred approach to work well, students will have to learn more than just the target language. They will need to learn about how language is structured and used, and about themselves as language learners. Thus, in addition to a given level of language competence, students should leave a course with a better understanding of language and of themselves as both language users and language learners. This is clearly an educational product, and helping students to acquire it can be very rewarding for teachers in both personal and professional terms.

*Originally published in Volume 47/1, 1993*

# 23

## The learner's contribution to
## the self-access centre

### GUY ASTON

## Introduction

### Economic and pedagogic motivations

Self-access centres for language learning have enjoyed growing popularity in recent years for both economic and pedagogic reasons. By providing an environment with a variety of machines and materials that users can exploit, and some kind of catalogue and advisory service to help them do so, such centres can offer a wider and more flexible range of opportunities for language use than is possible in most classrooms. In so far as the individual is free to choose the activities to carry out and the time to dedicate to them, learning is self-directed and autonomy is encouraged. On the other hand, because learners are largely left to their own devices, without the control of a teacher, such centres can also be seen as providing language learning on the cheap, potentially substituting for direct teaching operations. This economic argument is a compelling one for many institutions, notwithstanding warnings that if benefits to the learner are to be maximized through appropriate organization and qualified consultancy, self-access centres do not necessarily reduce staff loads with respect to conventional teaching (Dickinson 1987: 122).

There are, in other words, two ways of looking at self-access centres. One is as a means of improving learning, the other as a means of cutting teaching costs. Each has rather different implications for the priorities and organization of such centres and the underlying conflict between the two tends to be reflected in different pedagogic approaches:

If we believe that the chief responsibility for initiating and shaping the
language learning process rests with the teacher as the learner's chief
source of knowledge about the target language, we are likely to think
of self-instruction as an alternative to instruction by a teacher and of
self-access systems as a form of teacher-substitute. We shall probably
want to organize self-access systems so that learners can be taught as
it were by remote control, and the learning materials we shall mostly
provide will be fully-developed language courses of a more or less
traditional kind ...

However, things look very different from the learner-centred perspective of the 'analytic' approach to language course design. If ...
successful language learning depends on interaction with a large and
varied diet of textual materials and the development within the
learner of a capacity to take decisive initiatives, then we must provide
the learner with resources that he or she can draw on *as an individual*.
According to this view all language learning turns out to have a self-
instructional component, and the self-access system is seen not as an
alternative to the teacher but as a necessary resource for all language
learners.

(Singleton and Little 1989: 32–3)

## Teaching by remote control

This formulation is an extreme one, but the dichotomy remains. For
instance, rather than as a total substitute for teaching, self-access may be
proposed as providing pre-fabricated paths of self-instruction in certain
skills or practice areas—'Brush up your tenses' and the like, where the
individualized environment allows learners to work on those aspects of
the language which are particularly problematic for them (Sturtridge
1992). Such paths must be established a priori—by the teacher, materials producer, and cataloguer—so that materials are carefully selected
for particular types of learners and types of problems. The advisory and
cataloguing systems must enable learners to match their individual
requirements to the metalinguistic categories employed in this selection
process, so that appropriate paths can be identified among the closed set
placed on offer.[1]

## Encouraging learner initiative

Compare this with an approach to self-access which aims at providing a
'large and varied diet' and encouraging learner initiative. The aim will

be to create an open environment, within which learners can encounter instances of language in use and invent their own infinitely varied learning pathways through them. In this case less control of materials will be required, as the emphasis will be on providing a wide range of open-ended learning opportunities rather than specifying materials which focus on specific linguistic contents and subskills. The materials may indeed be totally uncontrolled by the centre, as with live satellite TV. The advisory system will encourage rather than prescribe. Cataloguing is likely to be in motivational terms, such as the type of material, topic, and general difficulty (Ferris *et al.* 1988), rather than in the metalinguistic terms of an expert analysis.

In the first case, the main criterion will probably be the ability of the system to offer solutions to specific problems. In the second case, it is likely to be the ability of the system to motivate learners and to develop autonomy. While these criteria are to some extent incompatible, they share one common feature, namely that materials, catalogues, and advisory structures should optimize results vis-à-vis the centre's objectives, whatever these may be. In either case, learners will need to be made aware of the facilities available, and shown their potential for language learning. The importance of this principle is reinforced by the fact that in practice, most self-access centres need to combine the two approaches described to some extent, for the good reason that not only centres but learners too vary in their philosophies. However much a centre may seek to invest in open, unstructured materials, it cannot deny users structured ones without going against the beliefs of many learners. If the centre aims to encourage and develop autonomy, it can hardly oblige learners to adopt a purely unstructured approach, since, as Holec (1980, 1985) points out, coercion and autonomy are incompatible. Thus, while self-access centres need to offer many resources which only some learners will in fact want to exploit, all learners still have to be placed in a position where they can evaluate the relevance of those facilities to them. The learner's knowledge and attitudes are key to the success of any self-access system, regardless of its underlying motivation and philosophy.

## *The learner as consumer and contributor*
### Learner involvement

Reconciling objectives in self-access centres is obviously a local matter, and decisions will vary according to circumstances. Funds, space and personnel have to be found, pedagogic approaches proposed, endorsed and put into practice. As McCafferty notes, there is a paradox here:

Ideally, everything in the self-access system would have been put there on the basis of its usefulness to learners. But before you have any learners you have no real evidence as to what a particular individual or group will find useful.

(McCafferty undated: 26)

Strikingly, these decisions do not as a rule involve learners, who tend to be seen simply as consumers of facilities provided for their benefit. Where learners are seen as potential contributors, this is generally in economic terms—for instance in acting as assistant librarians, policing the facilities and helping other users to locate materials (Sheerin 1989). They are not thought of as potential contributors to the pedagogy of the centre in a qualitative sense, as contributing to the design of the system. However, if we shift from an economic to a pedagogic perspective, other possibilities of learner involvement emerge. Holec (1985) lists three requirements for self-access centres: (a) an infrastructure of appropriate materials and resources; (b) teachers trained in providing support, and (c) effective means of informing potential users about the system. Learners themselves can be involved in satisfying all these requirements: in making materials available, in providing support to learners, and in publicizing its wares. Negotiation of the centre's objectives and activities with users can be a source of learning for themselves, for other users, and indeed for the centre and its staff.

A hint of this potential is provided in Sheerin's discussion of the advantages of involving users in the day-to-day running of self-access facilities:

students become more self-reliant and responsible, both as a body and as individuals, and they have more opportunities for getting to know the system well, and of influencing its development.

(Sheerin 1989: 33)

Sheerin formulates this potential as a pedagogic spin-off from an essentially economic contribution. However, the learner's possible contribution can instead be evaluated in primarily pedagogic terms, as implied, for instance, by the observation that 'teachers-only' access to materials means that the centre's staff 'spends a considerable amount of time doing a job which students benefit greatly from doing themselves' (Moulden 1988: 88). Activity which is designed to help the learner acquire the language and/or to learn how to learn can also be structured so that learners help to generate publicity for the self-access facility, and to optimize self-access infrastructure and levels of support for its users. Such a perspective clearly does not preclude the possibility of economic spin-offs, but is not primarily motivated by them.

## Learning management

As an illustration, consider the issue of support. Any self-access centre will be involved in training learners, and this will typically be carried out either through an advisory service, or by teachers in conventional lessons which potential users also attend. The optimization of either option will also involve training the teachers (O'Dell 1992), who themselves require support in their learning. Furthermore, there is a sense in which the institution itself needs to be trained, for instance in carrying out research and obtaining feedback on its learner-training and trainer-training procedures. Problems of learning management permeate the system on all levels. Holec (1980, 1987) indicates five areas where learning management requires decisions: spatio-temporal organization, techniques, materials, objectives, and evaluation. These areas concern all the levels of the system: the target user, the trainer, and the institution itself. Users need to assess their objectives, the means by which they can be achieved, and the results obtained; trainers need to consider these issues with respect to both users and their own learning-to-train; the institution needs to do so with respect to users, trainers, and its own learning *qua* organization.

These tasks tend to be seen as hierarchically structured in a downwards direction, where each level in the pyramid concerns itself with the needs of lower levels (and, in so far as autonomy is encouraged, its own: see Figure 1). But this is not necessarily the case. Trainers are frequently involved not just in supporting learners and in managing their own 'learning-to-train', but also in analysing the organization, and proposing and commenting on services (though in authoritarian structures this sort of feedback may be less common). The interaction need not stop there: users too can contribute to the learning of the higher levels of the pyramid, namely the institution and its trainers, as well as to the learning of other users. They too can provide feedback and suggestions, so that the overall pattern of learning support is an interactive one (Figure 2).

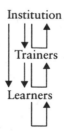

FIGURE 1 *Learning support: hierarchical model*

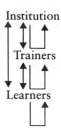

FIGURE 2 *Learning support: interactive model*

Just as they can contribute to requirements of support, the users of a self-access centre can also contribute to the other areas emphasized by Holec (1985)—the design of an appropriate environment, and its publicity. In the second part of this paper, I describe an experiment which involved learners in systematically evaluating self-access facilities, and outline the benefits which arguably derived from it—for the learners involved, for other learners, and for the centre and its staff.

## The setting

In 1991, a twelve-place self-access centre was set up within the Faculty of Economics at Ancona University for the learning of English, French, German, Spanish, and Italian as a foreign language. The centre is open 25 hours a week to all students in the faculty on a first-come first-served basis, and is run by a librarian and a technician, who advise on selecting materials and on technical problems. There are areas dedicated to audio, video (satellite and VCR), computers, and reading materials (chiefly reference works and magazines). The main aim is to provide an open environment in which learners have a wide range of opportunities to experience language in use, though some structured materials on specific problem areas are also available. Most users also attend language courses in the faculty, and although self-access work is not an official part of any course many of the teachers encourage their students to use the centre, taking time in class to discuss learning strategies, and to underline the value of extensive experience of language use of a relatively unstructured nature.

Response to the facilities has been positive, both as a means of preparing for faculty examinations and of improving general language ability. Over the first six months of 1992 overall occupation of the places available averaged 50 per cent, including vacations: most use concerned

English, the most widely-studied language in the faculty. However, some areas were clearly more popular than others, with the more complex materials and activities tending to be spurned in favour of 'telly-watching'. This may have been partly due to inadequacies of cataloguing and advice: not all the centre's staff have pedagogic experience, and it has not been possible to employ teachers as cataloguers and advisors (for further details, see Aston 1995). This apparent gap between supply and demand, and the need to improve support to learners and publicity for the full range of facilities, led to the experiment now to be described.

This experiment took the form of a seminar in which learners examined the use of the self-access centre, having as their objective the production of information and suggestions for the centre's users and staff. This seminar was programmed as one of five options offered to economics students doing their third-year English course with the aim of improving spoken fluency through intensive work in a supportive atmosphere. Each seminar involved spending two hours a week for eight weeks doing some kind of 'project work' in a specified area with the assistance of a native-speaking teacher-animator, working towards a 'real-world' outcome (Fried-Booth 1986; Legutke and Thomas 1991): English was to be the language both of the final product and the process by which it was prepared. Seminars were optional, and work done in them was not examined. At the end of the semester, however, the participants in each seminar presented results from their project to the entire course, in a collective feedback session.

## The project
### The process

The participants in the seminar were eight volunteers at an intermediate or upper-intermediate level of English. All of them had previously made some use of the self-access centre, and were aware of its aims in offering opportunities for learning and learning-how-to-learn. Their brief was to explore the centre—trying out new machines and materials, comparing their experiences, identifying difficulties and discussing ideas for use— and to come up with such products for the centre's staff and for other users as they saw fit: oral or written reports, notices, leaflets, recordings, etc. For help and advice they could call on the centre's staff (a necessary exception was made here to the rule that they should at all times use English), and on their teacher-animator (who was present at about half the sessions). The first four weeks were spent trying out activities and comparing experiences. Participants worked in twos and threes, the groups changing as students moved around to be shown and try out discoveries others had made. For the second half of the seminar, groups were fixed on the basis of individual interests, each producing materials about a specific area of the centre—video, computers, and magazines. In the final collective feedback session they presented these materials to the entire course: leaflets were distributed to those present, and practical demonstrations provided using video. Copies of the leaflets were also placed in the centre for consultation by users.

## The product

The computer area group produced a leaflet which:

- explained how to use the *Longman Mini Concordancer* (the available help having been judged inadequate for the naive user). It described loading, text selection and existing procedures, and illustrated some possible searches (using the wildcard option to find derivatives, such as *wide/width/widen/widening*, and hyphenated compounds; using collocation options to compare *few* with a *few*, and restrictive with non-restrictive relative clauses);

- presented and suggested how to use *Storyboard* (always read the complete text carefully before you start to reconstruct it, try playing competitively on two adjacent machines);

- strongly advised against using a maze programme at all ('it absolutely doesn't work').

The video area group also produced a leaflet. This involved a number of things:

- getting help from the duty technician in locating satellite channels, for which reception conditions could vary from day to day;

- discussing the relative difficulty of different types of satellite programme (if in doubt, watch the news);

- recording satellite programmes while watching them, and noting down the tape counter number when particularly interesting or difficult bits were encountered, so that these could be easily found and reviewed afterwards.

The reading area group produced an advertisement for some of the magazines available. This sang the praises of the *Authentik* series of newspapers and associated recordings from radio, whose multimedia nature the group had discovered with surprise and interest. While the least didactic, this pamphlet was good publicity, being quite the most attractive of the series.

The group as a whole also proposed modifications to the existing notices explaining how to use the catalogue, which they found confusing and incomplete. On the basis of their recommendations, these were rewritten by the centre's staff.

## Project outcomes: limits and benefits

Most of the suggestions made by the group may seem relatively obvious ones which staff might be expected to provide themselves. However, their formulation by users still seems a valuable way of encouraging learners to seek out and reflect on learning procedures. A more severe limitation is that these suggestions mainly concern Holec's (1987) simpler areas of decision, those of choosing techniques and materials, rather than the more complex ones of clarifying objectives and evaluating results. The seminar might have made progress in these directions given more time, however, and it would be interesting to repeat the experiment focusing on just one or two types of activity in greater depth. A last proviso in evaluating the results is that it is impossible to assess long-term effects.

With these reservations, the project would seem to have produced the following benefits:

1  Participants increased their knowledge and understanding of the resources available for self-directed self-access work, and became more aware of their own individual learning strategies, and the way these interacted with the facilities available. They also received substantial language practice in exploring and discussing materials and in preparing and presenting the final products: overall attitudes to English and to autonomous language learning seemed positively reinforced.

2  Other students benefited from the group's final presentation which communicated information on, interest in, and enthusiasm for many of the facilities; it also communicated ideas and enthusiasm for user control of the centre's activities. This control was practically demonstrated in the presentation, which constituted a piece of learner training carried out by other learners.

3  The centre and its staff benefited from direct improvements to the facilities (leaflets, organizational changes), and suggestions for future developments; critical feedback helped make staff more aware of

learners' problems and attitudes; and the experiment provided publicity, not least through the most effective channel, the grapevine.

## Conclusions

The experiment described is clearly a very limited attempt to involve the
learner in the development of a self-access centre. But it does illustrate
certain principles which seem important if such centres are to maintain
what Riley *et al.* (1989) call their essential 'catalytic' nature for all concerned. This presupposes personal and interpersonal involvement at all
levels, first and foremost of users:

> The learner needs people to talk to, to listen to, to discuss, argue and
> exchange information with, to write to, to practise with, to learn
> from. It is a function of the centre to bring learners together; to pro-
> vide a meeting place; initially at least to create the basis and purpose
> for activities and to provide either monitoring or endorsement of
> activities.
> (McCafferty undated: 24)

From such a perspective, it seems important for the learner's role not to
be limited to the consumption of services provided in a pre-established
framework. Learners can become animators and creators of self-access
facilities, taking greater control not only of their own learning, but also
of the institution whose task is to make such learning and control possible, negotiating the facilities, their use, and the support provided. In this
manner:

> The learner is no longer faced with an 'independent' reality that
> escapes him, to which he cannot but give way, but with a reality which
> he himself constructs and dominates.
> (Holec 1980: 21)

Such learner involvement seems systematically possible provided that
there are not too many students using the centre, and that they stay long
enough to take full advantage of it. Not only do the benefits to all parties
involved seem relevant from a pedagogic point of view: in the case
described here, where learners carried out the project as part of their faculty language course, they were also achieved at minimal economic cost
to the centre itself.

*Originally published in Volume 47/3, 1993*

# Note

1 For more detailed discussion of this distinction, see Holec (1988b), who contrasts 'distance-learning' and 'learner autonomy' approaches to self-access, and Sturtridge (1992), who subdivides the first category into 'instruction', 'practice', and 'skill' centres, contrasting these with 'learning centres' *tout court*.

# 24

# Feedback in the writing process: a model and methods for implementation

CLAUDIA L. KEH

## The 'process approach'

The 'process approach' to writing is not a new approach: it has been around since the early 1970s. Many readers of this paper may have a working definition of this approach—a multiple-draft process which consists of: generating ideas (pre-writing); writing a first draft with an emphasis on content (to 'discover' meaning/author's ideas); second and third (and possibly more) drafts to revise ideas and the communication of those ideas. Reader feedback on the various drafts is what pushes the writer through the writing process on to the eventual end-product.

An awareness of the term or concept described above may, however, be as far as some teachers get with the process approach for one reason or another. For some teachers (particularly those in exam-driven systems such as are found in Asia) such an approach may be viewed as impractical or 'too time consuming' (or perhaps not 'good' preparation for the exam). In such cases, teachers may equate endless hours of marking (particularly red-pen corrections at the surface level) with working hard. This 'traditional' method has great face-validity to on-lookers (e.g. fellow teachers; headmaster). Further, red marks on students' papers may also 'prove' the teacher's superiority over students and demonstrate that the teacher is 'doing his or her job'. Another reason for not implementing the process approach is that teachers simply have not worked out (or had time to work out) just *how* to implement such an approach. Or, finally, there may be teachers who have tried the approach but have 'run dry' or run into some form of difficulty in implementation and have given up.

## A definition of feedback

Feedback is a fundamental element of a process approach to writing. It can be defined as input from a reader to a writer with the effect of providing information to the writer for revision. In other words, it is the comments, questions, and suggestions a reader gives a writer to produce 'reader-based prose' (Flower 1979) as opposed to writer-based prose. Through feedback, the writer learns where he or she has misled or confused the reader by not supplying enough information, illogical organization, lack of development of ideas, or something like inappropriate word-choice or tense.

A review of the literature on writing reveals three major areas of feedback as revision. These areas are: peer feedback; conferences as feedback; and teachers' comments as feedback. (Evaluation and error correction—two other major areas of the literature—can also be considered as feedback in revision under some situations.) In the course 'Practical Writing' at the Language Centre of Baptist College, (tertiary level) Hong Kong, all three types of feedback options are used for each paper that the students write. (Students write four or five papers in all for one semester; each paper taking approximately three weeks to go through the process to the final product.) Figure 1, illustrates how the implementation takes place.

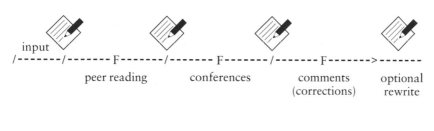

FIGURE 1 *Implementation of feedback (for one paper)*

'Input' on the continuum in Figure 1 means anything which helps students get ideas for writing. This includes invention strategies such as brainstorming, fast writing, clustering, and interviewing. This may also include readings for models of good writing (for a particular type of assignment such as compare/contrast) or readings related to a particular topic. Vocabulary development (brainstorming words associated with a particular topic) may also be included here. Once students have received input for writing, they write their first draft (D1). They are made aware that D1 is only a draft—it is not a sacred process. After D1 is written, students receive their first form of feedback—from peers.

## Peer feedback

In the literature on writing, peer feedback is referred to by many names, for example, peer response, peer editing, peer critiquing, and peer evaluation. Each name connotes a particular slant to the feedback, mainly in terms of where along the continuum this feedback is given, and the focus of the feedback. For example, peer response may come earlier on in the process (e.g. after D1) with a focus on content (organization of ideas, development with examples), and peer editing nearing the final stages of drafting (e.g. after D2 or D3) with a focus on grammar, punctuation, etc.

There are several advantages given for using peer feedback in whatever form it may take. It is said to save teachers time on certain tasks, freeing them for more helpful instruction. Feedback is considered to be more at the learner's own level of development. Learners can gain a greater sense of audience with several readers (i.e. readers other than the teacher). The reader learns more about writing through critically reading others' papers.

Results from a questionnaire given to my own students about peer feedback as well as end-of-course discussions support and augment some of the advantages mentioned above. Students felt the peer feedback was useful in gaining a conscious awareness that they were writing for more than just the teacher. That affected how and what they wrote. Now students write with a greater goal than just writing down as much as possible to cover the topic. They write with a more specific focus because they know that their peers will also be reading their paper. Students also found peer feedback useful for obtaining immediate feedback and 'detecting problems in others' papers'. Here are two comments from students:

> During peer reading, I know how readers feel and how they react.

> Peer evaluation are helpful for these can raise the analytical power of the student. [sic] When they read the essays of their classmates, they can find out their mistakes and at the same time, this helps to remind them to avoid and correct such mistakes.

## Lower and higher order concerns

The first step in implementing peer feedback is to train students for the task. Research shows that students have a tendency to read for surface, mechanical errors, usually referred to as 'lower order concerns' (LOCs). Students tend not to read for 'higher order concerns' (HOCs) such as the development of ideas, organization, and the overall focus of what they are writing.[1]

A comment from one of my students confirms her peers' focus on lower order concerns:

> Peer reading is rarely given a comment of 'good'. Usually, the readers keep an eye on finding grammar mistakes or choice of words.

The distinction between the teacher's management of LOCs and HOCs is crucial to the feedback process. But training students to read for more than lower order concerns is not easy, and, as the student's comment above suggests, not always successful. But the rewards—that is, getting student-readers to read with a writer in mind—are worth the problems or unsuccessful sessions.

Early in the course, I begin to instruct students to read critically in preparation for the peer feedback. I begin by showing examples of their first samples of writing, either on an overhead projector or by giving copies to the class. I focus on higher order concerns connected with lesson objectives. As the example below shows, if the lesson objective is on the logical presentation of ideas and use of appropriate transition words, then that is what the instruction includes:

*Assignment:* to develop a given topic sentence; either inductive or deductive organization.
*Place in syllabus:* first writing sample (pre-essay; first week).
*Focus:* transitions; elements of coherence.

---

Before many major examinations, like HKCEE, ACCA, etc., we can see many students studying in the library. Consultations with lecturers are especially more frequent during this time. Moreover, it is hard to find any student participating in any extra-curricular activity. ▼ *Transition* It is not uncommon to find students getting ill in this period. Therefore, ▼ *add a phrase which shows a connection between the key points and the generalization* students are very nervous before examinations.

---

The goal of such instruction is to give students an example of how to look for HOCs as well as the vocabulary and means to carry out such a focus on HOCs. Through this kind of instruction, students also become accustomed to the type of language (vocabulary such as cohesion, logic, restatement) later used in conferences and comments, making the teacher's work easier.

I also use group paragraph writing, followed by analysis, revision, and evaluation done by groups. For example, I assigned a group paragraph on defining an element of Chinese culture to a Westerner who had little or no experience with an Asian culture. Once paragraphs were completed, they were photocopied and compiled into a small booklet. The last page of the booklet included criteria for evaluation, suggestions for revision (HOCs), and finally instructions for identification of surface errors (LOCs).

For the peer feedback sessions (held during class time in pairs or groups), students are given guidelines. These guidelines begin as very structured check-lists, and progress to being less structured; finally, there are no guidelines, reflecting the place in the syllabus and students' growing competence in peer reading.[2] All guidelines used are based on lesson objectives and use vocabulary from readings and discussions. (See Figure 2 for an example.)

At the end of the course, I move to a 'no-guideline' method suggested by Chandrasegaran (1989). In this method, students write questions about their own drafts specifically to a reader in the wide ruled margins of their draft.

Once students have received feedback from their peers, they revise their papers and write a second draft. After the second draft, feedback is given in the form of conferences.

## Conferences

As with peer feedback, there are several advantages of conferences between the student-writer and teacher-reader.[3] One advantage mentioned is the interaction between the teacher and student. The teacher-reader is a 'live' audience, and thus is able to ask for clarification, check the comprehensibility of oral comments made, help the writer sort through problems, and assist the student in decision-making. Thus, the teacher's role can be perceived as a participant in the writing process rather than as a grade-giver. And compared to writing comments, conferences also allow more feedback and more accurate feedback to be given per minute.

*Type:* check-list/structured
*Objective/focus*
        TS: definition/function
        logical connectors
        support with examples
        restatement sentence

1 What is the author's purpose in writing?
  – to show the importance of something;
  – to convince the reader to do something;
  – to explain how something is done.

2 <u>Underline</u> the author's topic sentence
  Does the topic sentence tell you, the reader, what to
  expect in the remainder of the paper?   yes   no

3 Are the author's points clearly presented to the reader?
  Put a triangle $\triangle$ around every logical connector.
  Can you suggest any other connectors?

4 Does the author give enough examples to support his/her point?
  Put a question mark ? beside anything not clearly explained.
  Put an exclaimation mark ! beside a good example.

5 Does the author provide a good conclusion?
  As the reader, do you feel satisfied with the ending?
  <u>Underline</u> the author's restatement sentence.

FIGURE 2 *An example of guidelines/training for peer-group feedback*

Once again, results from my students' questionnaires and end-of-course discussions provided evidence to support these points. In answer to the question 'What has been the most helpful aspect of the conference sessions?', the majority of students said: feedback from teacher; interaction with teacher and fellow students; different ideas from teacher and students' points of view; and improved logic in writing. Students also wrote:

Students can ask questions; can have a chance to talk more in English.

Improving my writing technique by saying where my problems are and getting immediate feedback.

Questions or problems from the essay are solved more effectively and more information can be gained.

Another item on the questionnaire asked 'What has been the most significant thing you've learnt from the conferences?' The majority of students responded that word-choice, organization, grammar, and reader awareness were areas of significance. Students also added the following comments:

My speaking technique in English and writing technique has improved such as content organization.

Reader awareness—that means to have a better way to arouse readers' interest.

I found too that students valued the conferences not only for their beneficial effect on writing, but also because they helped to build up the students' confidence in oral work.

In implementing conferences with students, I have experimented with individual conferences which last 10–15 minutes and group conferences (2–3 students per group) which last 20–30 minutes. In both cases, I cancel class and have students sign up for appointments. Students not attending a conference on a particular conference day will instead go to class for group work. This group work usually consists of inductive, problem-solving grammar activities, assessed as problematic from students' own papers.

When individual conferences are used, students are given focus questions to prepare beforehand. The questions are designed to get students to focus first on content (HOCs), as more of the surface-type problems (LOCs) seem 'easier' for students to identify and discuss. The questions may include: What is the main point of your essay? How have you organized your points? Who are you writing to? Who is your audience? What do you hope to achieve? What specific area do you want the teacher to look at? Are there any words, phrases, etc. that you feel insecure about?

When group conferences are used, students are given sole responsibility in deciding the agenda for the conferences and how the conferences will be run. These agendas may include an outline of who will speak first, what questions will be asked and how they will be asked. Some groups read aloud portions of their own papers for feedback, others read aloud their peer's paper with a comment about where they feel the paper sounds 'wrong', and make suggestions for improvements.

## A non-directive approach

For whichever type of conference, I use what Duke (1975) calls a non-directive approach. This approach to conferencing is based on counselling techniques in which the teacher asks for more information, shows appreciation for what the student says, uses acceptance and approval words (such as 'I see' and 'I understand') and tells the students that their ideas are not strange. This helps build students' self-esteem, reassures them and gives them further confidence to write. I believe this approach to conferencing is particularly important with my Chinese students. From discussions with my Chinese colleagues, I have learnt that the Hong Kong Chinese do not separate one's work from one's self (as is the case in Western/American thinking). Thus, criticism of one's writing may be taken as criticism of oneself. In addition, my students are not accustomed to speaking with a Westerner on a personal level.

Some recent research (Schwertman 1987; Walker and Elias 1987) suggests that conferences fail when they are *not* non-directive (as described above). Conferences fail when teachers assume an authoritarian role, when they lead the conversation and ignore questions that do not fit into their preconceived 'ideal' agenda, rather than focusing on the concerns of the student as they emerge in dialogue.

The remedy for, or precaution against, such unsuccessful conferences is to give students time to formulate questions and give answers, simply listening to them. Following these recommendations is difficult particularly at the beginning of the course when students may not yet have learnt to separate HOCs from LOCs. I have had groups come in for conferences with an agenda full of mainly grammatical questions, when I know that more pressing and fundamental problems still exist at the content level. In such cases, I listen as students go through their agendas and respond. Once all their questions have been asked, I ask my own questions about the content of the paper, the main point or focus, or how the paper is introduced, concluded, or organized. I make a conscious effort to ask open-ended questions to avoid getting the answers I want to hear. In this way, I have respected students' own concerns (concerns not on my agenda), but have also been able to give some individual instruction on HOCs needing attention.

I have found that the group conferences have been more successful than the individual conferences. Students seem more comfortable speaking in a group than one-to-one with the teacher. More discussion takes place in a group, as questions can be directed not only to the writer, but to the readers as well, taking some pressure off the non-native speaker. In discussions with students, they too prefer group conferences because they 'enjoy classmates' ideas' and 'learn from others' problems'. However, I have also found that towards the end of the course, students are more willing to come on an individual basis to discuss papers in-process as well as 'finished' products that they want to rewrite. I follow the advice given by Harris (1986). The student and I decide together on the goals for the conference—we may discuss reasons for an overall mark given, or questions the student may have, or comments I have written. Finally, we look at the main problems of the paper. From there, I decide on a teaching strategy to help solve the major problems, for example, directing the student to exercises for practice in specific areas of grammar.

After students receive feedback from the (in-process) conferences, they write their third draft—their product.[4] Before handing in their final draft, for evaluation, students are told to edit their own work for LOCs—surface and mechanical problems. They refer to various grammatical input given throughout the course in the form of short, 5–10-minute grammar 'lessons', group problem-solving activities, or actual grammar lessons. In all cases, the grammar point focused on is one which has been identified as problematic in students' own writing, making it relevant. Also, such 'lessons' are meaning-focused rather than 'rules'-focused (see Keh 1989).

## Written comments

Most teachers of writing will agree that making comments on students' papers causes the most frustration and usually takes the most time. Teachers worry whether the comments will be understood, produce the desired results, or even be read. Such worries are justified if we believe the research.[5]

To avoid writing ineffective or inefficient comments, the first step is for the teacher to respond as a concerned reader to a writer—as a person, not a grammarian or grade-giver. Kehl, for example, urges the teacher to communicate '… in a distinctly human voice, with sincere respect for the writer as a person and a sincere interest in his improvement as a writer' (1970: 976). Another recommendation is to limit comments according to fundamental problems, keeping in mind that students cannot pay attention to everything at once. This again requires teachers to distinguish clearly between 'higher order' and 'lower order' concerns, not only when commenting on final drafts, but also when giving written comments as part of the writing process. The rationale here is that LOCs may disappear in a later draft as the writer changes content. For example, the writer may eliminate paragraphs or rewrite sentences where surface problems may have existed.

### Three roles

I have observed that I tend to write comments from three different roles or points of view. Firstly, I write as a reader interacting with a writer—

that is, responding to the content with comments such as 'good point' or 'I agree'. The next role is that of a writing teacher concerned with points of confusion and breaks in logic, but still maintaining the role of a reader. The types of comments written here refer to the specific point of confusion—the effect the confusion has on a reader (actually using the words, 'I as your reader am confused by ...'. They also refer to strategies for revision—choices of problem solving, options, or a possible example. The final role I play is that of a grammarian. These comments are written with reference to a grammar, giving a reason why a particular grammatical form is not appropriate (as with tense choice).

It is difficult to separate these roles when reading a student's paper. Therefore, I refer to an HOC list to help maintain a focus on overall problems, or to point out what a student has done well. I also remind myself of lesson objectives, so that I do not overwhelm students with marks and comments. Making these distinctions may also require reading through a paper twice. After writing comments in the margins of the draft, I write a summative comment at the end of the paper pointing out overall strengths and weaknesses and a suggested goal for the next paper.

## What students think

In my desire to improve my comment-writing and get feedback on how well I am communicating via comments, I asked students how useful they found each category of comment including one-word comments, phrasal comments, sentence-level comments, paragraph comments, and questions (as comments). The results were that students find one-word comments less helpful than comments with the most information (at least in terms of length).

Students further described helpful comments as those that point out specific problems and provide suggestions, examples, or guidelines for revision, and those that give overall strengths and weaknesses of the paper. Students told me, in discussions at the end of the course, that they tend to read these summative comments first and that it is very important to offer praise first followed by the problem areas.

> I think sentence comments and questions are most helpful. The reasons are the former can let me know about what is wrong with my sentence structure such as grammar, logical order, and ideas of the sentence. The latter can help me think about the reader and therefore help me write my essay more clearly.

Paragraphs plus question comments are actually ideas because the questions make me think about the possible solutions to the problems.

Questionnaires revealed that students actually read most if not all comments written on their papers. I was surprised by this, but found that the same applied to all their courses.

When I asked the students why they read the comments, some responded that they wanted to know what they did well, and how they could improve the paper. This was particularly true for students who chose to rewrite the same paper for a higher mark (provided improvement was made). What requires further investigation, however, is whether students actually apply the information and suggestions they read from comments to subsequent papers.

In discussions with students at the end of the course, one student reported that question comments were most useful, because they forced her to think about the answers. Another student reported that the most confusing type of comments I have written on their papers are one-word comments. I was not surprised by that comment. But what did surprise me were the examples given and the reasons for the lack of usefulness or confusion.

Comments such as 'good' or 'good point' were problematic. Reflecting back, I know that when I write comments such as 'good', I feel confident that they are clear and offer encouragement. However, my student pointed out that it was not clear if 'good' was meant to compliment the content, writing style, or grammar. My one-word questions, for example, 'Why?', were also problematic because they did not provide enough information to complete the question successfully leaving the student no way of providing an appropriate answer. From my point of view, 'Why?' is written to indicate the need for further development.

It would seem, therefore, that my roles mentioned above had become enmeshed. When I was responding as a reader to a writer at the content level, a one-word comment (even an 'encouraging' one) was in the end ineffectual because it didn't provide enough specific information. To help myself write more effective comments, I am now developing a list of recommendations (based on input from my students) for reference while I am writing comments. Six of these are:

1   connect comments to lesson objectives (vocabulary, etc.);

2   note improvements: 'good', plus reasons why;

3   refer to a specific problem, plus strategy for revision;

4   write questions with enough information for students to answer;

5  write summative comment of strengths and weaknesses;

6  ask 'honest' questions as a reader to a writer rather than statements which assume too much about the writer's intention/meaning.

## Conclusion

All three types of feedback discussed in this paper focus on 'higher order concerns' before 'lower order concerns'. All three can also be characterized as being 'student-centred' rather than 'teacher-centred'. Finally, all three types of feedback are consciously connected with lesson objectives.

I have found that each type of feedback has its own uses and advantages. Peer feedback is versatile, with regard to focus and implementation along the 'process writing' continuum. Overall, students felt peer feedback was valuable in gaining a wider sense of audience. Conferences may be used at the pre-writing stage, in-process stage, evaluation stage, or post-product stage and were felt by students to have a beneficial effect on both written and oral work. Finally, comments are useful for pointing out specific problems, for explaining the reasons for them, and for making suggestions. Here are some final remarks from my students:

> Peer learning is good for us. Through the discussion, we can discover our mistakes. I think if secondary school can provide such learning method to students it will be useful.

> The student–teacher conferencing is very helpful. If the student–teacher conferencing is used in secondary schools, it would be more helpful to the students, because only the written comments are not enough.

> I think this kind of conferencing/writing comments is helpful to secondary-school students. It would help students to know more clearly what is wrong with their writing: especially F5 and F7 students—they can discuss with their teacher about the skills in writing in public exams.

> When I was in secondary school, there were no conferences between student and teacher. I found it hard to finish the work that was assigned to me without a channel of inquiry. Moreover, I found it boring sometimes as teachers usually taught us by reading notes from a textbook.

These remarks reveal very clearly that, at least in the opinion of these students, the feedback processes described in this paper could be—and should be—taking place long before our students are adults.[6]

*Originally published in Volume 44/4, 1990*

## Notes

1 The need to train students in peer feedback is documented by, for example, Danis (1982), Flynn (1982), and Ziv (1983). For discussions of 'higher order concerns', see Krest (1988) and McDonald (1978).

2 This progression follows the suggestion of, for example, Beaven (1977), Hafernik (1984), and Ellman (1980).

3 See, for example, Duke (1975), Fassler (1978), Judy and Judy (1981), and Harris (1986).

4 For discussions about other conference options (e.g. at the pre-writing or product stage) see, for example, Harris (1986), Fassler (1978), Duke (1975).

5 See, for example, Hillocks (1986), Kehl (1970), Sommers (1982), Ziv (1982).

6 See Stewart (1989) for an example of a process approach to writing for secondary-school students.

# 25

## *The textbook as agent of change*[1]

### TOM HUTCHINSON &
### EUNICE G. HUTCHINSON[2]

## Introduction

The textbook is an almost universal element of ELT teaching.[3] Millions of copies are sold every year, and numerous aid projects have been set up to produce them in countries such as Sri Lanka, Yemen, and Peru. The growth of ESP has also generated an increasing number of textbooks for more specialized areas, such as English for Draughtsmen, English for Fisheries, etc. No teaching–learning situation, it seems, is complete until it has its relevant textbook. Yet this phenomenon—the ELT text-book—which has such an impact on ELT, has been little studied. And such papers as have been written about textbooks have been generally critical. Swan (1992: 33), for example, gives this warning:

> The danger with ready-made textbooks is that they can seem to absolve teachers of responsibility. Instead of participating in the day-to-day decisions that have to be made about what to teach and how to teach it, it is easy to just sit back and operate the system, secure in the belief that the wise and virtuous people who produced the textbook knew what was good for us. Unfortunately this is rarely the case.

## Contemporary views of pedagogy

The idea that textbooks produce a kind of dependency culture among teachers and learners is echoed by Littlejohn (1992: 84). In his study of some widely-used primary/lower secondary textbooks, he concludes that 'the precise instructions which the materials give reduce the teacher's role to one of managing or overseeing a preplanned classroom event'. This concern about the merits of textbooks is not restricted to ELT. Loewenberg Ball and Feiman-Nemser (1988) describe how in teacher pre-service education programmes (for all subjects) in the United States, textbooks are consistently criticized as inadequate to meet the needs of the classroom. Student teachers are taught that good teachers do not follow the textbook but devise their own curriculum and materials. Why, we might reasonably ask, given the extent of the influence of textbooks, does there appear to be at best apathy and at worst hostility to them in academic circles?

Lying at the heart of the unease appears to be a concern that the format of the textbook does not sit easily with the developments in ideas about teaching and learning that have come out of the applied linguistics debates of the last two decades. Having recognized the dynamic and interactive nature of the learning process, and having taken on board the individuality of any teaching–learning situation, we might reasonably expect the textbook to wither away in favour of negotiated syllabuses backed up by materials produced by teachers and learners working together. Indeed, the development of concepts such as the process syllabus (Breen 1984) should logically preclude the very idea of a fixed and permanent textbook. The textbook as a medium should have given way to resource packs and the like.

## The nature of contemporary textbooks

And yet the textbook not only survives, it thrives. The number of new textbooks being produced shows no sign of abating. Even more striking is the fact that each new generation of books is more comprehensive and more highly structured than the last. A comparison of two successful textbooks by the same author (with different co-authors) written a decade apart, illustrates this trend well. *Streamline* (Hartley and Viney 1978) consists almost entirely of texts, questions, and substitution drills. Its modern successor, *Grapevine* (Viney and Viney 1989), however, contains in addition an integrated video, information-gap activities, role play, further reading texts, songs, the development of reading, writing, and listening skills, games, grammar summaries, and tape transcripts. As well as containing a greater range of content, *Grapevine* has explicit rubrics for activities, whereas *Streamline* simply gives the exercise number and an example. The instructions in the *Grapevine* teacher's book are also more detailed and give more information about the 'why?' and the 'how?' of each activity. Far from becoming looser, the structure of the textbook is becoming much tighter and more explicit—more like a prepared script. Less and less appears to be left to the teacher to decide and work out.

How can we explain this apparent mismatch between the movement of language teaching theory towards greater negotiation and individual choice in the classroom on the one hand, and the development of ever more comprehensive and structured textbooks on the other? Are we perhaps just in a timelag between the evolution of ideas and their transference into the classroom? Are vulnerable teachers and learners being seduced and exploited by the attractive package deals offered by commercial publishers, as Littlejohn (1992) implies? Or is the market-place telling us that our theories about language teaching and learning are simply wrong?

## Structure in teaching and learning

Textbooks clearly survive because they satisfy certain needs. In this paper we wish to suggest that we have to take a much wider perspective on what those needs actually are. Principally we need to attach much more value to the importance of structure in people's lives. Textbooks, we shall argue, survive and prosper primarily because they are the most convenient means of providing the structure that the teaching–learning system—particularly the system in change—requires.

We shall first of all consider the role of the textbook in terms of normal day-to-day use and then consider its role in the process of change. We shall refer to data from a study carried out in the Philippines into the introduction of an ESP textbook for fisheries technology. Our analysis will illustrate the wide range of needs that textbooks fulfil. In the light of this analysis we shall challenge some of the assumptions that underlie the anti-textbook view. We shall argue that the textbook has a vital and positive part to play in the day-to-day job of teaching English, and that its importance becomes even greater in periods of change.[4] Finally, we shall consider the implications of a more informed and positive view of the role of the textbook, emphasizing, in particular, the need to see textbook creation and teacher education as complementary and mutually beneficial aspects of professional development.

## *The context of the classroom*

We generally think of textbooks as providers of input into classroom lessons in the form of texts, activities, explanations, and so on.

Allwright (1981), however, provides a model of the lesson which adds a further dimension to the role of the textbook. Allwright characterizes the lesson as an interaction among the three elements of teacher, learners, and materials. What this interaction produces are opportunities to learn.

Portraying the lesson as a dynamic interaction in this way might seem to imply that the greatest need is freedom for the dynamics of the interplay to take the lesson where it will. This might further imply that the less control the better. Such a view does not bode well for the textbook, which is generally seen as controlling lessons by providing a prepared script for the interaction. However, if we consider the full range of the needs of the people involved in the interaction we will arrive at a very different conclusion. As Allwright and Bailey (1991: 21) point out, the greatest need is in fact for the interaction to be effectively managed—by both teachers and learners—'to give everyone the best possible opportunities for learning the language'.

The importance of management and the role of the textbook in the management process are certainly recognized by both learners and teachers. In her questionnaire data, Hutchinson (in preparation) asked the question 'Why do you want to use a published textbook?' In the responses, management concerns accounted for 45.25 per cent of learners' reasons and 74.6 per cent of teachers'.

*(adapted from Allwright 1981)*

FIGURE 1 *A model of the lesson*

Although learners cite 'content' as their main reason for wanting a published textbook (with 51.89 per cent), management does not come far behind. Learners see the textbook as a 'framework' or 'guide' that helps them to organize their learning both inside and outside the classroom—during discussions in lessons, while doing activities and exercises, studying on their own, doing homework, and preparing for tests. It enables them to learn 'better, faster, clearer (sic), easier (sic), more'.

Teachers see managing their lessons as their greatest need. Most of their responses centre around the facilitating role of the textbook: it 'saves time, gives direction to lessons, guides discussion, facilitates giving of homework', making teaching 'easier, better organized, more convenient', and learning 'easier, faster, better'. Most of all the textbook provides confidence and security.

But what is it about the teaching–learning situation that makes management so important? We shall consider this question in terms of the context of the lesson, the wider learning context, and the context of the lives of the participants.

## Context of the lesson

Prabhu (1992), characterizes the lesson as, amongst other things, a social event. As such it is potentially threatening to the participants, since any social encounter is essentially unpredictable. However, in practice the level of unpredictability is low, because we find high levels of unpredictability difficult to tolerate. Any recurrent event such as a lesson is naturally and inevitably subject to what Prabhu calls 'social routinization': the encounter becomes increasingly stereotyped, to reduce the unpredictability, and thereby the stress, for those who are active participants in the event.

But it is important to recognize that this process of routinization is not a regrettable necessity that simply makes the interaction more tolerable to the participants—it also has positive advantages. Wong-Fillmore (1985) stresses the importance of structure to learners. She concludes from her observation of different lessons that the good lessons were characterized by a clear lesson format with lesson phases clearly marked and signposted, by regularly scheduled events, and by clear and fair turn allocation for student participation. The good lesson, in other words, is the clearly structured one.

Thus, although we may characterize the lesson as a dynamic interaction, through its nature as a social event the lesson will inevitably tend to routinization. Teachers and learners will actively seek ways of pinning down the procedures of the classroom. The fact, therefore, that textbooks impose a structure on the interaction of the lesson should be seen not as an undesirable constraint, but rather as a potentially beneficial phenomenon, which teachers and learners will welcome.

## Wider learning context

Prabhu (1992: 162) also characterizes the lesson as a curricular event in that it is one of 'an incremental sequence of teaching units, the sequence as a whole meant to achieve a larger objective'. A lesson is not a one-off, isolated event, but part of a series that has a long-term purpose relative both to the learners and, usually, to the requirements of interested bodies external to the classroom, such as education authorities, sponsors, parents, and (in the EAP case) other subject departments. Any lesson needs to be seen, therefore, in relation to what goes before it and what will come after it. There is a need, in other words, for a map or plan as a visible and accessible statement of where the individual lesson fits into the general development of the learning programme.

That there should be as clear and complete a map as possible is important for a number of reasons:

*Negotiation* This is an essential element of any interaction. It requires equal access for all to the content and procedures being negotiated. Only a textbook can show as fully as possible what will actually be done in the lesson. (Recognizing, of course, that the same material can also be interpreted in many different ways.) Although the existence of a textbook may be thought to constrain negotiation, in fact it makes it possible, by providing something to negotiate about. This does not just apply to negotiation within the classroom. Torres (1990) describes how the production of an ESP textbook for fisheries technology provided a basis for communication between ESP teachers and content teachers, and led to a better relationship both between the two groups of teachers and between the English and the Fisheries curricula. One ESP teacher commented: 'The content teachers and English teachers are now friends, where before [the English teachers] were always blamed by content teachers for the learners' poor language skill. This time they are now working together, and the fisheries textbook made this possible.'

*Accountability* Although only teacher, learners, and materials may actively participate in the classroom, they are not the only parties to the interaction. Each of the three active participants is subject to the influence of, and acts as a representative of, other stakeholders in the system. Teachers, for example, may act as representatives of the school staff, education authorities, or school owners who pay their salaries. Learners may be representatives of their parents or sponsors. These other stakeholders may not only need to know what is being done in their name in the closed and ephemeral world of the classroom, but may also justifiably claim the right to influence what is taught in the classroom in terms of content, methodology, and cultural or ideological values.

*Orientation* Teachers and learners need to be able to orient themselves in relation to what goes on in other classrooms. They need to know what is expected of them, what is regarded as acceptable or desirable in terms of content, what objectives should be reached, how much work should be covered in a given time, and so on. This knowledge helps teachers and learners to feel more secure by enabling them to assess their own performance in relation to the expectations of the authorities and to the performance of fellow teachers. Such shared knowledge may also be administratively necessary in order to maintain a degree of standardization across different classes or institutions.

As a shared enterprise with known goals the teaching–learning process demands a map. There are only three places where this map can reside—in the teacher's head, in a written syllabus (produced by external authorities or negotiated between teacher and learners), or in the form of pre-planned materials (i.e. a textbook). With the first two options, there are problems. If it is only in the teacher's head, it is inaccessible to anyone else. In the form of a syllabus, it is more accessible, but only to those who understand the code in which the syllabus is framed and even so it does not show what the actual content of the lessons will be like. A map needs to be as full and as accessible as possible. Only the textbook can fulfil this need.

## Context of the lives of the participants

Finally, while we may discuss the lesson in terms of interaction, creativity, learning processes, etc., we should not lose sight of the fact that the participants involved are people with their own busy and complicated lives to lead. However dedicated the teacher may be, the lesson is still only part of a job that has to be done to earn a living, and the amount of time and effort that can be put into any lesson has to be balanced against all the other competing interests of the individual's life—family, home, shopping, travel to and from work, leisure, and so on. We can make a similar case for the learners. One of the primary requirements that both teachers and learners have, therefore, is the means to make their working lives easier. As two teachers in Hutchinson's (in preparation) study say: '[The ESP textbook] enables the teacher to save time, especially when he or she is quite busy with other school matters' and 'Much to (sic) my desire to prepare my own instructional materials, I lack both the time and the materials/finances.'

To sum up, then, we can see the lesson as a dynamic interaction between teacher, materials, and learners. This interaction has to be managed in order to provide the structure and predictability that are necessary to make the event socially tolerable to the participants, to enable learners and teachers to know where the lesson fits into the general pattern of things, to save teachers and learners work, and to give legitimate external parties access to, and possibly influence upon, what takes place in the classroom. The very fact that a lesson is a dynamic interaction, therefore, leads not to a need for maximum freedom, but to a need for a predictable and visible structure both within the lesson and across lessons. The textbook, we suggest, is the best means of providing this structure.

We have looked in this section at the need for clear and accessible structure in the teaching–learning process, and have argued that the textbook is the best means of providing this structure. Turning now to the main point of this paper—the textbook's role in the change process—we shall see that if the visible structure that the textbook provides is important in the normal run of events, in the unsettled context of change it becomes essential.

## Context of change

Change has become almost endemic in ELT. The past two decades have seen a welter of new methodologies, new areas of interest, such as ESP, new approaches to syllabus design, new concepts, such as learner training, and so on. This rush of new ideas has created a need to understand the process of change, and its impact upon the individuals who must implement it.

The fundamental problem of change is that it disturbs the framework of meanings by which we make sense of the world. It challenges, and thereby potentially threatens, the values, attitudes, and beliefs that enable us to make experience meaningful and predictable. Yet, like growth, no development is possible without such disturbance. If people are to accommodate themselves to change, therefore, the disturbance that change inevitably brings must be kept within manageable limits. If it exceeds these limits, it will engender feelings of anxiety and insecurity and thereby provoke what Marris (1986) calls 'the conservative impulse', i.e. a determination to resist the change and maintain the existing context within which the individual feels secure.

## Conditions for effective change

Studies from management and social sciences (see, for example, Marris 1986; Blackler and Shimmin 1984) indicate that there are certain conditions for smooth and effective change:

1  Only a certain amount of change can be accommodated at any one time. The individual's network of meanings has to be given time to take new ideas and experiences on board.

2  Adjusting to change takes time and energy. To make the adjustment, therefore, individuals need relief from other pressures, and constant reassurance and support.

3  To reduce feelings of insecurity, people need as complete a picture as possible of what the change will look like in practice.

4  Individuals find it difficult to carry the burden of change alone. The support of a group helps individuals by sharing the burden. As a general rule, groups are more inclined to take risks than individuals (Handy 1985: 155) because they feel more secure through their mutual support for each other.

In sum, then, the most important requirement in the process of change is security. This reinforces the need for structure and visibility. Van den Akker (1988) illustrates this well.

## Implementing curriculum change

Van den Akker was interested in how written materials can help teachers in the implementation of a new curriculum, in this case a new science curriculum introducing a more enquiry-based approach. Two groups of teachers were given different materials. The control group's materials were more loosely structured, gave more options, and generally left most decision-making as to how they should implement the curriculum guidelines to the teachers. The experimental group's materials had fewer options, more 'how-to-do-it' advice and structured guidance, such as basic lesson plans giving sequences of activities, time estimates for each activity, and explanations of the function of each stage of the lesson.

The results of the research showed that the experimental group's lessons were much closer to the intentions of the curriculum developers, in that they were more successful in maintaining the enquiry-based approach. The control group teachers on the other hand frequently lost control and reverted to more traditional forms of teaching.

Furthermore, the experimental group reported greater satisfaction with the materials, their lessons, and their performance.

Van den Akker concluded that the highly structured approach is more effective in getting curriculum change into the classroom. He also concludes that, although this research was only concerned with the implementation phase, the change is likely to be more permanent: 'Certainly, if early experiences have been satisfying and yield positive results (both in teacher performance and in students' learning) there seems more chance of commitment to a programme and of stable and substantial changes in the direction of proposals for an innovation' (ibid.: 54).

## Creating a supportive environment

Change is a disruptive and threatening process. The crucial factor in achieving smooth and lasting change, therefore, is security. The most effective agents of change will thus be those that can create the supportive environment in which teachers will feel able and willing to take on the challenge of change. This would indicate that the textbook has the potential to be a very effective agent of change. We can relate its advantages back to the conditions for change noted above:

1 People can only accommodate a certain amount of change at any one time. The textbook can introduce changes gradually within a structured framework enabling teachers and learners to develop in harmony with the introduction of new ideas. In other words, the textbook can be not just a learning programme for language content, but also a vehicle for teacher and learner training.

2 Adjustment to change requires support and relief from other burdens. As we have already noted, the structure provided by the textbook saves the teacher work and helps him or her to manage the class. This frees the teacher to concentrate attention on coping with new content and procedures. Furthermore, since it is used on a daily basis, is portable and permanent, the textbook can provide constant support. In Torres (1990) the introduction of an ESP textbook meant that teachers were not spending their time scouring for materials and producing visual aids, but were free to concentrate on planning the lessons and understanding the subject matter. This resulted in better planned lessons, a more creative methodology, and more useful materials adaptation and supplementation.

3 People need to know what the change will look like. The textbook can provide as complete a picture as possible. Through structured

scripts (particularly when supported by a teacher's guide) it can show as explicitly as possible what to do, and because it is immediate to the actual context of use, there is no problem of transfer from training context, such as a seminar, to the classroom.

4 People feel more confident about change if supported by others. Adopted on a school basis, the textbook gets the support of the group behind the individual teacher, and thus relieves the teacher of much of the burden of responsibility for introducing changes. This was certainly the case in Hutchinson's study (in preparation), where ESP teachers drew a great deal of comfort from the fact that the textbook project involved a network of eight regional state colleges, and was supported by content teachers and college administrators.

## Textbooks as agents of change

There seems, then, to be a substantial case for regarding textbooks as effective agents of change. Far from being a problem, as some educationalists have concluded, the good textbook, properly used, can provide an excellent vehicle for effective and long-lasting change. Attempts to do without a textbook (unfortunately, the all too common strategy of many a reform programme) fly in the face of what is known about the process of change, and are more likely to create the damaging insecurity that will make it more difficult for the individual to accommodate the change. Only the textbook can really provide the level of structure that appears to be necessary for teachers to fully understand and 'routinize' change. Viewed in this way, the move to more highly structured textbooks that we noted in the introduction is not something to be deplored, but rather to be welcomed as a natural and beneficial response to a period of rapid change.

In the next section we shall draw together our conclusions so far in order to confront some of the assumptions that seem to underlie the textbook debate.

## Some assumptions challenged

If we take a wide perspective on the role of the textbook we can see that it can and does satisfy a very wide range of needs. It is hopefully clear why, apparently in the face of developments in ELT methodology, the textbook continues to be the mainstay of ELT provision. Furthermore, in a period of change the value of the textbook becomes even greater. We now wish to return to the earlier question that we posed in the introduction, namely why is the view of textbooks in academic discussion seemingly so negative?

The anti-textbook argument appears to be based on a number of assumptions, which, when probed, appear to have little or no evidence to support them. Let us look at some of these possible assumptions.

## Textbooks as a basis for negotiation

*Assumption 1: Textbooks are merely a pre-packaged form of classroom materials.* There is at the base of this assumption a belief that only the needs of the classroom interaction and more particularly the needs of the learner matter. We have seen, however, that textbooks satisfy a range of needs both within the classroom and beyond it. Principally, the textbook provides a structure for the management of the lesson as a social interaction and a basis for negotiation between all the relevant parties. Textbooks are not just classroom materials packaged in a particular format. Rather we need to see it the other way round: providing classroom materials is just one of the functions that textbooks have.

## Textbooks as a flexible framework

*Assumption 2: Maximum freedom of choice is both desirable and desired.* Or to look at it from the opposite perspective, structure constrains creativity. This is patently not true. Freedom of choice brings with it the responsibility of making decisions. This both confuses and frightens people. Thus, all the evidence indicates that both teachers and learners want and benefit from the security that a clear structure provides, even though this restricts the options available. This is particularly the case, as Van den Akker (1988) shows, during the process of change. We have to beware of confusing ends with means. As Owen *et al.* (1978: 388) say: 'It is important to distinguish between a structured learning environment and control ... A teacher may present a highly structured learning environment but allow students great flexibility, responsibility, and freedom of choice; in another classroom the learning environment may be devoid of structure yet rigidly dominated by a dictatorial instructor.'

Our purpose, in other words, may be to enable the individual to develop his or her talents as fully as possible, but the means of achieving this is to provide the secure framework within which learners and teachers can make informed choices.

## Textbooks and teacher development

*Assumption 3: The fixed format of a textbook makes negotiation more difficult*. In fact, the opposite is the case. For negotiation to happen, there has to be something to negotiate about, and that must be as complete as possible, and available equally to all parties to the interaction. The great benefit of a textbook is that it is visible and therefore can be freely negotiated. Without it the teacher is the only person who has the map. How can effective negotiation take place in such circumstances?

*Assumption 4: The development of more highly structured textbooks leads to the de-skilling of teachers*. (See Littlejohn 1992, for example.) The teacher becomes little more than a cipher for a prepared script. Again, we have to ask: Where is the evidence? Stodolsky (1988: 180), for example, dismisses the idea that teachers feel unduly constrained by textbooks: 'We have found little evidence in the literature or in the case studies to support the idea that teachers teach strictly by the book. Instead we have seen variation in practice that seems to result from teachers' own convictions and preferences, the nature of the materials they use, the school context in which they teach, the particular students in their class, and the subject matter and grade level they are teaching.'

This view is borne out by Hutchinson's study (in preparation) of the actual classroom use of the ESP textbook by two teachers. A task-by-task analysis of selected modules reveals that, even in the kind of teacher-fronted classrooms found in the study, teachers and learners do not follow the textbook script. Most often teachers follow their own scripts by adapting or changing textbook-based tasks, adding new tasks or deleting some, changing the management of the tasks, changing task inputs or expected outputs, and so on. Moreover, what is also clear from the study is that the teacher's planned task is reshaped and reinterpreted by the interaction of teacher and learners during the lesson.

It is indeed far more likely that the more secure teachers feel in what they are doing, the more inclined they are to depart from the given script. Furthermore, we might challenge the whole idea of 'de-skilling'. The more complex the textbook becomes, the more skill is required of the teacher in using it. They may need different skills to those they have traditionally employed, but, if anything, the more developed the textbook, the greater the skill required of the user. In fact, the 'de-skilling' argument misses the whole point about teacher development. Without the kind of structured guidance that a good textbook can provide, teachers are likely to carry on teaching in the same way as they have always done. The textbook makes it possible to bring changes into the classroom. The textbook, in other words, should be seen as a means of 're-skilling' not 'de-skilling'.

## Textbooks as a workable compromise

*Assumption 5: A textbook cannot meet the needs of any individual teaching–learning situation nor the needs of the individuals within it.* And this is true. A textbook can never be more than a workable compromise, but then, given the range of needs that exist within any learning context, so is everything else in the classroom. If we argue that textbooks should be done away with because they cannot meet all the needs of a given situation, are we also to argue that since no teacher can meet all the needs of any given learner, teachers should be done away with? Nothing that happens in education is anything more than a workable compromise, and we cannot uniquely condemn textbooks because they are not a perfect fit. Given that a reasonable amount of thought has gone into the creation of the textbook by the publisher, and to the choice of the textbook by the teachers, there is no reason to assume that any other materials would be any better, and many reasons why they may be worse.

To sum up, there are, we feel, a number of implicit assumptions in the arguments against textbooks—assumptions for which there is little or no support. It is difficult to avoid the conclusion that the anti-textbook arguments are based on ideological or cultural values, which do not accord with the reality of people's needs. O'Neill (1991) touches on this point. With regard to teacher training, he argues that rather than stressing individuality and creativity in the classroom, we should concentrate on getting teachers to do ordinary things well, such as ask effective and useful questions. But, he maintains, such an approach does not figure highly in the debate about teaching because it is not seen as desirable by the Western mind. We can see something similar in the attitude towards textbooks. There is an emphasis on individual freedom and creativity over effective performance. It's a sort of 'back to nature' appeal. Wouldn't it be better if we all baked our own bread, preferably from our own home-grown, organic wheat, rather than buying a cut-and-wrapped loaf at the supermarket? In reality, of course, the convenience of the supermarket is overwhelming in determining our choice. The important conclusion to draw, surely, is not that we should encourage everyone to make their own bread, but that we should educate people to be more informed, more discerning, and more influential consumers.

Let us now consider the implications of our arguments.

# Implications for action

We have focused in this paper on the value of the textbook, particularly in periods of change. Our concern throughout has been to see the textbook in relation to the needs of the various parties in the teaching–learning process, particularly the needs of the teacher. Teaching is a partnership between teacher and materials. Partnerships work best when each partner knows the strengths and weaknesses of the other and is able to complement them. If we are to understand the value of the textbook and fully exploit its potential as an agent of lasting and effective change, we need to see textbook development and teacher development as part of the same process. This has two implications.

## Textbook development

The teacher development potential of textbooks should be recognized and actively built into textbook design. This will require more research into what teachers and learners actually do with textbooks and teacher's guides in the classroom. It has been disheartening that in preparing this paper, we have had to rely largely on studies of textbook use in subject areas other than ELT. For an industry of this size and economic value, the amount of supported knowledge about textbooks and their use is lamentable. It is little wonder that such discussion as there is about ELT textbooks is generally so ill-informed. We need to know what the role of the textbook really is in ELT. We would suggest that publishers in particular, both in their own interests and those of the profession, should fund research into this very question. We have to know what needs the textbook satisfies, if we are to provide the secure and appropriate support that is required for development.

## Teacher development

Just as textbooks (or at least their producers) need to find out more about the teachers' needs, so teachers need to learn more about textbooks. Teachers should, as Prabhu (1992) maintains, become good 'theorists', who understand not only how, but also why something is done. This indicates a need for a better relationship between the textbook and teacher development, through courses, seminars, workshops, etc. In particular, we need to abandon the generally hostile attitude to textbooks that pervades much teacher training, and stop wasting so much time and effort on teaching teachers to do without or simply substitute for a textbook. Instead a central feature of all teacher training and development should be to help teachers become better consumers of textbooks by teaching them how to select and use textbooks effectively. This means helping them to be able to evaluate textbooks properly, exploit them in the class, and adapt and supplement them where necessary.

## Conclusion

We began by posing two questions. Why does there appear to be such apathy and even hostility to the ELT textbook in the literature? And why does the textbook survive and prosper apparently in contradiction to the development of ideas in applied linguistics? We have argued in this paper that the anti-textbook position rests on narrow and unsupported assumptions about the role that textbooks play. When we explored the ELT context more thoroughly, we discovered that far from being a problem, the textbook is an important means of satisfying the range of needs that emerge from the classroom and its wider context. Education is a complex and messy matter. What the textbook does is to create a degree of order within potential chaos. It is a visible and workable framework around which the many forces and demands of the teaching–learning process can cohere to provide the basis of security and accountability that is necessary for purposeful action in the classroom. This vital management role takes on even greater importance in the insecure context of change. Rather than denigrating and trying to do away with textbooks, we should recognize their importance in making the lives of teachers and learners easier, more secure and fruitful, and seek a fuller understanding of their use in order to exploit their full potential as agents of smooth and effective change.

*Originally published in Volume 48/4, 1994*

## Notes

1 This paper was presented at the 27th International Annual IATEFL Conference, Swansea, April 1993.

2 This article was originally published under the names of Tom Hutchinson and Eunice Torres.

3 The term 'textbook' is used in the broad sense of 'an organized and pre-packaged set of teaching/learning materials'. The materials may be bound in just one book or distributed in a package, such as the

familiar coursebook, workbook, teacher's guide, and cassettes. Our use of 'textbook' would encompass both the individual book and the package.

4 We are not concerned with the merits or otherwise of any particular textbooks. We recognize that there are bad textbooks and good textbooks. Our concern is with the textbook as a medium, which may be used well or badly.

5 We acknowledge that our arguments may not be relevant to some parts of the world (India and Pakistan have been cited to us as examples) where there is a justifiable concern about the stultifying effect of dull and outdated official textbooks backed by all the authority of the educational system and the academic hierarchy.

# 26

## Developing pragmatic awareness: closing the conversation[1]

### K. BARDOVI-HARLIG, B. A. S. HARTFORD, R. MAHAN-TAYLOR, M. J. MORGAN, & D. W. REYNOLDS

## Introduction

Frequently, neither the content nor the formula (the component parts) of speech acts can be felicitously transferred from one language to another, as House and Kasper (1981) and Takahashi and Beebe (1987) have shown for complaints and refusals, respectively. Face-threatening acts are not the only speech acts which take different forms and content in different languages, however. Even greetings and leave-takings show differences (Schmidt and Richards 1980).

### Pragmatic proficiency

Language learners interacting with speakers of a target language must be exposed to language samples which observe social, cultural, and discourse conventions—or in other words, which are pragmatically appropriate. Speakers who do not use pragmatically appropriate language run the risk of appearing unco-operative at the least, or, more seriously, rude or insulting. This is particularly true of advanced learners whose high linguistic proficiency leads other speakers to expect concomitantly high pragmatic competence. This is not to say, however, that classroom activities designed to increase pragmatic awareness are appropriate only for advanced learners; such activities can and should take place at lower levels as well.

Recent studies have resulted in valuable descriptions of a variety of speech acts including compliments (Wolfson 1988; Holmes and Brown

1987), direction giving (Scotton and Bernstern 1988), apologies (Borkin and Reinhart 1978), and expressions of gratitude (Eisenstein and Bodman, 1986). Yet descriptions are only the first step: facilitating the development of pragmatic competence with respect to a particular speech act or function necessarily entails both a description of the use of the speech acts in the target-language community and an approach for developing pragmatic competence in the language classroom.

A potential problem in teaching pragmatics is the sheer number of speech acts, as Williams (1988) observes. He argues that the large number of language functions and speech acts makes the teaching of specific acts an unattainable goal and instead suggests that 'the focus should ... be ... on using language in ongoing discourse, in a particular context, for a particular purpose, and as part of a strategy' (ibid.: 46). Although we agree with Williams that it is impossible to teach all language functions or speech acts, we further claim that there are also a large number of language contexts and purposes, and that teaching these is equally prohibitive. It is impossible to prepare students for every context, or even all of the most common situations they will face in natural language settings.

## The teacher's responsibility

Our position, therefore, is that the real responsibility of the classroom teacher is not to instruct students specifically in the intricacies of complimenting, direction-giving, or closing a conversation: rather, it is to make students more aware that pragmatic functions exist in language, specifically in discourse, in order that they may be more aware of these functions as learners. We, as teachers, must know about these speech acts and their component parts to determine what is naturalistic input for our students, even though it would be impossible to impart this knowledge concerning every speech act explicitly. We believe that if students are encouraged to think for themselves about culturally appropriate ways to compliment a friend or say goodbye to a teacher, then they may awaken their own lay abilities for pragmatic analysis.

## Four steps

There are four basic steps to integrating pragmatically appropriate language into the English classroom:

1  identification of the speech act;
2  data collection and description;

3 text and materials evaluation;
4 development of new materials.

The identification of a speech act for instruction can result from observing students' conversational or written language use, anticipating students' needs, or asking students to identify areas of difficulty. We emphasize that there is no 'best' or 'most crucial' speech act for instruction. Selections should be made according to the learners' needs or interests and by the current or future type of target-language contact.

Data collection may be accomplished by observing or recording spontaneous conversations or by collecting data through role plays or discourse completion questionnaires (written role plays)—see Takahashi and Beebe (1987)—or by a combination of both approaches. Available literature may be used to supplement data collection. This is an essential step for all teachers, including native speakers, because our intuitions are not sufficiently keen in this respect, as Wolfson (1986) claims.

Following the data collection, textbooks, tapes, and other instructional materials must be evaluated for authenticity. Depending on the speech act, teachers should check for representation of the speech act in different types and topics of conversations, and the status and relationship of the speakers, to name a few parameters.

We have found that the fourth step—modification of existing materials and creation of new materials and activities—is generally necessary. Even inappropriate or incomplete dialogues can be used profitably. We will illustrate each of these steps by examining conversational closings in American English.

## Identification of the speech act

Our pedagogical interest in closings developed from the discourse analysis of Hartford and Bardovi-Harlig (1989, and forthcoming) which revealed that learners of English are often unable to end, or close, conversations appropriately. Even advanced learners of English have difficulty recognizing when a native speaker is closing the conversation, providing the necessary responses, and initiating a closing. It was found that in extreme cases learners sometimes enter into social contracts without having the pragmatic competence to fulfil them. In one conversation, for example, an advanced learner responded perfectly to the other speaker's attempts to say 'goodbye', thus entering into a contract to leave, but did not leave and was finally ushered to the door. Their data suggest that closings which are overly brief or overly extended may make learners appear rude, by seeming either abrupt or hard to 'get rid of'.

## Data collection and description
### Saying 'goodbye'

Knowing how to close or say 'goodbye' in one's native language does not ensure success in another language. Closings are culture-specific, both in their obligatoriness and structure. For example, some cultures have apparently minimal or no closing requirements in some contexts, while others, including American English, have fairly elaborate ones. In Nepali, for instance, it is appropriate to employ minimal closings in certain contexts: a customer may end a service encounter after its completion with an optional short expression of thanks and simply leave. In Thai, according to Schmidt (1989), conversations may be closed with 'Goodbye, I'm leaving now.' In contrast, Swahili closings, like English closings, are more elaborate, exhibiting a minimum of three turns (Omar 1989). Although English closings may be quite extended, in this paper we present only the essential components of felicitous closings: the terminal exchange, the preclosing, and the shut-down.

An American English closing must have, at a bare minimum, a terminal pair. It is by use of this pair that speakers actually terminate conversations, as in Example 1:

Terminal exchange   A: All right. See ya.
                    B: See ya later.

Although the terminal exchange is central to saying goodbye, other turns are frequently involved. Speakers may take a turn to verify that the conversation has ended, as in Example 2:

Preclosing          A: All right.
                    B: OK.
Terminal exchange   A: So long.
                    B: See you later.

Arrangements are frequently reiterated in closing,[2] as is shown below in Example 3:

Preclosing          A: OK. Thank you very much.
                    B: All right.
Arrangements        A: Now I have to go to French, which is a lot
                       more complicated than this was. [laugh]
Terminal exchange   B: All right. Good-bye.
                    A: Bye-bye.

Additionally, and usually before any preclosings occur, a speaker may shut down the topic, as in Example 4:

| | |
|---|---|
| Shutting down the topic | A: Yeah, well, next time we come up, um … I'll bring our set and … you can go through 'em and pick the ones you want. |
| Preclosing 1 | B: OK. OK. |
| | A: So … |
| Preclosing 2 | B: That'll be fine. |
| | A: OK. |
| Closing | B: Give my love to David. |
| | A: OK. Tell And … Uncle Andy I hope /he feels/ better[3]. |
| | B: /I will/. |
| | B: OK. Thanks a lot for / calling /. |
| Terminal exchange | A:                              /Bye bye/. |
| | B: Bye, dear. |

The shutting-down of the topic and the preclosing both signal a speaker's intention to end the conversation, and provide the opportunity for a conversational partner to continue the conversation if desired. It is important for learners to recognize the function of these particular turns, because it is only here that they may extend the conversation without appearing rude.

The learner thus has to become familiar with the many parts of the closing in English. In order of importance, learners must first learn that all terminal exchanges have two parts: an initiation and a response. As an initiator of a closing, the learner must wait for a response. In response to the initiation of a closing, the learner must provide the second part. Secondly, learners must recognize that preclosings function to verify that no additional business remains to be negotiated in the conversation. If a speaker does not begin a new topic or reintroduce a previous one, then the conversation will end. Finally, learners must recognize that certain contributions shut down a topic after which the conversation may be ended.

## *Text and materials evaluation*

Given the preceding description of closings (see also Schegloff and Sacks 1973; Hartford and Bardovi-Harlig 1989 and 1992), we examined the presentation of closings by twenty current ESL textbooks which contain dialogues. A summary of our findings is presented in Table 1.

In surveying the textbooks, we discovered that only twelve included what we consider complete closings represented in at least one of the dialogues, and that very few did so on a consistent basis. The purpose of dialogues is generally to introduce a new grammatical structure and not to provide a source for realistic conversational input. They therefore typically represent conversations as getting only as far as shutting down a topic and occasionally as far as a preclosing, as is shown below in Examples 5 and 6:

| | | |
|---|---|---|
| Shut down of topic only | STANLEY: | Hi, Dick. |
| | DICK: | Hi Stanley. Did you go to the football game yesterday? |
| | STANLEY: | No, I went to the movies with my kids. Did our team win? |
| | DICK: | No, they didn't. They lost. |
| | STANLEY: | Did they lose by much? |
| | DICK: | They lost by twelve points. |
| Shutting-down | STANLEY: | Oh, that's awful. I'm glad I didn't go. (Lado 1989) |

| | | |
|---|---|---|
| Shut-down with preclosing | A: | Would you like to go dancing with me this evening? |
| | B: | I'd love to, but I'm just getting over the flu. |
| | A: | Well, why don't we do something else like go to a movie? |
| | B: | Oh, no thanks, really. I'm still too weak for anything. |
| | A: | OK. How about dinner and dancing next Friday night? |
| Shutting-down | B: | That sounds great. I'm sure I'll be all right by then. |
| Preclosing | A: | Great. See you then. (Harris and Hube 1989) |

We posit that this lack of complete conversational models leaves students unaware of both the proper way to end a conversation and the signals speakers may use when they are ready to terminate an exchange.

| Textbook* | Complete closings | | | Partial closings | Teaches closings | Claims about language used in textbook |
|---|---|---|---|---|---|---|
| | many | some | none | | | |
| *AKL: Intermediate* (O'Neill et al. 1978) | | | • | | no | no claims |
| *All Set for English* (Luukas et al. 1987) | | • | | • | no | EFL text |
| *Breaking the Ice* (Hynes and Baichmann 1989) | | • | | | no | 'authentic language; scripted passages' |
| *Culture Puzzle* (Levine et al. 1987) | | • | | | yes | 'realistic examples' |
| *Express Ways (3)* (Molinsky and Bliss 1986) | | • | | • | yes | 'content of real-life contexts and situations' |
| *Get Ready* (Abraham and Mackey 1986) | | • | | • | yes | 'contextualized practice; strategies for social interaction; conversational management' |
| *Idioms in American Life* (Howard 1987) | | | • | • | no | 'real-life situations' |
| *Improving Oral Communication* (Handschuh et al. 1985) | • | | | • | yes | 'carefully constructed dialogues' |
| *Interactions* (to follow) | | | • | • | no | no claims |
| *Lado English Series 2* (Lado 1989) | | | • | | no | 'communication skills' |

| Textbook* | Complete closings | | | Partial closings | Teaches closings | Claims about language used in textbook |
| --- | --- | --- | --- | --- | --- | --- |
| | many | some | none | | | |
| Life in English (Braun 1984) | | • | | • | yes | 'typical American behavior' |
| Mosaic I (Ferrer and Whalley 1986) | | | • | | no | 'realistic academic lectures and sample conversations' |
| Mosaic II (Ferrer and Whalley 1986) | | • | | • | no | 'realistic academic lectures and sample conversations' |
| Moving On (2) (Huizenaga 1989) | | • | | • | no | 'contextualized dialogues; situational authenticity' |
| Moving Up (Lackstrom and White 1983) | | • | | • | no | goal: 'authentic functional communication' |
| On Speaking Terms (Harris and Hube 1989) | | | • | • | no | 'natural conversational English' |
| Real-Life English (4)† (Jolly and Robinson 1988) | | | • | • | no | 'realistic, meaningful dialogues' |
| Say it Naturally! (Wall 1987) | | | • | • | yes | 'verbal strategies for authentic conversation' |
| Speak Freely (Glass and Arcario 1985) | | • | | • | no | 'demonstrates use of colloquial English' |
| Talking with Americans (Text to follow) | | • | | • | no | no claims |

* All the texts reviewed contain dialogues.
† None of the *Real-Life English* texts (1–4) teaches closings according to the list of language functions provided for the series.

TABLE 1 *Closings in ESL textbooks*

## *Development of new materials*
### Pragmatically-centred activities

Given that the burden of providing authentic input in the classroom falls to the teacher, what is the best way to incorporate such material? Holmes and Brown (1987) provide seven activities for teaching compliments. In addition to role plays, their suggestions include: filling in blanks on charts containing data on compliments; asking students to devise different situations in which particular compliments can be used; and identifying compliment formulas and relative frequency of occurrence. While it is promising to see suggestions being made for teaching pragmatics, we feel that most of Holmes and Brown's lessons focus on the development of specific meta-pragmatic rules and information rather than on the ability to use compliments. Much work is still needed on how best to teach speech acts.

Thus far we have made two claims: that instruction can heighten students' pragmatic awareness; and that teachers often lack adequate textbook materials that focus on pragmatic functions. While this may at first seem discouraging, there are, in fact, a variety of ways to introduce pragmatics in the language classroom. Before making specific suggestions for presenting closings, we will briefly discuss the activities we have used with our high-intermediate-level students in a speaking–listening class in the Intensive English Program at Indiana University.

### Introducing speech acts

One way of introducing a speech act and encouraging students to think about how it functions is to examine that function in their own language and culture, as suggested in the ESL text *The Culture Puzzle* (Levine *et al.* 1987). We found that a successful discussion concerning closings was easily generated and did not require the introduction of technical vocabulary. This type of activity gives students not only a basis of comparison, but also the opportunity to share a speech act, at which they are clearly expert, with their classmates. Through guided discussion, students become aware of the pragmatic rules governing their native language and the ramifications of enacting such rules appropriately and inappropriately. The awareness of communication goals that this activity generates can then be applied to the target language in the instructional setting.

The students in our class, after participating in just such an activity, agreed that their languages, like English, require speakers to announce their intention to close. They maintained that in their native languages abrupt closings were impolite, as were speakers who refused to respond to other speakers' attempts to shut down a conversation.

The students were then asked to comment on the naturalness of a set of classroom dialogues, an activity which we describe more fully in the section entitled 'Structured activities', below. Initially, the class did not notice that the conversations in question lacked adequate closings. This response could have been caused by a variety of factors, including: their previous exposure to contrived rather than authentic dialogues; the fact that students are unaware of this distinction; or, perhaps, simply because students (and teachers) do not expect classroom language to conform to the same pragmatic rules that govern authentic conversations.

Judging from their comments, it is very likely that the students did not recognize the infelicitous closings for a combination of these reasons. Moreover, their knowledge of closings in English seemed to be limited to terminal exchanges, most notably 'goodbye, goodbye', or simple variations. When led through a discussion of the closings, they recognized the patterned speech found in preclosings and shut-downs, but did not seem to know when or why to include them. Student responses tended to focus on substituting alternative word choices. By and large, they were hesitant or unable to alter the ordering or timing of the dialogues in order to affect the communication that was taking place. In other words, these students were linguistically competent, but pragmatically deficient.

At this point, the students were prepared to experiment with the pragmatic component of closings. During class activities, they were able to choose appropriate vocabulary and speech patterns, and to utilize them as native speakers would at the proper time during practice closings. Student contributions, such as the use of 'well ...' to shut down conversations, signalled the emergence of pragmatic awareness of this particular language function. We will now turn to specific activities for fostering pragmatic competence. The activities incorporate natural models, structured approaches, role play, and data-collection by students, and all include discussion.

## Natural models: 'The Classroom Guest'

Natural language samples can be introduced into the classroom in a variety of ways. For beginning students, activities such as 'The Classroom Guest' help develop listening, speaking, and pragmatic skills. In 'The Classroom Guest', the instructor arranges for someone to interrupt the class—to deliver a message, ask a question, or make any other brief and believable exchange. Before the arranged interruption, the instructor turns on a tape-recorder that can pick up the voices of both the teacher and the visitor and records the entire exchange. When the visitor leaves, the teacher asks the students what was said. After the class discussion, two students are asked to recreate the scene through role play, with help from the rest of the class. The teacher also records the re-enactment. Next, both exchanges are played to the class and the differences between the 'real' exchange and the students' re-enactment are discussed.

## Structured approaches

Activities that are more structured are also useful, particularly for beginning speakers. We suggest two here: in the first, students act out and compare felicitous and infelicitous closings in textbook dialogues; and in the second, they construct complete closings from individual turns. Acting out textbook dialogues with incomplete closings emphasizes the difference between appropriate and inappropriate ways to end conversations. Having the actors walk away at the end of a conversation illustrates the abruptness of some of the dialogues. Comparing felicitous and infelicitous closings gives students practice in informal pragmatic analysis and helps to raise students' awareness of why certain closings are inappropriate. Incomplete dialogues can be found in many textbooks and are especially useful for this activity. We have chosen three dialogues for comparison: a dialogue that merely ends with a shut-down of the topic (see Example 5, above); one which includes a preclosing but not a terminal pair (see Example 6, above); and one with a felicitous closing (see Example 7, below).

> A: I'd love to continue this conversation, but I really need to go now. I have to get back to the office.
> B: Well, let's get together soon.
> A: How about Friday?
> B: Friday sounds good. Where should we meet?
> A: (looks at watch) You know, I really must be going now or I'll be very late. Can you give me a call tomorrow and we'll decide?
> B: Fine. Speak to you then.
> A: Sorry I have to rush off like this.
> B: That's okay. I understand.
> A: Good-bye.
> B: So long.
> (adapted from Molinsky and Bliss 1986)

Students from the class are chosen to act out the dialogues, which are given to them on separate pieces of paper so they can more easily incorporate body language while performing. The remainder of the students are asked to close their books, so that they can concentrate on the performance. The teacher asks the students to pay particular attention to whether the conversation seems natural, but does not focus their attention on the closing.

Incomplete dialogues, such as Examples 5 and 6, are performed first and discussed. The discussion might begin with questions like 'Did this seem natural to you?', or 'Do you think you might have a conversation that would end like this?'. The students are asked to supply closings that seem more natural as endings for the particular conversations.

After performing the dialogues with incomplete closings, students perform a dialogue with a complete closing. The discussion of this dialogue focuses on what made it better than the others. If time permits, this discussion can be used to launch a more general discussion of what makes the students perceive another speaker as rude or awkward, and of uncomfortable experiences the students may have had when they were unintentionally perceived as rude or awkward.

In the second structured activity, the students reconstruct closings. The class is divided into small groups of three or four. The groups are each given a set of paper strips, with one sentence from a closing written on each strip. Each group is assigned a different situation, and uses the strips to reconstruct a 'goodbye' appropriate for that particular situation. For example, the group writing a closing between a professor and a student would use strips with more formal expressions than would the group writing a closing between two friends. After the groups finish writing, two members from each group act out their closing. Following the presentations, the appropriateness of each dialogue is discussed.

## Role play

Role playing is perhaps the most straightforward approach, and requires the least amount of teacher preparation. Role-play situations can be developed to focus on virtually any speech act—for example, compliments, greetings, apologies—and they provide an excellent way for students to practise both their pragmatic skills and their speaking skills. (We include a selection of role plays in the Appendix.) Variations of the role play, such as the one we call 'Never Can Say Goodbye', can be used to explore ways of closing in a timely fashion. We set up the following scene between two students:

Two friends have been talking about a forthcoming event (party, football game, or exam). One student has another appointment, and must try to end the conversation politely, while the second student wants to continue the exchange.

A time limit is set for the role play, and if the conversation does not end within that period, the students sit down and two different students repeat the exercise. After several rounds, the class discusses which of the role plays was the most polite yet still offered the most effective approach to ending a conversation.

## Data collection by students

Teachers of intermediate and advanced learners may find that asking students to gather linguistic data outside the classroom is a challenging follow-up to in-class activities. Students may be asked to focus on specific speech acts by gathering examples themselves. For example, following classroom work on closings, students can record endings of phone calls, dinner-time conversations, leave-takings after classes, or conversations they overhear. Radio, television, and films, as well as books and plays, offer alternative sources for EFL students. Once these samples have been recorded (either taped or written down from memory), students can compare different ways of saying goodbye in different contexts.

## *Conclusion*

Our suggestions by no means exhaust the possible ways of incorporating the development of pragmatic awareness into the classroom. Specific teaching contexts, students' needs, and instructor creativity will suggest other possibilities.

In closing, we would like to suggest a fifth step for integrating pragmatics into the language classroom, and that is to share the results of the first four steps (identification, data collection, evaluation, and new materials) with colleagues through in-service programmes or informal conversations.

Teaching pragmatics empowers students to experience and experiment with the language at a deeper level, and thereby to participate in the purpose of language—communication, rather than just words. When we approach the language class as an opportunity for learners to expand their communication across cultural boundaries, we, as teachers, have the responsibility to equip them with not only the structural aspects of the language, but with the pragmatics as well: more simply, the right words to say at the proper time.

*Originally published in Volume 45/1, 1991*

## Notes

1  An earlier version of this paper, 'What textbooks don't say about saying goodbye', was presented at The Eleventh Annual INTESOL Conference. We thank Nancy A. Quinn for her assistance with our computer programs. This research was supported in part by a research development grant to K. Bardovi-Harlig from the College of Arts and Sciences at Indiana University.

2  Making arrangements may also function to shut down the topic. The content of the shut-down generally reflects the main purpose of the conversation. It is here that speakers reiterate their appreciation, confirm arrangements, or otherwise summarize the conversation.

3  The obliques indicate overlapping speech.

## Appendix

*Role plays ('Goodbye' scenes)*

1  *Roles: student, townsperson*
   Scene: The student and townsperson are waiting for a bus. They have started a conversation about the weather when the student's bus pulls up. The townsperson must wait for the next bus. What happens next?

2  *Roles: student, a new friend*
   Scene: The student has been talking to a new friend. The friend pauses, then says, 'Well, it was nice talking with you.' What happens next?

3  *Roles: cashier at the supermarket, shopper in the check-out line*
   Scene: The shopper pays the cashier, and the cashier thanks the shopper. The shopper responds.

4  *Roles: student, a good friend*
   Scene: A student and his or her friend have been talking. The student must leave for class. What happens next?

5  *Roles: professor, student*
   Scene: The professor and student have been discussing an exam that the student failed. The professor looks at her watch and says that she has a class in fifteen minutes. The student responds.

6  *Roles: student, stranger*
   Scene: At the airport, the student must go from the ticket counter to the departure gate, but has more bags than she or he can carry. A stranger offers to help, and to walk the student to the gate. What happens next?

# 27

# Undertaking ESL/EFL programme review for accountability and improvement

RONALD MACKAY

## Programme evaluation

The practice of evaluation is fast becoming an indispensable activity within the context of new and old programmes alike (Rea-Dickins and Germaine 1992). However, in the field of second language teaching, the term 'programme evaluation' is used to refer to a wide variety of activities, ranging from academic, theory-driven research to informal enquiries carried out by a single teacher in a single classroom. For the purposes of this paper, I restrict my comments to activities

- which systematically collect information;
- which are about the context, activities, characteristics, and outcomes of individual programmes;
- which are for use by specific people;
- which enable specific decisions to be made; and
- which give regard to what these programmes are doing, and who they are affecting.

## Dichotomies in evaluation terminology

In the evaluation literature, distinctions between 'formative' and 'summative' evaluation, and between 'evaluation for accountability' and 'evaluation for improvement', are usually more apparent than real—at least for the world of ESL/EFL. As Cronbach (1982) points out, summative or accountability evaluations which provide evidence of disappointing outcomes ought, by definition, to lead administrators to cut off programme funds. In my experience, this seldom happens. Once programmes are in place, they generate their own impetus and their own political support. Almost invariably, evaluation findings, irrespective of the label attached to them, are used to lobby for better programmes, or at the very least as evidence that programme improvement is needed.

It is the case, however, that evaluations with different focuses on different questions will provide information which is more or less useful for programme improvement purposes (Mackay and Weir 1991). In my experience, evaluations which address discrete issues over which programme personnel have some or total control are the ones that generate information useful for programme improvement. Included in this category would be questions such as 'To what extent are the programme objectives relevant to the participants?'; 'Are the activities of the programme consistent with its objectives?'; 'Are the programme activities plausibly linked to the attainment of the programme goals?'.

On the other hand, are the evaluations which address gross 'bureaucratic' concerns (e.g. 'Have the target budgets for the periods concerned been over- or under-spent?') or restrict themselves solely to outcome concerns ('How do students in programme X perform relative to students in programme Y?'). These tend to provide relatively little information of direct use to those responsible for altering, modifying, or otherwise improving their programmes. Moreover, because of differences in the contexts in which ESL language instruction is often offered (e.g. the immediate availability of textbooks and other pedagogic resources, the socio-economic and previous educational background of the students, the facilities available within the school, the experience and qualifications of the teachers, etc.), answers to even such apparently sensible questions as those posed in parenthesis above do not always provide the bureaucracy with sufficient appropriate information on which to base decisions about terminating certain programmes or promoting others.

In my experience the bureaucratic approach to programme review is most common where programme personnel have not been invited to contribute to the design or focus of the evaluation study. That is, in situations where the evaluation questions have been formulated virtually entirely by the funder or the bureaucracy in isolation from the school principals, directors of studies, teachers, communities of language learners, and other beneficiaries who make up the front line of any second language programme.

It is, I believe, more realistic to distinguish between extrinsically motivated evaluations (Figure 1) which are conceived, motivated, and designed at the bureaucratic level, and intrinsically motivated evaluations which are conceived, motivated, and designed at the programme level, with or without the direct involvement of the bureaucracy (Figure 2).

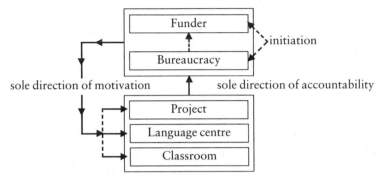

FIGURE 1 *Extrinsically motivated evaluation*

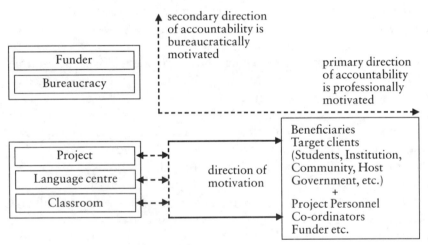

FIGURE 2 *Intrinsically motivated evaluation*

It is important that evaluations generate information which can be used by project personnel (teachers, trainers, materials writers, etc.) since the task of programme improvement will be devolved to them, not the bureaucrats. The programme is the locus in which change will usually be required to be made, and it is important that those responsible for undertaking such change have the information they need to allow them to act appropriately and effectively (Rea-Dickins and Germaine 1992: 7–8).

## Problems of extrinsically motivated evaluations

Why is it then, that 'bureaucratic', extrinsically motivated evaluations are so often carried out, leaving programme personnel dissatisfied, frustrated, confused, and even hostile—in the worst possible mental state to consider undertaking programme improvement? There are various reasons. Some of them, it must be said, may even be perfectly justified. After all, funders and bureaucrats are entitled to seek the information they require and which they know they can use regarding any project for which they are responsible. Such information *may* be of a different order from the information which can be used by a programme manager or teacher.

However, I believe that evaluations of the extrinsically motivated type are often carried out for two less defensible reasons, both of which can be addressed by us as professional applied linguists and teachers willing to acquire an understanding of the purposes and principles of programme evaluation (Cumming 1987; Rea-Dickins and Germaine 1992). The first reason is that there is a dearth of appropriate programme evaluation models or even guidelines generated for specific use within our field of second language teaching and learning. The recent work by Rea-Dickins and Germaine (1992) addresses this dearth directly and effectively by providing language teaching professionals with a basic introduction to evaluation practice and principles.

The second reason why the bureaucracy may be encouraged to mount extrinsically motivated evaluations is because, in most second language projects, *intrinsically* motivated evaluation efforts are conspicuously absent. The bureaucracy tends, understandably, to become increasingly nervous when programme personnel are not able to show evidence of adequately monitoring programme progress and direction. It is often this discomfort experienced as a result of the obvious lack of internal programme monitoring that encourages the bureaucracy to impose the only kind of evaluation framework with which it is familiar and comfortable.

I strongly believe that if language programme personnel—principals, directors of studies, head teachers, and teachers—were pro-active, and more ready to accept the responsibility for undertaking self-motivated, internal, improvement-focused reviews, the bureaucracy would feel less need to impose its own extrinsically motivated evaluations—evaluations whose focuses, methodologies, questions, and indicators are often alien to the implementation and improvement concerns of the front-line staff of the programmes concerned.

One immediate benefit of programme personnel initiating evaluations would be that much of the information generated would inevitably be found to be satisfactory to the bureaucracy for its own accountability purposes, and so reduce the perceived need to impose an evaluation from the outside. (See Figure 2.)

## The ideal management-evaluation-development cycle versus reality

The inclusion, *in principle*, of an evaluation component as an intrinsic part of the cycle of good management is a commonplace. Figure 3 is an example of a classic evaluation-in-management cycle model.

*In practice*, however, it is equally common to find the evaluation component absent from the management cycle. Managers of language programmes, often for very plausible reasons (lack of time, money, expertise, or available personnel), can spend their entire effort just keeping the existing system going, with little thought for programme improvement or innovation.

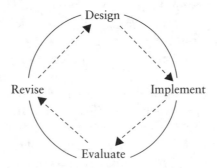

FIGURE 3 *Evaluation-in-management cycle*

## An evaluation approach that satisfies both accountability and improvement

Elsewhere, with others, (Mackay 1991b, 1992; McMahon *et al.* 1984, Scottish Office Education Department 1991, HMSO 1988), I have suggested that a systematic internal evaluation system 'owned' by the project, involving project personnel in a co-operative exercise, to overcome obstacles and resolve problems standing in the way of programme excellence, can meet most of the requirements of both (internal) improvement and (external) accountability. Figure 4 lists some of the strengths and advantages of an intrinsically motivated internal evaluation system of programme/project-based review.

---

Undertaking a programme project-based review will enable project personnel to
– determine how well the project is performing in relation to its aims
– identify strengths on which to build
– identify areas which put the sustainability of the project at risk and which therefore demand attention
– identify other areas of concern requiring improvement
– identify priorities for subsequent action
– report the project performance to appropriate bodies such as funders, host government, host institution, etc.
– provide the funder and beneficiary with valuable information on which to base decisions, e.g. targeting resources
– answer questions concerning the accountability of the project posed by other interest groups/principal stakeholders
– detect improvements in project performance since the previous review
– contribute to the identification of staff development needs

---

FIGURE 4 *Strengths and advantages of programme/project-based review*

This is in keeping with the views on internal evaluation of Love (1991), Hopkins (1989), and Adelman and Alexander (1982).

## What does a programme/project-based review model look like?

Figure 5 is based on a current project in Indonesia in which the author has been recently involved in order to assist with programme evaluation efforts. Several years ago, fourteen language centres were established in different government institutions and universities. The goals of these language centres included the enhancement of communication within fourteen economic development projects dealing with such areas as forestry, rice storage, fishing, public works, etc. as well as the preparation of technical and scientific personnel to undertake professional development training in English-speaking countries, principally the UK.

The project managers, the programme personnel in each language centre, and an enlightened bureaucracy, jointly decided that before external project funding ended, in about two years' time, an evaluation framework was required. The purpose of the framework would be to direct an evaluation undertaking which would permit those on the front line within each centre to identify and report upon the perceived threats to the sustainability of their individual language centres. An early and pro-active review of threats to sustainability would permit centre personnel to take appropriate remedial action while funding was still available from the project sponsor—the British Government.

Extensive programme documentation was supplied to the author by the two project managers who co-ordinated the fourteen centres, and investigative question-and-answer sessions were conducted by mail and fax prior to the author's visit to Indonesia. On the basis of these it was decided that the most appropriate framework within which practicable and useful evaluations of the language centres could be carried out would be one which employed indicators of the particular strengths and

FIGURE 5 *A framework for project-based review*

weaknesses which centre directors and teachers (i.e. the front-line programme personnel) believed to be important, and which involved these same persons in the evaluation undertaking, with or without the assistance of facilitators who could act as expert resources during the process.

The use of indicators of strengths and weaknesses has been widely used in reviewing educational programmes for at least the past decade (Bryk and Hermanson 1993). One of the distinct advantages of adopting a performance indicator model in this case was felt to be the motivational value of having language centre directors and teachers decide not only which components of their projects required scrutiny but also the criteria by which these components would be judged.

Programme/project-based review begins with the conceptualization of the language teaching project as a whole, made up of its interrelated but discrete parts, along the lines of traditional organizational structure. This conceptualization is represented in Figure 5 by the first three levels, where the entire project can be broken down into smaller administrative units (in this case the fourteen different language centres) each of which in turn presents logical and possible focuses for scrutiny. In this case, five focuses were identified by language centre personnel as requiring review—programmes, staff, institution, resources, and finances. It is important that the focuses identified represent areas over which project personnel have some influence or control—preferably more rather than less! For example, in the case of the Indonesian project, each language centre had a mandate (and governmental authorization) to generate revenue by marketing ESL courses to external clients. Thus, if the review indicates that the sustainability of one or more particular language centres is at risk due (in part) to inadequate financial resources, the directors of these language centres, in conjunction with their staff, are able to formulate plans to seek additional paying clients in order to generate more revenue.

Factors over which project personnel have no control are 'background' factors—that is, they are simply constraints which have to be acknowledged and accommodated to. If background factors are made the focus of a review, the result is simply frustrated for all concerned. Since project personnel cannot influence such factors, there is a risk that their energies and efforts will deteriorate into complaints which simply cannot be addressed. The craft of good programme/project-based review is to focus attention and energy onto areas which require improvement and which can be directly affected by project personnel. The craft of good management, following a programme/project-based review is to channel the enthusiasm and energy of programme personnel into those areas where a difference can be made, and where improvement will have the most salutory impact.

Within each focus, a number of key areas can be identified. In the Indonesian project it was felt by the directors and personnel of the language centres that the focus 'programmes' could be broken down into the quality of each course offered in the language-centre, the quality of the teaching, and student performance (see Figure 5).

Key areas represent a level of detail accessible to measurement for the purpose of estimating adequacy or effectiveness. The criteria on which key areas are measured are unique and appropriate to each. The Indonesian project personnel felt that the key area 'quality of each course' could be measured by collecting appropriate data on seven performance indicators (see Figure 5).

Once the data corresponding to each of these performance indicators has been collected and organized, the project personnel as a group are in a position to examine and interpret it and, after due deliberation, to arrive at judgements regarding the level of performance of their respective language centres in each of the key areas. Priorities for subsequent action by programme personnel can then be set, based on a clear appreciation of the strengths and weaknesses of the individual language-centre.

An additional advantage of the information generated by programme-based review is that some of it can be presented in an appropriate and summarized form to meet the interests and concerns of the bureaucracy. A project or programme which can show the bureaucracy what its strengths and weaknesses are, and how it plans to reinforce the former and overcome the latter, cannot fail to impress the 'powers that be', and runs less risk of having an extrinsically motivated evaluation imposed upon it.

*Originally published in Volume 48/2, 1994*

# CONCLUSION

One of the aims of *ELT Journal*, since its inception, has been 'to bridge the gap between the everyday concerns of teachers in their classrooms and the various disciplines such as psychology, sociology and linguistics that may offer significant insights'. The selection of articles in this volume certainly might be said to bridge the gap and to bring a richness of insights from a range of disciplines. If we take Stern's (1983) four key concepts of ELT, language, learning, teaching, and context, it is immediately possible to appreciate the ways in which our understanding of these concepts has been enriched.

In terms of *language*, we have seen attempts to refine our knowledge of the structure and use of the English language. Considerations of language varieties and the concern of pragmatics with the use of language in context have both generated new perspectives within ELT.

In terms of *learning*, the ELT profession has received useful insights from second-language acquisition studies, not least the need to provide a rich input and opportunities for interaction in the classroom.

In terms of *teaching*, the influence of educational thinking is clearly perceived in the growing interest in the management of curriculum evaluation and renewal, in process approaches, in critical pedagogy, in reflective practice, and in ideas for encouraging a greater degree of independence in learners.

In terms of *context*, the last decade has seen much discussion of the political, cultural and social settings within which the increasing internationalization of English must be viewed and the implications for principles and practice considered.

Perhaps, too, this collection demonstrates a 'bridging of the gap' in another, significant way. Many of the articles pay testament to the fact that the applied science model of research and dissemination has been supplemented by another, persuasive model, that of the teacher as class-room researcher. It is no longer the case that teachers depend solely on the passing on of insights from empirical work in the contributing disciplines. They are, themselves, capable of developing a research approach, of formulating research questions and of carrying out enquiries into their own professional practice. Our hope is that the articles in this volume, whatever their focus and whatever the approach to enquiry they exhibit, will provide a map of recent issues in ELT, that they will point the way to further explorations, and that the references and the topic index will enable our readers to begin a journey along whatever routes are professionally and personally relevant.

# CONTRIBUTORS

GERRY ABBOTT started teaching EFL in 1958. After four years in Thailand and two years as British Council Education Officer in Jordan, he took up a lectureship at Manchester University, where he is now an Honorary Fellow. Other posts have included Head of the Department of Language Methods at Makerere University, Kampala; Unesco expert in English, PDR Yemen; English language adviser, Sarawak; and, most recently, senior lecturer in English, University of Mandalay. He co-edited and contributed to *The Teaching of English as an International Language* (Collins, 1981). *Back to Mandalay* (Impact Books, 1990) is an account of his experiences in Burma.

CEM ALPTEKIN is Professor of Applied Linguistics and TEFL at Bogaziçi University, Istanbul. He obtained his PhD from New York University. His research interests include the neuro- and socio-pyschological aspects of second language acquisition. He has published in a number of journals including *Canadian Modern Language Review*, *ITL Review of Applied Linguistics*, *Language Learning*, *Second Language Research*, and *TESOL Quarterly*.

GUY ASTON studied applied linguistics at Edinburgh University, and obtained his PhD, on the description and teaching of conversational interaction, from the University of London. He was formerly co-ordinator of the PIXI research project on the pragmatics of cross-cultural interaction and director of the University of Ancona Language Centre. He is currently Associate Professor of English Language at the School for Interpreters and Translators, University of Bologna, where he directs a research group into the uses of computerized text corpora in language teaching and self-access learning, on which he has published a number of articles. He is co-author (with L. D. Burnard) of *The British National Corpus Handbook* (Oxford University Computing Services, forthcoming).

KATHLEEN BARDOVI-HARLIG is Associate Professor of TESOL and Applied Linguistics at Indiana University. Her areas of investigation include second language acquisition, interlanguage pragmatics, and teacher education. She has taught applied linguistics in Hungary and Japan, and at the TESOL Institute. Her work on language teaching has appeared in *ELT Journal*, *TESOL Quarterly*, *Pragmatics and Language Learning* (monograph series), *TESOL France Journal*, and edited volumes. With B. A. S. Hartford she has written several articles on interlanguage pragmatics. Their most recent work includes a thematic issue of *Studies in Second Language Acquisition: The Construction of Discourse by Nonnative Speakers*. They are also co-editors of a book currently under review: *Beyond Methods: Components of Language Teacher Education*.

CAROLINE BODÓCZKY and ANGI MALDEREZ work at the Centre for English Teacher Training, Eötvös Loránd University, Budapest. They continue to be involved in mentoring work and the design and evaluation of teaching practice. Their publications include 'The INSET impact of a mentoring course' in *In-service Teacher Development: International Perspectives*; edited by Chris Kennedy (Macmillan, forthcoming) and 'Out into schools' in *Changing Perspectives* edited by A. Medgyes and P. Medgyes (Heinemann, forthcoming). They are also writing a resource book for mentor development courses (Cambridge University Press, forthcoming).

DONARD BRITTEN is currently the British Council's Regional ELT Adviser for Western Romania, and teaches at the University of Timisoara. Before that, he trained teachers and inspectors in West and North Africa, where he was also involved in curriculum development and materials writing. He is co-author of the national Moroccan English course, *English in Life*, and, with Gwendolyn Dellar, of *Using Phrasal Verbs*, which takes a narrative and system-based approach to lexical development. His main current interest is in language awareness work in teacher development, particularly as a basis for teaching the lexical system.

LESLIE DICKINSON currently divides his time between the School of Liberal Arts, King Mongkut's Institute of Technology, Thonburi (KMITT), Bangkok, and Edinburgh. Until he took early retirement in 1993, he was a Senior Lecturer at the Scottish Centre for International Education at Moray House Institute of Education, Heriot-Watt University, Edinburgh. In 1995 he collaborated with Anita Wenden in editing a special number of the journal *System* on the topic of autonomy, and in 1996 he organized an international conference at KMITT on autonomy in language learning. He is currently researching language learning motivation, its enhancement, and its relationship with learning independence.

ROD ELLIS is Professor of TESOL in the Department of Curriculum, Instruction and Technology in Education, College of Education, Temple University, Philadelphia. He has been a teacher and teacher trainer in the UK, Europe, Africa, Latin America, and the Far East. He has published widely in the area of second language acquisition and in the application of research and theory to language teaching. His publications include *Understanding Second Language Acquisition* (OUP), which won the BAAL Prize in 1986, and *The Study of Second Language Acquisition* (OUP), which won the English Speaking Union's Duke of Edinburgh Book Competition in 1994.

ULRICH GERBER has been teaching English at pre-university level in Switzerland for twenty years. He received his lic.phil. (licentiate) from Zürich University in 1977 and his teaching diploma in 1978. He teaches students aged 15 to 19 at the Kantonsschule Zürcher Unterland in Bülach. He is interested in finding more efficient and motivating ways of teaching English and has published several articles on this subject. He is especially interested in South Africa, both the country and its people. He publishes in newspapers and periodicals and gives courses on this topic at his school and in public.

BEVERLY A. S. HARTFORD is Associate Professor of TESOL and Applied Linguistics at Indiana University. She has taught applied linguistics in Poland and Nepal, and has conducted workshops in Venezuela and Malaysia. She has published in the areas of interlanguage pragmatics and World Englishes. She is co-author of *Issues in International Bilingual Education: The Role of the Vernacular* with Albert Valdman and Charles Foster.

EUNICE G. HUTCHINSON (formerly TORRES) was Assistant Professor of English and Head of the English Program at the College of Arts and

Sciences, University of the Philippines in the Visayas (UPV), Iloilo City. She was also actively involved in the training of English teachers throughout the Philippines. From 1987 to 1991 she was the project co-ordinator of the UPV/British Council 'English for Fisheries' materials development project and co-authored the project textbook *English for Fisheries Technology*. She is currently completing her PhD at Lancaster University on teachers' and learners' classroom use of textbooks.

TOM HUTCHINSON is Associate Director of the Institute for English Language Education, Lancaster University. He has taught in the UK, Germany, and Croatia, and has given teacher training seminars in many countries, including Brazil, Sri Lanka, and the Phillipines. He is the author of a number of successful textbooks, including *Lifelines, Hotline, Project Video*, and *Project English* (all published by Oxford University Press). He is also the author of *ESP: A Learning-Centred Approach* (Cambridge University Press, 1987). Apart from writing textbooks, he is currently interested in the management of change.

JENNIFER JARVIS is Senior Lecturer in Education (TESOL) and Postgraduate Research Tutor at the School of Education, University of Leeds. She has teaching qualifications in TESOL, a Masters degree, and state teaching qualifications. She has had wide experience as a teacher trainer and trainer trainer in many parts of the world. Her current research is in the interaction of teachers and pupils in young learner classrooms. She has worked extensively in the area of primary reading skills and in designing and implementing school-focused in-service training. She is also involved in work on analysing educational discourse.

CLAUDIA KEH has an MA in TESL from the University of California at Los Angeles. She is currently the Senior Language Consultant for Professional and Educational Services International, Hong Kong. She conducts research, designs and writes curricula and materials for ESL and Business English programmes for Hong Kong and China, and trains teachers to use these materials. She has also taught refugee children, adult immigrants, secondary school and university students, and business professionals in the USA, Hong Kong, and China. Her current interests include curriculum design, materials development, writing skills for Business English, and learning strategies.

JUDITH KENNEDY is currently a lecturer in applied linguistics at the Centre for English Language Teacher Education, University of Warwick, where she is responsible for the initial training of English language teachers. She has lived and worked in many countries, including Côte d'Ivoire, Tunisia, Malaysia, Russia, and Hong Kong. Her current interests include change and innovation in education systems, and teacher development. She is a committee member of IATEFL and founder editor of *English Language Teacher Education and Development Journal*, published jointly by the universities of Warwick and Birmingham.

B. KUMARAVADIVELU is currently Professor of Applied Linguistics at San José State University. He has an MA from Lancaster University and a PhD from the University of Michigan. He has taught at the Central Institute of English and Foreign Languages in India, and at the universities of Alabama and Minnesota. His research interests include teacher education and the socio-political aspects of second language education. He has published widely in a number of journals, and is a member of the Editorial Board of *TESOL Quarterly*.

MARTIN LAMB qualified as a history teacher in 1982 and went to Sweden to teach EFL, planning to return to the UK after one year. Instead he stayed in Sweden for a second year, and then moved to Indonesia, where he taught for six years. After that he worked in Bulgaria for five years as a teacher and teacher trainer. Along the way, he acquired an RSA Diploma in TEFL and an MA in Linguistics from Lancaster University. He is now back in Indonesia, working as a language consultant on a higher education project managed by the British Council, and pursuing his interest in all aspects of teacher training and development.

RONALD MACKAY is Professor of Education and Director of the TESL Centre at Concordia University, Montreal. He studied in Aberdeen and Edinburgh and obtained his PhD from l'Université de Montréal. He started his career as an English teacher in Spain. He was a lecturer at the University of Newcastle upon Tyne, and Director of the Research and Development Unit, UNAM, Mexico City. Since 1992 he has carried out evaluations and/or trained evaluators in Canada, Indonesia, Kuwait, Mexico, UK, and Venezuela. He also plans, manages, and evaluates Canadian and international educational projects. From January to May 1995 he was a Visiting Scholar at the Scottish Council for Research in Education.

REBECCA MAHAN-TAYLOR has an MA in Applied Linguistics and has been teaching ESL for nine years at the Intensive English Program at Indiana University. She has given workshops and presentations at

TESOL in the areas of listening strategies and pragmatic competency. In addition to these topics, her interests include cross-cultural communication, ESL and American slang, and the role of authentic media in the classroom. Her suggestions for using the community as a teaching resource can be found in the TESOL series, *New Ways in Teaching Speaking*. She is currently co-authoring a text with Shelly Ridder which will promote the teaching of issues in the ESL classroom through the use of feature films.

PÉTER MEDGYES is Director of the Centre for English Teacher Training at Eötvös Loránd University, Budapest, where he teaches applied linguistics and EFL methodology. He was a teacher trainer at a secondary school level for more than a decade. He has written several ELT textbooks and articles. His most recent publication, *The Non-Native Teacher* (Macmillan, 1994), won the 1995 Duke of Edinburgh English Language Book Competition. He is currently interested in investigating collaborative practices in teacher education and the teaching of academic writing skills.

MARY J. MORGAN received her MA in Linguistics from Indiana University in 1989. She served in the Peace Corps, training English teachers and teaching English to secondary school students in the Central African Republic. She was an editor for the Educational Resources Information Center's Clearinghouse on Reading and Communications Skills, where her publications included 'Critical Thinking, Reading and Writing'. From 1990 to 1992, she taught English to medical professionals at Xi'an Medical University's English Language Center in the People's Republic of China. She is currently a reporter and assistant editor at the *Rochester Business Journal*, a weekly newspaper covering the business community in Rochester, New York. She is also editor of the *Rochester Business Journal NewsLink*, an electronic multimedia version of the newspaper.

BARBRA NAIDU is a senior lecturer at St Joseph's College, Bangalore. She has an MA in English and American literature from the University of San Diego, and is currently working on a PhD at Bangalore University on the teaching of English prose at the tertiary level. She has served on two syllabus committees which have designed learner-friendly textbooks for general English. She has been involved in a number of non-formal projects, particularly on the challenges of large classes.

K. NEERAJA is Senior Lecturer and Head of the Department of English at Maharani Lakshmi Ammanni College, Bangalore. She has an MA in

English language and literature and has been teaching since 1972. She has worked on a number of non-formal research projects on several aspects of large classes, and has been involved in developing an open-ended resource book for teachers. Some of her current interests include the production of learning-centred teaching materials, learner perspectives and learner strategies, and the multi-faceted role of the teacher in the current educational context.

JUNKO NOBUYOSHI has an MA in TESOL from Temple University, Japan. She has been teaching at Simul Academy in Tokyo since 1994. Before that she worked at the Kanda Institute of Foreign Languages and at Kanda University of International Studies.

DAVID NUNAN is Professor of Applied Linguistics and Director of the English Centre at the University of Hong Kong. Before this he was Director of Research and Development, NCELTR, and Co-ordinator of Postgraduate Programs in Linguistics at Macquarie University, Sydney. He has published over 100 books and articles in the areas of curriculum and materials development, classroom-based research, and discourse analysis. His recent publications include *The Self-Directed Teacher* (Cambridge University Press, 1996), and, with K. M. Bailey, *Voices from the Language Classroom* (Cambridge University Press, 1996). His most recent major textbook project is *Atlas: Learning Centered-Communication*, a multi-level, task-based series (Heinle and Heinle, 1995).

ROBERT PHILLIPSON studied at Cambridge University and Leeds University, and has a PhD from the University of Amsterdam. He has worked for the British Council in ELT posts in Algeria, UK, Yugoslavia, and, since 1973, has worked at the Department of Languages and Culture, University of Roskilde, Denmark. His main research interests are language policy, English worldwide, and theories of linguistic dominance and language rights. He is co-editor, with Tove Skutnabb-Kangas, of *Linguistic Human Rights: Overcoming Linguistic Discrimination* (de Gruyter, 1994). He is currently working on language policy in Europe at the supranational, national, and subnational levels.

M. B. H. RAMPTON is a Principal Lecturer at the Centre for Applied Linguistic Research at Thames Valley University. He was an ESL teacher in Britain for five years and subsequently did a PhD in sociolinguistics at the University of London. He is interested in ethnography, multilingualism, ethnicity, and language education. He co-authored *Researching Language: Issues of Power and Method* (Routledge, 1992).

His book *Crossing: Language and Ethnicity Among Adolescents* (Longman) was published in 1995.

DUDLEY W. REYNOLDS is a PhD candidate in Linguistics and an Associate Instructor at the Center for English Language Training at Indiana University. He has taught English to speakers of other languages in the United States and Egypt. His research interests include the acquisition of discourse structure by second language learners, methods for teaching pragmatics, and World Englishes. Most recently his work has focused on the uses of repetition in second language writing. He has published in *Studies in Second Language Acquisition*, *TESOL Quarterly*, and *World Englishes*.

PETER SHEAL has an MA from Lancaster University and has worked for the British Council in Libya and Nigeria. He has worked in staff development and management training since 1980. He is currently a management trainer and consultant in the Middle East. His publications include *The Staff Development Handbook* (1992) and *How to Develop and Present Staff Training Courses* (1994), both published by Kogan Page. His current interests are in management skills training and team building in business and educational organizations.

JAYAGOWRI SHIVAKUMAR has been a lecturer at NMKRV College for Women, India since 1981. She has an MA from Bangalore University, a postgraduate teaching qualification from CIEFI, Hyderabad, and is currently engaged in PhD research on non-formal approaches to teacher development. She is also interested in co-operative learning, and in examining the notion of standardness in Indian varieties of English.

ELLEN SPOLSKY is Professor of English and Director of the Lechter Institute for Literary Research at Bar-Ilan University, Israel. Her interest in linguistics and cognitive science colours her understanding of how interpretation works and keeps her alert to the implications for the teaching of literature that her theoretical studies produce. Her book *Gaps in Nature: Literary Interpretation and the Modular Mind* (SUNY Press, 1993) explains the relationship between the ideologies of different schools of literary criticism and cognitive processing preferences. She is currently working on a book which deals with versions of scepticism in the Renaissance, as revealed in art and literature.

HELEN STEPHENSON has an MEd in TESOL from the University of Manchester. From 1982 to 1989 she worked in TEFL in Europe. From 1989 to 1992 she was an ELT co-ordinator at the Ministry of Education in São Tomé and Príncipe, and later set up the Voice of America training programme, also in São Tomé and Príncipe. Her current interests include the role of learner-selected activities in intensive language programmes, and language versus subject skills in vocational training.

JANE SUNDERLAND is currently a teaching fellow in the Department of Linguistics and Modern English Language, Lancaster University, where she teaches courses on language and gender and language in society. She also co-ordinates a research group called 'Language and Gender in the Classroom'. She is about to complete her PhD, entitled 'Learning Gender in the Foreign Language Classroom: Its Shaping and its Relation with Language Learning Opportunities'. She edited *Exploring Gender: Questions and Implications for English Language Education* (Prentice Hall, 1994). Her current interests include the role of gender in language teacher education, with specific reference to culture, and gender and discourse roles in language textbook dialogues.

IAN TUDOR is currently Head of the English Department at the Institut de Langues Vivantes et de Phonétique, Université Libre de Bruxelles. He has an MSc and a PhD in applied linguistics from the University of Edinburgh, and has taught in Libya, Germany, and the UK. His current interests are in learner-centredness, self-direction in language learning, and teacher education. He has published on a number of aspects of L2 methodology, including reading skills, and the use of L1 materials in L2 teaching. He is the author of *Learner-centredness as Language Education* (Cambridge University Press, 1996).

VANAMALA VISWANATHA is a Reader in English at Bangalore University, where she teaches ELT and translation studies. She has an MA in English language and literature, a postgraduate teaching qualification, and a PhD for work on the teaching of literature. She has designed and taught ESP courses, in-service teacher training programmes, and business courses for executives. In 1995 she was awarded a British Council visitorship to the UK. She is currently editing and translating an anthology of women's writing in English, and working on ELT and multilingualism.

H. G. WIDDOWSON worked as an English Language Officer with the British Council for a number of years before taking up a post in the Department of Linguistics at Edinburgh University, where he obtained his PhD in 1973. At present he has professorial appointments at the University of London Institute of Education and the University of Essex. He has lectured and published extensively in the field of applied linguistics, discourse analysis, literary stylistics, and language education. Among his books are *Aspects of Language Teaching* (1990), *Practical Stylistics* (1994), published by Oxford University Press. He is the editor of a new series, 'Oxford Introductions to Language Study', published by Oxford University Press, and author of the first title in the series, *Introduction to Linguistics* (1996).

# BIBLIOGRAPHY

ABBOTT, G. 1984. 'Should we start digging new holes?' *ELT Journal* 38/2: 98–102.

ABBOTT, G. 1992. 'Development, education, and English language teaching'. *ELT Journal* 46/2: 172–9.

ABERCROMBIE, D. 1956. *Problems and Principles: Studies in the Teaching of English as a Second Language.* London: Longman.

ABRAHAM, P. and D. MACKEY. 1986. *Get Ready: Interactive Listening and Speaking.* Englewood Cliffs, NJ.: Prentice Hall.

ADASKOU, K., D. BRITTEN and B. FAHSI. 1990. 'Design decisions on the cultural content of a secondary English course for Morocco'. *ELT Journal* 44/1: 3–10.

ADELMAN, C. and R. J. ALEXANDER. 1982. *The Self Evaluating Institution: Practice and Principles in the Management of Educational Change.* London: Methuen.

ALLWRIGHT, R. L. 1981. 'What do we want teaching materials for?' *ELT Journal* 36/1: 5–18.

ALLWRIGHT, R. L. 1988. 'Is class size a problem?' Report No. 3 of the Lancaster–Leeds Large Classes Project. Lancaster: University of Lancaster.

ALLWRIGHT, R. L. and K. BAILEY. 1991. *Focus on the Language Classroom.* Cambridge: Cambridge University Press.

ALPTEKIN, C. 1981. 'Socio-pyschological and pedagogic considerations in L2 acquisition'. *TESOL Quarterly* 15/3: 275–84.

ALPTEKIN, C. 1988. 'Chinese formal schemata in ESL composition'. *British Journal of Language Teaching* 26/2: 112–15.

ALPTEKIN, C. 1990. 'A look into the use of native-speaker teachers in EFL programs'. *TEFL Turkey Reporter* 1/1: 5–9.

ALPTEKIN, C. 1993. 'Target-language in EFL materials'. *ELT Journal* 47/2: 136–43.

ANSRE, G. 1979. 'Four rationalisations for maintaining European languages in education in Africa'. *African Languages* 5/2: 10–17.

ASSINDER, W. 1991. 'Peer teaching, peer learning: one model'. *ELT Journal* 45/3: 218–29.

ASTON, G. 1993. 'The learner's contribution to the self-access centre'. *ELT Journal* 47/3: 219–27.

ASTON, G. 1995. 'Starting a self-access centre' in C. Cecioni and C. Cheselka (eds.). *Proceedings of the Symposium on Language and Technology, Florence, 11–13 December 1991*. Florence: CUSL.

ATKINSON, D. 1989. '"Humanistic" approaches in the adult classroom: an effective reaction'. *ELT Journal* 43/4: 268–73.

AUERBACH, N. 1985. 'Engorging the Patriarchy' in J. J. McGann (ed.). *Historical Studies and Literary Criticism*. Madison: University of Wisconsin Press.

BAHNS, J. 1993. 'Lexical collocations: a contrastive view'. *ELT Journal* 47/1: 56–63.

BAILEY, K. M. 1983. 'Competitiveness and anxiety in adult second language learning: looking *at* and *through* the diary studies' in H. W. Seliger and M. H. Long (eds.). *Classroom Oriented Research in Second Language Acquisition*. Rowley, MA.: Newbury House.

BAMBER, B. 1987. 'Training the trainers' in *Language Teacher Education*. ELT Documents 125. London: Modern English Publications/British Council.

BARDOVI-HARLIG, K. and B. S. HARTFORD. 1989. 'Speaking out of turn: negotiating potentially disruptive speech acts'. Paper presented at TESOL San Antonio.

BARDOVI-HARLIG, K. and B. S. HARTFORD. 1990. 'Congruence in native and nonnative conversations: status balance in the academic advising session'. *Language Learning* 40/4: 467–501.

BARDOVI-HARLIG, K., B. S. HARTFORD, R. MAHAN-TAYLOR, M. J. MORGAN, and D. W. REYNOLDS. 1991. 'Developing pragmatic awareness: closing the conversation'. *ELT Journal* 45/1: 4–15.

BARNES, D. 1976. *From Communication to Curriculum*. Harmondsworth: Penguin.

BARNETT, L. and G. JORDAN 1991. 'Self-access facilities: what are they for?' *ELT Journal* 45/4: 305–12.

BATE, B. 1978. 'Non-sexist language use in transition'. *Journal of Communication* 28: 139–49.

BEAVEN, M. 1977. 'The effects of between-draft teacher evaluation versus students' self evaluation on high school revising of rough drafts'. *Research in Teaching English* 13: 111–19.

BERRY, R. 1991. 'Rearticulating the articles'. *ELT Journal* 45/3: 252–9.

BISONG, J. 1995. 'Language choice and cultural imperialism'. *ELT Journal* 49/2: 122–31.

BLACKLER, F. and S. SHIMMIN. 1984. *Applying Psychology in Organizations*. London: Methuen.

BLANCHARD, K. and S. JOHNSON. 1983. *The One-Minute Manager*. Glasgow: Collins.

BODÓCZKY, C. and A. MALDEREZ. 1994. 'Talking Shop: pre-service experience and the training of supervisors'. *ELT Journal* 48/1: 66–79.

BOLITHO, R. 1979. 'On Demonstration Lessons' in S. Holden (ed.). *Teacher Training*. London: Modern English Publications.

BORKIN, A. and S. REINHART. 1978. 'Excuse me and I'm sorry'. *TESOL Quarterly* 12/1: 57–69.

BOURNE, J. 1988. '"Natural acquisition" and "masked pedagogy"'. *Applied Linguistics* 9/1: 83–99.

BOWERS, R. 1983. 'Project planning and performance' in *Language Teaching Projects for the Third World*. ELT Documents 116. London: British Council/Macmillan.

BOWERS, R. 1986. 'English in the world: aims and achievements in English language teaching'. *TESOL Quarterly* 20/3: 393–409.

BOWERS, R. 1987. 'Developing perception of the classroom' in *Language Teacher Education*. ELT Documents 125. London: Modern English Publications/British Council.

BOWERS, R. 1992. 'Memories, metaphors, maxims, and myths: language learning and cultural awareness'. *ELT Journal* 46/1: 29–38.

BRAUN, S. W. 1984. *Life in English*. New York: Harcourt Brace Jovanovich.

BRAY, M. 1991. *Making Small Practical: The Organization and Management of Ministries of Education in Small States*. London: The Commonwealth Secretariat.

BREEN, M. 1984. 'Process syllabuses for the language classroom' in C. J. Brumfit (ed.). *General English Syllabus Design*. ELT Documents 118. London: Modern English Publications/British Council.

BREEN, M. 1987. 'Learner contributions to task design' in C. Candlin and D. Murphy (eds.). *Lancaster Practical Papers in ELT*. Vol. 2. London: Prentice Hall.

BREND, R. 1975. 'Male–female intonation patterns in American English' in B. Thorne and N. Henley (eds.). *Language and Sex: Difference and Dominance*. Rowley, MA.: Newbury House.

BRINDLEY, G. 1984. *Needs Analysis and Objective Setting in the Adult Migrant Education Program*. Report of the New South Wales Adult Migrant Education Program for the Joint Commonwealth/States Committee on the A.M.E.P.: Sydney.

BRITISH COUNCIL. 1988. *ELT in Development Aid: Defining Aims and Measuring Results*. Dunford House Seminar Report. London: British Council.

BRITTEN, D. 1988. 'Three stages in teacher training'. *ELT Journal* 42/1: 3–8.

BROOKES, A. and P. GRUNDY. (eds.). 1988. *Autonomy and Individualisation in Language Learning*. ELT Documents 131. London: Modern English Publications/British Council.

BROWN, A. 1989. 'Giving your students' /ɪ/'. *ELT Journal* 43/4: 294–301.

BROWN A., S. S. SMILEY, J. D. DAY, M. A. TOWNSEND, and S. C. LAWTON. 1977. 'Intrusion of a thematic idea in children's comprehension and retention of stories'. *Child Development* 48: 1454–66.

BRUMFIT, C. 1980. *Problems and Principles in English Teaching*. Oxford: Pergamon.

BRUMFIT, C. 1982. 'Some humanistic doubts about humanistic language teaching' in *Humanistic Approaches: An Empirical View*. ELT Documents 113. London: Modern English Publications/British Council.

BRUMFIT, C. 1984. *Communicative Methodology in Language Teaching*. Cambridge: Cambridge University Press.

BRUMFIT, C. 1987. 'Concepts and Categories in Language Teaching Methodology'. *AILA Review* 4.

BRUNDAGE, D. H. and D. MACKERACHER. 1980. *Adult Learning Principles and their Application to Program Planning*. Ontario: Ontario Institute for Studies in Education.

BRUNER, J. 1985. 'Vygotsky: a historical and conceptual perspective' in J. V. Wertsch (ed.). *Culture, Communication and Cognition: Vygotskian Perspectives*. Cambridge: Cambridge University Press.

BRYK, A. S. and K. HERMANSON. 1993. 'Educational indicator systems: observations on their structure, interpretation, and use'. *Review of Educational Research* 19: Chapter 10.

BURKE, P. 1969. *The Renaissance Sense of the Past*. Oxford: Blackwell.

BURNABY, B. and Y. SUN. 1989. 'Chinese teachers' views of western language teaching: context informs paradigms'. *TESOL Quarterly* 23/2: 219–38.

BURSTALL, C. 1974. *Primary French in the Balance*. Windsor: National Foundation for Educational Research.

BYRAM, M. 1988. 'Foreign language education and cultural studies'. *Language Culture and Curriculum* 1/1: 15–31.

BYRAM, M. 1989. *Cultural Studies in Foreign Language Education*. Clevedon: Multilingual Matters.

CALDERHEAD, J. 1989. 'Reflective teacher and teacher education'. *Teaching and Teacher Education* 5/1: 43–51.

CALHOUN, J. B. 1972. 'Plight of the Ik and Kaiadilt is seen as a chilling possible end for Man'. *Smithsonian*, November issue, reprinted in P. Whitten (ed.). 1977. *Being Human Today: Psychological Perspectives*. San Francisco, CA.: Canfield.

CAMERON, D. 1985. *Feminism and Linguistic Theory*. London: Macmillan.

CANALE, M. 1983. 'From communicative competence to language pedagogy' in J. Richards and R. Schmidt (eds.). *Language and Communication*. London: Longman.

CANDLIN, C. and C. EDELHOFF. 1982. *Challenges: Teacher's Handbook*. Harlow: Longman.

CARDINAL, H. 1969. *The Unjust Society: the Tragedy of Canada's Indians*. Edmonton: M. G. Hurtig.

CARRELL, P. L. 1987. 'Content and formal schemata in ESL reading'. *TESOL Quarterly* 21/3: 461–81.

CARRELL, P. L. and J. C. EISTERHOLD. 1983. 'Schema theory and ESL reading pedagogy'. *TESOL Quarterly* 17/4: 553–73.

CHANDRASEGARAN, A. 1989. 'Developing, planning, and reviewing skills in composition'. Paper presented at the RELC Conference, Singapore.

CHARLES, M. 1990. 'Responding to problems in written English using a student self-monitoring technique'. *ELT Journal* 44/4: 286–93.

CHAUDRON, C. 1988. *Second Language Classrooms: Research on Teaching and Learning*. Cambridge: Cambridge University Press.

CLARKE, J. and M. CLARKE. 1990. 'Stereotyping in TESOL materials' in B. Harrison (ed.). *Culture and the Language Classroom*. ELT Documents 132. London: Modern English Publications/British Council.

CLARKE, M. A. 1976. 'Second language acquisition as a clash of consciousness'. *Language Learning* 26/2: 377–90.

CLARKE, R. 1985. *Science and Technology in World Development*. Oxford: Oxford University Press, in association with UNESCO.

CLYNE, M. 1981. 'Culture and discourse structure'. *Journal of Pragmatics* 5/1: 61–66.

CLYNE, M. 1985. 'Medium or object–different contexts of (school-based) second language acquisition' in K. Hyltenstam and M. Pienemann (eds.). *Modelling and Assessing Second Language Acquisition*. Clevedon: Multilingual Matters.

COLEMAN, H. 1987. 'A study of large classes'. Report No. 2 of the Lancaster–Leeds Large Classes Project. Leeds: University of Leeds.

COLLIE, J. and S. SLATER. 1987. *Literature in the Language Classroom*. Cambridge: Cambridge University Press.

CONNOR, U. and R. B. KAPLAN (eds.). 1987. *Writing Across Languages: Analysis of L2 Text*. Reading, MA.: Addison Wesley.

COOPER, J. M. (ed.). 1984. *Developing Skills for Instructional Supervision*. New York and London: Longman.

COOPER, R. 1984. 'The avoidance of androcentric generics'. *International Journal of Social Language* 50: 5–20.

CORDER, S. P. 1986. 'Talking shop: language teaching and applied linguistics'. *ELT Journal* 40/3: 185–90.

COULMAS, F. (ed.). 1981a. *Conversational Routine: Explorations in Standardized Communication Situations and Prepatterned Speech*. The Hague: Mouton.

COULMAS, F. (ed.). 1981b *A Festschrift for Native Speakers*. The Hague: Mouton.

COX REPORT. 1989. *English From Ages 5 to 16*. London: Department of Education and Science and Welsh Office.

CREWE, W. J. 1990. 'The illogic of logical connectives'. *ELT Journal* 44/4: 316–25.

CRONBACH, L. J. 1982. *Designing Evaluations of Educational and Social Programs*. San Francisco, CA.: Jossey-Bass.

CRYSTAL, D. 1985. *A Dictionary of Linguistics and Phonetics*. Oxford: Blackwell.

CRYSTAL, D. 1995. 'In search of English: a traveller's guide'. *ELT Journal* 49/2: 107–21.

CUMMING, A. 1987. 'What is second language program evaluation?' *Canadian Modern Language Review* 43/4: 678–99.

CUMMINS, A. and R. MACKAY. 1994. 'Learning processes in a Canadian exchange program for multicultural/anti-racist education'. *Canadian Journal of Education* 19/4: 399–417.

CUNNINGSWORTH, A. and P. KUSEL. 1991. 'Evaluating teachers' guides'. *ELT Journal* 45/2: 128–39.

DAM, L. and G. GABRIELSON. 1988. 'Developing learner autonomy in a school context: a six year experiment beginning in the learners' first year of English' in H. Holec (ed.).

DANIS, F. 1982. 'Weaving the web of meaning: interaction patterns in peer-response groups'. Paper presented at the Annual Meeting of the Conference on College Composition and Communication, San Francisco, CA.

DHERAM, P. 1995. 'Feedback as a two-bullock cart: a case study of teaching writing'. *ELT Journal* 49/2: 160–8.

DICKINSON, L. 1987. *Self-instruction in Language Learning*. Cambridge: Cambridge University Press.

DICKINSON, L. 1992. *Learner Training for Language Learning*. Dublin: Authentik.

DICKINSON, L. 1993. 'Talking Shop: aspects of autonomous learning'. *ELT Journal* 47/4: 330–6.

DORE, R. 1976. *The Diploma Disease*. London: Allen and Unwin.

DÖRNYEI, Z. and S. THURRELL. 1991. 'Strategic competence and how to teach it'. *ELT Journal* 45/1: 16–23.

DUKE, C. 1975. 'The student-centered conference and the writing process'. *English Journal* 64: 44–47.

EDELSKY, C. 1981. 'Who's got the floor?' *Language in Society* 10: 383–421.

EDGE, J. 1987. 'From Julian Edge'. *ELT Journal* 41/4: 308–9.

EDGE, J. 1988. 'Natives, speakers, and models'. *JALT Journal* 9/2: 153–7.

EDWARDS, J. R. 1977. 'Ethnic identity and bilingual education' in H. Giles (ed.). *Language, Ethnicity and Intergroup Relations*. New York: Academic Press.

EISENSTEIN, M. and J. W. BODMAN. 1986. ' "I very appreciate": expressions of gratitude by native and non-native speakers of American English'. *Applied Linguistics* 7/2: 167–85.

EISLER, R. 1987. *The Chalice and the Blade*. San Francisco, CA.: Harper and Row.

ELLIOT, J. 1991. *Action Research for Educational Change*. Milton Keynes: Open University Press.

ELLIOT, J. 1993. 'Professional education and the idea of a practical educational science' in J. Elliot (ed.). *Reconstructing Teacher Education*. London: Falmer.

ELLIS, G. and B. SINCLAIR. 1989. *Learning to Learn English*. Cambridge: Cambridge University Press. (Student's Book and Teacher's Book.)

ELLIS, R. 1982. 'Informal and formal approaches to communicative language teaching'. *ELT Journal* 36/1: 73–81.

ELLIS, R. 1986. 'Activities and procedures for teacher training'. *ELT Journal* 40/2: 91–9.

ELLIS, R. 1993. 'Talking Shop: second language acquisition research: how does it help teachers?' *ELT Journal* 47/1: 3–11.

ELLMAN, N. 1980. 'Structuring peer evaluation for greater student independence' in Gene Stanford (ed.). *How to Handle the Paper Load: Classroom Practices in Teaching English*. Urbana, IL.: National Council of Teachers of English.

ETHEL. 1980. 'Ethel in genderland' 5 (A newsletter for feminist teachers of EFL: no longer in publication.)

EVERARD, K. B. and G. MORRIS. 1985. *Effective School Management*. London: Harper and Row.

FAIRCLOUGH, N. 1992. *Critical Language Awareness*. Harlow: Longman.

FASSLER, B. 1978. 'The red-open revisited: teaching composition through student conferences'. *College English* 40: 186–90.

FEIMAN-NEMSER, S. and M. BUCHMANN. 1987. 'When is student teaching teacher education?' *Teaching and Teacher Education* 13: 255–73.

FERGUSON, C. A. 1982. 'Introduction' in B. B. Kachru (ed.).

FERRER, J. and E. WHALLEY. 1985. *Mosaic I: A Listening/Speaking Skills Book*. New York: Random House.

FERRER, J. and E. WHALLEY. 1985. *Mosaic II: A Listening/Speaking Skills Book*. New York: Random House.

FERRIS, D., B. NORTH, B. SUTER, H. MAXWELL-HYSLOP, K. SHAW, and S. DAWSON. 1988. 'Autonomy and self-directed learning: application in different European pedagogical contexts' in H. Holec (ed.).

FETTERLEY, J. 1978. *The Resisting Reader*. Bloomington, Ind.: Indiana University Press.

FISH, D. 1989. *Learning through Practice in Initial Teacher Training*. London: Routledge and Kegan Paul.

FISHMAN, J. A., C. A. FERGUSON, and J. DAS GUPTA (eds.). 1968. *Language Problems of Developing Nations*: New York: Wiley.

FLORENT, J. and C. WALTER. 1989. 'A better role for women in TEFL'. *ELT Journal* 43/3: 180–4.

FLOWER, L. 1979. 'Writer-based prose: a cognitive basis for problems in writing'. *College English* 41/1: 19–37.

FLYNN, E. 1982. 'Freedom, restraint, and peer group interaction'. Paper presented at the Annual Meeting of the Conference on College Composition and Communication, San Francisco, CA.

FORTUNE, A. 1992. 'Self-study grammar practice: learners' views and preferences'. *ELT Journal* 46/2: 160–71.

FREEMAN, D. 1991. 'Language Teacher Education, Emerging Discourse, and Change in Classroom Practice'. Plenary Address at the 1st International Conference on Teacher Education in Second Language Teaching, City University of Hong Kong.

FREIRE, P. 1972. *Pedagogy of the Oppressed*. Harmondsworth: Penguin.

FREUDENSTEIN, R. (ed.). 1990. *Error in Foreign Languages*. FIPLV–Eurocentres.

FREUDENSTEIN, R. 1991. 'Europe after 1992. Chances and problems for the less commonly taught languages'. *FIPLV World News* 55/21: 1–3.

FRIED-BOOTH, D. L. 1986. *Project Work*. Oxford: Oxford University Press.

FRIEDLANDER, A. 1990. 'Composing in English: effects of a first language on writing in English as a second language' in B. Kroll (ed.). *Second Language Writing: Research Insights for the Classroom*. Cambridge: Cambridge University Press.

FULCHER, G. 1991. 'Conditionals revisited'. *ELT Journal* 45/2: 164–8.

GARY. A. and J. COWAN. 1986. *Learning from Experience*. FEU/PICKUP Occasional Paper. Middlesex: Further Education Unit.

GEBHARD, J. C. 1990. 'Models of supervision: Choices' in J. Richards and D. Nunan (eds.).

GERBER, U. 1990a. 'A good way to use plays in the classroom'. *English Teaching Forum* 28/2: 49–50. Washington D.C.: United States Information Agency.

GERBER, U. 1990b. 'Literary role play'. *ELT Journal* 44/3: 199–203.

GILBERT, S. M. 1979. 'Life studies, or, speech after long silence: feminist critics today'. *College English* 40/8: 849–63.

GILBERT, S. M. 1984. 'The education of Henrietta Adams' in *Profession 84*. Modern Language Association of America.

GITLIN, A. and J. SMYTH. 1989. *Teacher Evaluation: Educative Alternatives*. London: Falmer.

GLASS, E. and P. ARCARIO. 1985. *Speak Freely: Conversational American English*. San Diego: Harcourt Brace Jovanovich.

GOLDHAMMER, R. 1969. *Clinical Supervision: Special Methods for the Supervision of Teachers*. New York: Holt, Rinehart and Winston.

GREEN, M. F. 1977. 'Regression in adult learning of a second language'. *Foreign Language Annals* 10/2: 173–83.

GUNSTONE, R., F. RICHARD, J. R. BAIRD, P. J. FENSHAM, and R. T. WHITE. 1988. 'Understanding Teacher Education'. Paper given at the International Council of Associations of Science Education World Conference, Canberra.

GUPTA, A. F. and A. L. S. YIN. 1990. *Language and Education* 4/1: 29–52.

GUTHRIE, E. 1984. 'Intake, communication, and second language teaching' in S. J. Savignon and M. S. Berns (eds.). *Initiatives in Communicative Language Teaching*. Reading, MA.: Addison-Wesley.

HADFIELD, C. and J. HADFIELD. 1990. *Writing Games*. Walton-on-Thames: Nelson.

HAFERNIK, J. J. 1984. 'The hows and whys of peer editing in the ESL writing class'. *CATSOL Occasional Papers* 4: 48–55.

HALLAK, J. 1990. *Investing in the Future*. Paris: International Institute for Educational Planning, UNESCO/Pergamon.

HALLIDAY, M. A. K., A. MCINTOSH, and P. STREVENS. 1964. *The Linguistic Sciences and Language Teaching*. London: Longman.

HANDSCHUH, J. DE GEIGEL and A. SIMOUNET. 1985. *Improving Oral Communication: A Pronunciation Oral-Communication Manual*. Englewood Cliffs, NJ.: Prentice Hall.

HANDY, C. 1985. *Understanding Organizations*. London: Penguin.

HARGREAVES, A. 1982. 'The rhetoric of school centred innovation'. *Journal of Curriculum Studies* 14/3: 251–66.

HARMAN, I. P. 1990. 'Teaching indirect speech: deixis points the way'. *ELT Journal* 44/3: 230–8.

HARRIS, B. 1975. *Supervising Behavior in Education.* New York: Prentice Hall.

HARRIS, J. G. and R. HUBE. 1989. *On Speaking Terms.* Revised by S. Vogel. New York: Collier Macmillan.

HARRIS, M. 1979. 'The overgraded paper: another case of more is less' in G. Stanford (ed.). *How to Handle the Paper Load.* Urbana, IL.: National Council of Teachers of English.

HARRIS, M. 1986. *Teaching One-to-One.* Urbana, IL.: National Council of Teachers of English.

HARRISON, P. 1987. *The Greening of Africa.* London: Paladin (Harper Collins).

HARTFORD, B. S. and K. BARDOVI-HARLIG. 1989. 'Structuring the interview: an examination of native and non-native participation'. Paper presented at the Third Annual Conference on Pragmatics and Language Learning, Urbana, IL.

HARTFORD, B. S. and K. BARDOVI-HARLIG. 1992. 'Closing the conversation: Evidence from the academic advising session'. *Discourse Processes* 15: 93–116.

HARTLEY, B. and P. VINEY. 1978. *Streamline.* Oxford: Oxford University Press.

HARTMAN, P. L. and E. L. JUDD. 1978. 'Sexism and TESOL materials'. *TESOL Quarterly* 12/4: 383–93.

HAWES, H. and T. COOMBE (eds.). 1986. *Education Priorities and Aid Responses in Sub-Saharan Africa.* London: HMSO (for Overseas Development Administration and University of London Institute of Education).

HILLOCKS, G. 1986. *Research on Written Composition: New Directions for Teaching.* Urbana, IL.: ERIC Clearinghouse on Reading and Communication Skills.

HINDS, J. 1983. 'Contrastive rhetoric: Japanese and English'. *Text* 3/2: 183–95.

HINDS, J. 1984. 'Retention of information using a Japanese style of presentation'. *Studies in Language* 8/1: 45–69.

HMSO. 1988. *Secondary Schools: An Appraisal by Her Majesty's Inspectorate.* London: Department of Education and Science.

HO, B. 1995. 'Using lesson plans as a means of reflection'. *ELT Journal* 49/1: 66–71.

HOLEC, H. 1979. *Autonomy and Foreign Language Learning.* Strasbourg: Council of Europe.

HOLEC, H. 1980. 'Learner-centred communicative language teaching: needs analysis revisited'. *Studies in Second Language Acquisition* 3/1: 26–33.

HOLEC, H. 1985. On autonomy: some elementary concepts' in P. Riley (ed.).

HOLEC, H. 1987. 'The learner as manager: managing learning or managing to learn?' in A.L. Wenden and J. Rubin (eds.).

HOLEC, H. (ed.). 1988a. *Autonomy and Self-directed Learning: Present Fields of Application*. Strasbourg: Council of Europe.

HOLEC, H. 1988b. 'General presentation. Prospects' in H. Holec (ed).

HOLMES, J. 1989. 'Stirring up the dust: the importance of sex as a variable in the ESL classroom'. *Proceedings of the ATESOL 6th Summer School, Sydney* 1–4: 4–39.

HOLMES, J. and D. BROWN. 1987. 'Teachers and students learning about compliments'. *TESOL Quarterly* 21/3: 523–46.

HOPKINS, D. 1989. *Evaluation for School Development*. Milton Keynes: Open University Press.

HORNBY, A. S. 1946a. 'Foreign Language Studies: Their Place in the National Life'. *English Language Teaching* 1/1: 3–6.

HORNBY, A. S. 1946b. 'Balance and proportion'. Editorial. *ELT Journal* 1/2: 31–3

HOUSE, J. and G. KASPER. 1981. 'Politeness markers in English and German' in F. Coulmas (ed.).

HOWARD, J. 1987. *Idioms in American Life*. Englewood Cliffs, NJ.: Prentice Hall.

HOWATT, A. P. R. 1984. *A History of English Language Teaching*. Oxford: Oxford University Press.

HOWELL-RICHARDSON, C. and B. PARKINSON. 1988. 'Learner Diaries: Possibilities and Pitfalls' in P. Grunwell (ed.). *Applied Linguistics in Society*. Papers from the Twentieth Anniversary Meeting of The British Association for Applied Linguistics. London: CILT/BAAL.

HUBERMAN, M. 1985. 'What knowledge is of most use to teachers? A knowledge-use perspective'. *Teaching and Teacher Education* 1/3: 251–62.

HUDSON, R. A. 1980. *Sociolinguistics*. Cambridge: Cambridge University Press.

HUIZENGA, J. 1989. *Moving On: Beginning Listening, Book 2*. White Plains, NY: Longman.

HUNDLEBY, S. and F. BREET. 1988. 'Using methodology notebooks on in-service teacher-training courses'. *ELT Journal* 42/1: 34–6.

HUTCHINSON, E. G. (in preparation). 'The role of textbooks in classroom second language teaching: Teachers' and learners' classroom use of a fisheries-based ESP textbook in the Philippines'. PhD thesis, Lancaster University.

HUTCHINSON, T. and E. G. HUTCHINSON. 1994. 'The textbook as agent of change'. *ELT Journal* 48/4: 315–28.

HYLAND, K. 1990. 'Providing productive feedback'. *ELT Journal* 44/4: 279–85.

HYNES, M. and M. BAICHMANN. 1989. *Breaking the Ice: Basic Communication Strategies*. White Plains, NY: Longman.

INAYATULLAH. 1967. 'Towards a non-western model of development' in D. Lerner and W. Schramm (eds.).

JARVIS, J. 1992. 'Using diaries for teacher reflection on in-service courses. *ELT Journal* 46/2: 133–43.

JENKINS, S. and J. HINDS. 1987. 'Business letter writing: English, French and Japanese'. *TESOL Quarterly* 21/2: 327–49.

JOHN, P. D. 1991. 'A qualitative study of British student teachers' lesson planning perspectives'. *Journal of Education for Teaching* 17/4: 359–72.

JOHNSON, K. 1981. *Communicate in Writing*. Harlow: Longman.

JOHNSON, P. 1982. 'Effects on reading comprehension of building background knowledge'. *TESOL Quarterly* 16/4: 503–16.

JOHNSTONE, B. 1986. 'Arguments with Khomeni: rhetorical situation and persuasive style in cross-cultural perspective'. *Text* 6/2: 171–87.

JOLLY, J. and L. ROBINSON. 1988. *Real-Life English*. Austin, Tex.: Steck-Vaughn.

JONES, L. 1977. *Functions of English*. Cambridge: Cambridge University Press.

JUDY, S. and S. JUDY. 1981. *An Introduction to the Teaching of Writing*. Urbana, IL.: National Council of Teachers of English.

KACHRU, B. B. 1982a. 'Meaning in deviation: towards understanding non-native English texts' in Kachru (ed.). 1982b.

KACHRU, B. B. (ed.). 1982b. *The Other Tongue: English Across Cultures*. Oxford: Pergamon.

KACHRU, B. B. 1985. 'Standards, codification, and sociolinguistic realism: the English language in the outer circle' in R. Quirk and H. G. Widdowson (eds.).

KACHRU, B. B. 1986. *The Alchemy of English: The Spread, Functions and Models of Non-native Englishes*. Oxford: Pergamon.

KACHRU, Y. 1985. 'Discourse analysis, non-native Englishes and second language acquisition research'. *World Englishes* 4/2: 223–32.

KAYE, P. 1989a. 'Laughter, ladies, and linguistics: a light-hearted quiz for language lovers and language learners'. *ELT Journal* 43/3: 185–91.

KAYE, P. 1989b. '"Women are alcoholics and drug addicts", says dictionary'. *ELT Journal* 43/1: 192–5.

KEH, C. 1989. 'Teaching proofreading: analysis, diagnosis and production'. Paper presented at the RELC Conference, Singapore.

KEH, C. 1990. 'Feedback in the writing process: a model and methods for implementation'. *ELT Journal* 44/4: 294–304.

KEHL, D. G. 1970. 'The art of writing evaluative comments on students' themes'. *English Journal* 59: 972–80.

KENNEDY, C. 1987. 'Innovating for a change: teacher development and innovation'. *ELT Journal* 41/3: 163–70.

KENNEDY, C. 1988. 'Evaluation of the management of change in ELT projects'. *Applied Linguistics* 9/4: 329–42.

KENNEDY, J. 1993. 'Meeting the needs of teacher trainees on teaching practice'. *ELT Journal* 47/2: 157–65.

KERR, S. T. 1982. 'Appropriate technology for education in developing countries'. *Programmed Learning and Educational Technology* 19/3: 228–33.

KINGMAN REPORT. 1988. *Report of the Committee of Enquiry into the Teaching of English Language*. London: HMSO.

KIRKBY, J. 1971 (1746). *A New English Grammar*. Menston: The Scholar Press.

KLIPPEL, F. 1983. *Ideas*. Dortmund: Lambert Lensing.

KLIPPEL, F. 1985. *Keep Talking*. Cambridge: Cambridge University Press.

KNOWLES, M. 1975. *Self-Directed Learning: A Guide for Learners and Teachers*. New York: Association Press.

KNOWLES, M. 1983. *The Adult Learner: A Neglected Species*. Houston: Gulf.

KOBAYASHI, H. 1984. 'Rhetorical patterns in English and Japanese'. *TESOL Quarterly* 18/4: 737–38.

KOCH, B. J. 1983. 'Presentation as proof: the language of Arabic rhetoric'. *Anthropological Linguistics* 25/1: 47–60.

KOURAOGO, P. 1987. 'Curriculum renewal and INSET in difficult circumstances'. *ELT Journal* 41/3: 171–78.

KRAMER, C. 1975. 'Women's speech: separate but unequal?' in B. Thorne and N. Henley (eds.). *Language and Sex: Difference and Dominance*. Rowley, MA.: Newbury House.

KREST, M. 1988. 'Monitoring student writing: how not to avoid the draft'. *Journal of Teaching Writing* 7/1: 27–39.

KUHN, T. S. 1970. (2nd edn.). *The Structure of Scientific Revolutions*. Chicago: University of Chicago Press.

KUMARAVADIVELU, B. 1991. 'Language learning tasks: teacher intention and learner interpretation'. *ELT Journal* 45/2: 98–107.

KUMARAVADIVELU, B. 1992. 'Macrostrategies for the second/foreign language teacher'. *Modern Language Journal*, June 1975.

KUMARAVADIVELU, B. 1993. 'Maximizing learning potential in the communicative classroom'. *ELT Journal* 47/1: 12–21.

LACKSTROM, J. E. and R. V. WHITE. 1983. *Moving Up: Intermediate Functional English*. London: Heinle and Heinle/Nelson.

LADO, R. 1989. *Lado English Series 2*. Englewood Cliffs, NJ.: Prentice Hall.

LAMB, M. 1991. 'Reflections on a Short INSET Course'. Unpublished MA dissertation, Lancaster University.

LAMB, M. 1995. 'The consequences of INSET'. *ELT Journal* 49/1: 72–80.

LANGE, D. 1990. 'A blueprint for a teacher development program' in J. Richards and D. Nunan (eds.).

LAWTON, D. 1989. 'The future of teacher education' in N. J. Graves (ed.). *Initial Teacher Education: Policies and Progress*. London Education Studies.

LEECH, G. 1989. *An A–Z of English Grammar and Usage*. London: Edward Arnold.

LEGUTKE, M. and H. THOMAS. 1991. *Process and Experience in the Language Classroom*. London: Longman.

LERNER, D. and W. SCHRAMM (eds.). 1967. *Communication and Change in the Developing Countries*. Honolulu: East-West Center Press.

LEVINE, D. R., J. BAXTER, and P. MCNULTY. 1987. *The Culture Puzzle: Cross-Cultural Communication for English as a Second Language*. Englewood Cliffs, NJ.: Prentice Hall.

LIN, L. Y. and R. BROWN. 1994. 'Guidelines for the production of in-house self-access materials'. *ELT Journal* 48/2: 150–6.

LITTLE, D. (ed.). 1989. *Self-Access Systems for Language Learning*. Dublin: Authentik.

LITTLEJOHN, A. L. 1992. 'Why are ELT materials the way they are?' Unpublished PhD thesis, Lancaster University.

LOEWENBERG BALL, D. and S. FEIMAN-NEMSER. 1988. 'Using textbooks and teachers's guides'. *Curriculum Inquiry* 18/4: 401–23.

LONG, M. 1983. 'Native speaker/non-native speaker conversation in the second language classroom' in M. Clarke and J. Handscombe (eds.). *On TESOL '82*: 207–25. Washington D.C.: TESOL.

LOSCHKY, L. and R. BLEY-VROMAN. 1990. 'Creating structure-based communication tasks for second language development'. *University of Hawaii Working Papers in ESL* 9: 161–209.

LOULIDI, R. 1990. 'Is language learning really a female business?' *Language Learning Journal* 1: 40–3.

LOVE, A. J. 1991. *Internal Evaluation: Building Organizations from Within*. Newbury Park, CA.: Sage.

LOWE, T. 1987. 'An experiment in role reversal: teachers as language learners'. *ELT Journal* 41/2: 89–96.

LUCERO, T. D. 1983. 'Clinical supervision versus traditional supervision'. *The Technology Teacher*. November 1983.

LUUKAS, A., M. HEINONEN, and A. PRICE. 1987. *All Set for English*. Finland: Otva.

MABOGUNJE, A. L. 1980. *The Development Process: A Spatial Perspective*. London: Hutchinson.

McCAFFERTY, J. (undated). *A Consideration of a Self-Access Approach to the Learning of English*. Mimeo, London: the British Council.

McDONALD, W. U. 1978. 'The revising process and the marking of student papers'. *College Composition and Communication* 24: 167–70.

McDONOUGH, J. and S. MCDONOUGH. 1990. 'What's the use of research?' *ELT Journal* 44/2: 102–9.

MACKAY, R. 1991a. 'Programme evaluation: staking your claim!' Paper presented at IATEFL Annual Conference, Exeter.

MACKAY, R. 1991b. 'Project-based review: Intrinsically motivated evaluation for LSP projects'. Paper presented at AVEPLEFE, Universidad del Zulia, Maracaibo, Venezuela.

MACKAY, R. 1992. 'Historias de Guerras y Romances o Expectativas Frustradas? Un caso de evaluación como tendencia en ESP'. Paper prepared for Congreso Internacional sobre la Enseñanza de Idiomas Extranjeros, Havana, Cuba.

MACKAY, R. 1993. 'Designing Evaluations to Assess Project Sustainability'. Paper presented at Overseas Development Administration/British Council sponsored workshop, Bali, Indonesia.

MACKAY, R. 1994. 'Undertaking ESL/EFL programme review for accountability and improvement'. *ELT Journal* 48/2: 142–9.

MACKAY, R. and C. WEIR. 1991. 'Evaluation of second language projects and programmes: an overview' in Weir and Roberts 1994.

McMAHON, A. *et al.* 1984. *GRIDS Primary School Handbook*. London: SCDC Publications.

MANGELSDORF, K. 1992. 'Peer reviews in the ESL classroom: what do the students think?' *ELT Journal* 46/3: 274–84.

MARRIS, P. 1986. *Loss and Change*. London: Routledge and Kegan Paul.

MATALENE, C. 1985. 'Contrastive rhetoric: an American writing teacher in China'. *College English* 47/8: 789–808.

MATEENE, K. 1985. 'Colonial languages as compulsory means of domination, and indigenous languages, as necessary factors of liberation and development' in K. Mateene, J. Kalema, and B. Chomba (eds.). *Linguistic Liberation and Unity of Africa*. Kampala: OAU Bureau of Languages. OAU/BIL Publication 6.

MAULE, D. 1988. '"Sorry, but if he comes, I go": teaching conditionals'. *ELT Journal* 42/2: 117–23.

MEARA, P. 1977. 'Schizophrenic symptoms in foreign language learners'. Paper given at BAAL Annual Conference, Colchester.

MEDGYES, P. 1983. 'The schizophrenic teacher'. *ELT Journal* 37/1: 2–6.

MEDGYES, P. 1986. 'Queries from a communicative teacher'. *ELT Journal* 40/2: 107–12.

MEDGYES, P. 1990. 'Error and the communicative approach' in R. Freudenstein (ed.). 1990. *Error in Foreign Languages*. FIPLV–Eurocentres.

MEDGYES, P. 1992. 'Native or non-native: who's worth more?' *ELT Journal* 46/4: 340–9.

MEDLEY, D. M., H. COKER, and R. S. SOAR. 1984. *Measurement-based Evaluation of Teacher Performance*. New York and London: Longman.

MEHAN, H. 1979. *Learning Lessons: Social Organization in the Classroom*. Cambridge: Cambridge University Press.

MEISEL, H., H. CLAHSEN, and M. PIENEMANN. 1981. 'On determining developmental stages in natural second language acquisition'. *Studies in Second Language Acquisition* 3: 109–35.

MILLER, C. and K. SWIFT. 1989. *The Handbook of Non-Sexist Writing*. London: The Women's Press.

MILLER, L. and P. ROGERSON-REVELL. 1993. 'Self-access systems'. *ELT Journal* 47/3: 228–33.

MOLINSKY, S. J. and B. BLISS. 1986. *ExpressWays: English for Communication*. Englewood Cliffs, NJ.: Prentice Hall.

MOON, J. 1994. 'Teachers as mentors: a route to in-service development'. *ELT Journal* 48/4: 347–55.

MORROW, K. and M. SCHOCKER. 1993. 'Process evaluation on an INSET course'. *ELT Journal* 47/1: 47–54.

MOULDEN, H. 1988. 'Self-directed learning of English for French students of computer applications in business management' in H. Holec (ed.).

MURPHY-O'DWYER, L. 1985. 'Diary studies as a matter for evaluating teacher training' in J.C. Alderson (ed.). *Evaluation*. Lancaster Practical Papers in English Language Education, Vol. 6. Oxford: Pergamon.

NAIDU, B., K. NEERAJA, J. SHIVAKUMAR, and V. VISWANATHA. 1992. 'Researching heterogeneity: an account of teacher-initiated research into large classes'. *ELT Journal* 46/3: 252–63.

NATIONAL CENTER FOR RESEARCH IN VOCATIONAL EDUCATION, OHIO STATE UNIVERSITY. 1980. *A Competency-Based Vocational Education Administrator Program. Module LT 58 B-3.* Athens, GA.: American Association for Vocational Instructional Materials.

NAYSMITH, J. H. 1986/7. 'English as imperialism'. *Language Issues* 1/2: 3–5.

NELSON, G. L. 1987. 'Culture's role in reading comprehension: a schema theoretical approach'. *Journal of Reading* 30: 424–28.

NGŨGĨ WA THIONG'O. 1986. *Decolonising the Mind: The Politics of Language in African Literature.* London: James Currey.

NIHALANI, P., R. K. TONGUE, and P. HOSALI. 1979. *Indian and British English.* New Delhi: Oxford University Press.

NISHIMURA, Y. K. 1986. 'Prose-organizing strategies of Japanese college students: contrastive analysis'. *Descriptive and Applied Linguistics* 19: 207–18.

NOBUYOSHI, J. and R. ELLIS. 1993. 'Focused communication tasks and second language acquisition'. *ELT Journal* 47/3: 203–10.

NORMAN, N. 1984. 'Contrastive analyses of organizational structures and cohesive elements in native and ESL Chinese, English and Spanish writing'. Unpublished PhD dissertation, Fordham University.

NOSTRAND, H. L. 1989. 'Authentic texts and cultural authenticity: an editorial'. *The Modern Language Journal* 73/1: 49–52.

NUNAN, D. 1985. 'Content familiarity and the perception of textual relationships in second language reading'. *RELC Journal* 16/1: 43–51.

NUNAN, D. 1987. 'Communicative language teaching: making it work'. *ELT Journal* 41/2: 136–45.

NUNAN, D. 1989a. 'A client-centred approach to teacher development'. *ELT Journal* 43/2: 111–18.

NUNAN, D. 1989b. *Designing Tasks for the Communicative Classroom.* Cambridge: Cambridge University Press.

NUNAN, D. 1989c. *The Learner-Centred Curriculum.* Cambridge: Cambridge University Press.

NUTTALL, C. 1982. *Teaching Reading Skills in a Foreign Language.* London: Heinemann.

O'DELL, F. 1992. 'Helping teachers to use a self-access centre to its full potential'. *ELT Journal* 46/2: 153–9.

O'NEILL, R. 1982. 'Why use textbooks?' *ELT Journal* 36/2: 104–11.

O'NEILL, R. 1991. 'The plausible myth of learner-centredness: or the importance of doing ordinary things well'. *ELT Journal* 45/4: 293–304.

O'NEILL, R. and R. SCOTT. 1974. *Viewpoints.* London: Longman.

O'NEILL, R., R. KINGSBURY, T. YEADON, and E. T. CORNELIUS, JR. 19 *American Kernel Lessons: Intermediate.* New York: Longman.

OVERSEAS DEVELOPMENT ADMINISTRATION. 1990. *Into the Nineties: An Education Policy for British Aid.* London: Overseas Development Administration.

OLSEN, T. 1976. 'I stand here ironing' in T. Olsen, *Tell Me a Riddle.* New York: Dell.

OMAR, A. 1989. 'How learners greet and take leave in Kiswahili.' Unpublished manuscript, Indiana University.

OMODIAOGBE, S. A. 1992. 'One hundred and fifty years on: English in the Nigerian school system-past, present, and future'. *ELT Journal* 46/1: 19–28.

OSKARSSON, M. 1978. *Approaches to Self-Assessment in Foreign Language Learning*. Oxford: Pergamon.

OWEN, S. V., R. D. FROMAN, and H. MOSCOW. 1978. (2nd edn.). *Educational Psychology: An Introduction*. Boston: Little, Brown and Co.

OXFORD, R., M. NYIKOS, and M. EHRMAN. 1988. 'Vive la différence? Reflections on sex differences in use of language strategies'. *Foreign Language Annals* 21/4: 321–9.

PAIKEDAY, T. M. 1985. *The Native Speaker is Dead!* Toronto and New York: Paikeday.

PALMER, C. 1993. 'Innovation and the experienced teacher'. *ELT Journal* 47/2: 166–71.

PARKINSON, B. and C. HOWELL-RICHARDSON. 1990. 'Learner diaries' in C. Brumfit and R. Mitchell (eds.). *Research in the Language Classroom*. ELT Documents 133. London: Modern English Publications/British Council.

PAVIO, A. 1971. *Imagery and Verbal Processes*. New York: Holt, Rinehart and Winston.

PEARSON, E. 1988. 'Learner strategies and learner interviews'. *ELT Journal* 42/3: 173–8.

PENNYCOOK, A. 1989. 'The concept of method, interested knowledge, and the politics of language teaching'. *TESOL Quarterly* 23/4: 589–617.

PERREN, G. 1963. 'Teaching English literature overseas: historical notes and present instances' in J. Press (ed.). *The Teaching of English Literature Overseas*. London: Methuen.

PERREN, G. and M. F. HOLLOWAY. 1965. *Language and Communication in the Commonwealth*. London: HMSO (for Commonwealth Education Liaison Committee).

PETRIE, H. G. 1979. 'Metaphor and learning' in A. Ortony (ed.). *Metaphor and Thought*. Cambridge: Cambridge University Press.

PHILLIPSON, R. 1990a. 'Glottopolitics and linguistic warfare'. *World Englishes* 9/1: 85–94.

PHILLIPSON, R. 1990b. *English Language Teaching and Imperialism*. Tronninge, Denmark: Transcultura.

PHILLIPSON, R. 1992a. 'ELT: The native speaker's burden?' *ELT Journal* 46/1: 12–18.

PHILLIPSON, R. 1992b. *Linguistic Imperialism*. Oxford: Oxford University Press.

PIRSIG, R. M. 1974. *Zen and the Art of Motorcycle Maintenance*. London: Corgi (Transworld).

POCIECHA, S. H. 1988. 'Action and condition in the post-elementary classroom'. *ELT Journal* 42/4: 288–93.

PORECCA, K. 1984. 'Sexism in current ESL textbooks'. *TESOL Quarterly* 18/4: 705–24.

PORTE, G. 1988. 'Poor language learners and their strategies for dealing with new vocabulary'. *ELT Journal* 42/3: 167–72.

PRABHU, N. S. 1992. 'The dynamics of the language lesson'. *TESOL Quarterly* 26/2: 161–76.

PRATOR, C. H. 1968. 'The British heresy in TESOL' in J. A. Fishman, C. A. Ferguson, and J. Das Gupta (eds.).

PRODROMOU, L. 1988. 'English as cultural action'. *ELT Journal* 42/2: 73–83.

PRODROMOU, L. 1992. 'What culture? Which culture? Cross-cultural factors in language learning'. *ELT Journal* 46/1: 39–50.

PURNELL, S. 1978. 'Politically speaking, do women exist?' *Journal of Communication* Winter: 150–5.

QUIRK, R. 1990. 'Language varieties and standard language'. *English Today* 21, 6/1: 3–10.

QUIRK, R. and S. GREENBAUM. 1973. *A University Grammar of English.* London: Longman.

QUIRK, R., S. GREENBAUM, G. LEECH, and J. SVARTVIK. 1985. *A Comprehensive Grammar of the English Language.* London: Longman.

QUIRK, R. and H. G. WIDDOWSON, (eds.). 1985. *English in the World: Teaching and Learning the Language and Literatures.* Cambridge: Cambridge University Press/British Council.

RAMANI, E. 1986. 'The role of classroom interaction in the classroom community'. *RELC Anthology Series* 19. Singapore: RELC/Singapore University Press.

RAMANI, E. 1987. 'Theorizing from the classroom'. *ELT Journal* 41/1: 3–11.

RAMPTON, M. B. H. 1990. 'Displacing the "native speaker": expertise, affiliation, and inheritance'. *ELT Journal* 44/2: 97–101.

REA-DICKINS, P. and K. GERMAINE. 1992. *Evaluation.* Oxford: Oxford University Press.

REASOR, A.W. 1986. 'Dominant administrative styles of ESL administrators'. *TESOL Quarterly* 20/2: 338–43.

REYNOLDS, R. E., M. A. TAYLOR, M. S. STEFFENSEN, L. I. SHIREY, and R. C. ANDERSON. 1982. 'Cultural schemata and reading comprehension'. *Reading Research Quarterly* 17: 353–66.

RICHARDS, J. and D. NUNAN (eds.). 1990. *Second Language Teacher Education.* Cambridge: Cambridge University Press.

RICHARDS, J., J. PLATT, and H. WEBER. 1985. *Longman Dictionary of Applied Linguistics.* London: Longman.

RIDJANOVIC, M. 1983. 'How to learn a language, say English, in a couple of months'. *English Teaching Forum* 21/1: 8–13.

RILEY, P. (ed.). 1985. *Discourse and Learning.* Harlow: Longman.

RILEY, P., M-J. GREMMO, and H. MOULDEN. 1989. 'Pulling yourself together: the practicalities of setting up and running self-access systems' in D. Little (ed.).

RINVOLUCRI, M. 1981. 'Resistance to change on in-service teacher training courses'. *Recherches et Échanges* 6/1: 45–52.

ROGERS, C. 1969. *Freedom to Learn.* Columbus, Ohio: Merrill.

ROSEN, H. 1983, 'The professional development of teachers' in M. Torbe and R. Protherough (eds.). *Classroom Encounters*. London: Allen and Unwin.

ROSSNER, R. and R. BOLITHO (eds.). 1990. *Currents of Change in English Language Teaching*. Oxford: Oxford University Press.

SANTOS, T. 1988. 'Professors' reaction to the academic writing of non-native students'. *TESOL Quarterly* 22/1: 69–90.

SAVIGNON, S. J. 1991. 'Communicative language teaching: state of the art'. *TESOL Quarterly* 25/2: 261–77.

SCHEGLOFF, E. A. and H. SACKS. 1973. 'Opening up closings'. *Semiotica* 8/4: 289–327.

SCHMIDT, R. 1989. 'TESOL and Sociolinguistics Colloquium.' TESOL, San Antonio.

SCHMIDT, R. and J. RICHARDS. 1980. 'Speech acts and second language learning'. *Applied Linguistics* 1/2: 127–57.

SCHMITT, N. and D. SCHMITT. 1995. 'Vocabulary notebooks: theoretical underpinnings and practical suggestions'. *ELT Journal* 49/2: 133–43.

SCHÖN, D. A. 1983. *The Reflective Practitioner*. London: Temple Smith.

SCHÖN, D. A. 1987. *Educating the Reflective Practitioner*. San Francisco, CA./London: Jossey-Bass.

SCHULZ, M. 1975. 'The semantic derogation of women' in B. Thorne and N. Henley (eds.). *Language and Sex: Difference and Dominance*. Rowley, MA.: Newbury House.

SCHWERTMAN, K. A. 1987. 'The mystery of misconnecting agendas'. Paper presented at the Annual Meeting of the Conference on College Composition and Communication (Atlanta, GA).

SCOTTISH OFFICE EDUCATION DEPARTMENT. 1991. *Using Performance Indicators in Secondary School Self-Evaluation*. Edinburgh: Scottish Office Education Department.

SCOTTON, C. M. and J. BERNSTERN. 1988. 'Natural conversations as a model for textbook dialogue'. *Applied Linguistics* 9/4: 372–84.

SELINKER, L. 1972. 'Interlanguage'. *IRAL* 10: 219–31.

SHARP, A. 1990. 'Staff/student participation in course evaluation: a procedure for improving course design'. *ELT Journal* 44/2: 132–7.

SHARPE, P. J. 1984. *Talking with Americans: Conversation and Friendship Strategies for Learners of English*. Boston: Little, Brown and Co.

SHAVELSON, R. J. and P. STERN. 1981. 'Research on teachers' pedagogical thoughts, judgements and behaviour'. *Review of Educational Research* 51/4.

SHEAL, P. 1989. 'Classroom observation: training the observers'. *ELT Journal* 43/2: 92–104.

SHEERIN, S. 1989. *Self-access*. Oxford: Oxford University Press.

SHELDON, L. 1988. 'Evaluating ELT textbooks and materials'. *ELT Journal* 42/4: 237–46.

SIDE, R. 1990. 'Phrasal verbs: sorting them out'. *ELT Journal* 44/2: 144–52.

SIMMONS, J. (ed.). 1980. *The Education Dilemma*. Oxford: Pergamon.

SINCLAIR, J. (ed.). 1987. *Collins COBUILD English Language Dictionary*. London: Collins.

SINGLETON, D. and D. LITTLE. 1989. 'Setting the context: language learning, self-instruction and autonomy' in D. Little (ed.).

SKEHAN, P. 1989. *Individual Differences in Second Language Learning*. London: Edward Arnold.

SKUTNABB-KANGAS, T. 1981. 'Guest worker or immigrant–different ways of reproducing an underclass'. *Journal of Multilingual and Multicultural Development* 2/2: 89–115.

SMITH, L. E. (ed.). 1987. *Discourse Across Cultures*. New York: Prentice Hall.

SOLOMON, J. 1987. 'New thoughts on teacher education'. *Oxford Review of Education* 13/3: 267–74.

SOMMERS, N. 1982. 'Responding to students' writing'. *College Composition and Communication* 33: 48–156.

SPENDER, D. 1982. *Invisible Women*. London: The Women's Press.

SPOLSKY, B. 1989. '"I come to bury Caesar, not to praise him": teaching resisting reading'. *ELT Journal* 43/3: 173–9.

STANWORTH, M. 1983. *Gender and Schooling*. London: Hutchinson.

STEFFENSEN, M. S., C. JOAG-DEV, and R. C. ANDERSON. 1979. 'A cross-cultural perspective on reading comprehension'. *Reading Research Quarterly* 15: 10–29.

STEPHENS, K. 1990. 'The world of John and Mary Smith: a study of Quirk and Greenbaum's *University Grammar of English*' 1973. *CLE Working Papers* 1: 91–107.

STEPHENSON, H. 1994. 'Management and participation in ELT projects'. *ELT Journal* 48/3: 225–32.

STERN, H. H. 1983. *Fundamental Concepts of Language Teaching*. Oxford: Oxford University Press.

STEVICK, E. 1990. *Humanism in Language Teaching*. Oxford: Oxford University Press.

STEWART, M. 1989. *The Process of Writing*. London: Macmillan.

STEWART, S. 1982. 'Language and culture'. *USF Language Quarterly* 20/3: 7–10.

STODOLSKY, S. S. 1988. 'Is teaching really by the book?' in P. W. Jackson and S. Horoutunian-Gordon (eds.). *From Socrates to Software: The Teacher as Text and the Text as Teacher*. 88th Yearbook of the National Society for the Study of Education: 159–84.

STREVENS, P. 1980. *Teaching English as an International Language: From Practice to Principle*. Oxford: Pergamon.

STURTRIDGE, G. 1992. *Self-Access: Preparation and Training*. Manchester: British Council.

SUNDERLAND, J. 1986. 'The grammar book and the invisible woman'. Unpublished MA dissertation, Lancaster University.

SUNDERLAND, J. 1992. 'Gender in the EFL classroom'. *ELT Journal* 46/1: 81–91.

SWAIN, M. 1985. 'Communicative competence: some roles of comprehensible input and comprehensible output in its development' in S. Gass and C. Madden (eds.). *Input in Second Language Acquisition*. Rowley, MA.: Newbury House.

SWAN, J. 1993. 'Metaphor in action: the observation schedule in a reflective approach to teacher education'. *ELT Journal* 47/3: 242–9.

SWAN, M. 1980. *Practical English Usage*. Oxford: Oxford University Press.

SWAN, M. 1985a. 'A critical look at the Communicative Approach (1)' *ELT Journal* 39/1: 2–12.

SWAN, M. 1985b. 'A critical look at the Communicative Approach (2)'. *ELT Journal* 39/2: 76–87.

SWAN, M. 1992. 'The textbook: bridge or wall?' *Applied Linguistics and Language Teaching* 2/1: 32–5.

SWATRIDGE, C. 1985. *Delivering the Goods: Education as Cargo in Papua New Guinea*. Manchester: Manchester University Press.

TAKAHASHI, T. and L. BEEBE. 1987. 'The development of pragmatic competence by Japanese learners of English'. *JALT Journal* 8/2: 131–55.

TALANSKY, S. 1986. 'Sex role stereotyping in TEFL teaching materials'. *Perspectives* XI/3: 32–42.

TANKA, J. and P. MOST. 1985. *Interactions: A Listening/Speaking Skills Book*. San Francisco, CA.: Random House.

TAYLOR, D. 1991. 'Compound word stress'. *ELT Journal* 45/1: 67–73.

THOMPSON, A. R. 1981. *Education and Development in Africa*. London: Macmillan.

THOMSON, A. J. and A. V. MARTINET. 1980 (3rd edn.) and 1986 (4th edn.). *A Practical English Grammar*. Oxford: Oxford University Press.

THORNBURY, S. 1991. 'Watching the whites of their eyes: the use of teaching practice logs'. *ELT Journal* 45/2: 140–6.

TODD, F. 1987. *Planning Continuing Professional Development*. London: Croom Helm.

TODD, R. 1988. 'Continuing professional development in British universities' in T. Bilham, M. Carboni, and F. Todd (eds.). *The PICKUP Papers*. 2nd National PICKUP in Universities Conference, Lancaster. London: Department of Education and Science.

TOMLINSON, B. 1988. 'In-service TEFL: is it worth the risk?' *The Teacher Trainer* 2/2: 17–19.

TOMLINSON, B. 1990. 'Managing change in Indonesian high schools'. *ELT Journal* 44/1: 25–37.

TORRES, E. 1990. 'If you cannot understand into your teacher you can depend into the book: the role of textbooks in challenging English language teaching and learning situations'. Paper presented at the first international conference of the Malaysian English Teachers Association, Kuala Lumpur, Malaysia.

TRIM, J. L. M. 1978. *Developing a Unit/Credit Scheme for Adult Language Learning*. Strasbourg: Council of Europe.

TUDOR, I. 1992. 'Learner-centredness in language teaching: finding the right balance'. *System* 20/1: 31–44.

TUDOR, I. 1993. 'Teacher roles in the learner-centred classroom'. *ELT Journal* 47/1: 22–31.

UNDERHILL, A. 1987. 'Learning to change'. *Teacher Development*

(Newsletter of the IATEFL Teacher Development Special Interest Group) No. 6: 1.

UNDERHILL, A. 1989. 'Process in humanistic education'. *ELT Journal* 43/4: 250–60.

UNDERHILL, A. 1992. 'The role of groups in developing teacher self-awareness'. *ELT Journal* 46/1: 71–80.

UNESCO. 1953. *The Use of the Vernacular Languages in Education.* Paris: UNESCO.

VALDES, J. M. (ed.). 1986. *Culture Bound: Bridging the Cultural Gap in Language Teaching.* Cambridge: Cambridge University Press.

VAN DEN AKKER, J. J. 1988. 'The teacher as learner in curriculum implementation'. *Journal of Curriculum Studies* 20/1: 47–55.

VAN EK, J. and N. ROBAT. 1984. *The Student's Grammar of English.* Oxford: Blackwell.

VAN LIER, L. 1987. *The Classroom and the Language Learner: Ethnography and Second-Language Classroom Research.* London: Longman.

VINEY, K. and P. VINEY. 1989. *Grapevine.* Oxford: Oxford University Press.

VINEY, P. 1985. *Streamline English: Directions.* Oxford: Oxford University Press.

WAITE, S. 1994. 'Low-resourced self-access with EAP in the developing world: the great enabler?' *ELT Journal* 48/3: 233–42.

WALKER, C. and D. ELIAS. 1987. 'Writing conference talk: factors associated with high- and low-rated writing conferences'. *Research in the Teaching of English* 21/3: 266–85.

WALL, A. P. 1987. *Say it Naturally! Verbal Strategies for Authentic Communication.* New York: CBS College Publishing.

WALLACE, C. 1988. *Learning to Read in a Multicultural Society.* New York: Prentice Hall.

WALLACE, M. and D. WOOLGER. 1991. 'Improving the ELT supervisory dialogue: the Sri Lankan experience'. *ELT Journal* 45/4: 320–7.

WALZ, J. 1989. 'Context and contextualized language practice in foreign language teaching'. *Modern Language Journal* 73: 160–8.

WARDHAUGH, R. 1987. *Languages in Competition: Dominance, Diversity and Decline.* Oxford: Blackwell.

WEBB, J. and J. SINCLAIR. 1985. 'Educational project management: survey of communications skills requirements in aid projects in Indonesia' in *Communication Skills in Bilateral Aid Projects.* Dunford House Seminar Report. London: British Council.

WEINREICH, U. 1953. *Languages in Contact.* The Hague: Mouton.

WEIR, C. and J. R. ROBERTS. 1994. *Evaluation in ELT.* Oxford: Blackwell.

WENDEN, A. and R. J. RUBIN. 1987. *Learner Strategies in Language Learning.* London: Prentice Hall.

WESSELS, C. 1991. 'From improvisation to publication on an English through Drama course'. *ELT Journal* 45/3: 230–6.

WHITE, L. 1987. 'Against comprehensible input: the Input Hypothesis and the development of language competence'. *Applied Linguistics* 8: 95–110.

WHITE, R. 1993. '"Saying please": pragmalinguistic failure in English interaction'. *ELT Journal* 47/3: 193–202.

WHORF, B. L. 1941. 'Language, mind and reality'. *The Theosophist* 63/1 and 63/2, Madras. Reprinted in J. B. Carroll. (ed.). 1956. *Language, Thought and Reality*. Cambridge, MA.: MIT Press.

WIDDOWSON, H. G. 1985. 'Against dogma: a reply to Michael Swan'. *ELT Journal* 39/3: 158–61.

WIDDOWSON, H. G. 1986. 'Forty years on …'. *ELT Journal* 40/4: 265–69.

WIDDOWSON, H. G. 1987. 'A rationale for teacher education' in Council of Europe Project No.12. Strasbourg: Council of Europe.

WIDDOWSON, H. G. 1990. *Aspects of Language Teaching*. Oxford: Oxford University Press.

WIDDOWSON, H. G. 1993. 'Proper words in proper places'. *ELT Journal* 47/4: 317–29.

WIERZBICKA, A. 1990. 'Antitotalitarian language in Poland: some mechanisms in linguistic self-defence'. *Language in Society* 19/1: 1–59.

WILLIAMS, M. 1988. 'Language taught for meetings and language used in meetings: is there anything in common?' *Applied Linguistics* 9/1: 45–8.

WILLIAMS, M. 1989. 'A developmental view of classroom observations'. *ELT Journal* 43/2: 85–91.

WILLIAMS, M. and R. BURDEN. 1994. 'The role of evaluation in ELT project design'. *ELT Journal* 48/1: 22–7.

WILLING, K. 1988. *Learning Styles in Adult Migrant Education*. Adelaide: National Curriculum Resource Centre.

WILSON, P. and L. HARRISON. 1983. 'Materials design in Africa with particular reference to the Francophone Primary School Project, Cameroon' in *Language Teaching Projects for the Third World*. ELT Documents 116. London: Modern English Publications/British Council.

WINFIELD, F. E. and P. BARNES-FELFELI. 1982. 'The effects of familiar and unfamiliar cultural content on foreign language composition'. *The Modern Language Journal* 66/4: 373–8.

WOLFSON, N. 1986. 'Research methodology and the question of validity'. *TESOL Quarterly* 20/4: 689–99.

WOLFSON, N 1988. 'Native and non-native variation in complimenting behavior'. Paper presented at the Conference on Pragmatics and Language Learning, Urbana, IL.

WONG-FILLMORE, L. 1985. 'When does teacher talk work as input?' in S. Gass and C. Madden (eds.). *Input in Second Language Acquisition*. Rowley, MA.: Newbury House.

WOODS, E. and N. McLEOD. 1990. *Using English Grammar: Meaning and Form*. London: Prentice Hall.

WOODS, P. 1988. 'Pulling out of a project'. *ELT Journal* 42/3: 196–201.

WRAGG, E. C. 1982. *A Review of Research in Teacher Education*. Windsor: National Foundation for Educational Research/Nelson.

WRIGHT, T. 1990. 'Understanding classroom role relationships' in J. Richards and D. Nunan (eds.).

YOUNG, R. 1987. 'The cultural content of TESOL: a review of research into Chinese classrooms'. *RELC Journal* 18/2: 15–30.

YOUNG, R. and C. DOUGHTY. 1987. 'Negotiation in context: a review of research' in J. Lantolf and A. Labarca (eds.). *Research in Second Language Learning: Focus on the Classroom*. Norwood, NJ.: Ablex.

YULE, G., T. MATTHIS, and M. HOPKINS. 1992. 'On reporting what was said'. *ELT Journal* 46/3: 245–51.

ZIV, N. 1982. 'What she thought I said: How students misperceive teachers' written comments'. Paper presented at the Annual Meeting of the Confederation on College Composition and Communication, San Francisco, CA.

ZIV, N. 1983. 'Peer groups in the composition classroom: A case study'. Paper presented at the Annual Meeting of the Conference on College Composition and Communication, Detroit, MI.

ZOGRAFOU, A. 1990. 'Explore the way language supports and generates sexist values, concepts and models in the ELT textbook'. *Turning Point*. Unpublished essay, Lancaster University.

ZUCK, J. G. 1984. 'The dynamics of classroom observation: evening the odds through information'. *TESOL Quarterly* 18/2: 337–41.

# TOPIC INDEX
## *to Volumes 42–49*